SIR CHRISTOPHER HATTON

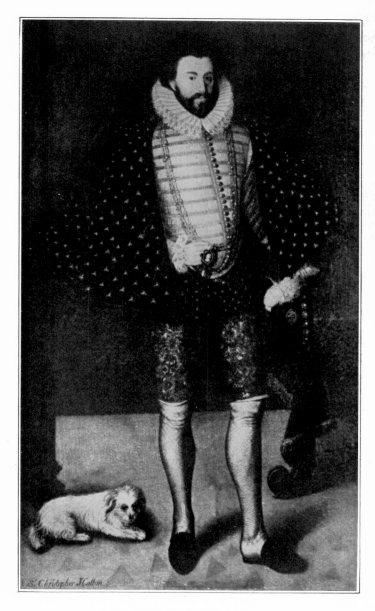

SIR CHRISTOPHER HATTON
From the portrait in the Inner Temple

SIR CHRISTOPHER HATTON

Queen Elizabeth's Favourite

by

ERIC ST. JOHN BROOKS

M.A., LITT.D.

'No scandal about Queen Elizabeth, I hope?'
THE CRITIC

JONATHAN CAPE
THIRTY BEDFORD SQUARE
LONDON

FIRST PUBLISHED JUNE 1946
SECOND IMPRESSION JANUARY 1947

PRINTED IN GREAT BRITAIN IN THE CITY OF OXFORD
AT THE ALDEN PRESS
BOUND BY A. W. BAIN & CO. LTD., LONDON

CONTENTS

CONTENTS

APPENDICES

ILLUSTRATIONS

For
NICHOLAS

PREFACE

OF the four most influential statesmen of Queen Elizabeth's reign, Burghley, Leicester, Walsingham and Hatton, only Walsingham has had the distinction of a modern full-length biography. No life of Sir Christopher Hatton could claim the importance for historians of Dr. Conyers Read's great biography of Walsingham. For Walsingham, as Secretary, held, more than anyone save Burghley, the threads of Elizabethan policy in his hands. But Hatton is a much more picturesque figure than Walsingham, and his life yields a different and in many respects more colourful picture of the Elizabethan scene. Moreover, Hatton's part in the history of his times has been largely misunderstood. He has come down to us merely as a favourite of Elizabeth's, a man who made his position at Court by his skill in dancing, a courtier unlearned in the law, who owed to the partiality of his Queen his promotion to the high office of Lord Chancellor. His solid merits have been overlooked, though so discriminating a historian as Professor Neale has done something to brush aside Froude's contemptuous estimate of him. It is in an effort to redress the balance that this study has been undertaken; and it is believed that the portrait of Hatton here presented, both as man of affairs and consummate courtier, as typical Elizabethan in fact, is just.

No previous life of Hatton, apart from brief sketches, has been written, for Sir Harris Nicolas's life is not really a biography. It is a transcript, made by Hatton's secretary Samuel Cox, of letters written by and to Hatton during the years 1577-88, with a running commentary by Nicolas. But, while in no proper sense a life of Hatton, it is invaluable as illustrating his official duties, his activities and his friendships. Nicolas's work, which will be referred to in these pages as the Letter Book, is the most important source for Hatton's everyday life. But much other relevant material, both published and in manuscript, has been consulted in the preparation of this book. I have avoided the use of footnotes, but in an appendix the principal sources have been indicated, chapter by chapter. It is hoped that the authority for every major statement, at any rate, has been given.

My thanks are due to the courteous officials of the Public

9

PREFACE

Record Office, British Museum, Somerset House and London Library for much general assistance. More specifically, for permission to quote from their works, I have to thank Sir Edmund Chambers for some passages about the masks and the tilt-yard, from his *Elizabethan Stage*; Professor J. E. Neale for a part of Hatton's speech after the defeat of the Armada, from his *Queen Elizabeth*; and Miss Tenison for Hatton's letter to Leicester about the latter's marriage, from her *Elizabethan England*. For permission to reproduce illustrations, I am indebted to the Treasurer, Inner Temple, for the portrait of Hatton there; and to the Northamptonshire Record Society for the photograph of the Holdenby estate map from the Finch-Hatton collection. I have to thank the Society also for facilities in examining this collection, which was deposited with it by the 13th Earl of Winchilsea; and Mr. J. Steegmann, late of the National Portrait Gallery, for assistance in preparing the list of Hatton's portraits.

Tapping House
Great Missenden

SIR CHRISTOPHER HATTON

CHAPTER I

HATTON AND HIS AGE

'HATTON danced, and that is all we know of him.' Lytton
Strachey has summed up in a phrase the popular conception of
Sir Christopher Hatton, Gentleman Pensioner, Captain of the
Queen's Guard, Gentleman of the Privy Chamber, Vice-Chamberlain, High Steward of the University of Cambridge, Chancellor
of the University of Oxford, Knight of the Garter, Privy Councillor
and Lord High Chancellor of England. The mere enumeration
of these titles and offices suggests that we know a great deal more
about him than his accomplishments as a dancer. But it is true
that Christopher Hatton is chiefly remembered to-day as a man
who danced his way into his Queen's heart. And, if we add to
this popular estimate that he has left behind him a number of
impassioned letters addressed to Elizabeth, which at any rate
suggest that he was her lover; that he robbed the Bishop of Ely
of his London residence where Hatton Garden is to-day; that he
ruined himself in building one of the most stately palaces in the
realm, 'the last and greatest monument of his youth'; that his
infatuated Queen made him Lord Chancellor to the dismay and
derision of the lawyers who had watched him wasting, in acting
and dancing, his opportunities as a law student; and that he died
at a comparatively early age, overwhelmed in debt to the Crown,
we have said all of Hatton that the average reader is likely to
recall.

Such is the Hatton legend, promoted by his earliest biographer,
Robert Naunton, and fostered by Lord Campbell in his *Lives of
the Lord Chancellors*. Like all legends it has some foundation in fact.
Hatton, no more scrupulous than the age in which he lived, did
take advantage of the Queen's dislike of the Bishop of Ely to steal
the Naboth's vineyard that he coveted. It was a discreditable act
in a life that has been minutely searched, generally speaking
without result, for damaging episodes. He built beyond his
means, and died leaving his estate heavily encumbered. And his
so-called love-letters to Elizabeth, if they will not bear the
construction of guilty passion that has been laid upon them, carry

13

the cult of Elizabethan adulation to ridiculous heights. But when we have said all this, we have said the worst that hostile criticism has been able to bring against him. That Hatton was an accomplished dancer and a skilled performer in the tilt-yard is true enough. But a study of his life dispels the legend that he owed his astonishing progress from an obscure country squire to a dazzling position, with the Woolsack as crowning achievement, to such adventitious graces. Charm and address might help any young man to a foothold in Elizabeth's Court, but more solid gifts were needed if he were to make his way in that glittering circle. Hatton's fascinating figure in the galliard has as much or as little significance as the gallantry of Ralegh's happy gesture with his cloak.

Whether one takes the extreme view of a Froude, to whom Elizabeth was but a vacillating figure, carried to final triumph by sagacious counsellors, or whether one assumes, more reasonably, that the glorious issues of her reign were due in greater or less measure to her own sagacity, all historians have agreed that Elizabeth was a supremely good judge of men. And she cannot in fairness be denied the merit of choosing her instruments, and loyally supporting them. Of statesmen proper, the commanding figures of her era are Burghley and Walsingham, both men who, judged by any standards, are among the greatest of English men of affairs. These men were chosen for their gifts alone. Elizabeth was often at variance with Burghley, but she never wavered in the trust she reposed in him. She had little sympathy with his Protestant leanings; none at all with the Puritanism of Walsingham. But, though Walsingham was antipathetic to her, he could count as a rule upon her steady confidence. Her contrary moods might break the hearts of the two statesmen, but she did not think of throwing them over, as her father had thrown over Cromwell, Wolsey and More.

When she chose her men for more personal reasons she was less fortunate. Her two principal failures in judgment were betrayals of her head by her heart. Leicester, the light of her youth, perhaps the only man who claimed her love as man claims woman's, had few gifts and no character. Essex held the love of her old age, part maternal, part the warmth that fading fires claim from glowing youth. Apart from these two, and from the erratic Oxford, whom she quickly summed up for what he was, Elizabeth's favourites were creditable and even remarkable figures.

Two were outstanding, Hatton in the earlier days, Ralegh in the latter. The more brilliant Ralegh overshadows his rival in our eyes. But Elizabeth never had any confidence in Ralegh's statesmanship, while she recognized Hatton's more solid qualities by entrusting him with important duties, and securing him the promotion which she denied to the more showy man.

Sir Robert Naunton, who first gave currency to the Hatton legend, is not a trustworthy witness against him. Naunton had married the granddaughter of Sir John Perrot, and Perrot is the one man for whom there is evidence that Hatton had a real antipathy. The explanation given for that dislike, that Perrot had seduced Hatton's daughter, will be discussed in its proper place; but, whatever the reason, the enmity seems to have been a fact. Hatton is said to have been one of the most active agents in bringing about Perrot's downfall, though the unwise actions and indiscreet utterances of that boisterous old soldier sufficiently account for his misfortunes. Perrot's contemptuous saying that Hatton had come to Court by the galliard, an allusion to the favourite's talent for dancing, started the story that Hatton owed everything to his ornamental qualities. Naunton, who has preserved the phrase, adds that Hatton's entry into Elizabeth's circle was due to his performance in a mask as a student of the Inns of Court, and that the Queen's favour was extended to him on account of his 'activity and person which was tall and proportionable'. While admitting that 'besides the graces of his person and dancing', Hatton possessed also 'a strong and nimble capacity, and that he could soon learn the discipline and garb both of the times and Court', Naunton qualifies his praise by adding, 'The truth is he had a large proportion of gifts and endowments, but too much the season of envy; and he was a mere vegetable of the Court that sprang up at night and sank again at his noon'. Lord Campbell has taken Hatton's skill in dancing as the clue to his career; and to dancing and acting he adds as a matter of course that Hatton must have been idle, ignorant and profligate. He draws imaginary pictures of the reactions of his people at home to the news of the son's excesses in town; and, jealous of the dignity of the Lord Chancellor's office, he is never tired of laughing at Hatton's scant knowledge of the law. But, as will be suggested in what follows, Hatton's was a political rather than a legal appointment. He was chosen for a State emergency, and fulfilled the

Queen's requirements in that respect, while the legal part of his duties was competently performed with the assistance of skilled advisers.

Of modern historians Froude is the most hostile to Hatton. He sees in him only 'a handsome, innocent, rather absurd person' attached to the Queen 'on the footing of a human lap-dog', who 'repaid her caresses with a genuine devotion, ridiculous only in the language in which it was expressed'. But this contemptuous estimate is rejected by probably all historians to-day. There is a return to the better tradition of Hatton's contemporary Camden, who says that 'for his modest sweetness of condition' the Queen took him into

> the number of the Gentlemen of her Privy Chamber, made him Captain of her Guard, Vice-Chamberlain and one of her Privy Council, and lastly made him Lord Chancellor of England, and honoured him with the Order of St. George. A man he was of a pious nature, a great reliever of the poor, of singular bounty and munificence to students and learned men (for which reason those of Oxford chose him Chancellor of their University) and one who in the execution of that high and weighty office of Lord Chancellor of England could satisfy his conscience in the constant integrity of his endeavours to do all with right and equity.

Camden, in enumerating the successive posts to which the Queen appointed Hatton, suggests that it was Elizabeth who through the years moulded the raw material into the statesman. The same note is struck in the rude verses which Hatton's follower, Francis Flower, wrote for a tablet near his tomb in Old St. Paul's. They tell how the Queen 'first trained him in the stately band of Pensioners' (Flower himself was a member of the corps), and gradually advanced him: 'now doth she prune this vine'. Professor Neale, the latest biographer of Queen Elizabeth, writes, that 'like other favourites', Hatton was 'a man of real capacity, and Elizabeth had turned him into a counsellor and statesman, who by his work and influence had come latterly to rank with Leicester, Burghley, and Walsingham as one of the four most influential men in the Government, a person deserving of great office'. And of his elevation to the Woolsack he adds 'the appointment was not unreasonable, and if it emphasized the political side of the Chancellor's office, Hatton's prudence saved it from failure on the legal side'.

From purely decorative functions at Court, dancing, masking and tilting, with occasional minor parts in such picturesque pageants as the baptism of the future James I, Elizabeth thus gradually turned her favourite to more serious work. He entered Parliament in 1571, and after a time had allotted to him the role of Queen's mouthpiece in the House of Commons. By the time he became Vice-Chamberlain in 1577 he was in full authority in that capacity, told the House what it was to discuss and what not, rebuked such ardent apostles of free speech in Parliament as Peter Wentworth, and generally kept a controlling hand on matters of special interest to the Queen. He moved the House on one occasion to recite prayers for her Majesty, and led it in such intercession, repeating the petition written by a friend of his, the dutiful Commons all kneeling. He also represented the Queen in the examination of those charged with high treason. The Duke of Norfolk is the earliest case of Hatton's employment in this capacity of investigating plots aimed at the Queen's life. Thenceforward, such conspiracies became more frequent as a result of the Catholic Counter-Reformation inaugurated by the mission of the Jesuits Campion and Parsons, and Hatton's duties in this respect became more arduous. He was present at the examination of Dr. Parry, of the Babington conspirators and others, and sat as a commissioner at the trials of these men, being indeed the dominating figure in the Court. At the same time it fell to him in such cases to put to Parliament the point of view of the Crown. He spoke, for instance, in the House of the crimes of Mary Queen of Scots, besides being one of the commissioners at her trial. For his indictment of Mary in Parliament and for his speech after the defeat of the Spanish Armada, the notes he prepared have been preserved, and may be compared with the orator's finished performance in the House.

Hatton was also specially charged by the Queen to endeavour to secure uniformity in worship and to keep Puritan tendencies in check. He it was who communicated to the Bishops Elizabeth's wishes in matters of Church discipline; and it was apparently to further her policy that he secured the appointment of John Aylmer to the Bishopric of London. When Aylmer showed signs of interfering too much with the Catholics, then in favour or at least tolerated, as well as with the Puritans, Hatton rapped him sharply over the knuckles. For there is good evidence that Hatton had been brought up as a Catholic and, if in the earlier part of his life he was not actively one, he, like his mistress the Queen, had

B

Catholic sympathies. Richard Bancroft, a future Archbishop of Canterbury, was Hatton's chaplain; and Bancroft, Hatton and Whitgift, the then Archbishop, worked together to carry out the Queen's anti-Puritan policy. Whitgift had been specially entrusted with this task, and when the Chancellorship fell vacant, the Queen, it is said, chose him for this post also, so that combining the authority of Archbishop and Chancellor like his medieval predecessors, he would be in a supreme position to tackle a task which Elizabeth regarded as vital. When Whitgift declined the post, her choice fell upon Hatton, and there can be little doubt that he was chosen as a sympathetic supporter of Whitgift.

Hatton's career thus illustrates many of the panels of Elizabethan life. His earlier days at Court, dancing in a stately mask, or sharing in the medieval splendours of the tilt-yard, bring before our eyes the brilliant colours of the life of palaces. Every New Year's Day Hatton with the other courtiers presented the Queen with some costly confection of jewellery, receiving in return a handsome present of plate. As Vice-Chamberlain he assisted in the arrangements for the progresses in which Elizabeth delighted. Combining business with pleasure, she showed herself to her enthusiastic people, and lived for a season at the expense of her wealthier lieges. On such a progress the Tudor fancy revelled in pageantry. Poets were engaged to write allegorical plays, welcoming Gloriana to her loyal subjects' town or castle; and besides such well-known men as George Gascoigne and Gabriel Harvey, who composed the pageants for the entertainments at Kenilworth and Audley End, a minor poet, Thomas Churchyard, was chosen for a number of other progresses. Churchyard had close relations with Hatton, who employed him on occasion on diplomatic missions, and seems to have been responsible for his selection as pageant-maker.

Exalted personages were the natural patrons of the literary men of the Elizabethan age. Hatton himself had been in his earlier days an amateur author, writing part of a play that was acted before the Queen. He continued to take an interest in letters, and Burghley as well as Camden called him a lover of learned men. Besides Churchyard, who dedicated some books to him, he was the patron of many other writers. Dr. Dee the alchemist and geographer, Byrd the musician, Gabriel Harvey and many more inscribed works to him. Spenser wrote a sonnet to him. Bynneman, the leading printer of his day, described himself as Hatton's servant, and used his cognizance as an ornament on his title-pages; and Hatton had close connections also with Thomas Norton, counsellor to the Stationers' Company and licenser of books. He was a patron of Cornelius Ketel, the painter, to whom he sat for his portrait. Following his Queen's lead, he helped to finance the enterprises of Drake and, as a part promoter of the great voyage of circumnavigation, he is commemorated in the *Golden Hind*, named from his cognizance.

It is this combination of solid qualities with the lighter graces of Court life that makes Hatton so interesting a figure. He is the representative Elizabethan in his love of pageantry, his toying with literature, his passion for building, his political activity, his concern with his family history. For, like Burghley and the other new men of the Tudor world, he sought to trace his family to a Norman origin and to embellish his coat of arms with numerous quarterings. If the Norman founder of his race was fictitious, and his quarterings doubtful heraldry, it was but in keeping with the credulous pretentiousness of the age. If he could not rival Burghley or Walsingham as a statesman, Ralegh or Dyer as a literary figure, he was more interested in letters than the two former, a greater influence in affairs than the two latter.

Hatton's character is summed up in Camden's phrases, 'modest sweetness of condition . . . pious nature, a great reliever of the poor, of singular bounty and munificence to students and learned men'. There are numerous witnesses in his correspondence to his amiable disposition. Letter after letter mentions his courtesy and fair dealing, and although the tributes of the afflicted to those capable of relieving their sufferings may be common form, the volume of this testimony to Hatton's goodness of heart is impressive. Inclined to be jealous of Burghley and in general a supporter of Leicester's and Walsingham's policies, he had his clashes with the elder statesman. But Burghley himself is witness to his lack of rancour. 'I find you readier', he says, 'to change offence taken than any other with whom I have had like occasion.' And, as he was no learned lawyer, yet a hard-working and common-sense Lord Chancellor, so was he in no sense a scholar, though we need not accept Lord Campbell's sneers at his want of learning. When he was not writing his extravagant letters to Elizabeth, he was able to pen a straightforward communication which makes its points sensibly and without flourish, with little of the customary Tudor tortuousness and the involved and crabbed metaphors of his infinitely more learned Queen. Occasionally, as in a dignified communication to Samuel Cox, his quarrelsome secretary, or in a charming note to his friend Sir Richard Knightley, when he stood godfather to Knightley's son, he rises to a more than respectable height as a letter-writer. His speeches in Parliament are sufficiently eloquent, and there is evidence from the Bardon Papers, that he prepared his material with care. His oratory, like his correspondence, is sprinkled with the Latin tags that the fashion of the age demanded; and his general culture is witnessed by the Scots Jesuit Crichton who, in conversation, made a weighty astronomical allusion, which Hatton, 'being a learned man', immediately took.

His failings are most conspicuous in his subservience to the Queen. Ralegh's famous extravagance excepted, Hatton's letters to Elizabeth are perhaps the most shameless examples of that pandering to her love of adulation that the custom of the Court demanded. That his relations with her were innocent probably few historians doubt to-day. Hatton's passionate protestations must be taken with a grain of salt. They are but illustrations of the insincerity of the Elizabethan cult, and even the passages in Dyer's letter to him, which on their face seem to have a guilty implication, take on a much more innocuous hue when coolly considered. To keep Elizabeth's favour, it seems that he denied himself marriage. Lady Shrewsbury, as reported by the Queen of Scots, is the sole authority for this conclusion, but the statement that Hatton at one time aspired to the hand of Elizabeth Cavendish, and withdrew from his suit for fear of offending the Queen seems likely enough. David Lloyd, who wrote a brief memoir of Hatton, affirms that he was chaste in his life, but Lloyd is not a good witness for events that happened a hundred years before his time; and there is some evidence that Hatton had an illegitimate daughter, the lady whom Sir John Perrot seduced.

If extravagance is a fault, Hatton's opulence in building and love of pageantry, which left him over £50,000 in the Queen's debt, must be counted among his vices. The most unscrupulous act of his life is his filching of Ely House from the Bishop; the least chivalrous his acquiescence in the disgrace of his old friend William Davison the Secretary, whom Elizabeth made the scapegoat for the execution of Mary Stuart. Partisans of the Scots Queen will not forgive Hatton for his share in her trial and that of the Babington conspirators, and for his speeches against her in Parliament. But Hatton, like Walsingham, was but doing his duty as he saw it, and the impartial historian will acquit him of blame on that score. In his strength and in his weakness, his virtues and his faults, he remains a man of his age, that tantalizing age which the more it is studied seems the more remote from our own.

CHAPTER II

HATTONS AND HOLDENBYS

THE herald's pedigrees derive the family of Sir Christopher
Hatton from the Hattons of Cheshire, a numerous race in that
county. In early days they had been of some importance, but for
a couple of centuries before Sir Christopher's time had been
reduced to the position of minor landowners and small farmers.
There are two places named Hatton in Cheshire; and the fact that
the one family owned property in both tends to make their origin
and descent confusing. Briefly, it seems to be established that the
first place, Hatton in Daresbury, was given in medieval times to
one William son of Huthi, and that his descendants took the name
of Hatton. Later, a Hatton of Daresbury acquired the other
manor of Hatton in Waverton; and the old county historians
regarded it as 'a happy coincidence' that a Hatton of Hatton in
Daresbury should have settled in another place of the same name.

Hatton in Waverton became the principal possession of the
family, and a long line of Hattons succeeded until the male line
failed and the estate came through heiresses to the ancient family
of Dutton of Dutton, who thus became the Duttons of Dutton and
Hatton. But junior branches of the Hattons persisted, among them
the Hattons of Quisty Birches in Daresbury.

The pedigree that the heralds finally adopted derived Sir Christopher Hatton's immediate ancestors, the Hattons of Holdenby
in Northamptonshire, from the Hattons of Quisty Birches; and
this descent was elaborated until the Hattons were brought back to
Normandy, the Mecca of all Tudor heralds. The pedigree is set
forth in the Heralds' Visitation of Cheshire made in the year 1580
by Robert Glover, Somerset Herald, and William Flower, Norroy
King of Arms. The heralds' business was to visit the county,
determine which families were entitled to bear arms and ascertain
what those arms were, and obtain a statement from the head of
each family of his descent. This they were supposed to check
against their own records.

In this Visitation we find an exposition of the Hatton pedigree so
unusual in its minuteness as to suggest that there must be some

special significance in the circumstance in which it was prepared. That circumstance was unquestionably the influence of Sir Christopher Hatton. He was an important man in 1580, and no doubt the heralds were anxious to oblige Mr. Vice-Chamberlain, as he then was. It will be shown, indeed, in a later chapter that the preparation of the pedigree was prompted by Hatton himself, who, when he rose in the world, sent an agent to Cheshire to inquire into his family origins. For, though a member of the smaller landed gentry in virtue of his ownership of the manor of Holdenby and his descent from the feudal family of Holdenby of that place, he was anxious to prove that the Hattons too were of gentle extraction, and he was determined that the name of Hatton, raised by his exertions from obscurity to fame, should live. Being childless, he named his sister's son, William Newport, as his heir, adopted him and had him change his name to Hatton. He sought out his first cousins, Hattons in Kent, promoting the marriage of their representative, John Hatton, to the daughter of Sir Robert Shute, Baron of the Exchequer, and named him after his nephew in the settlement of his estates. Sought out too his second cousins, three brothers, humble Northamptonshire folk, whom he put next in the settlement, and his third cousin, Thomas Hatton of Shrewsbury, whom he chose as his heir if all these lines should fail.

All this, however, is not to suggest that the heralds' pedigree is necessarily false, or that Sir Christopher Hatton was not, in fact, descended from this ancient race. It is certain, however, that save for his own ownership of the manor of Holdenby, the circumstances of the family, as revealed in their wills, were humble if respectable. And his own descent, so far as it can be traced in the documents (other than heralds' pedigrees) that have come down to us, begins no farther back than his great-grandfather, whose Christian name is not certainly known. In the pedigrees he is given as a younger brother of Piers Hatton of Quisty Birches and is named Henry Hatton of Holdenby. Whoever he was, and whatever his Christian name, it is certain that he married Elizabeth, sister and eventually heiress of William Holdenby of Holdenby.

As Holdenby was the ancestral seat of this branch of the Hatton family and the only hereditary property of Sir Christopher's, its surroundings and history may be briefly noted at this stage, reserving for a later page an account of the great mansion built by Sir Christopher Hatton on the site of his ancient manor house.

Holdenby is a parish in the Hundred of Newbottle, Northampton-shire. The name is spelt in the earlier records Haldenby, and it means the *by* or township of Halfdan or Haldan. The local pro-nunciation, however, has been shortened to Holmby, and it is as Holmby House that it was later familiar as the place where Charles I was a prisoner in 1646. From the place-name the local lords of the manor took their surname, de Haldenby, later Haldenby or Holdenby. They had owned it from the thirteenth century at least, the long line of male Holdenbys ending with William, who died in 1498, in possession of the manor.

When the Hattons first appear on the scene Holdenby is in the possession of Joyce, daughter of William Holdenby, the last Holdenby of Holdenby. Joyce had married a kinsman, John Holdenby of Ravensthorpe, a neighbouring property, and died about the year 1512, without issue. The heiress was Elizabeth, sister of the above William Holdenby of Holdenby. She had married a Hatton and was the mother of three sons. Of these, George died without issue, and the next son, John Hatton, of Blechingley in Surrey, became the heir to Holdenby. He was the father of William Hatton, the first Hatton of Holdenby, who in turn was father of Sir Christopher, the subject of this memoir. Of Richard, the third son of Elizabeth Hatton, it will suffice here to say that he was grandfather of Sir Christopher Hatton's second cousins whom, in later life, he named in the remainder to his estates.

John Holdenby of Ravensthorpe, the husband of the last Holdenby of Holdenby continued to hold the manor for life, according to the custom known as the courtesy of England. He married again, and had a family of daughters by his second wife. He now made an offer to John Hatton, that he would take charge of Hatton's son and heir, William, and marry him to one of these daughters. In this way he hoped to secure the possession of the family manor in his own descendants. The arrangements made illustrate the rather humble circumstances of John Hatton of Blechingley and also the customs of the age.

By two agreements, made in 1514 and 1516, Holdenby pur-chased the wardship of Hatton's heir and the right to marry him to one of his daughters. Provision was also made that if William Hatton should die before the marriage could take place, or 'before carnal knowledge had with any of the daughters of the said

John Holdenby', Hatton was to deliver his next son and heir apparent to marry one of Holdenby's daughters; and so from heir to heir until a son of Hatton's should marry a daughter of Holdenby's and consummate the marriage. So were boys and girls disposed of in the Tudor marriage market. Holdenby further agreed to find William Hatton at 'convenient learning, and well and honestly according to his degree' during his minority. He also released the father from a bond of £200 for money owing for merchandise which Hatton had bought of him in the Staple of Westminster. One may hazard a guess that Hatton was a merchant or smallholder, and had purchased of Holdenby wool or other products of the manor. By another agreement, made in 1518, Holdenby promised to pay Hatton £4 a year during the life of his mother (Elizabeth Hatton, the heiress), with another 10s. a year 'toward a cote clothe' for him.

And so young William Hatton passes into John Holdenby's keeping to be brought up as a gentleman and married to the squire's daughter, on whose death the manor will, of course, revert to the Hattons, and will eventually go to William Hatton and his wife, Holdenby's daughter.

These arrangements made, John Hatton left Blechingley, and settled in the town of Northampton, close to Holdenby. In the rolls for the subsidy collected in 1522-4, John Hatton gentleman, is found there paying a tax of 6s. 8d. on his lands valued at £6 13s. 4d. a year. It is certain that he died before John Holdenby, and so never succeeded to the estate. For, when Holdenby died in 1534, the inquisition taken after his death records that he held his land of Ravensthorpe (which was a part of the Holdenby fee) of William Hatton. William Hatton was therefore lord of the fee, which shows that his father must have been dead. Among the wills, now at Birmingham, of the Northampton Archdeaconry Court, is one that is partly unreadable owing to damage by damp, but which can scarcely be other than this John Hatton's. It is dated July 12th, but the year is illegible. It is, however, in the book of wills that belong to the period 1524-7, and it adjoins wills of the year 1526. It may therefore be dated at about that year, and though there is no date of probate, it may be concluded that John Hatton died about this time. The will is that of John Hatton of the Sepulchre, Northampton. It names his son, William Hatton, to whom he leaves his 'searsnett dowbelett' and a furred . . .; and his (wife?) Joan, whom he makes executrix, leaving her the residue of his estate.

As the John Hatton, with whom we are concerned, had a wife Joan and a son William, the father of Sir Christopher, the probability that this will is his is exceedingly strong. In fact, it is almost certain that these humble bequests are those of the grandfather of the future Lord Chancellor of England.

According to the pedigrees, Joan, the wife of John Hatton, was the daughter of one John Westby of Kent. When Hatton's genealogical agent, Laurence Bostock, visited Holdenby in February, 1573, as will be told later, he made some inquiries about her. He interviewed John Dalton and John Fletcher, who had lived in Northampton for sixty years; also the vicar of St. Giles, who had been a monk in the Abbey before it was suppressed, and knew her well. She had boarded at Dalton's house after the death of her last husband, and had told Dalton that she was born in Kent, and that she and her two sisters were heirs to her father and had shared his lands between them. After the death of John Hatton, her first husband, she married Thomas Sadler, a sergeant of Northampton, and on his death John Farrington, a tallower of the same town. She died in Queen Mary's days (1553-8). Bostock's evidence that her last husband was John Farrington is borne out by the will of her son, William Hatton, made in 1546, who names in it his mother Faryngton, to whom he leaves 40s.

The efforts of John Holdenby to keep Holdenby in his family were unsuccessful. His daughter Mary who married William Hatton died without issue, and William Hatton married again. His new wife was Alice, daughter of Laurence Saunders of Harrington, Northamptonshire, a member of a numerous and well-connected clan. William Hatton died in 1547, and in his will asked that he should be buried in the chapel of our Lady within the church of Holdenby before the image of St. Catherine, and that his executrix should cause to be graved in brass and set in a fair stone in the wall under St. Catherine's image the words: 'Here lieth William Hatton, son of John Hatton, son of Elizabeth Hatton, daughter of William Holdenby and sister and heir to William Holdenby, sometime lord of the manor of Holdenby, upon whose soul Jesus have mercy.' There is still a brass plate in Holdenby Church, with an inscription much to this effect.

William's eldest son and heir was Francis Hatton, aged, according to the inquisition taken at his father's death, fourteen years. He died young, and nothing more is known of him. His tomb is in Holdenby Church, with a Latin inscription of four lines of verse. When next we hear of Holdenby, it is in the possession of Christopher Hatton, the second son. There was also a third son, Thomas, and a daughter Dorothy, who married John Newport of Hunningham, Warwickshire, and was the mother of William Newport *alias* Hatton, Christopher Hatton's heir. Dorothy Hatton's second husband was William Underhill of Idlicote, whose son William sold New Place in Stratford to Shakespeare.

There is but little to record of Christopher Hatton's younger brother Thomas. On November 6th, 1564, William Saunders of Harrington, leased that manor with the advowson of the church to his nephews Christopher Hatton of Holdenby, one of the Queen's Majesty's Gentlemen Pensioners, and to Thomas Hatton, his brother, of the Middle Temple, gentleman, until the year 1602. This record serves to correct the statement of the biographers that Thomas was the elder brother of Christopher, and, dying young, left Christopher his heir. Thomas was alive in January, 1567, when on his marriage with Ursula Newport (sister of John Newport, who married the Hattons' sister Dorothy) his brother Christopher gave him the rents of Hall Close in Holdenby, further proof that Christopher was the elder brother and owner of Holdenby. Thomas must have died soon after and without issue, since he is not named in the settlement of his estates made in 1573 by Sir Christopher Hatton, whose heir was his sister's son. Like his eldest brother Francis, Thomas lies buried in Holdenby Church with a Latin inscription on his tomb.

CHAPTER III

EARLY YEARS: OXFORD AND THE LAW

CHRISTOPHER, the eldest surviving son of William Hatton, of Holdenby, Northamptonshire, by his wife Alice, the daughter of Laurence Saunders of Harrington in the same county, was born about the year 1540, when Henry VIII had still seven years to live. This we know from the inscription on his monument, which states that he was 51 at the time of his death in 1591. He was therefore but seven years of age when his father died in 1547. Sir Harris Nicolas, who edited Hatton's Letter Book, says that there is some reason to believe that his maternal uncle, William Saunders, superintended his education; but he quotes no authority. Nothing, indeed, of Hatton's early life is known until, according to Anthony Wood, he entered as a Gentleman Commoner at St. Mary Hall, Oxford. He would then have been about 15 or 16 years of age, so that the year of his matriculation was probably 1555 or 1556. He left Oxford without taking a degree, a singular enough record for one who was to become Chancellor of the University.

Lord Campbell in his life of Hatton, among his *Lives of the Lord Chancellors*, purports to give some details of Hatton's career at Oxford; but his imaginative reconstruction of these early years is obviously biased by the prejudices of a lawyer who felt some mortification in having to admit the dancing Chancellor, 'this minion', as he calls him, to the select company of the grave worthies whose careers on the Woolsack he was chronicling, a company Campbell was afterwards himself to join. He tells us, for instance, that, under the care of his mother, Hatton imbibed with difficulty from a domestic tutor the first rudiments of knowledge; that he is said to have been idle and volatile, but to have been remarkable for good humour and vivacity, as well as for comeliness; that at the University he was exceedingly popular with his companions, but that he spent much more time in fencing and archery than in perusing Aristotle and Aquinas; and that from fear of being 'plucked', he left Oxford without trying for a degree.

All this is based upon no more than the known fact that Hatton left Oxford without a degree. It is possibly a not inaccurate, if unsympathetic, picture of a young gentleman of the period, of some birth and fashion, not remarkable for learning, but whose good looks and amiable disposition are sufficiently attested in his after life. His addiction to fencing and archery rests only in Lord Campbell's imagination, though they are likely enough pastimes for a young man in Hatton's position; it is certain that he was an expert in the tilt-yard.

Again we lose sight of Hatton in the year or two that may have elapsed after he went down from Oxford, until, on May 26th, 1560, when he was twenty years of age, he became a member of the Inner Temple, being described on his admission as of Holdenby in Northamptonshire. Fuller in his *Worthies of England* records that 'he rather took a bait than made a meal at the Inns of Court, whilst he studied the lawe therein'. Fuller wrote about half a century after Hatton's death; but he had known and conversed with many of his contemporaries, and he delighted in collecting such epigrammatic sayings. The suggestion is that Hatton did not enter the Temple with the view to studying the law as a profession, but rather to acquire a knowledge of the world and of the arts of social intercourse. A training in such accomplishments was certainly part of the curriculum in the Inns of Court. Fortescue, the author of the celebrated *De Laudibus Legum Angliae*, writing about a century before Hatton's time, describes the Inns as existing not only for the study of law, but as providing 'as it were a university or school of all commendable qualities requisite for noblemen. There they learn to sing and to exercise themselves in all kind of harmony. There also they practise dancing and other noblemen's pastimes'. Such young men of birth were placed in the Inns of Court, as Fortescue observes, not necessarily to learn law or adopt a legal calling; and it was customary in Hatton's day for ambitious men, desirous of entering upon a public career, to spend some years there in completing their education. William Harrison in his *Description of England* (1577) indeed regards the Inns of Court as the third university of the country.

It is possible, however, as Lord Campbell observes, that it was intended that Hatton should earn his bread as a lawyer. The family estate was small, and it is perhaps unlikely that he would have been put to the Bar merely to acquire a polish which would have been out of place in an obscure young country squire. Moreover, Hatton had a family connection, overlooked by his biographers, which would be likely to determine the law as his obvious career. His great-uncle, Thomas Saunders of the Harrington family, had a son, Sir Edward Saunders, who had risen to great eminence in that profession. He was of the Middle Temple, and had been Reader there. He was a Catholic, and had been appointed by Mary Chief Justice of the Queen's Bench. To this position he was immediately reappointed by Elizabeth on her succession, though shortly after removed to the Court of Exchequer as Chief Baron. He was a learned Judge, whose abilities were amply recognized; and his influence must have been thought likely to be of value to a young cousin adopting the law as a career. However that may be, the possibility must not be excluded that Hatton was from the first intended for public life. For besides his cousin the Judge, there is some evidence, as will appear presently, that he had powerful backing in the family of Lord Northampton, which was closely allied to the Queen.

It has been supposed that Hatton was never called to the Bar. There can be no proof one way or the other, because the Inner Temple Register of such calls does not begin until 1567, three years after he had entered the Queen's service. He became eligible to be called, according to Nicolas's information, within five if not three years of his admission as a student. It is just possible, therefore, that he may have been called some little time before 1564, when his service with the Queen began. It is unlikely that he studied in the Temple after that.

Lord Campbell at this stage of Hatton's career again draws on his imagination, giving in the manner of to-day's popular biography a highly coloured account of the young lawyer's life. He was in truth, says Campbell, a noted roisterer and swashbuckler, hearing the chimes at midnight, knowing where the *bona-robas* were and sometimes lying all night in the Windmill in St. George's Fields. This is, of course, only Campbell's paraphrase of Shallow's life at the Inns of Court, as he tells it in *Henry the Fourth*, to which play Campbell refers us for his local colour. 'But while he spent much of his time in dicing and gallantry', he proceeds, 'there were two amusements to which he particularly devoted himself, and which laid the foundation of his future fortunes. The first was dancing, which he studied under the best masters, and in which he excelled beyond any man of his time. The other was the stage; he constantly frequented the theatres ... and he himself used to assist in writing masques, and he took a part in performing them.'

As for dancing, henceforth to be inseparably associated with the name of Queen Elizabeth's favourite, the known fact of Hatton's excellence in this art seems to be the sole grounds for the guess that he studied under the best masters: the names of his teachers have not come down to us. But dancing was at that time a usual accomplishment and indeed a tradition of the Bar. It was a part of the entertainment provided in the Revels to be described below; and the passage from Fortescue, already quoted, is evidence that it was included in the education provided by the Inns of Court.

That it was Hatton's dancing that first attracted Elizabeth rests not only on tradition but on contemporary evidence. Sir Robert Naunton, his first biographer, is the earliest source of the story. He says, 'Sir Christopher Hatton came into Court as Sir John Perrot's opposite; as Perrot was used to say, "by the galliard", for he came thither as a private gentleman of the Inns of Court in a masque; and for his activity and person, which was tall and proportionable, taken into her favour'. Here we have the first form of the story which has persisted throughout the centuries, finding its latest expression in Lytton Strachey's phrase, 'the stately Hatton so comely in a galliard'. Naunton's tale is therefore worth examining a little more closely.

His account of Hatton, though short, is of value as being a contemporary picture. Naunton was by twenty-three years the younger man; but before Hatton's death was old enough to move in the great world, and had acquired some experience of public affairs. He died in 1635. He wrote in his *Fragmenta Regalia* short lives of Queen Elizabeth and her principal servants, including Hatton. This work, though first published in 1641, was, according to Fuller, a fruit of his younger years. He is thus a contemporary witness, who must have known in the flesh most of those of whom he wrote and have had many opportunities of hearing what other contemporaries had to say about them. His short sketch of Hatton contains the remark quoted above, which he gives on the authority of Sir John Perrot. That Perrot actually used these words is the more likely, seeing that Naunton was married to his granddaughter, and presumably had an intimate knowledge of his history. In his pages on Perrot's own life, Naunton tells us that his boldness and freedom of speech incurred 'the spleen and advantage of his enemies, amongst whom Sir Christopher Hatton was professed'; that the Queen had a great liking for the bluff soldier, who was indeed reputed (and Naunton seems to believe the story) to be an illegitimate son of Henry VIII, whom he resembled in his stature and choleric mien; and that to get him out of the way his enemies manœuvred him into that grave of reputations, the Lord Deputyship of Ireland, where he succeeded Lord Grey of Wilton, a distant kinsman of Hatton's. Perrot remained in Ireland from 1583 to 1588. On his return the Queen showed him much graciousness, but he withdrew from Court to the Welsh castle of Carew, partly on account of 'the hatred and practice of Hatton, then in high favour, whom he had not long before bitterly taunted for his dancing'.

Perrot was presently put on his trial, a trumped-up charge of treasonable correspondence with Spain being brought against him. In addition, it was alleged, apparently with truth, that he had used coarse and unmannerly language about the Queen. It was generally believed that Hatton, whose enmity Perrot is supposed to have incurred by seducing his illegitimate daughter, was the leading spirit among his persecutors. A news-letter, mentioning Perrot's arrest, says that some 'ascribe it to the Chancellor [i.e. Hatton], Sir John's adversary'. Be that as it may, he was found guilty, and died in the Tower in 1592 before sentence had been decided upon. When he heard the view of the Court he is reported to have said, 'God's death; will the Queen suffer her brother to be offered up a sacrifice to the envy of his frisking adversary?' Perrot's taunts, to which Naunton refers, numbered among them, no doubt, the statement already quoted that Hatton came to Court 'by the galliard'. If this statement and Naunton's addition, 'as a private gentleman of the Inns of Court in a masque', can be trusted, they afford a clue, as will be seen below, to the occasion when Hatton first came under Elizabeth's notice.

'The stately Hatton so comely in a galliard.' Perhaps it will help us the better to place him against the courtly background of his life if we consider for a moment the famous dance with which Perrot's phrase has for all time associated him, the measure that Queen Elizabeth trod, six or seven in a morning, 'after the Florentine style, with a high magnificence that astonished beholders'. The galliard was one of the favourite dances of the age, quicker and gayer than the solemn and stately pavane. In its simplest form it consisted of five steps, with a leap into the air and beating of the feet together after the fifth. From its five steps it was originally called the cinquepace, and the leap was the cabriole or caper. The literature of the period is full of allusions to it. In *Henry V* Shakespeare speaks of 'the nimble galliard', and in *Much Ado* Beatrice refers to it as the cinquepace. *Twelfth Night* brings galliard and caper together:

> SIR TOBY What is thy excellence in a galliard, knight?
> SIR ANDREW Faith, I can cut a caper.
> SIR TOBY And I can cut the mutton to't.

Fresh steps and various modifications came and went, being added as fashion dictated, and the galliard tended, as dances have done at all times, to become rather complicated. Barnabe Rich, who dedicated one of his works to Hatton and has given us a glimpse of the appearance of Holdenby House at the time of Hatton's rebuilding in 1581, has some plaintive remarks in *Riche His Farewell to Military Profession* on the difficulties of the dances of the day. Of the galliard he says:

> Our galliards are so curious that they are not for my dancing, for they are so full of tricks and turns that he which hath no more than the plain cinquepace is no better accounted of than a very bungler; and for my part they might as soon teach me to make a capricornus as a caper in the right kind that it should be.

But Hatton and his Queen felt no such diffidence as they trod the lively measure, perfect exponents of the graceful art that had brought them together.

From dancing it is but a step to the other interest with which Lord Campbell credits Hatton. He was undoubtedly attracted to the drama, for the statement that he assisted in writing masks and took a part in performing them is true, and is in fact the only detail known of his life at this point, before he became a Court official and began to figure in the entries in the State papers. As with his dancing, his interest in the drama came about through his connection with the Temple. Part of the social life of that society centred in the keeping of the Christmas season. From the earliest times, as Stow tells us, Christmas was kept in the Royal palace and in the houses of noblemen and men of position such as the Mayor and Sheriffs of London. A Lord of Misrule or

Master of Merry Disports was chosen yearly, who continued in office from All Hallows Eve to Candlemas (February 2nd). Masks and mumming were the order of the day during this season.

The Inns of Court followed in the same tradition with the Revels which also lasted until Candlemas, on which day the judges and sergeants-at-law feasted, while on every Saturday after supper the benchers danced their solemn revels in their gowns, with a song or carol begun by a Brother of the House. After the revels were finished the young gentlemen fell to dancing 'the measure galliard etc. in very laudable manner, the benchers beholding it'. For the Christmas festival special officers were appointed. Both Inns had a Steward, Marshal, Butler and Master of the Revels. At the Middle Temple there was also a Constable of the Tower; and at the Inner Temple a Clerk of the Kitchen, and in later times a Common Sergeant, a Constable Marshal and a Master of the Game.

But by the time Elizabeth came to the throne, there are indications that the customary Christmas masks and celebrations were beginning to die out. In 1552, at the Middle Temple it was ordered that the ensuing Christmas should not be kept in the usual way on account of the scarcity and dearness then prevailing; and from 1559 onwards an entry generally appears in the minutes to the effect that Christmas should not be solemnly kept, but that a cartload of coals and an allowance of forty shillings for minstrels should be provided for the benefit of those remaining in residence. The Inner Temple was, however, more faithful to the old tradition, and in the year 1561 a special effort was made, Christmas being kept with a richness of display and an extravagance in feasting probably never before equalled.

The reason for the unusual magnificence of the Christmas revels of that year was the settlement in favour of the Inner Temple of a dispute between the two societies. It turned on the efforts made by the Middle Temple to secure the transfer to it of Lyon's Inn, one of the three inns of Chancery under the control of the rival society. Through the powerful aid of Robert Dudley (afterwards the Earl of Leicester), Master of the Queen's Horse and Her Majesty's favourite, the Inner Temple was able successfully to resist the transfer. In gratitude it resolved that no one belonging to the society should ever be retained as counsel or give any help

34

in any action against Dudley or his heirs, and ordered that his arms should be set up in their Hall 'as a continual monument of his Lordship's goodness and great goodwill towards this House'. In addition they elected Dudley as Governor of their Christmas celebration that year, and in the festivities which followed he himself was enrolled a Member of the House.

The details of this festival, in which for a moment Christopher Hatton emerges from the routine of his life in the Inner Temple, have been preserved by Gerard Legh in his *Accedens of Armory*, published in the following year. Legh puts his narrative into the mouth of a traveller returning to London from abroad. This pilgrim hears a description of the Temple from a citizen, who tells him of the gentlemen who go there to learn law and 'also to use all other exercises of body and mind whereunto nature most aptly serveth to adorn, by speaking, countenance, gesture and use of apparel, the person of a gentleman', a further illustration of the social training that the Inns of Court afforded. Fired by this description, the stranger enters the Temple Gate, noticing the church, monuments and coats of arms. He is met by a herald and conducted to the Inner Temple Hall where Dudley holds his Court in the style and title of 'the mighty Palaphilos, Prince of Sophie, High Constable Marshal of the Knights Templars, Patron of the Honourable Order of Pegasus'. Dinner is served in state:

> The Prince so served with tender meats, sweet fruits and dainty delicates, confectioned with curious cookery, as it seemed wonder a world to observe the provision; and at every course the trumpets blew the courageous blast of deadly war, with noise of drum and fife, with the sweet harmony of violins, sackbuts, recorders and cornets, with other instruments of music as it seemed Apollo's harp had tuned their stroke.

At other tables sat the officers of the Revels, among them the Master of the Game, with his Chief Ranger, Masters of the Household and Clerks of the Green Cloth and Check. The records tell us that on this occasion Master Hatton was Master of the Game. He was possibly one of the twenty-four gentlemen, apparelled in long white vestures, with each a scarf of Pallas colours, whom Legh's imaginary traveller saw dubbed knights of the fabled Order of Pegasus and invested with the helm of fortitude, the breastplate of courage, the sword of justice, the spurs of speed 'to prick therewith the horse of fame', and the targe, mantle and collar of Pallas with pendant Pegasus. If Hatton were one of these, the act was symbolical of his future career, courtly and dignified, attended with the fame that comes to royal favourites and culminating in the splendour of the highest office of the law.

So far Gerard Legh on the Christmas Revels at the Inner Temple in 1561. That the account is not exaggerated appears from the course of these ceremonies, as laid down in the Temple records. The duties and dress of each officer are described, and we read that the Master of the Game was apparelled in green velvet, and the Ranger of the Forest in green satin, each wearing a hunting horn about his neck, the Ranger carrying also a green bow and arrows. 'Blowing together three blasts of venery, they pace round about the fire three times.' The Master of the Game makes three curtsies, and kneeling before the Lord Chancellor, declares the cause of his coming and desires to be admitted into his service. 'A huntsman cometh into the Hall, with a fox and a purse-net; with a cat, both bound at the end of a staff; and with them nine or ten couple of hounds, with the blowing of hunting-horns. And the fox and cat are by the hounds set upon, and killed beneath the fire.' Dancing and revelry follow, the dishes for each meal on the several days of the feasting being minutely described. There was a banquet on New Year's Eve, with a play and a mask, to which ladies were admitted. The official records tell us that Master Hatton was to have a special admission to this Christmas festival of 1561, without payment in respect of his charges as Master of the Game.

It has generally been supposed that on this occasion one of the most famous of the Inner Temple plays, *The Tragedy of Gorboduc*, was acted. It is certain that it was presented on Twelfth Night (January 6th, 1562), and it was probably part of the preceding Christmas festival. Its fame reached the Queen, and the gentlemen of the Inner Temple had the honour of acting it before her at Whitehall on January 18th. May not this have been the occasion when Christopher Hatton first came to the Queen's notice? It is probable that he was one of the actors in this piece. He was Master of the Game, and during the festivities had been associated with Robert Dudley, the Queen's favourite. But there are difficulties in the dates. It is not known that Hatton was in Elizabeth's service much before June, 1564, when he was a recently appointed

Gentleman Pensioner. His appointment was therefore at least two years later than the date of the 'great mask'. Yet, if we accept Naunton's story that he came to Court as a private gentleman of the Inns of Court in a mask, the festivities of 1561-2 seem to be almost certainly the occasion. This is Sir Edmund Chambers's view: 'It was presumably at the mask of 18th January that Hatton danced his way into Elizabeth's heart.'

CHAPTER IV

THE MASKS

'THE Mask', says Sir Edmund Chambers, 'is not primarily a drama; it is an episode in an indoor revel of dancing.' It is characterized by the presence of masked and otherwise disguised persons, who come into the hall accompanied by torch-bearers and musicians, often bringing gifts to the hosts and principal guests; generally also there is a spokesman or presenter, the 'truchman' or 'trounchman'. The maskers dance before the company and then, mingling with the guests, invite them to join in dancing. The mask may be simple, the kind favoured by Elizabeth, the decoration being supplied by the gaily-dressed performers, the torch-bearers and musicians, or it may be more spectacular, with the addition of a moving or stationary pageant. The actors are amateurs, not professionals, and the mask finally evolves into the masked ball, not the play or opera.

A well-known illustration is provided by a remarkable painting in the National Portrait Gallery, which represents episodes in the life of Sir Henry Unton, English Ambassador to France and a friend of Hatton's. One of these scenes is the mask at Unton's wedding, which took place about the year 1580. The wedding party is shown seated at a table in a great chamber overlooking the hall in which sit the minstrels. Maskers pass to and fro, and with them a drummer, a 'trounchman' holding a paper in his hand, Mercury, Diana, nymphs, and white and black Cupids as the torch-bearers.

Such was the kind of spectacle which the Inner Temple revellers brought to the Court on January 18th, 1562, the 'great mask' at Whitehall that followed the performance of *Gorboduc*. Hatton may or may not have acted in *Gorboduc*; it is fairly certain, as indicated in the last chapter, that he was one of the maskers. And it is possible that this was the occasion when, to quote Camden, 'being young and of a comely tallness of body and amiable countenance, he got into such favour with the Queen'. There is no proof that Elizabeth ever masked in person, as her father and brother did; but Sir Edmund Chambers thinks it extremely probable that she did so; and we may, if we wish, imagine her dancing at this mask, with the youthful Christopher Hatton.

It seems worth while, therefore, to say something about *Gorboduc* and its authors, the play that preceded the 'great mask' on January 18th, 1562. And it has other claims on our notice than the accident that Hatton may have acted in it. For it was the first historical play brought upon the stage in this country, the earliest regular English tragedy, and the first play in English to be written in blank verse. Moreover, it was in great part the work of one of the leading poets of the early Elizabethan age, Thomas Sackville, the Queen's cousin.

Gorboduc was not printed until 1565, and then without the consent of the authors, under the title of *The Tragedy of Gorboduc*. In that edition it is stated on the title-page that three acts were written by Thomas Norton and the two last by Thomas Sackville. Norton, eight years Hatton's senior, had entered the Inner Temple in 1555. Besides his share in *Gorboduc*, he is known as a translator and poet, among his works being twenty-eight of the Psalms contributed to Sternhold and Hopkins's version of the Psalter in English metre. He became a member of Parliament and a stern Calvinist, translated some of Calvin's sermons, and wrote many works against Popery. In 1562 he was appointed counsel to the Stationers' Company and also to the City of London, as well as a licenser of books. He was in favour with Burghley and Hatton, and four of his letters to the latter are preserved in Hatton's Letter Book. Later he became City Remembrancer, an office which he held until his death. He was one of the commissioners for examining Campion, the Jesuit martyr, and was present when he was racked. In consequence he got into some trouble and was confined to his house, but was released through the influence of Burghley and Hatton. These events will be related more fully in a later chapter.

Sackville is too well known to call for much mention here. Grandson of Anne Boleyn, the Queen's great-aunt, this connection added to his talents, literary and other, secured his rapid advancement at Court. Four years older than Hatton, he too had entered, in 1554 or 1555, the Inner Temple. In after years he came to some extent into contact with Hatton and was, with him, one of the commissioners for the trial of Mary Queen of Scots. He succeeded Hatton as Chancellor of the University of Oxford.

The story of *Gorboduc* is shortly summed up in the argument of the tragedy as follows:

> Gorboduc, king of Britain, divided his realms in his life-time to his sons Ferrex and Porrex. The sons fell to dissension. The younger killed the elder. The mother, that more dearly loved the elder, for revenge killed the younger. The people, moved with the cruelty of the fact, rose in rebellion and slew both father and mother. The nobility assembled and most terribly destroyed the rebels, and afterwards for want of issue of the prince whereby the succession of the crown became uncertain, they fell to civil war, in which both they and many of their issues were slain, and the land for a long time almost desolate and miserably wasted.

The topical interest of the play turns on the uncertainty of the succession to the crown in default of issue of the reigning monarch. The reference is of course to Elizabeth and the Queen of Scots, and the fifth act is an attack on Mary's title to the succession. This, no doubt, was its interest for Sir Philip Sidney, who praised it far beyond its merits. From the above it may be concluded that it was not a very lively piece. Nor is it. In fact a recent writer regards it as 'of so repellently gloomy and artificial a character that few but students of pre-Elizabethan drama could be expected to read it with even a pretence of pleasure'. It is now available in the World's Classics, and readers may judge for themselves. The play was re-issued about the year 1570, under the title of *The Tragedie of Ferrex and Porrex*, 'set forth without addition or alteration but altogether as the same was shewed on stage before the Queen's Majesty about nine years past, viz. the 18th day of January, 1561, by the Gentlemen of the Inner Temple'. The date is January, 1561-2, or, as we should write it, 1562.

The first mention of Christopher Hatton in the State Papers is in a warrant under date June 30th, 1564, from the Queen to Sir George Howard, Master of the Armoury, 'to make a complete suit of armour for Christopher Hatton, Gentleman Pensioner, to be delivered to him on his paying the just value thereof'. It is clear that he had only just been appointed a Gentleman Pensioner, for his name does not appear on the roll of the corps made up at Lady Day (March 25th) 1564. If it is correct to assume that he first came under Elizabeth's notice two and a half years before, it seems that it was a long time before she did anything for him. It is possible, of course, that he had been in attendance at Court in the interval, but it is difficult to suggest in what capacity.

This consideration suggests that we ought to examine a little more closely the inferences based on Naunton's statement and Perrot's remark that Hatton owed his first appointment at Court to his dancing. There is, of course, little doubt that his rapid promotion was due to his person and accomplishments, but it does not necessarily follow that he was offered his post at Court solely because the Queen had been attracted by him when he acted in *Gorboduc*, or took part in the mask that followed. Then, as now, we must look if we can find any influence to account for the choice of one man, among others as well qualified, for a coveted post. Perhaps we can find it in the Parr family, the widowed Queen of Henry VIII, and her brother, William Parr.

Hatton's connection with the Parrs was indeed slight. But the two families were neighbours, and they were remotely related by marriage. The Parrs were cousins of William, Lord Parr of Horton in Northamptonshire, whose grandson, Ralph Lane, the future Governor of Virginia, called Christopher Hatton his cousin. And there is, moreover, proof that Catherine Parr was willing to employ her influence on behalf of the Hattons. In 1548 she wrote to her new husband and Edward VI's uncle, Thomas Seymour, the Lord Admiral and the romping friend of Queen Elizabeth's youth; in a footnote she asked him to use his good offices with Lord Dacre for Master Hatton. Dacre had been Warden of the West Marches, and was to be Warden again in the following year. And, though Master Hatton cannot be Christopher, who was only eight years old at this time, it is quite likely that he was his elder brother, Francis, then about sixteen, recently left an orphan, and presumably looking around for a calling and a position in the world. The facts that there were no other Hattons at that time of any social standing whom the Queen Dowager would be likely to know, and that she was a distant connection, make it almost certain that Francis Hatton is meant. But Francis died, and his brother Christopher succeeded to the family estate; and Catherine Parr died in 1548, shortly after writing this letter. But her brother, William Parr, later Marquis of Northampton, was living. This man had been Captain of the corps of Gentlemen Pensioners in Edward VI's reign, and, although he had been dismissed and attainted by Mary, he was in some favour with Elizabeth. If he did exert himself for the young Christopher Hatton, it might well be that it was he who thought of having him appointed to his old corps.

The band of Gentlemen Pensioners was one of the royal guards, two corps of which were first established in Tudor times. Henry VII at his coronation had founded the Yeomen of the Guard, a body of fifty archers. Henry VIII in 1509 constituted a new guard of fifty mounted gentlemen, drawn from such as 'be comen and extracte of noble blood', for the purpose of encouraging among this class the handling of the spear and other feats of arms. For this reason they were called 'Spears'. Each man had to furnish himself with a complete harness of armour and other equipment, and with two horses (later increased to three) for himself and his page. He had also to find an archer and a custrel, that is an attendant armed with a 'coustille' or long sword, sharp from guard to point and having three edges, and with a javelin or demi-lance, armed and horsed. When unmounted, the guard were equipped with battle-axes; and the battle-axe, soon superseded by the more decorative processional axe with a spear-point above, became the distinctive weapon of the corps, as it still is of the Gentlemen-at-Arms, their successors, the King's bodyguard of to-day.

Though called Spears in Henry VIII's ordinance, the new guard soon became known as the Gentlemen Pensioners, being modelled on the French *Pensionnaires*. Apart from being chosen men who were expected to joust in the tilt-yard, their duties were to be in attendance on the sovereign with their axes, and to accompany him to chapel and on progresses. It was a fairly exacting service, and in recognition of this each Pensioner was allowed three months' leave in the year. The pay was fixed at 3s. 4d. a day, and there were also board wages of 2s. 6d. a day. Not large salaries even for those times; but the Pensioners were normally men of means, who sought this position for the prestige of an appointment about the Court. In the *Midsummer Night's Dream*, the cowslips tall are the Fairy Queen's Pensioners; and the popular esteem in which the corps was held is shown by another reference (an anachronism) of Shakespeare's in the *Merry Wives of Windsor*, where Mistress Quickly says to Falstaff:

> There have been Earls, nay, what is more, Pensioners here.

There is evidence that the Pensioners' costume changed from

time to time; and it may have altered during the period of Hatton's service from 1564 to 1577. In 1509 they were, according to the chronicler Hall, 'apparelled and trapped in gold, silver and goldsmiths' work'. In 1544 Strype reports them at the siege of Boulogne 'on barded horses, in one suit of red and yellow damask, the bards of their horses and plumes of feathers being of the same colours'. The same chronicler tells us that at a muster in Hyde Park in Edward VI's reign, 1551, they were 'in complete harness and great array, in white and black, five and five in a rank. And after them came their servants, in number an hundred, with great horses and harness, in white and black, with spears'. In Mary's time, they wore at musters the Tudor colours of white and green. In an illustration of one of Elizabeth's progresses, of uncertain date but perhaps during the term of Hatton's service, they are soberly clad in black cloaks with ruffs and long gold chains, a ceremonial dress; the portrait of Hatton by Cornelius Ketel shows him dressed either as a Gentleman Pensioner or in a similar costume. At other times the Pensioners appear before the Queen in armour on horseback. When on foot they were armed with gilt battle-axes.

Hatton, on being appointed a Gentleman Pensioner, had, as the record of June 30th, 1564 shows, to purchase a complete suit of armour from the Armoury. And it has been held that Elizabeth here showed her usual parsimony in not supplying her young favourite with his armour. But it is fairly certain that this was the ordinary arrangement; for Henry VIII's regulations laid it down that each Pensioner was 'to have his harness complete and all other habiliments meet and necessary'.

Hatton had arrived. His face had indeed been his fortune, and his dancing and acting had, at any rate, helped to secure him a coveted post which more than retrieved the lost opportunities of Oxford and the Inns of Court. He figures in all the bravery of his new style in November of the same year (1564) when, as already recorded, his uncle, William Saunders of Harrington, released to him as Christopher Hatton of Holdenby, co. Northampton, one of the Queen's Majesty's Gentlemen Pensioners, and to his brother, Thomas Hatton of the Middle Temple, gentleman, his manor of Harrington for a term of years to expire in 1603. No monetary consideration is mentioned, and the precise nature of the transaction is uncertain. It was probably a family arrangement, possibly occasioned by the rising fortunes of the young Court favourite.

A couple of months before this, Hatton is mentioned for the first time in a private memoir, and in circumstances which show that he was already of some importance and was employed by the Queen to welcome distinguished visitors to London. In September, 1564, Mary Queen of Scots sent James Melville on a mission to Elizabeth. It was the year in which Mary was manœuvring to get Darnley across the Border into Scotland in order to marry him, and when Elizabeth instead offered her the hand of Robert Dudley, whom she created Earl of Leicester to fit him for his proposed position.

Sir James Melville in his Memoirs has left us a lively account of his meeting with Elizabeth, and of the English Queen's questions concerning the relative beauties and accomplishments of herself and her rival sovereign. Melville tells us that, on his arrival in London, the Queen sent 'Mr. Hatton, afterwards Governor of the Isle of Wight, in her name to welcome me, and to show me that the next morning she would give me audience in her garden at eight of the clock'. Melville's memory has here played him false, for Hatton was never Governor of the Isle of Wight; he is confusing him with Sir Edward Horsey. 'The next morning', Melville continues, 'Mr. Hatton and Mr. Randolph, late agent for the Queen of England in Scotland, came to my lodging to convey me to Her Majesty, who was, as they said, already in the garden. With them came a servant of my Lord Robert's [Dudley], with a horse and footmantle of velvet laced with gold, for me to ride upon.' He found Elizabeth walking in the alley. There followed the first of the celebrated interviews, in which Elizabeth spoke of her wish for Mary to marry Dudley and announced her intention of making him Earl of Leicester, comparing him to his advantage with 'yonder long lad', pointing to Darnley. Elizabeth contrived that Melville should surprise her playing the virginals; inquired whether she or Mary played the better, danced the better, which was the taller, which the fairer? To all of which questions the courtly young Scotsman returned diplomatic answers. Two years later, at the baptism of Mary's and Darnley's son, the future King James, Melville, as we shall see, gives us another and more intimate glimpse of Hatton, who by then had climbed still higher the ladder of success.

Some writers have implied that Hatton remained for a time at the Temple, notwithstanding his new appointment. It is possible that he wished to keep the law as a second string to his bow; but it seems unlikely that he could have contrived to continue as a law student. In spite of some evidence to that effect, it is more probable that his appointment at Court terminated his studies at the Temple, though he would have remained a member. That evidence turns on Hatton's association with another of the Inner Temple plays, the tragedy of *Tancred and Gismund*. It is certain that this play was acted before the Queen in 1566 or 1567. Hatton wrote the Fourth Act; and the authors are stated to have been Gentlemen of the Inner Temple. That seems to mean no more than that Hatton was a member of the Inner Temple, as indeed he styles himself twenty years later, when he was Lord Chancellor, in a letter to that Society.

Tancred and Gismund is of great interest in the story of Hatton's life, for the Act in it, assigned to him, is his sole dramatic effort; and, if we set aside Mr. B. M. Ward's arguments for his part authorship of *A Hundreth Sundrie Flowres*, his solitary literary flight. The story is taken from Boccaccio's *Decameron*; its plot may be gathered from the argument of the play, which tells both in verse and prose of the inordinate love of Tancred, Prince of Salerne, for his widowed daughter, Gismund. This causes him to oppose her love for Guiscard, the County (or Earl) Palurin. Love, however, will not be denied; the father surprises the lovers and condemns the Earl to be strangled. He sends his daughter her lover's heart in a goblet, which she, filling with her tears and adding poison, drinks and dies. Whereupon the unhappy father kills himself also.

Boccaccio's tale was turned into English verse by William Walter and printed by Wynkyn de Worde in 1532. The play with which Hatton was concerned, based on this version, was first published in 1591: 'The Tragedie of Tancred and Gismund. Compiled by the Gentlemen of the Inner Temple, and by them presented before her Majestie. Newly revived and polished according to the decorum of these daies. By R. W. London . . . 1591.' The date is of interest, for it is the year of Hatton's death, and the printing of the book may have been intended as a memorial to Hatton, one of the many pieces which his death called forth.

'R. W.' is Robert Wilmot, one of the authors of the play that he resurrected. He was a member of the Inner Temple in Hatton's day, and when he comes before us in 1591 he was an Essex clergyman. Little is known of him, but he is mentioned by William Webbe in his *Discourse of English Poetrie* (1586) as one of the poets of that time. Prefatory to the play is printed a letter from this William Webbe to his friend, Robert Wilmot, in which he calls for 'a peremptory performance of an old intention of yours, the publishing I mean of those waste papers (as it pleaseth you to call them, but as I esteem them, a most exquisite invention) of Gismund's tragedy'. Of the Inner Temple gentlemen the writer says:

> The tragedy was by them most pithily framed, and no less curiously acted in view of her Majesty, by whom it was then as princely accepted, as of the whole honourable audience notably applauded . . . The brave youths that then (to their high praises) so feelingly performed the same in action, did shortly after lay up the book unregarded, or perhaps let it run abroad (as many parents do their children once past dandling) not respecting so much what hard fortune might befall it being out of their fingers, as how their heroical wits might again be quickly conceived with new inventions of like worthiness, whereof they have been ever since wonderful fertile.

He proceeds, therefore, to praise Wilmot for rescuing the play from 'the devouring jaws of oblivion', and for improving it and adorning it with 'the approved guise of our stateliest English terms'.

There follows an address from Wilmot 'To the Worshipful and Learned Society, the Gentlemen Students of the Inner Temple, with the rest of his singular good Friends, the Gentlemen of the Middle Temple . . .' In this Wilmot defends his action, which some might think indecorous in a clergyman in reviving this play; and, personifying it as 'Gismund', speaks of 'the love that hath been these twenty-four years betwixt us'. This phrase would date the composition of the play as about the year 1567. But Sir Edmund Chambers suggests Shrovetide, 1566, as the date of its performance, for the Court was then at Greenwich, where there is evidence that the play was given.

This evidence is contained in the Dedication and the prefatory sonnets. Wilmot dedicated the play to 'the Right Worshipful and Virtuous Ladies, the Lady Mary Peter and the Lady Anne

Gray', and speaks of 'these gentlemen, which with what sweetness of voice and liveliness of action they then expressed it, they which were of her Majesty's right Honourable maidens can testify'. There is also a Preface to the Queen's Maidens of Honour, consisting of three sonnets which indicate that the play was performed 'by the pleasant side of famous Thames at Greenwich Court', and in the Queen's presence. This agrees with Webbe's statement that the play was acted before the Queen, and adds that the audience included the maids of honour, among them Mary Petre and Anne Grey.

Now, who were these writers, and what evidence have we to identify them? Each Act is assigned in the text to a different hand. Thus, at the end of Act I is written, 'Exegit Rod. Staf.' Act II concludes, 'Per Hen. No.' Act III is signed 'G. Al.' Act IV has the ascription, 'Composuit Ch. Hat.' Act V alone has no indication of authorship, but is followed by an Epilogue initialed 'R. W.', so that Wilmot himself was probably the writer. 'Ch. Hat.' is almost certainly Christopher Hatton; 'G. Al.' has not been identified; 'Rod. Staf.' is likely to be the 'Master Stafford', who was fined £5 for refusing to act as Marshal at the Inner Temple in 1556-7. 'Hen. No.', though he has not been traced as a member of the Inner Temple, may be Henry Noel, a Gentleman Pensioner in Hatton's time, and, like Hatton, very extravagant. Elizabeth herself is said to have punned on his name:

No. L.
The word of denial, and the letter of fifty
Makes the gentleman's name that will never be thrifty.

Though perhaps not a very inspiring effusion, *Tancred and Gismund* is well wrought and readable, and with the musical introductions to each Act must have been pleasant enough to see and hear. The principal characters are Tancred, the King, Gismund, his daughter, and Guiscard, her lover. There are also a Captain of the Guard, Chamberlain, Cupid and the Furies. For the introduction to the First Act, 'Cupid cometh out of the heavens in a cradle of flowers, drawing forth upon the stage, in a blue twist of silk from his left hand, Vain Hope, Brittle Joy, and with a carnation twist of silk from his right hand, Fair Resemblance, Late Repentance'. Cupid soliloquizes, and then Gismund enters. She bewails her widowed lot; the King seeks to comfort

47

her, pointing out that though her husband is dead, her father is happily alive. We come to the Fourth Act, after Guiscard has followed Gismund to her chamber, being led by a letter from her concealed in a hollow cane.

This is Hatton's Act, in which the King discovers his daughter with her lover. There follows Tancred's soliloquy which is perhaps the best of Hatton's writing:

> Should I destroy them both? O gods ye know
> How near and dear our daughter is to us.
> And yet my rage persuades me to imbrue
> My thirsty hands in both their trembling bloods,
> Therewith to cool my wrathful fury's heat . . .
> But still, methinks, if I should see her die,
> And therewithal reflex her dying eyes
> Upon mine eyes, that sight would slit my heart:
> Not much unlike the cockatrice, that slays
> The object of his foul infections . . .

with much more in the same strain, a bit clumsy, but good ranting verse.

Guiscard is thrown into prison and the Act closes with a eulogy, intended for the listening ears of Elizabeth, upon the chaste service due from lover to lady and sovereign. There is lots of it, sad stuff; and the following passage will suffice:

> The love of virtue in thy lady's looks,
> The love of virtue in her learned talk;
> This love yields matter for eternal books,
> This love enticeth him abroad to walk,
> There to invent and write new roundelays
> Of learn's conceit, her fancies to allure
> To vain delights: such humours he allays,
> And sings of virtue and her garments pure . . .
> So whilom did the learned Tuscan serve
> His fair lady: and glory was their end.
> Such are the praises lovers done deserve,
> Whose service doth to virtue and honour tend.

And with this allusion to the loves of Petrarch and Laura, Christopher Hatton's Act comes to an end.

In the last Act Guiscard is strangled, and his heart brought to Gismund in a cup of gold. Here Wilmot, if his were the hand,

completes the story and shows himself the best poet of them all.
The Captain of the Guard laments the Earl's passing:

> For violent is death, when he devours
> Young men or virgins, when their hearts be green . . .

Gismund receives her lover's heart, rejoicing in the cruel gift,
which she takes as a token of her father's 'princely care and
tender love', surely a false note, but redeemed by the lines that
follow:

> To send me this, mine own dear heart, to me.
> Wert thou not mine, dear heart whilst that my love
> Danced and played upon thy golden strings?
> Art thou not mine, dear heart, now that my love
> Is fled to heaven, and got him golden wings?

And so it ends, with Gismund taking poison and the King killing
himself.

CHAPTER V

THE COURTIER

'To the band of Gentlemen Pensioners', says Sir Edmund Chambers, 'the Court looked for its supply of accomplished tilters.' The tilt was a survival of the medieval tournament. It served the double purpose of a pageant, dear to the hearts of the Tudors, and an exercise in military arts, a part of the courtly training of a gentleman. Henry VIII was an ardent supporter of pageantry of this kind, which reached its zenith in the splendours of the Field of the Cloth of Gold. The Gentlemen Pensioners, to which corps Hatton now belonged, had been founded by Henry, as has been shown above, largely to keep alive the tradition of the spear, with which they were armed and which gave them their name of 'Spears'. As a survival, the tilt clung to the use of armour, which the invention of gunpowder was rendering obsolete on the field of battle. Abandoned in the real army, save as a decoration on parade, it lived on in the tilt-yard, where it reached the height of costly perfection.

Elizabeth inherited her love of the tilt-yard from her father; and in 1562 she revised the rules for courtly combat, which had been laid down in 1466. Sir Edmund Chambers gives a classification of these 'jousts of peace', which at this time played so important a part in Hatton's life. They were of three kinds:

> The most important was the tilt, in which horsemen met in the shock of blunted spears across the 'tilt' or *toile*, a barrier covered with cloths, which ran longitudinally down the centre of the 'lists' or space staked out for the encounter. A record was kept of the courses run, in which marks were credited to the competitors for spears fairly broken or for 'attaints' on the head or body, and corresponding deductions made for spears ill-broken. The tourney was also on horseback, with swords instead of spears; while in the foot-tourney or 'barriers' the assailants were dismounted and fought alternately with push of pike and stroke of sword across a wooden obstacle.

The lists where the tournament took place and the preliminary ceremonies are described by Sir William Segar, Garter King of Arms, in his *Honour Military and Civil*, published in 1602, and earlier (1590) in *The Book of Honour and Arms,* of which Segar was probably also the author, dedicated to Hatton. The lists, he tells us, were sixty paces in length and forty in width, running east and west, with a gate at each end. The knights and gentlemen participating were grouped as challengers and defendants, whose pledges or hostages were placed before the royal box, and remained there until redeemed by the valour of their champion. When the challenger arrived, usually at the east gate of the lists, the Constable called out to him, 'For what cause art thou come hither thus armed? And what is thy name?' The challenger then gave his name, and said, 'I am hither come armed and mounted to perform my challenge', naming the defendant, 'and acquit my pledges.' The Constable then identified the challenger by opening the visor of his headpiece. The defendant now appeared at the west gate, and the Constable, after measuring their lances, administered the oaths to each. The first oath ran:

> Dost thou conceive the effect of this bill? Here is also thine own gauntlet of defiance. Thou shalt swear by the Holy Evangelists that all things therein contained be true; and that thou maintain it so to be upon the person of thine adversary, as God shall help thee and the Holy Evangelists.

In the second oath the opponents pledged themselves that they had not brought with them any unlawful weapon, 'engine, instrument, herb, charm or enchantment', and that they would put their trust in God alone. The heralds then cleared the lists, admonishing the spectators not to take sides. Finally, the Constable cried out in a loud voice, 'Let them go, let them go, let them go and do their best'.

And so, to quote from George Peele's *Polyhymnia*:

> Together went these champions, horse and man,
> Thundering along the tilt; that at the shock
> The hollow gyring vault of heaven resounds,
> Six horses spent, and spears in shivers split.

The first record we have of Hatton's tilting is when he performed before the Queen at Westminster in 1565, the year following his appointment as Gentleman Pensioner. This entertainment was arranged in honour of the marriage to the Lady Anne Russell of Ambrose Dudley, Earl of Warwick, elder brother of Robert Dudley, now Earl of Leicester, Hatton's principal as leader of the Inner Temple revels in 1561. An account of the preliminary challenge and acceptance has been preserved by Stow. In August the Queen was at the house of the Earl of Bedford, the bride's father, at Ivy Bridge in the Strand. York Herald entered to say that there was a messenger without who craved to speak with her. Permission being given, in came Richard Edwardes of the Chapel Royal, booted and spurred to represent a postboy. Kneeling down, he announced that four valiant knights, Henry Knollys, Christopher Hatton, Thomas Leighton, and Robert Colsett, wished to 'hold joust and barriers' at the marriage. The Queen consenting, up stepped Leicester, Lord Herbert, Arthur Lord Grey of Wilton and twenty other gentlemen to accept the challenge.

The tournament, which took place on Sunday, November 11th, is thus briefly described:

> A goodly challenge was made and observed at Westminster at the tilt, each one six courses: at the tourney twelve strokes with the sword, three pushes with the puncheon staff: and twelve blows with the sword at barriers, or twenty if any were so disposed.

It lasted three days, one for the tilt, one for tourney and one for barriers. One of the defendants on this occasion was Henry MacWilliam, a Gentleman Pensioner, then a follower of Leicester's but later closely connected with Hatton's affairs.

Hatton jousted again before the Queen at Westminster in May, 1571, as one of the four challengers in 'a solemn joust at the tilt, tourney and barriers', his colleagues being the Earl of Oxford, Charles Howard, later Lord Howard of Effingham, the Admiral commanding against the Armada, and Sir Henry Lee. The defendants included Ralph Lane, afterwards the first Governor of Virginia, who called Hatton his cousin, George Delves, a Gentleman Pensioner, whose lively account of this entertainment is quoted below, and Henry MacWilliam.

This pageant also lasted three days, devoted to tilt, tourney and barriers. The Queen bestowed a prize on each of the challengers, who were led armed by two ladies into the Presence Chamber. Oxford was given a tablet of diamonds, Howard a chain, Lee a diamond and Hatton a gold bell and chain. He was already, perhaps, the Queen's 'bell wether', one of her pet names for him. It was reported that all the challengers did 'very valiantly, but the chief honour was given to the Earl of Oxford'. We have a brief first-hand account of this tourney from the pen of one of the defendants, who does not agree that Oxford was pre-eminent. George Delves, a Gentleman Pensioner, writing to the Earl of Rutland from Court on May 14th, 1571, says:

> Lord Oxford has performed his challenge at tilt, tourn and barriers far above expectation of the world, and not much inferior to the other three challengers. Their furniture was very fair and costly. The Earl's livery was crimson velvet, very costly. He himself and the furniture were in some more colours, yet he was the Red Knight. Charles Howard was the White Knight; Sir Henry Lee the Green Knight. Mr. Hatton was the Black Knight, whose horses were all trimmed with caparisons of black feathers, which did passing well. There were twenty-seven defendants, whereof your servant was one . . .

The scoring sheet of this tilt is preserved among the Ashmolean Manuscripts in the Bodleian Library. Against each name the herald has tricked the bearer's arms. Those here ascribed to Hatton are of great interest, for they are quite different from the ancient arms of Hatton of Hatton in Cheshire, which he subsequently adopted. This point will be discussed in a subsequent chapter.

In 1568 Hatton had been appointed by the Queen Keeper of the royal park of Eltham; and here in 1576 he was visited by the Sieur de Champagny, a Flemish Catholic agent, whom he entertained with *force musiques et comedies*. On the following day Hatton took him to Greenwich, where he saw a tilt specially arranged for him. Sir William Segar gives us an account of Champagny's impressions on this occasion:

> I was (quoth he) one day by Sir Christopher Hatton, Captain of her Majesty's Guard, invited to Eltham, an house of the Queen's, whereof he was guardian; at which time I heard and saw three things that in all my travel of France, Italy and Spain, I never heard or saw the like. The first was a concert of music, so excellent and sweet as cannot be expressed. The second, a course at a buck, with the best and most beautiful greyhounds that ever I did behold. And the third, a man of arms excellently mounted, richly armed, and indeed the most accomplished Cavaliero I had ever seen. This knight was called Sir Henry Lee, who that day (accompanied with other gentlemen of the Court) only to do me

honour, vouchsafed at my return to Greenwich to break certain lances: which action was performed with great dexterity and commendation.

George Delves's few lines of description give us some idea of the costliness and magnificence of these entertainments in which Hatton took a leading part. Such details enable us to appreciate the great expense to which a man of fashion was put, and help to explain the chronic indebtedness from which Hatton suffered. His tilting armour, richly chased and engraved, must alone have involved a heavy outlay. We know a good deal about Hatton's armour.

Our principal source of information is a manuscript, now in the Victoria and Albert Museum, known as the Jacobe Manuscript. It was described by the late Lord Dillon in *An Elizabethan Armourer's Album*. It once formed part of the Harleian Library; was in 1790 in the possession of the Duchess of Portland, daughter of Edward Harley, Earl of Oxford; passed to the Continent, and was finally purchased for the nation at the Spitzer sale of armour. It contains drawings, seventeen inches in height, in ink and water-colour, of twenty-nine suits of armour and extra pieces. Most of the drawings are titled 'Jacobe'; and Lord Dillon and others believe them to be the work of Jacob Halder, or Jacobe, the Master Armourer at the Greenwich Armoury in Elizabeth's reign.

The suits depicted in the manuscript were made for those who took part in tournaments, and the illustrations show the wearers with the right hand grasping a mace or truncheon, while the left hand holds the sword hilt. Of the twenty-nine suits illustrated, three were made for Sir Christopher Hatton, and among the others there are two suits for Leicester, three for Sir Henry Lee and one for 'Mr. Macke Williams', in whom we recognize Henry MacWilliam, Gentleman Pensioner and Hatton's friend.

The ornamentation of the various suits is shown in detail, and in some cases it is possible to identify existing suits of armour with the drawings, and so to assign them to their owners. Sir Christopher Hatton's first suit is russet with gold bands, between which are pierced lozenge-shaped designs. On the tapul of the breast-plate is a figure of Mercury, and two capital E's regardant, surmounted by a crown, the monograph of Queen Elizabeth. Lord Dillon, whose description this is, identified the suit with a

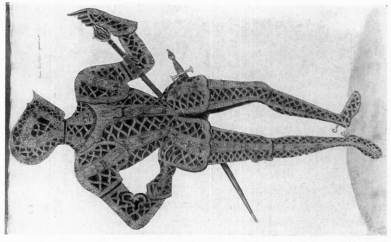

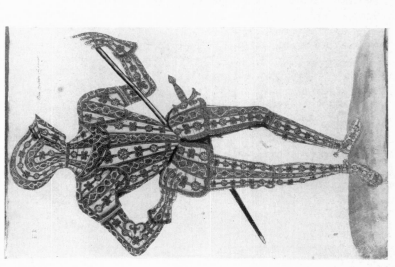

TWO SUITS OF ARMOUR FOR SIR CHRISTOPHER HATTON

From the contemporary manuscript in the Victoria and Albert Museum

(Crown Copyright Reserved)

suit bearing the date 1585, now at Windsor; but this has been disputed. It is a remarkably fine armour, and gives, says Lord Dillon, a good idea of the large stature of Elizabeth's favourite.

The second Hatton suit in the manuscript is described by Lord Dillon as white with gilt bands of ornament, between which are strings of roses and knots. He identified a vamplate of a lance in the Tower of London as belonging to this suit; but this has also been disputed. The third Hatton suit is white, with narrow gilt bands. It too has disappeared, so that it would seem that none of Hatton's armour is now in existence, and we only know of its appearance from the Jacobe Manuscript. One of Hatton's suits of armour he gave to Leicester. This we know from Leicester's will, in which he leaves to Hatton, 'mine old dear friend', his best George and Garter and 'one of his armours which he gave me'.

In December 1566 James, the infant son of Mary Queen of Scots, the future King James VI and I, was baptized at Stirling. It is again from Sir James Melville's Memoirs that we learn that Hatton was a member of the suite of the Earl of Bedford, who represented Elizabeth, bringing with him from her a massive font of gold. Mary dispatched Melville to meet Bedford at Coldingham and conducted him to Stirling, where he arrived with an escort of eighty horsemen. With him rode George Carey, eldest son of Lord Hunsdon, Elizabeth's first cousin, 'Mr. Hatton, greatest in favour with the Queen of England for the time', and a Mr. Lignish, a favourite of the Duke of Norfolk, whom he represented.

The baptism ceremony was celebrated in all its traditional medieval splendour. The royal horses were caparisoned in cloth of gold, silver-fringed. The baptismal Cloth of Estate was of crimson velvet, edged with gold thread and braid and crimson silk. The infant prince's bedspread was wrought of ten yards of figured cloth of silver. The evening of Sunday, December 17th, 1566, was chosen for the ceremony, James being carried to the royal chapel by the French Ambassador. Two rows of barons and gentlemen, holding wax candles, lined the aisle. Nobles followed, carrying the basin and ewer and the other paraphernalia of the rite, at the celebration of which an archbishop, three bishops, a prior, deans and archdeacons were present. The French Ambassador handed the child across the golden font to the Countess of Argyll, acting as Queen Elizabeth's proxy. Darnley, the young father of the infant prince, was absent, sulking — it was just after Rizzio's murder — and it had fallen to Bothwell, soon to supplant Darnley in Mary's affections, to receive the ambassadors and the other foreign visitors.

Feasting, dancing and other entertainments occupied the ensuing days; and on Thursday the 21st there was a great banquet and mask, in which we catch an unexpected glimpse of Hatton. Mary's Auvergnat *valet de chambre*, Sebastien Pagaz, the Bastian of Melville's narrative, and George Buchanan, afterwards famous or infamous as Mary's traducer, collaborated to present a splendid spectacle. Sebastien contrived a scene in which the banquet was brought in, through the great hall, upon a platform decorated with laurel on which reclined musicians clad as maidens, singing and playing upon a variety of instruments. Running before the platform were a number of other men dressed as satyrs, with long tails, and whips in their hands. As the nymphs sang Buchanan's verses, the satyrs served the guests. All went gaily until a joke perpetrated by the satyrs was taken in bad part by the English visitors. For not content with their role of waiting on the feasters, they 'put their hands behind them to their tails, which they wagged with their hands in such sort as the Englishmen supposed it had been devised and done in derision of them, weakly apprehending that which they should not have appeared to understand'. For the touchy English guests well knew that the improper gesture was an allusion to the belief, widely held by foreigners, that the English had tails bestowed upon them as a divine punishment for the martyrdom of Thomas Becket. It would have been more dignified, as Melville hints, to ignore the satyrs' rudeness.

But Hatton, Lignish, and the other gentlemen, who had already dined (too well perhaps) so as to be free to watch the spectacle, when they saw what was happening, turned their backs and sat down on the floor behind the great table. Hatton told Melville that 'if it were not in the Queen's presence, he would put a dagger to the heart of that French knave, Bastian, who, he alleged, had done it out of despite that the Queen made more of them than of the Frenchmen'. Melville tried to keep the peace, but the Queen, sitting with Bedford, was attracted by the clamour behind her, and turned to inquire what was the matter. Melville explained, and Mary and Bedford, with some difficulty soothed the irate Englishmen. Melville blames Hatton, Lignish and the others who 'committed a great oversight to notice it was done against them. But my Lord of Bedford was discreet and interpreted all things for the best'.

The English envoys did not leave Stirling empty-handed. Mary gave Bedford a rich chain of diamonds, worth 2000 crowns; Carey got a chain of pearl and a ring with a fair diamond; Hatton a chain with the Queen's picture and a ring; Lignish and five others of quality received chains. Melville and an escort speeded them on their homeward way.

Such was Hatton's first contact with the Queen of Scots. Six years later he was to be concerned with inquiries concerning her and the Duke of Norfolk's treason following the Ridolfi Plot; and it may be that, as is suggested later, he then visited her, a captive at Sheffield Castle. Another fourteen years, and Mary was to write Elizabeth the scandalous letter in which she accused her of guilty love for Hatton and others. Three years more, and Hatton was to be present as one of the commissioners at the trial at Fotheringay which sent Mary to the block.

From now onwards Elizabeth began to load Hatton with lands and offices. In April, 1568 she gave him the site of the Abbey and demesne lands of Sulby in Northamptonshire, nominally in exchange for his hereditary manor of Holdenby. But on the same day she leased Holdenby to him for forty years, and two years later reconveyed it to him in fee. In July of that year (1568) he was appointed Keeper of Eltham Park in Kent and of Horne Park in Surrey. In 1569 the farm of the chapel of Monkton in Pembrokeshire was granted to him; and in a list of justices of the peace in October, 1569 his name appears for his native county. He was granted also the reversion of the office of Queen's Remembrancer of the Exchequer in February, 1571, and in the same year was given an inn near Temple Bar called the Ship, lands in Yorkshire and Dorsetshire, and the wardship of a minor, a valuable perquisite since it carried with it the power to sell the ward's marriage. The minor in question was a connection, William son of William Underhill (who owned New Place, Stratford-on-Avon, sold by his son to Shakespeare) and who had married as his second wife Hatton's sister, Dorothy Newport. In 1572 he was given woods in Herefordshire, the manor of Frampton in Dorsetshire, the reversion of the house of the monastery of St. Mary de Pratis near Leicester, the stewardship of the manor of Wellingborough in Northamptonshire, and the wardship of two more minors.

Hatton was returned to Parliament for Higham Ferrers, Northamptonshire in April, 1571, but in that Parliament he was a silent member. It was characteristic of the man to proceed cautiously. He would be an observer only until he had learned the ropes. So, when he became Lord Chancellor, he was careful to feel his way in unfamiliar surroundings, and to lean on the advice of learned friends until he could stand on his own feet. In 1572 he was again returned to Parliament, as Knight of the Shire for Northamptonshire, and continued to represent that county until he went to the Woolsack. Gradually he began to take a more active part in the work of the House of Commons, and came eventually to be recognized as the Queen's mouthpiece there.

Before this time, though the precise date is unknown, he had been made one of the Gentlemen of the Queen's Privy Chamber. There is an interesting record of his costume in that office in 1574, when the Queen issued a warrant for the delivery to Christopher Hatton, Esquire, Gentleman of the Privy Chamber, of six yards of tawney medley at 13s. 4d. a yard, with black fur for the same, and also five yards each for the Grooms and Pages of the Chamber.

In 1572 Hatton was appointed, in succession to Sir Francis Knollys, Captain of the Queen's Bodyguard. This, the famous Yeomen of the Guard, was one of the two corps of royal guards, in the other of which, the Gentlemen Pensioners, he had been enlisted eight years before. The Yeomen were a footguard established by Henry VII in 1485, a working Palace guard, not recruited as were the Pensioners from the gentry but from the yeoman class. Their Captain, however, was a man of position; Knollys, whom Hatton succeeded, was married to the Queen's first cousin, and Hatton's successor was Sir Walter Ralegh. Hatton had now added to his position as Gentleman Pensioner this coveted post about the Queen's person. He held it, with the Vice-Chamberlainship, to which he succeeded in 1577, until he became Lord Chancellor in 1587. According to John Phillips, who published a eulogistic poem on Hatton after his death, he took great care of his men of the Queen's Guard, and induced Elizabeth to raise their pay from 1s. 4d. to 1s. 8d. a day, and for three months of the year to 2s.

In 1572 Hatton presented the Queen with the customary New Year's gift which she expected from her courtiers. This was his first recorded offering, and it took the form of 'a fair jewel called pizands of gold, fully garnished with rubies and diamonds, and flowers set with rubies, with one pearl pendant and another in the top', weighing three and a half ounces. 'Pizand' is presumably a variant of 'pesant', a weight of fine gold, and hence a coin or roundel. From now onward, like the rest of the Court, Hatton made these customary New Year's gifts of jewellery, receiving from the Queen in return a present of silver plate, her usual mark of regard. He was specially favoured, for he always received four hundred ounces at these times, while even the highest dignitaries never got more than two hundred, the usual gift being fifty ounces.

Such royal notice of course made Hatton an object of envy; and Leicester in particular is said to have shown his jealousy of the new favourite. Miss Strickland, in her life of Queen Elizabeth, gives a story about the two men which, as she quotes no authority, we need not necessarily regard as authentic. Leicester, the story goes, sought to bring ridicule on Hatton by proposing to introduce to the Queen a dancing-master who excelled him in his art. But Elizabeth drew a proper distinction between the professional and the amateur. 'Pish', she said contemptuously, 'I will not see your man: it is his *trade*.'

CHAPTER VI

HATTON'S PLACE IN PARLIAMENT

HATTON's first appearance on the larger stage of public life is as an actor, though a minor one, in the drama of Mary Queen of Scots, who had been a virtual captive in England since 1568. The problem of Mary Stuart was the chief issue in English politics, and no one connected with affairs could be indifferent to it, or not seek to take a part. Unfortunately, although there are unmistakable traces of Hatton's activities in these matters in the early days of Mary's captivity, there is little direct evidence of their exact nature. It appears from a letter of his to Queen Elizabeth, of which the date is probably October, 1572, that he was officially engaged in the affairs of the Queen of Scots, the Duke of Norfolk and the Parliamentary debate of that year concerning the Prayer Book. When the Duke was under sentence of death for his share in the Ridolfi Plot he acknowledged Hatton's kindness to him. This is probably a reference to an examination of the Duke by Hatton, undertaken on Elizabeth's commission. There is some reason also to think that Hatton's business with Mary's affairs may have brought him to Sheffield Castle where she was then in the custody of the Earl of Shrewsbury.

All this is vague enough, and is mainly concerned with Hatton's official activities. But, if there is little evidence for the precise part that he may have played behind the scenes, there are indications that he was of Leicester's party, which had at first favoured the marriage of the Queen of Scots to the Duke of Norfolk, and that he was one of those who, up to a point, worked against Burghley, at whom Norfolk's plotting was largely directed. May it not have been that the young courtier, not content with the merely ornamental role of an Oxford or a Dyer, cherished the ambition to be more than just a royal favourite and sought to play an important part in directing policy, perhaps even thought that he might be the man to supplant Burghley? Such evidence as there is will be given below. But, whatever the facts, Elizabeth's loyalty to Burghley, the indignation of Lords and Commons against Mary Stuart and the Duke of Norfolk, and Burghley's renewed grip of affairs, after a temporary period of eclipse, must have convinced Hatton that he was not marked out for the larger spheres of statesmanship, for the moment at any rate. His cue was to support the elder statesmen, and by personal service and attendance on the Queen, to acquire a confidential position not the less influential for being unofficial. It was a wise decision. It led him to the Woolsack.

As a preliminary to an attempt to suggest the role that Hatton played in this drama, it is suggestive to note that, though he conformed to the Elizabethan settlement and was in the latter part of his life an orthodox and even an aggressive Protestant, he was almost certainly brought up as a Catholic, and was probably at this time a crypto-Catholic if not an open one. His mother's family, Saunders of Harrington, was Catholic, if we may judge by the record of her first cousin, Sir Edward Saunders the judge, though it is true that Sir Edward's younger brother, Laurence, was a Protestant martyr under Mary Tudor. Of Hatton's own sympathies there is a good deal of evidence. In June, 1573, when he was in Antwerp, an unknown correspondent, 'T.G.', no doubt a Catholic *émigré*, wrote to him from that town and, reminding him that he was first baptized in the Catholic faith and had continued in it for many years, warned him of the danger of leaving it. He urged him to use his influence with Elizabeth, being concerned at 'the cutting off of the rightful succession' to the throne, a reference to the claims of Mary Stuart to be recognized as Elizabeth's heir. On Hatton's return from abroad in October of the same year, Peter Burchet, a fanatical Puritan, conceived the notion of assassinating him as 'a wilful Papist', one that 'hindereth the glory of God so much as in him lieth'.

That Hatton was brought up as a Catholic seems the more likely from the fact that he was sent as a student to St. Mary Hall, Oxford, about the year 1556, when William, later Cardinal Allen, was Principal there. Even in his later life there is evidence that he was regarded by the Catholics as one of their faith who had strayed from the fold for reasons of State. He had, in fact, like thousands of others, perhaps even the Queen herself, ceased to be a Catholic because it had become impossible for Queen or for loyal statesman to continue as such. To foreign ambassadors Elizabeth represented herself as a Catholic in everything except allegiance to the Pope. She disliked the Puritans, despised her own Bishops and, so far as so secularly minded a person could have a religion, was Catholic in sympathies.

Many of her Council seem to have been in the same position. The evidence in Hatton's case, at any rate, is too significant to be ignored. Allen himself wrote of him that he was one of those who had no doubt of the Catholic faith being true. But whatever association there may have been at one time between the two men, Hatton, by the compulsion of events, was eventually to move with his Queen to an anti-Papal and indeed Protestant position; and in his Armada speech as he thundered against the Pope, he took the opportunity to speak of the former head of his old College, at this time, under the calamitous influence of Father Parsons, the chief of those exiled Englishmen who were planning the overthrow of their Queen and country, as 'that shameless atheist and bloody Cardinal Allen, a savage and barbarous priest'.

Other reports which add to the cumulative evidence for Hatton's Catholicism are those of Peter Ribadeneira who, as quoted by Anthony Wood, wrote in the Appendix to Father Nicholas Sanders's *De Origine ac Progressu Schismatis Anglicani* that Hatton was always *in animo Catholicus*; of the anonymous author of *Leycester's Commonwealth*, who quotes an English Catholic *émigré*, one of the Pope's pensioners, as saying that he was of such credit and favour in Rome as if he was the greatest Papist in England; and of Camden who, in recording Hatton's death, states that the Catholics commended him 'as a man more inclinable to their side, who was of opinion that in matters of religion neither fire nor sword was to be used', a sentiment that reflects at any rate his clemency and tolerance.

More circumstantial is the remarkable record left by Father Crichton, the Scottish Jesuit, of a conversation he had with Hatton as late as about the year 1587, which seems to leave no doubt on the point. He says of himself:

> Father Crichton dealt by letter with Sir Christopher Hatton, the Councillor and the most familiar of all with the Queen. He knew him to be a Catholic at heart, and he accommodated himself to his humour. Hatton obtained liberty for him from the Queen, and used him with very great humanity. He asked Crichton what princes and Catholics thought about himself. Crichton answered that they felt about him what mathematicians think about the

motions of heavenly bodies. They have a natural motion from west to east, but still they are drawn by the *primum mobile*, and carried by motion to the west. Being a learned man, he at once understood what Crichton would have liked to say, that he had embraced heresy to please the Queen; and, taking out his purse, he gave him twenty angels and let him go.

The coming of the Queen of Scots to England in 1568 initiated a stern time of testing for those of the older faith. The year after her arrival the Northern Rebellion broke out. That rebellion ultimately derived from a suggestion that the Duke of Norfolk should marry the Queen of Scots, and that Mary should be restored, with Elizabeth's approval, to the throne of Scotland. But the proceedings soon developed and ramified until they became a plot to recognize Mary as Elizabeth's successor, resume friendship with Spain and withdraw all support from the French Huguenots. The plan appealed to the old conservative and Catholic party. It attracted to it the northern Catholics, including the Earls of Northumberland and Westmorland. It involved the overthrow of Burghley and the new men, mostly Protestants, whom he had gathered round him. Leicester was among those who were to be thrust aside, but he went over to the malcontents. It is at least conceivable that Hatton went with him to avoid the fate of these new men, of whom he was one, and attracted by the Catholic atmosphere of the plot. But Elizabeth learned of the conspiracy, supported Burghley and committed Norfolk to the Tower. The revolt of the northern Earls followed, and was soon broken. Burghley was in the ascendant again.

A Parliament was summoned in the spring of 1571 to attaint the leaders of the revolt, vote supplies and make provision against the dangers of the general situation. It was in this Parliament that Hatton made his first appearance, as Member for Higham Ferrers. Thomas Norton, joint author of *Gorboduc*, the play in which Hatton, when a student of the Inner Temple, may have acted, was a member too. The Fifth Act of *Gorboduc* is simply a political tract directed against Mary's title to the succession; and it is noteworthy that in this Parliament Norton introduced a Bill having for its object the barring of Mary's claims.

Later in the same year, 1571, Norfolk, released from the Tower, played a prominent part in the Ridolfi Plot. It had much the same objectives as the Northern Rebellion: an insurrection aided by a Spanish invading army, the seizure of Elizabeth's person, the restoration of the Catholic faith and the marriage of Norfolk to the Queen of Scots. Burghley, with his network of spies, got wind of the plot, unravelled its details and had Norfolk arrested. He was brought to trial on January 16th, 1572, found guilty of high treason and sentenced to death.

On January 20th, the day before his execution was expected, the Duke of Norfolk, a weak and vain man whose ambition had lured him on to forget his better nature and, in the prospects of marriage with the Scots Queen, to forgo his allegiance to his own sovereign, wrote to his son Philip, Earl of Surrey: 'Mr. Hatton is a marvellous constant friend, one that I have been much beholden unto. Write unto him and seek his goodwill, and I believe you will find him assured.' This probably means, as Hatton suggests in his letter to Elizabeth already referred to, that he had been commissioned by her to examine Norfolk, and in the course of examination had shown himself a humane and friendly official. This is the more likely, as the examination of those charged with high treason was later to become one of his special functions. How far he may have made an effort to influence the Queen on Norfolk's behalf is unknown. Certainly Elizabeth shrank from the execution and three times countermanded it. The Parliament that assembled in May, 1572, led by Thomas Norton, called loudly for the heads of Norfolk and Mary; and eventually in June Norfolk was hurried to the block on Tower Hill. No doubt the Yeomen of the Guard and their captain, Hatton, were present at the execution. A copy of Norfolk's touching letter of farewell to his son finds a place in Hatton's Letter Book.

Hatton sat in this Parliament as Member for Northampton-shire. The letter from him to Queen Elizabeth, mentioned above — the first to be preserved of his letters to her — belongs to this period, and is probably to be dated October, 1572. Its interest at this point is that it refers to his activities in the matters just dis-cussed. He says 'these last great causes that most displeased your nobles, as of the D. of N. and Q. of S., the Acts of Parliament for religion, and other strange courses in these things taken were all laid on my weak shoulders'. The references to Mary and the Duke show that he is writing of the Parliamentary events of this year. That he was busy in Norfolk's affairs had already appeared from the Duke's references to him. As for Mary, the Parliamentary records show that he was one of the Commons Committee appointed to confer with the Lords on 'the great matter touching the Queen of Scots' in May, 1572. And it is possible that her affairs brought him on a mission of inquiry to Sheffield Castle where Mary was. Such a mission was actually sent to Sheffield Castle in June, to make certain charges against Mary and to demand her answers to them. The commissioners were Lord de la Warre, Sir Ralph Sadler, Chancellor of the Duchy of Lancaster, Dr. Thomas Wilson, Master of Requests, and Thomas Bromley, Solicitor-General.

It is possible that Hatton was attached to this deputation; and this supposition gains some support from the fact that a copy of the warrant appointing the commission, in fact, the only known copy, is preserved among the Bardon Papers, more particularly described later, a collection of documents about the Queen of Scots, which was made in whole or in part for Hatton's use. The reason for thinking that Hatton may have been at Sheffield Castle is Mary Stuart's statement, considered in a later chapter, that he had once toyed with the idea of marrying Lady Shrewsbury's daughter, Elizabeth Cavendish, who two years later married Mary's brother-in-law, the Earl of Lennox; and Elizabeth Cavendish was then at Sheffield Castle with her mother and stepfather, the Earl of Shrewsbury. Mr. B. M. Ward has supposed that the 'Master F.I.' of George Gascoigne's story, *The Adventures of Master F.I.*, is Hatton; and the present writer has suggested that, if this identification is accepted, the story may have reference to Hatton's wooing of Elizabeth Cavendish at Sheffield Castle in June, 1572. The latest writer on Gascoigne, Dr. C. T. Prouty, whose arguments carry great weight, rejects this identification. It may be, therefore, no more than a coincidence that the dates agree: *A Hundreth Sundrie Flowres*, which contains the story of 'Master F.I.', was published in the Spring of 1573. The whole matter is discussed in a later chapter.

If Hatton had indeed such an adventure in love as Mary suggested, it would not have added to his favour with Elizabeth and would help to explain the Queen's anger to which the letter bears testimony. But, apart from these speculations, there can be little doubt about the letter's date. The mention in it of the Acts for Religion confirms the view that this Parliament is meant. For in that Session, a 'Bill for Rites and Ceremonies' to supersede the Book of Common Prayer was debated until Elizabeth sent down a message forbidding its discussion. That Hatton was the bearer of this message seems a likely inference from his statement, and from his later Parliamentary history. In subsequent Parliaments he was to reprimand the Commons for discussing matters of religion, discussions which Elizabeth held to be an infringement of her prerogative.

Hatton's letter to the Queen is written in an untidy hand, and does not give the impression that the writer is a man of much education. The spelling is even more erratic than is usual in letters of the sixteenth century. Hatton, for instance, habitually wrote, and probably said, 'axe' for 'ask'. But in his rustic pronunciation he was not probably different from many others at Court. Leicester is a case in point. He wrote 'hit' for 'it' and misplaced his h's in some other words. Henry Bradley says that it is probably safe to assume that even in Elizabeth's inmost circle there were many whose speech was strongly marked by the dialectical peculiarities of the parts of England from which they came. As George Gordon puts it, the courtiers 'carried their county about with them on their tongues'.

It would take too much space to quote this or Hatton's other letters in full. Most of them will be found in Nicolas's *Memoirs*. The most interesting passages are as follows, in modern spelling:

> Madam, in striving to withstand your violent course of evil opinion towards me, I might perhaps the more offend you, because the truth of my cause disagreeth with the rigour of your judgment. But the bitterness of my heart in humble complaints I trust you will hear, for your goodness and justice sake. May it therefore please you, my faults are said to be these: unthankfulness, covetousness and ambition.
>
> To the first, I speak the truth before our God. That I have most entirely loved your person and service, to the which, without exception, I have everlastingly vowed my whole life, liberty and fortune. Even so am I yours, as whatever God and you should have made me, the same had been your own ... Spare your poor prostrate servant from this pronounced vengeance.

He then defends himself from the charge of covetousness, and proceeds:

> To the third, God knoweth I never sought place but to serve you; though indeed, to shield my poor self, both nature and reason

would have taught me to ask refuge at your strong and mighty hand. These last great causes that most displeased your nobles, as of the D. of N. and Q. of S., the Acts of Parliament for religion and other strange (?) courses in those things taken, were all laid on my weak shoulders; under which when I shall fall, behold then the wretched man how he shall pass all pointed at. But to my purpose, if ever I inordinately sought either honour or riches, place, calling or dignity, I pray to God that hell might swallow me. Believe not, I humbly beseech you for your wisdom and worthiness, the tale so evil told of your most faithful: be not led by lewdness of others to lose your own that truly loveth you. These most unkind conceits wonderfully wring me: reserve me more graciously to be bestowed on some honourable enterprise for you; and so shall I die a most joyful man and eternally bound to you . . . I fear your too great trouble in reading this blotted letter. I will therefore with my most dutiful submission pray for your long and happy life. I pray God bless you for ever.

Your despairing, most wretched bondman,

Ch. Hatton.

Jealousy of Lord Oxford has been held to have been the occasion of this letter; but though Hatton may have been resentful of Oxford, then rising in favour, the reasons he himself gives for the Queen's annoyance, his faults of unthankfulness, covetousness and ambition, suggest that Elizabeth was vexed because he had been mixed up in the intrigues directed against Burghley, intrigues that she deeply resented.

For that there was a faction, however unimportant, that sought to pit Hatton against Burghley, is shown by the reported opinions of his relatives in Northamptonshire. In January, 1573, one of his agents sent Burghley some interesting information from that county. John Osborne of Kelmarsh had told this agent that about Easter last (1572) he was in the company of Thomas Haselrigge of Noseley, co. Leicester, and William Saunders of Harrington. Haselrigge 'sore railed' on Burghley and, among other things, affirmed that he had destroyed and spoiled three noble houses: the Duke of Norfolk and the Earls that fled out of the north (i.e. Westmorland and Northumberland of the Northern Rebellion). And he asked, 'now that Burghley had erected his pile at Burghley, who should destroy that?' Osborne declared also that William Saunders and Francis, his brother, 'in all their doings prefer Mr. Hatton above the Lord Treasurer [Burghley], saying that one day they looked to see wherein Mr. Hatton should have one step before him and give him the glike', that is get the better of him.

The interesting point of this document is that these disgruntled gentry were neighbours, connections and some of them close relations of Christopher Hatton. William Saunders of Harrington was his uncle. Francis, called here William's brother, was William's first cousin. John Osborne of Kelmarsh had a Saunders grandmother, and was Hatton's second cousin. He was a brother-in-law of Sir Ralph Lane, the first Governor of Virginia, who, in one of his letters, calls Hatton his cousin, in virtue, no doubt, of this connection. Thomas Haselrigge was a connection of Osborne's through the Lanes. So here we have evidence of dislike of Burghley and his policy on the part of Hatton's relatives, who seem to have nursed a vain ambition that he would one day overthrow the Lord Treasurer. The pedigree-mad Burghley, reading this report, would recognize immediately that these were Hatton's kinsmen and, smiling as he reflected on the futility of the plot that his agents had unearthed, would docket the letter with the rest of his vast correspondence.

In the Parliament of 1576 Hatton played a more active part than he had yet assumed. He was now the Queen's representative there, charged with the task of keeping procedure on lines agreeable to her, discouraging certain subjects of debate, prominent in castigating any member who might offend. He began also to secure seats in Parliament for some of his personal friends and retainers. It would not, perhaps, be accurate to say that he was forming a party in the modern sense of that term. Parties had scarcely arisen as yet in a Parliament whose business it was to vote supplies and register the decisions of the Executive. But Hatton's embryo party was at least a source of influence and an indication of growing importance.

In the Parliament of 1572, in which Hatton sat for Northampton County, three of his friends and followers had seats. They were Henry MacWilliam, Robert Colshill and Bartholomew Tate. Henry MacWilliam, a Gentleman Pensioner, sat for Liskeard in Cornwall, along with Paul Wentworth, one of two independently minded brothers, with whom Hatton, as Leader of the House, was often in conflict. Robert Colshill, also a Gentleman Pensioner, is mentioned occasionally in the Hatton Letter Book; his seat was Portsmouth. Bartholomew Tate represented Coventry. He was

Hatton's first cousin, being the son of Sir Bartholomew Tate by Anne, sister of Hatton's mother, Alice Saunders.

Henry MacWilliam turns up occasionally in Hatton's history. He was a fellow performer in the tilt-yard, and was placed by Hatton, at Walsingham's instigation, in charge of the Earl of Arundel when a prisoner in the Tower in 1585. He had a seat in the House for many years. In the next Parliament, that of 1584, he represented Appleby, and in that of 1586 Carlisle. His name declares him of Irish extraction, presumably a Burke of Mayo, a branch of whom had the name MacWilliam, but the family had long been settled in Essex. He married the widow of Sir John Cheke, the famous classical scholar, tutor of Edward VI and brother-in-law of Burghley. One of MacWilliam's daughters by her married Hatton's friend Sir John Stanhope, and another his first cousin Edward Saunders. Robert Colshill is absent from the Parliament of 1584; and it appears from a letter in the Hatton Letter Book that he was dead by 1581. Not much is known of his service with Hatton. With Hatton's uncle, William Saunders and his cousin, Tate, Colshill was at Holdenby in 1579 to welcome Lord Burghley in Hatton's enforced absence at Court. Bartholomew Tate also disappears from the Parliament of 1584.

. In that Parliament, however, others of Hatton's followers occur. Corfe Castle, which had been granted to him in 1572, was represented by two men, one of whom, Francis Hawley, was Hatton's deputy Admiral for Corfe Castle and the Isle of Purbeck. One of the two members for the Borough of Huntingdon was Francis Flower, who was a Gentleman Pensioner and a follower of Hatton's. He had a house at Eltham, where Hatton was Keeper of the Palace and a room in Hatton's house in Ely Place; had a grant to print books in Latin, Greek and Hebrew including school books such as Lilye's Grammar; was one of the authors of *The Misfortunes of Arthur* (1587), a play called forth apparently by the execution of Mary Queen of Scots; promoted or patronized the writing by Robert Greene of a lament on Hatton's death; and composed a long epitaph for a pillar beside Hatton's tomb in St. Paul's. His son, Sir George Flower, went to Ireland, and was ancestor of the Barons Ashbrook. Flower held the same seat in the Parliament of 1586, when Corfe Castle was represented by Francis Hawley and Hatton's nephew, Sir William Hatton;

while Samuel Cocks, gentleman, of London, that is Hatton's secretary, Samuel Cox, sat for Richmond in Yorkshire. This was Cox's only appearance in Parliament. He is gone in the Parliament of 1588, when Sir William Hatton and Francis Hawley still represented Corfe Castle; Francis Flower, Huntingdon; and Richard Swale, LL.D., a Master in Chancery, Hatton's legal adviser when Lord Chancellor, sat for Hatton's old seat of Higham Ferrers. In the Parliament of 1592 when Hatton was dead, most of the names have gone. But Flower, who had transferred his services to Sir William Hatton, the Lord Chancellor's heir, now sat for Corfe Castle along with William Tate, son of Bartholomew Tate.

Hatton's activity in the Parliament of 1576 concerned in particular the behaviour of an irrepressible but attractive Parliamentary figure, Peter Wentworth of Lillingstone Lovell in Buckinghamshire. He was a sort of connection of Hatton's, for his first wife was Letitia, daughter of Sir Ralph Lane of Horton by Maud Parr, cousin of Queen Catherine Parr. He was thus brother-in-law of John Osborne of Kelmarsh, Hatton's second cousin and brother-in-law of Sir Ralph Lane, who called Hatton his cousin. Wentworth's second wife was Walsingham's sister. As Member of Parliament for Tregony in the 1572 Parliament, Wentworth had been one of the most active of those who demanded the execution of Mary Stuart. He called her the most notorious whore in all the world; and when Elizabeth made a disarming speech to those who clamoured for her rival's death and the Commons, though disappointed, proposed sending her a message of thanks, Wentworth rose to say that she deserved no thanks.

That seems to have been passed over. But his action in Parliament in 1576 got him into trouble. He made an impassioned defence of free speech, complaining of two matters in particular: one 'a rumour which runneth about the House, and this it is, "Take heed what you do, the Queen liketh not such a matter; whosoever prefereth it she will be offended with him"; or the contrary, "her Majesty liketh of such a matter, whosoever speaketh against it, she will be much offended with him"'. The other was 'a message brought the last Session into the House that we should not deal with any matters of religion', but to leave such to the Bishops who had their instructions from the Queen. Hatton had, in all probability, been the bearer of this message in the Session of 1572, as suggested above; he is certainly recorded in the Parliamentary Debates as bringing such messages to the House in later years. Wentworth went on to say that he had always understood that the banishment from England of the Pope and Popery had been the work of Parliament and not of the Bishops. When, during the last Parliament, he and other Members had interviewed the Archbishop of Canterbury concerning the Articles of Religion, the Archbishop had said to them: 'Surely, you mistook the matter; you will refer yourselves wholly to us therein?' To which Wentworth made the memorable reply: 'No, by the faith I bear to God, we will pass nothing before we understand what it is, for that were but to make you Pope.'

At this point he was stopped by the outraged House, 'out of a reverend regard of her Majesty's honour'. He was sequestrated, committed a prisoner to the Serjeant's ward and examined by a Committee of the House, of whom Hatton was one. As a result he was sent to the Tower, but was released after three days, Hatton being the bearer of a gracious message from the Queen, announcing that she was pleased to remit her 'justly occasioned displeasure'.

From all this it is obvious that Wentworth was a Puritan, one of the tribe that Elizabeth most detested; and his claim that Parliament should discuss all and sundry, even against the Queen's wishes, and particularly matters of religion, was intolerable to her. It will be convenient to collect here the later references to Parliamentary contacts between Hatton and Wentworth and his brother, because they illustrate the sort of work in the Commons that Hatton was charged by the Queen to do.

In January, 1581, it was the turn of Paul Wentworth to get into trouble. He moved and carried a motion in Parliament for a public fast and for daily preaching. A few days later the Speaker had to express himself as very sorry for the error that had been made. The Queen, he said, greatly disliked the House's action, and he advised it to make submission. Hatton, who was now Vice-Chamberlain, made a speech in which he delivered a message from the Queen, declaring her annoyance with 'the rashness of the House in ordering a fast without her privity and pleasure first known', though setting forth 'very eloquently and amply' her recognition of Parliament's zeal for religion. The Queen, he said, attributed Paul Wentworth's behaviour partly to her own lenience towards his brother. He recommended the House to acknowledge its offence, ask for pardon and forbear from committing such a fault again. The House had to submit.

In 1587 Peter Wentworth again argued his favourite topic of the right of the House to free speech, and also their need to know just what their liberties were. He demanded also to be told whether the Speaker or any other (Hatton?) could interrupt a Member. The Speaker refused to put these questions, but showed them to Sir Thomas Heneage, the Treasurer of the Queen's Chamber; and soon afterwards Wentworth was committed a prisoner in the Tower. He was followed by Anthony Cope and three other Members who were sponsoring a Bill concerning the Sacraments and Ceremonies of the Church. A few days later a motion was made that these 'good and necessary Members' should be restored to the House. Mr. Vice-Chamberlain Hatton answered that 'if the gentlemen were committed for matter within the compass of the privilege of the House, then there might be room for a petition. But if not, we shall occasion her Majesty's further displeasure'.

We have a last glimpse of Hatton and Wentworth in September, 1591, two months before Hatton's death. Wentworth had been engaged in expatiating upon a favourite subject, the need of establishing the succession to the Crown, of all matters the one whose discussion annoyed Elizabeth the most. He had been questioned about a book, possibly his *Pithy Exhortation to her Majesty* on this question, which he had written four years before. He seems to have denied knowledge of it, but later thought better of his denial. So much we can deduce from his letter to Burghley, in which he says that 'the title that the Lord Chancellor [i.e. Hatton] gave it, "A Book of the Heir Apparent", and his saying that it came out of clothiers' and tailors' shops' had caused him to think that it had been some other. Two years after this, Wentworth, supported by three other Members, asked leave to introduce a Bill entailing the succession to the Crown. They were sent to the Tower, and there four years later Peter Wentworth, in whom the flame of liberty and patriotism burned so brightly, died at the age of 73.

CHAPTER VII

MR. HATTON IN SEARCH OF A PEDIGREE

WHEN the heralds visited Northamptonshire in 1564 to record the pedigrees of the gentlemen of the shire and to investigate their right to the arms they bore, Christopher Hatton of Holdenby, Esquire, lord of that manor, entered his descent with the rest. He was then aged twenty-four, a student of the Inner Temple, who, having performed in a mask before the Queen, had perhaps already entered her service. In that year, at any rate, he was appointed one of her Majesty's Gentlemen Pensioners; but possibly the appointment was later in the year than the Heralds' Visitation, for Hatton merely entered his name as Christopher Hatton of Holdenby, Esquire, not yet married.

In this pedigree he named his father, William Hatton, as son and heir of John Hatton of Blechingley, co. Surrey, and stated that John was son and heir of Henry Hatton by Elizabeth Holdenby, the heiress of Holdenby. Henry Hatton's father he gave as Laurence Hatton of Dowden (that is Duddon) in Cheshire, who married Joan, daughter of John Danyell of Daresbury in that county, gentleman. He apparently claimed no arms, and the heralds assigned him none. Later he adopted the arms, Sable, a cross Ermine, bordered Argent, as we know from the scoring sheet of the tilt of May, 1571. These arms, which are also recorded as being in the manor house of Holdenby in 1573, are quite different from the ancient coat of Hatton of Hatton in Cheshire, which Christopher Hatton subsequently assumed.

The later details of the above pedigree can be checked by record evidence, but there is nothing to substantiate the earlier. The Christian name of Hatton's great-grandfather, whom he calls Henry, is not discoverable from any known records (as distinct from family pedigrees), nor is the name of Henry's father and the statement that he came from Duddon in Cheshire otherwise ascertainable. Besides this son Henry, the pedigree gives Laurence Hatton a younger son, John.

There seems, however, to be no reason to doubt the general accuracy of Hatton's statements. A country gentleman might be expected to know his descent so far back as four generations.

Hatton's information cannot be disproved, and, failing evidence to the contrary, may be taken as fact.

Now where does this lead us? Through the Holdenbys Hatton unquestionably came of gentle stock. But what about the Hattons? Duddon is in the parish of Waverton, Cheshire, and Waverton and its hamlet of Hatton had once been owned by a family of Hatton. From the Hattons, Waverton and Hatton had passed by an heiress to the Duttons of Dutton, and henceforth of Hatton also. Junior lines of Hattons continued in the neighbourhood, and in Christopher Hatton's time were still living there, unimportant people, tenants of lands which had once been owned by the Hattons, presumably their ancestors. The great-grandfather, named in Christopher Hatton's pedigree, Laurence Hatton of Duddon, was no doubt one of these. How his son Henry came to marry Elizabeth Holdenby, then but a small country squire's daughter with no expectation of succeeding to the manor, but later, through the failure of her brother's line, the heiress, does not appear. If Christopher Hatton had not risen in his world and attained to a position of importance at Court, we should have heard no more of his pedigree, nothing of the claims of the Hattons to ancient splendours.

About the year 1567, when Hatton had been some years at Court, Mr. Ralph Dutton of Hatton, owning the Cheshire manor from which Christopher Hatton's presumed forbears had derived, and aware that it had come to his Dutton ancestors through an heiress of the name of Hatton, thought to write to the rising young Court favourite, make some vague claims to relationship, and suggest that through Mr. Hatton's influence he might be 'eased' of the loan of a hundred pounds 'which I was required amongst others to lend unto her Majesty'. It was worth trying; and, no doubt much to Mr. Dutton's surprise, Mr. Hatton was both able and willing to use his influence, and succeeded in having the sum remitted.

This contact again bore fruit, when five years later, in 1572, Hatton, already a Gentleman of the Queen's Privy Chamber, was appointed Captain of her Guard and bethought himself of his pedigree. For a man in his position it would be fitting to show an ancient descent, enrol it on the parchments of the College of Arms, and emblazon it with the arms and quarterings of heiresses, real or imaginary. The meagre entry of eight years earlier at the

Heralds' Visitation of Northamptonshire, which showed but five generations and claimed no coat of arms for the Hattons of Holdenby, was really not good enough.

It was an age of new men; and, as the rising families established themselves among the nobility and the governing classes, they showed all eagerness to prove that they too, like the feudal baronage they were supplanting, were men of ancient lineage. Though Burghley might tell his son that gentility is nothing else but ancient riches, he hankered after gentle descent. As J. H. Round, who spent his life among musty parchments, 'deliciously gnawing at the pedigrees of the proudest families of England', has it, he was 'pedigree-mad and sought for the upstart Cecils' ancestors in all directions'. Sir Henry Lee, to name another, the Queen's self-appointed champion and Hatton's friend, though but descended from a line of Buckinghamshire freeholders sought (or the heralds for him) to link his family with the feudal Leighs of Cheshire. The heralds were complacent, and much could be done to establish an ancient descent for a gentleman of consideration by forged charters and bold statements that called in aid mythical companions of William the Conqueror. Hatton would be in the fashion too.

He employed an agent to make genealogical inquiries, one Laurence Bostock, a Cheshire gentleman, an antiquary interested in genealogy and heraldry. Bostock was a cousin of Ralph Dutton of Hatton, and, being friendly with him and other Cheshire gentry, was made free of muniment rooms. He diligently searched for and copied ancient deeds, recorded inscriptions and coats of arms in churches, interviewed heads of families and laboriously wrote down their pedigrees. The results of his researches are embodied in a valuable collection preserved among the Harleian Manuscripts in the British Museum. It includes miscellaneous genealogical and heraldic matter, but is mainly concerned with the search for Hatton's ancestors:

> Here followeth the copies of some of the records of the Barony of Halton and also divers ancient deeds belonging to sundry gentlemen within the county palatine of Chester, gathered in the year of grace 1572 *et anno* Eliz. 14, touching Hatton and for Mr. Christopher Hatton, Esquire and Captain of the Queen's Majesty's Guard and one of the Gentlemen of her said Majesty's Privy Chamber, *per* L. de Bostock.

Bostock, having called in aid Ralph Dutton of Hatton, Christopher Hatton in July, 1572 wrote to Dutton as follows:

> My very good friend, Mr. Dutton: Your gentle promise to me at your last being at St. James, touching the search of such ancient records, monuments, ensigns and escutcheons as may lead me to some descent of the house and line whereof I myself am descended, moved me to trouble you with these letters. The bearer whereof, Laurence Bostoke I have (of self purpose) sent down unto you to gather and take notice of all such emblazons as serve to my purpose for a true pedigree of my name and alliance, to whom when I shall understand that you are so aiding and assisting (as for your acquaintance I know you may be and for friendship sake I trust you will be) you shall find me ever as ready to pleasure you and yours. So in hope he shall find your helping hand and I have cause to be thankful for his entertainment, I end wishing you well. From the Court the xvth. of July, 1572.

All during the year Bostock's researches continued, and a formidable body of documents was collected. Bostock, besides scouring the Cheshire churches and manor houses, made a journey to Northamptonshire and gathered what he could from the monuments in the church of Holdenby and from inquiries of old people of the village. His researches extended for another year and yet another; the aid of the professional heralds was called in; and Ralph Dutton was so pressed for information that he showed signs of taking alarm. This passion for pedigrees might be pure and disinterested, but in the process of disinterring these old bones was it not conceivable that something might be dug up that would cast doubt on his own title to the manor and lands of Hatton? A generation had passed since the Suppression of the Monasteries and the granting of their lands to laymen. But it was years before the new settlement was complete. There was some legitimate confusion; and in the reign of Elizabeth an attempt was made by unscrupulous people, with the connivance of the Government, to make capital out of legal uncertainties. England was convulsed by inquisitions for the searching out of so-called 'concealed lands', lands which the Crown sought to claim by questioning the titles of holders. None was safe, whether he held by grant from Abbot and Prior, or had actually been given monastic lands by the Crown. Even those who had no such connection might suffer. Old attainders and confiscations might be dragged to light at any

moment. Titles were in confusion. There was a regular office for
investigating them; and a patent for 'discovering' such lands was
farmed out by the Crown to patentees who made what they could
by a species of blackmail, to which the frightened tenant often
thought best to submit — to pay and be quit. In Ireland, a few
years before this, there had arisen an extraordinary state of affairs,
comic in its absurdity, though serious enough for the unfortunate
occupiers whose titles to lands held for centuries were impugned.
Sir Peter Carew, a Devon squire, poring over his ancient muniments (which, however, he could not himself read) had discovered
that his ancestors (or rather those whom he thought to be such)
had owned immense baronies and even kingdoms in Ireland.
Armed with the Queen's permission and encouragement he set
sail, landed in Ireland and proceeded to levy war on Butlers and
other great families who had held the lands he claimed for hundreds of years, winning vast tracts of territory by sword and process
of law.

Might not the Captain of the Queen's Guard be thinking the
thoughts of Sir Peter Carew? Sir Peter had not hesitated to go
back two hundred and fifty years in his antiquarian claims. Sir
Christopher Hatton might be contemplating similar preposterous
claims to the manor of Hatton which Hattons had owned in the
days of Edward III. It was necessary to reassure the alarmed
squire, and Henry Townsend, brother of Ralph Dutton's wife,
was chosen to write to him.

Townsend begins by telling his brother-in-law that Dutton's
son, Rowland, and Dutton's son-in-law (unnamed), whom he
calls great students, had informed him that Hatton wished the
writer to read and forward a letter to him 'to the intent I might
frame your answer in that degree that it might stand both with
your worship and answer his contentation according to the justice
of his claim'.

> I have seen [he continued] those records and books to warrant
> that which his worship doth challenge, which in duty and reason
> you are to yield unto, your estate, living and calling nothing
> therein impaired, but your descent better affirmed and furnished
> with rich roots, and also now a worshipful kinsman to be a pillar to
> you and yours. Wherefore doubt you not of my credit and words,
> he meaneth nothing towards you nor your lands, no more to
> endanger you than I do, but in respect you would not seem to give

[i.e. bear] those arms that his enemy should say he could not warrant them nor the college of the heralds justly confirm them.

This last sentence suggests that Hatton had objected to Dutton quartering the ancient arms of Hatton, as Dutton had a right to do, being descended from the heiress of Hatton.

For Mr. Hatton [Townsend continues] is descended (as it doth appear by the pedigree which Mr. Bostoke will show you) of the second house, and withal you have fines and recoveries which doth bar him albeit he had right. Wherefore the matter to you is not vaylable [? valuable], and yet of the other part (refusing this to do) he may have just cause of mislike and unkindness in you, and yet in the end give the arms. Wherefore I wish you to send this letter inclosed, by me herein drawn, to Mr. Hatton. . . .

Dutton was reassured by these arguments, and hastened to forward the letter drafted by his brother-in-law, assuring the Captain of the Guard of his sympathy and help. After acknowledging Hatton's letter and a communication from Clarenceux King of Arms, as well as Bostock's pedigrees he proceeds:

And for my part, touching the same, I and mine have just cause to think worship in you and wisdom of your carefulness of the preservation of that lineage and blood whereof you are descended, and albeit by your late instructions I do understand more than afore I did, yet of the affinity of our houses I was not ignorant of, and the same I did import unto your worship a seven years past, at which time I required your friendship to be my mean for the discharge of the loan of an hundreth pounds which I was required amongst others to lend unto her Majesty, of which sum by your good means I then was eased of, and for the which for my part I mean not to be unmindful. . . .

Townsend adds a postscript to his draft: 'Brother, let this letter be fair written, word by word, and delivered to Mr. Bostoke, and desire him to further your suit to Mr. Hatton for your son Hugh to serve him. I have partly moved the matter already.' So Dutton, satisfied that nothing prejudicial to his interest is contemplated, signs himself kinsman, and grateful with the sense of favours to come, seeks Hatton's patronage for his son. Nothing more is recorded in Hatton's correspondence of Ralph Dutton of Hatton and his sons Rowland and Hugh. But Hatton's friendship was extended to Ralph's nephew, John Dutton of Dutton. He called him cousin also, and took his son Peter into his service.

And now for Laurence Bostock's researches and conclusions. As Hatton's own information was that his great-great-grandfather was Laurence Hatton of Duddon, no doubt Bostock began by probing into the pedigree of that family. There were still Hattons living at Duddon, but investigation gave rather unpromising results. Bostock found a man there, Thomas Hatton, the bastard son of John Hatton of Duddon, son of another Thomas, son of another John. They were quite unimportant people, of whom we should never have heard but for Bostock's diligent inquiries. It is possible that this was the actual family from which the Hattons of Holdenby descended. Christopher Hatton's own information was that his ancestor, Laurence Hatton of Duddon had a younger son John. This may be the John Hatton who heads the pedigree of Hatton of Duddon, though the relationship may have been more distant.

But this pedigree was not good enough for the Captain of the Queen's Guard. It was necessary to construct one which would show a connected descent from the feudal Hattons of Hatton. The elder male line had died out, and was represented by the Duttons. But there was a family of Hatton still existing, more respectable than those of Duddon, small landowners in Quisty Birches, a hamlet of the other Cheshire Hatton in the parish of Daresbury. To this line Bostock proposed to link his distinguished client's family.

Here is his report:

> The town or lordship of Hatton is in the parish of Daresbury, and in the same parish is a manor house called Coysty birches, wherein one Laurence Hatton now dwelleth; and it is his own inheritance. How long his ancestors had continued there he cannot tell, and yet he is about eighty years old. His descent or pedigree hereafter following, so much as he, his wife and son's son can tell of.

Laurence Hatton whose recollections went no farther back than his grandfather, Piers Hatton, had an uncle, Hugh, who had settled in London, and another uncle, Richard, who had migrated to Shrewsbury. Richard is of interest, as his descendants were recognized by Christopher Hatton when he entailed his estates in 1584, being put in remainder after his undoubted relatives, the descendants of his father's and grandfather's brothers. Laurence Hatton did not find any place for the Hattons of Holdenby in his pedigree. He mentioned, however, that he had had other uncles but did not know what had become of them. Here was the missing link. Laurence Hatton of Duddon of the 1564 pedigree was thrown overboard as father of Henry, Christopher's great-grandfather, and Henry was turned into one of these missing uncles.

The heralds seem to have assigned to the Hattons of Quisty Birches for arms, Ermine, on a chevron three stars. But the ancient arms of the Hattons were, or were said to be, Azure, a chevron Or between three garbs Or, one of a series of coats based on that of the feudal Earls of Chester. So the arms of the Hattons of Quisty Birches were changed to this, and to Christopher Hatton Laurence Bostock assigned the same coat among the ten quarterings which he gave him.

The College of Arms agreed to all this, and when Robert Glover, Somerset Herald, and William Flower, Norroy King of Arms, visited Cheshire in 1580, a wonderful pedigree of Hatton was drawn up. First of all, a Conquest ancestor had to be discovered, and this was provided in the person of Ivon, a nobleman of Normandy who came to England in the train of the Conqueror, with his six sons. One of these was the ancestor of the FitzNigels, Barons of Halton, the feudal lords, under the Earls of Chester, of a large part of the county. A second was ancestor of the Duttons of Dutton; and a third, Wolfayth, of the Hattons of Hatton. Of this ancestry J. H. Round has pointed out that 'Yvon' is a lady's name, and is therefore as absurd for 'a noble of Normandy' as 'Wolfayth' for his son. At any rate, the pedigree provided Hattons and Duttons with yet another common ancestor.

Round couples this pedigree with Burghley's as among the frauds of the Elizabethan heralds, which he set himself to expose, 'nailing them up one by one as a gamekeeper nails his vermin'. But he made no critical examination of the Hatton pedigree, and his strictures only apply to this Conquest origin of the family, which he saw at once was absurd. But, though Bostock's pedigree is open to criticism, that is not to say that his work is either wholly venal or useless. On the contrary, his abstracts of deeds, copies of monumental inscriptions and the rest seem to be carefully done, and though he may have been led away by enthusiasm to advance unprovable claims, a great deal of his work seems accurate enough. In particular, the pedigree makes no effort to conceal the fact that many of Hatton's contemporary namesakes, with whom he claimed kinship by virtue of these researches, were of such humble occupations as cattle drover, butcher, cook (to John Dutton of Dutton), goldsmith and mason. It is evident that a great deal of trouble has been taken with the details of these contemporary lines, and that every effort has been made to include all living Hattons who could by any means be made to fit into the scheme.

The pedigree concluded, Bostock set forth the arms of his influential client as 'justly descended unto him and marshalled in his shield as he may rightly bear them'. He assigned to him a coat quarterly of ten, consisting of the arms that Hatton of Hatton was said to bear in virtue of their descent from several Cheshire families, as well as those of Holdenby and its alliances. This coat was the basis of the signet of six quarterings, with which Christopher Hatton sealed his deeds; the shield of fourteen quarterings on the archways of Holdenby House; and the arms marshalled in the plates of various books dedicated to him, on some of his portraits and on his monument in St. Paul's.

Efforts were also made in other directions to gather information about the Hatton family. Thus in 1578 Hatton asked for permission to search the muniments of Christ Church, Oxford, presumably on family matters, though what he expected to discover is unknown. He approached Dr. Toby Mathew, President of St. John's and canon of Christ Church, a man who looked to him for advancement and pestered him for the Deanery of Durham, which he eventually obtained. Mathew and his colleagues were agreeable, but the result of the search is unknown. In 1580 Hatton wrote to the Lord Mayor of London requesting that a Mr. Smith might be allowed to make copies of certain deeds, wills, etc. enrolled in the London Court of Husting. Again, the result of the search is unknown. Among the Finch-Hatton muniments deposited with the Northamptonshire Record Society is a copy of the will of Richard Hatton, LL.D., who died in 1509. The will reveals that he was the son of a certain Nicholas and Isabella Hatton, but there is no evidence that he was in any way related to Christopher Hatton. It was probably copied in the hope that it might throw light on the family history.

CHAPTER VIII

HATTON AND ELIZABETH

'I DO not live in a corner — a thousand eyes see all I do, and calumny will not fasten on me for ever.' So Elizabeth passionately protested to the Spanish Ambassador; and however slander might traduce her in her lifetime, she is to-day in the eyes of most historians cleared of the grosser accusations of a Sanders or an Allen, the petty scurrilities of a dozen obscure scandal-mongers. Responsible opinion, even in her lifetime, held such charges to be untrue. De Silva, the Spanish Ambassador in London, closely inquired into the rumours that were flying about, and convinced himself that they had no foundation; and, as Froude sums up, the fact that in the enormous mass of Mendoza's correspondence there is not a single imputation upon the personal character of Elizabeth is a conclusive answer to the polemics of Allen and Sanders. Such charges were made for political purposes; Allen's, for instance, on the eve of the Armada in his pastoral letter justifying the proposed invasion and calling on the faithful to rise and welcome their deliverers.

For a brief period at the beginning of her reign the conduct of Elizabeth and Leicester caused some alarm among her Ministers; and it must be confessed that her behaviour, coarse and familiar even for that age, helped to lend colour to some of the stories about her. Hatton's name is often coupled with Leicester's in the tittle-tattle of a handful of nonentities, whose sayings were reported to the authorities, and only survive because they concerned the greatest figure in England. Such hole-in-a-corner gossip is scarcely worth repeating, but unimportant as it is it does perhaps reflect a certain stratum of popular opinion, what possibly the market-place and the tap-room thought of the two men, and it may be set forth for what it is worth.

Leicester had already, in 1570, been the subject of scandalous rumours. At Norwich in that year, a loose-tongued fellow, having said that 'my Lord of Leicester had two children by the Queen', was sentenced to lose both his ears or to pay a fine of a hundred pounds. We do not know which alternative the poor man chose.

REMAINS OF THE PALACE OF HOLDENBY

From the drawing by Edward Blore in Baker's *History of Northamptonshire*

Scandal about Hatton, who was believed to be a serious rival of Leicester's, is chronicled in January, 1572, when a plot by two men named Mather and Berney to release the imprisoned Duke of Norfolk and to assassinate Elizabeth and Burghley came to light. Mather, being examined, said of Elizabeth that she

> desireth nothing but to feed her own lewd fantasy, and to cut off such of her nobility as were not perfumed and court-like to please her delicate eye, and place such as were for her turn, meaning dancers, and meaning you my Lord of Leicester and one Mr. Hatton who, he said, had more recourse unto her Majesty in her Privy Chamber than reason would suffer, if she were so virtuous and well inclined as some noiseth her; with other such vile words as I am ashamed to speak, much more to write.

Archbishop Parker writes to Burghley in November, 1572, to repeat that, on examination by the Mayor of Dover, a certain man had uttered 'most shameful words against her [the Queen] namely that the Earl of Leicester and Mr. Hatton should be [i.e. were] such towards her as the matter is so horrible that they would not write down the words, but would have uttered them in a speech to your lordship if you could have been at leisure'.

Such stories as these — and there are others — may be brushed aside. What credit they had at the time can in Leicester's case be attributed largely to the mysterious circumstances attending the death of his wife. There were not — there are not now — wanting those who declared that she had been murdered to clear the way for Leicester's marriage to the Queen. If these two were indeed bent on matrimony, that argument takes something from the force of the suggestion that they were lovers. And it ignores the psychological probabilities. The death of Amy Robsart and the rumours to which it gave rise made, in fact, the marriage of the supposed lovers impossible; and Elizabeth, at any rate, was intelligent enough to have foreseen this.

There is no such dramatic episode in Hatton's relations with Elizabeth. But there are his letters, surely among the most re-markable ever penned by a subject to a monarch. What would contemporary eyes have made of them could they have seen them, fresh from the glowing pen, not covered with the dust of three hundred years? Even to-day some commentators have drawn the conclusion that there must have been guilty passion between these two. But coolly considered, they cannot seriously be held to prove anything of the sort. They are indeed of a passionate and intensely personal nature. Written to any woman but the Queen they could have no other label attached to them but that of love letters. In the highly artificial atmosphere in which Elizabeth and her admirers moved, they must be regarded as no more than unusually exaggerated specimens of an epistolary style which her vanity had made customary and indeed compulsory.

The gossip about Leicester and Hatton was not entirely confined to the common people. Apart from Sanders, Allen and their fellows, whose vituperation falls into a different category, Mary Queen of Scots is the most famous of Elizabeth's accusers. She specifically mentions Hatton in her indictment. Writing to Elizabeth many years after the events to which she refers, Mary repeats a deal of malicious gossip that she had heard from the Countess of Shrewsbury. In 1568 Mary had fled to England and had been in Elizabeth's power ever since, being kept a prisoner, in the custody, for the greater part of the time, of Lord Shrewsbury. George Talbot, the sixth Earl, had in the same year married the redoubtable Bess of Hardwick, widow of William Cavendish; and in 1574 his wife's daughter, Elizabeth Cavendish, married Charles Stuart, Earl of Lennox, brother of Darnley, the husband of the Queen of Scots. According to Lady Shrewsbury's statement, Elizabeth Cavendish had once been the object of Hatton's tender regard, but he had withdrawn his suit for fear of Queen Elizabeth's wrath.

There was no love lost between the Queens of England and Scotland and the formidable Countess of Shrewsbury; and Mary must have derived the keenest satisfaction in repeating the old termagant's ill-natured charges. It seems, however, that Elizabeth never received this spiteful letter. Though written, it was never delivered. With Mary's other papers it came into the possession of Burghley and lies at Hatfield with the rest of his voluminous correspondence. Familiar with all the gossip of the English Court — she had been a Lady of the Bedchamber — Lady Shrewsbury was capable of giving it a peculiarly mischievous turn. For this personal reason her information has rightly been held to be suspect. But it is possible, by careful sifting, to draw some fairly safe conclusions from it.

Mary writes in French from Sheffield Castle where she was in Lord Shrewsbury's custody. She begins by quoting Lady Shrewsbury's charges against Elizabeth of immoral behaviour with

Leicester, Simier, Alençon, and the rest. The courtship of Elizabeth by the Duke of Alençon in 1572-6 and again in 1578 need not detain us. It will be discussed later. The impetuous Alençon and his bawdy go-between, Simier, had not escaped scandal in their relations with Elizabeth, and the common gossip was repeated by Lady Shrewsbury to Mary and by her to Elizabeth.

Mary goes on to say that Lady Shrewsbury had regretted that Elizabeth had not contented herself with Master Hatton and another [Leicester] of this kingdom. Her other references to Hatton or to matters that concern him are three, and belong to different periods; for her letter, written in 1584, refers to events of different times. Lady Shrewsbury's comments represent the gleanings of a persistent gossip over a period of years, poured at one time or another into the willing ears of the Queen of Scots. Mary refers to Hatton's courtship, frustrated by Elizabeth, of Lady Shrewsbury's daughter, which must have occurred some time before 1574; to Elizabeth's favours to the Earl of Oxford, which seem to have occasioned a difference between her and Hatton in 1572; and to Hatton's quarrel with the Queen on account of his jealousy of Ralegh in 1582.

Hatton's proposal to marry Lady Shrewsbury's daughter has some bearing on the subject of his connection with the publication of the anthology *A Hundreth Sundrie Flowres* in 1573. This will be discussed in a later chapter. The Queen's interest in Oxford dates from an earlier period, and its repercussion on the relations between her and Hatton belongs to the year we have now reached, 1572, when it is supposed to have led to a coolness between Queen and favourite.

Mary's comment on Elizabeth's friendship with Oxford is peculiarly vindictive, but there is evidence that in this case, at any rate, the gossip she repeated had some foundation in fact, and illustrated only too well Elizabeth's jealousy when her admirers wooed or married. Hatton, having once thought of marriage, was forced to turn aside and, remaining a bachelor, received at the Queen's hands material rewards of the most splendid kind. But Oxford, though his marriage had had Elizabeth's approval and had been graced by her presence, had later attracted her fancy, with the result that the unstable young man had injured his wife in the cruellest way. Mary's allegation was that he dared not cohabit with her for fear of losing Elizabeth's favour. Whatever the truth of this, there is no doubt that Oxford got on very badly with his wife and his father-in-law.

The erratic Edward de Vere, seventeenth Earl of Oxford, ten years Hatton's junior, had married in December, 1571, Anne Cecil, Burghley's daughter. Handsome and like Hatton an expert in dancing and the tilt-yard, he was much in the Queen's favour, and his wife was apparently jealous of Elizabeth's interest. In May, 1573, Gilbert Talbot wrote to his father, the Earl of Shrewsbury, that

> My Lord of Oxford is lately grown into great credit, for the Queen's Majesty delighteth more in his personage and his dancing and his valiantness than any other . . . If it were not for his fickle head he would pass any of them shortly. My Lady Burghley [his mother-in-law] hath unwisely declared herself, as it were, jealous, which is come to the Queen's ear, whereat she hath not been a little offended with her, but now she is reconciled again.

Hatton's jealousy seems to have been aroused in 1572, for a letter to him from Edward Dyer, the poet and friend of Philip Sidney, written in October of that year, shows that he was seriously upset by the Queen's partiality to a new favourite; and that favourite was perhaps Oxford, though he was possibly the Earl of Ormond. His identity does not greatly matter; whoever he was, Hatton had thought of reproaching Elizabeth for her fickleness. He consulted Dyer; and Dyer, with good common sense sought to dissuade him from so foolish a course. Dyer was one of Leicester's followers; and Leicester at one time, when jealous of Hatton, seems to have thought of putting Dyer forward as a rival to him. But that was six months later, and at this date the two men were friends, and, as Dyer's letter shows, Hatton had come to him for disinterested advice.

Dyer, having thought over the questions propounded by Hatton at a previous meeting, begins by saying that 'one that standeth by shall see more in the game than one that is much more skilful, whose mind is too earnestly occupied'. The passages that concern Hatton's relations with Elizabeth are worth quoting: 'First of all, you must consider with whom you have to deal, and what we be towards her; who, though she do descend very much in her sex as a woman, yet we may not forget her place, and the nature of it as our Sovereign.' Carefully choosing his words, he proceeds, 'now if a man, of secret cause known to himself, might in common reason challenge it . . .'; or, to use less tortuous language, he considers the case of one such as Hatton, so intimate with the Queen that he might feel himself justified in ignoring the difference in their positions. He concludes that the Queen would 'mislike' such a course; and advises a different one:

> But the best and soundest way in mine opinions, to put on another mind; to use your suits towards her Majesty in words, behaviour and deeds; to acknowledge your duty, declaring the reverence which in heart you bear, and never seem deeply to condemn her frailties, but rather joyfully to commend such things as should be in her, as though they were in her indeed; hating my L. of Crm. in the Queen's understanding for affection's sake, and blaming him openly for seeking the Queen's favour. For though in the beginning when her Majesty sought you (after her good manner), she did bear with rugged dealing of yours, until she had what she fancied, yet now, after satiety and fulness, it will rather hurt than help you; whereas, behaving yourself as I said before, your place shall keep you in worship, your presence in favour, your followers will stand to you, at the least you shall have no bold enemies, and you shall dwell in the ways to take all advantages wisely, and honestly to serve your turn at times.

Here again, there is a passage that seems to say that Hatton was the successful lover of Elizabeth; but it ought probably to be read as only one more specimen of the inflated language of the time, and can mean no more than, 'the Queen, having won your admiration, has grown tired of you'. For it is impossible to think that, if Hatton were really Elizabeth's lover, Dyer would blurt out the fact in such a way, or advise him, as he does, to discuss the whole matter with his 'best and most accounted friends', and canvass their advice. Sir Harris Nicolas notices this damaging passage and remarks how dangerous it was to write so, if it meant what it seems to mean. That consideration, he thinks, might be some reason for doubting the genuineness of the letter, unless we give the words a very different construction. That is just what we must do.

The letter seems to be genuine enough. It found its way in some manner unknown, into the hands of a Mr. Dell, who had been Archbishop Laud's secretary; or at any rate he had or made a transcript of it, which is all we now possess. Nor is there any reason to doubt its general accuracy. But 'my L[ord] of Crm.' is puzzling. Nicolas reads it in error as 'Ctm.', and thinks Oxford must be meant. It seems to fit Oxford well enough; and it may be that the word was 'Oxon' in the original, and misread by the copyist. But there is at least a possibility that the Earl of Ormond is the mysterious 'my L[ord] of Crm.', 'Orm.' being misread as 'Crm.' Thomas Butler, Earl of Ormond, a connection of the Queen's through the Boleyns, became a great favourite of Elizabeth's when he was at the English Court for five years from 1565 to 1569. He spent some months again in England in 1572, and was there at the date of this letter, and presumably still in the Queen's favour.

Dyer concludes, 'you may perchance be advised and encouraged to the other way by some kind friends that will be glad to see whether the Queen will make an apple or a crab of you, which, as they find, will deal accordingly with you; following if your fortune be good; if not, leave and go to your enemy'. Hatton no doubt pondered this advice, took counsel with his friends, and concluded that apples were pleasanter than crabs; but his abject letter to the Queen, quoted in a previous chapter, though it seems to belong to this period, has no connection with affairs of the heart. There is no hint in it of reproach for real or fancied neglect on Elizabeth's part; and the reasons given for the disfavour into which he had fallen are the faults charged against him. An explanation of the circumstances in which it was written has already been attempted. On the other hand — and this is what concerns a biographer of Hatton — the idea that, moved by jealousy, he remained Oxford's bitter and secret enemy, is not borne out by such facts as we have. Briefly, they are these. In June, 1574, Oxford went abroad without the Queen's permission. Elizabeth was furious and sent a messenger to fetch him back. He returned in July. Burghley in August interceded with the Queen for his son-in-law, appealed to Walsingham for support, and begged him to ask Hatton to continue his interest on Oxford's behalf. Burghley concludes, 'I cannot well end, neither will I end, without also praying you to remember Master Hatton to continue my Lord's friend, as he hath manifestly been, and as my Lord confesseth to me that he hopeth assuredly so to prove him. . . .'

For a short space Oxford returned to a normal life; and he and his wife were together at Hampton Court in October. In January,

1575, he again went abroad, this time with the Queen's permission. In March Lady Oxford was known to be with child, and the news being communicated to her husband, then in Paris, he wrote to Burghley, expressing his joy. Yet at the same time Dr. Richard Masters, the Queen's physician, reported to Burghley that the Queen had said to him that Oxford had protested to her that if his wife were with child, it was not his. On July 2nd a girl was born to them. In January following Burghley made a note in his diary that 'he [Oxford] confessed to my Lord Howard that he lay not with his wife but at Hampton Court, and that then the child could not be his, because the child was born in July, which was not the space of twelve months'. There seems to be something wrong with these calculations; and, as a matter of fact, since Oxford was with his wife at Hampton Court in October and their daughter was born in July, there is nothing abnormal in the course of events. But the two stories, if correctly reported, are evidence that he was anxious for the sake of keeping the Queen's favour, to deny his relations with his wife. Mary Stuart, therefore, seems to have had some justification for charging Elizabeth in her relations with Oxford with jealousy of a most exacting kind.

This episode in Oxford's life has little direct connection with Hatton, but it has been briefly recalled because a knowledge of Oxford's history is necessary to follow Hatton's attitude towards him. This has been misunderstood by some writers. That Hatton's interest in Oxford's affairs was consistently friendly and helpful is shown in his correspondence and is vouched for by Burghley. In another chapter Oxford's conversion to Catholicism at the time of the mission of the Jesuits Campion and Parsons and his subsequent return in 1581 to the Protestant fold will be referred to, because these events have a bearing on Hatton's relations with the Catholic conspirators, Lord Henry Howard and Charles Arundel. They concern this period of Oxford's life, and coincide in date with a scandalous episode in it.

Oxford, who had been converted to Catholicism at the same time as Howard and Arundel and who now accused them of plotting against the State (as in fact they were doing) fell out of favour with the Queen, on account of this accusation. Howard and Arundel brought counter-charges against him, and in 1581 he was sent to the Tower. A week later Burghley wrote to say he thought Oxford ought to confront his accusers. Oxford, however, was not sent to the Tower on account of Howard's and Arundel's charges; and though Burghley may have included these two men in the list of Oxford's accusers, it is more likely that his letter refers to his son-in-law's intrigue with Anne Vavasour. This scandal brings together a little group of Elizabethans who had frequent contacts with each other, Oxford, Hatton and Sir Henry Lee.

Anne Vavasour, later mistress of Sir Henry Lee of Ditchley, Hatton's associate in the tilt-yard, was a lady of loose reputation, who is celebrated in some ribald verses preserved in the pages of John Aubrey. She was the daughter of Henry Vavasour of Copmanthorpe in Yorkshire by Margaret, daughter of Henry Knyvet. Her history has been told by Sir Edmund Chambers in his life of Lee. In 1580 she had been appointed a Lady of the Bedchamber. In March of the following year she gave birth to a son in 'the maidens' chamber' at the Court. She was committed to the Tower by the scandalized Queen, and Oxford, who was alleged to be the father, attempted to flee the country. He was apprehended, sent to the Tower, released on June 8th, then confined to his house for two years and debarred from Court.

It was this affair that again lost him the Queen's favour, and led also to brawls with the Knyvets, Anne's relations. Burghley and Hatton busied themselves in intercession on Oxford's behalf. On July 13th Burghley writes to Hatton:

> Yesterday, being advertised of your good and honourable dealing with her Majesty in the case of my daughter of Oxford, I could not suffer my thanks to grow above one day old; and therefore in these few lines I do presently thank you, and do pray you in any proceeding therein not to have the Earl dealt with strainably, but only by way of advice as good for himself; for otherwise he may suspect that I regard myself more for my daughter than he is regarded for his liberty.

In March, 1582, Oxford, who had been credited with the design of assassinating Thomas Knyvet, Groom of the Privy Chamber and Anne Vavasour's uncle, fought a duel with him. They were both hurt, Oxford the more badly. He recovered, however, and soon attempted violence again. In June two of his men, Gastrell and another, were wounded in a fight with Knyvet's men in Lambeth Marsh. Later in the same month an attack was made on Knyvet at Blackfriars Stairs, as he was returning from a dinner party. In July there was another brawl in which Knyvet killed one of his assailants. The Coroner's Jury returned a verdict of *se defendendo.* Knyvet approached the Lord Chancellor, Sir Thomas Bromley, to shorten the legal proceedings for obtaining the pardon to which he was entitled by the verdict. Bromley refused to stir from the constitutional position; and the Queen, taking the part of her Groom of the Privy Chamber, directed Hatton to write to him. It was one of Elizabeth's stiffest letters, well calculated to bring a recalcitrant official to heel.

> Her Majesty [Hatton wrote] marvelleth not a little that your Lordship should deny her servant . . . She looked for justice, with favour at your hands towards this gentleman. 'You know', saith she, 'who he is and where he serveth; and therefore, in a cause so little important as this, you might have restrained the malice of his enemies well enough' . . . My good Lord, it is very necessary you take care to please the Queen in this case, for, in truth, she taketh it unkindly at your hands that she should be strained to meddle and be seen in the matter.

Bromley, however, still refused to budge, and returned a dignified answer, setting forth the legal position. The Queen, with good sense, expressed herself as satisfied, and Hatton was commanded to write him a conciliatory reply. But the brabbles and frays, as Burghley calls them, continued. In March, 1583, Gastrell killed one of Knyvet's servants. The Queen again laid the blame on Oxford; and Burghley, who was working not too successfully for his son-in-law's restoration to favour, wrote a long letter to Hatton in which he entered into details of these affairs and sought to prove that Oxford was not responsible for them. Having pointed out that he had been doubly punished, first by the Queen and then by 'the drab's friend, in revenge, to the peril of his life', he concluded with pardonable bitterness:

> And if his own punishment past and his humble seeking of forgiveness cannot recover her Majesty's favour, yet some, yea many, may think that the intercession of me and my poor wife, so long and importunately continued, might have obtained some spark of favour of her Majesty. . . .

In following these events we have been carried forward some years from the point at which they began. But the story of Oxford does illustrate the position that Hatton now held at Court. Among other duties, he was engaged as Vice-Chamberlain in rebuking, arranging, smoothing things out, appealed to on all sides for advice and assistance.

Let us now go back a few years to consider those extraordinary letters from Hatton to the Queen, by which perhaps he is best remembered to-day.

CHAPTER IX

HATTON'S LETTERS TO THE QUEEN

IN May, 1573, Hatton fell seriously ill. It was believed that his kidneys were affected. And this seems likely enough; for his death eighteen years later was said to be from 'diabetes', this term then being used in a sense different from to-day's, and indicating kidney trouble or some kindred complaint. We first hear of his illness in a letter from Gilbert Talbot to his father, Lord Shrewsbury. Talbot writes from Court on May 11th, and is full of news of happenings there. He says that Leicester is very much with the Queen and in as great favour as ever, but that Elizabeth dislikes the attentions to him of two young sisters, Lady Sheffield whom he afterwards married (though there is some doubt if it were a legal marriage) and Frances Howard, daughters of Lord Howard of Effingham.

The letter contains a passage which has already been quoted about the Queen's fancy for Lord Oxford, and proceeds:

> Hatton is sick still; it is thought he will very hardly recover his disease, for it is doubted [i.e. thought] it is in his kidneys: the Queen goeth almost every day to see how he doth. Now is there devices, chiefly by Leicester (as I suppose), and not without Burghley's knowledge, how to make Mr. Edward Dyer as great as ever was Hatton, for now, in this time of Hatton's sickness, the time is convenient. It is brought thus to pass: Dyer lately was sick of a consumption, in great danger; and, as your Lordship knoweth, he hath been in displeasure these two years: it was made the Queen believe that his sickness came because of the continuance of her displeasure towards him, that, unless she would forgive him, he was not like to recover; and hereupon her Majesty hath forgiven him, and sent unto him a very comfortable message: now he is recovered again, and this is the beginning of this device. These things I learn of such young fellows as myself.

So here we see some of the kaleidoscopic changes of Courts. Hatton grows in favour till he is regarded as a rival to Leicester; then Oxford comes to the fore for a time, and Hatton's star wanes; his friend Dyer advises him to act sensibly and not to show his jealousy; Hatton complies and apparently recovers some of his lost ground, but Leicester remains in favour; then Hatton falls sick, and Leicester conceives the idea of finally eliminating him by promoting Dyer to the Queen's favour as a counterpoise. But he had forgotten the real kindness of Elizabeth's heart. She visits the sick Hatton, comforts and helps him in his illness, and pardons the ailing Dyer, the more readily since she is persuaded to believe his illness is due to her displeasure.

It has been suggested that Coridon, Charimell and Amarillis of Edward Dyer's poem 'Amarillis' are Dyer himself, Hatton and Queen Elizabeth. The rivalry of Hatton and Dyer for the Queen's favour is the point of contact between the lives of the two courtiers and the characters of Dyer's poem. In the story Charimell and Coridon are fast friends, each smitten with love for Amarillis; the rivals pine and die of despair, and by Amarillis's supplication to Diana are metamorphosed, Coridon to an owl that fled to the wilderness and Charimell to a yellow flower which Amarillis plucked, and 'wore it on her head; sometime she laid it on her lap, and sometime on her bed'. Sometimes, however, she would repair to the wood and delight to hear 'the lay and tune' of Coridon's despair. That Coridon is Dyer is accepted by some other scholars, who equate him with the Coredens of Sidney's *Arcadia*, and if the poem treats of real events, as Dyer hints, the identification of Charimell with Hatton seems plausible enough.

On May 23rd Gilbert Talbot again wrote to his father that 'Mr. Hatton, by reason of his great sickness, is minded to go to the Spa for the better recovery of his health'. On the 29th the Privy Council signed an order to allow Hatton 'to pass over the seas for the recovery of his health', and the Queen showed her practical sympathy by permitting one of her physicians to accompany him. Strype, quoting from a letter from Francis Talbot to his father, Lord Shrewsbury, says that 'Mr. Hatton (not well in health) took this opportunity [one of the Queen's progresses] to get leave to go to the Spa, and Dr. Julio (a great Court physician) with him; whereat the Queen showed herself very pensive, and very unwilling to grant him leave, for he was a favourite'.

Hatton took his leave of Elizabeth on June 5th, the date being determined by the fact that, writing on the 17th, he says that it is the twelfth day since he saw her. Within two days of his departure he had more than one letter from her — now lost; and on June 7th wrote her in reply. He wrote again from Antwerp on June 17th; and again on August 10th (no address). An undated letter, written in illness, may also belong to this period. He was back in England before October 11th.

Three of these four letters, as well as the letter already quoted of the year 1572, are superscribed with a curious cipher. It consists of four triangles, and it seems likely that it is intended for a representation of one of the Queen's nicknames for him. For Elizabeth gave all her intimate friends affectionate, though rather absurd, names, drawn mostly from the animal kingdom. She had a fondness for curious imagery. Her portraits, as Froude observes, show her in robes broidered with eyes and ears as emblematic of omnipresence, or with lizards, crocodiles, serpents and other monsters, significant, whatever they meant besides, of her own extraordinary taste. So with her nicknames. Simier was her Monkey, Alençon her Frog, Burghley her Spirit, Robert Cecil her Pygmy, Walter Ralegh 'Water', the dark Walsingham her Moor, the presumably equally dark Lady Norris her Crow (or perhaps by the word Elizabeth meant a familiar friend), Sir Thomas Heneage 'Sanguine'. Leicester is the closest parallel to Hatton in the matter of the cipher, for his nickname was 'Eyes', and he ornamented his letters with a pair of eyes. Hatton was called by the Queen 'Lids' and also her Sheep, Mutton, and Bell Wether. That the first of these names had reference to his eyelids is proved by various passages in his letters to Elizabeth. They may have had some peculiarity of shape or trick, but a more ingenious explanation has been advanced by Mrs. Aubrey Richardson in *The Lover of Queen Elizabeth*, a life of Leicester. She explains Leicester's name of 'Eyes' as meaning that he was Elizabeth's clear-visioned deputy, her 'look-out man'; and she argues that 'Leicester being the "eyes" of the Argus of her people's needs, Hatton, by a natural sequence, became the "lids" of those "eyes" '.

And one might go farther. The eyes and ears of Elizabeth's costumes were symbols of omnipresence. One of her favourite sayings was *video sed taceo*, 'I see, yet am silent'. If Leicester represented the eyes of this omniscience, Hatton, who had special duties in the tactful handling of personal matters concerning the Court, may well have been called 'Lids' from the Queen's other claim of refusing to see when occasion demanded. And, as Leicester had a symbol in his letters for his 'eyes' something like õ õ, so we may believe with Mr. Martin Hume and Professor Neale that the triangles with which Hatton begins his letters to the Queen represented crudely drawn eyelids.

The letters are of an extraordinarily tender and lover-like quality. It may be presumed that Hatton's illness and absence from his sovereign inspired their unusually extravagant style. The first of them is dated '1573, June', and no place of writing is given. It was presumably written on June 7th, for the reasons already given; and it was possibly sent from Dover while he was waiting to take ship. Though, as he says, only two days had elapsed since he had said farewell to Elizabeth, she had already written to him, and more than once. He mentions his illness and his prospective journey; and the whole letter is couched in the hysterical language of an invalid, fearful of his health and of the danger of being forgotten in absence. It must be quoted in full:

> If I could express my feelings of your gracious letters, I should utter unto you matter of strange effect. In reading of them, with my tears I blot them. In thinking of them I feel so great comfort, that I find cause, as God knoweth, to thank you on my knees. Death had been much more my advantage than to win health and life by so loathsome a pilgrimage.
>
> The time of two days hath drawn me further from you than ten, when I return, can lead me towards you. Madam, I find the greatest lack that ever poor wretch sustained. No death, no, not hell, no fear of death shall ever win of me my consent so far to wrong myself again as to be absent from you one day. God grant my return. I will perform this vow. I lack that I live by. The more I find this lack, the further I go from you. Shame whippeth me forward. Shame take them that counselled me to it. The life (as you will remember) is too long that loathsomely lasteth. A true saying, Madam. Believe him that hath proved it. The great wisdom I find in your letters, with your contrary counsels are very notable, but the last word is worth the bible. Truth, truth, truth. Ever may it dwell in you. I will ever deserve it. My spirit and soul (I feel) agreeth with my body and life, that to serve you is a heaven, but to lack you is more than hell's torment unto them. My heart is full of woe. Pardon (for God's sake) my tedious writing. It doth much diminish (for the time) my great griefs. I will wash away the faults of these letters with the drops from your poor Lydds and so inclose them. Would God I were with you but for one hour. My wits are overwrought with thoughts. I find myself amazed. Bear with me, my most dear sweet Lady. Passion overcometh me.

I can write no more. Love me; for I love you. God, I beseech thee witness the same on the behalf of thy poor servant. Live for ever. Shall I utter this familiar term [farewell?] yea, ten thousand thousand farewells. He speaketh it that most dearly loveth you. I hold you too long. Once again I crave pardon, and so bid your own poor Lidds farewell. 1573 June.

Your bondman everlastingly tied, Ch. Hatton.

The next letter is from Antwerp and is dated June 17th. It is the twelfth day, Hatton says, since he saw Elizabeth. Again he alludes to his name of 'Lidds'. Hatton shows that he has made use of his visit to Antwerp to observe the attitude of the Netherlands to his country and sovereign, and sends an appreciation of the position by Thomas Heneage, Treasurer of the Queen's Chamber, who had accompanied him. Heneage had been one of the Queen's favourites some eight years before this, a handsome man who for a time had looked like being a serious rival to Leicester. He was a confidant of Hatton's, and later was to be a bearer of some remarkable letters between him and Elizabeth. From this letter the usual cipher superscription is absent:

... This is the twelfth day since I saw the brightness of that Sun that giveth light unto my sense and soul. I wax an amazed creature. Give me leave, Madam, to remove myself out of this irksome shadow, so far as my imagination with these good means may lead me towards you, and let me thus salute you: Live for ever, most excellent creature; and love some man, to show yourself thankful for God his high labour in you. I am too far off to hear your answer to this salutation; I know it would be full of virtue and great wisdom, but I fear for some part thereof I should have but small thanks. Pardon me; I will leave these matters, because I think you mislike them. ...

I would I saw your world at home, how some seek that I have done, which they shall find never. Some hope well and haste them on, but waste shall be their hire; and some despair whom I allow the wisest, but not the most happy of these men. But, Madam, forget not your Lidds that are so often bathed with tears for your sake. A more wise man may seek you, but a more faithful and worthy can never have you. Pardon me, my most dear sweet Lady, I will no more write of these matters. I wish you like welfare your presence might give me; it is, I assure you, the best farewell that ever was given you. Antwerp, the 17th. of June, 1573.

Yours all and ever yours, Ch. Hatton.

The next letter is in reply to one that the Queen had sent him under cover to Sir Thomas Heneage. It is dated August 10th, 1573, and was presumably written from Spa, which place he must by then have reached. It records an improvement in health, and shows that Dr. Julio had been sending reports of his progress to the Queen. Headed with the usual cipher, it runs:

Madam, as your most rare works confirm in me an irremovable faith, so is my love and band [bond] enlarged to an infinite serviceable thankfulness. The lining of Mr. Heneage letter warmeth the heart's blood with joys above joys. Full sweet will such a life be, that by so noble a sweet creature is with so glad and kind devotion asked at the Almighty's hands. God grant it you. Not for myself I ask it; but that your everlasting bandman [bondman], with pure love and careful diligent faith, may everlastingly serve you. . . .

The contentment of mind you give me doth most of all recure me. By your great bounty and most liberal charge I purchase life and health withal. By your oft messengers, carriers of your endless cares for my recovery's sake, I enjoy so great a comfort in life as never God hath blessed man withal before. For all these I can yield you nothing but the beggar's phrase, though indeed his best thanks, God save your life for EveR, and bless you with His glorious thanks for your divine merits towards me your so poor and discomforted despairing servant. My dear Lady, I amend: some proof thereof hath Julio sent unto you. I find cause to think that much greater effects will follow. God be blessed in all His works, and you in your most royal gifts. Upon the knees of my heart I most humbly commend my most faithful love and service unto you. Adieu, most dear sweet Lady. This 10th. of August, 1573. All and EveR yours, your most happy bandman,

Lyddes.

The highly artificial, even childish nature of this correspondence is illustrated by Hatton's trick of writing the word 'ever' as 'EveR', where the capitals stand for Elizabetha Regina.

There is one other letter about his illness from Hatton to the Queen, but it is without date, and it is uncertain if it belongs to this time. Sir Harris Nicolas thought that it probably did so, and that it was sent from Spa in July or early in August. But he agrees that it may belong to an earlier period of his illness, before he left England. On the other hand, there are some indications to suggest that it does not belong to this, but to another time of illness.

In the first place, Hatton is no longer 'Lids', as in the others of the series, but the Queen's Mutton, another pet name of Elizabeth's for him. Secondly, there is the puzzling reference to his illness: 'your Mutton is black; scarcely will you know your own, so much hath this disease dashed me'. That does not seem to fit the kidney or bladder complaint which had apparently brought Hatton to Spa. Nor does it fit the other circumstances. The context shows that Elizabeth had not seen him in this black condition, and it suggests that Hatton had been taken with some sort of fever when away from her. However, the references to the Boar seem to fit Oxford better than any other, and so the letter perhaps falls within the period of Hatton's jealousy of Oxford, which would, so far as we know, put it in the early 'seventies. It is preceded by the familiar cipher:

> The lack I feel doth make me know your greatest worth. I speak in the presence of God. I find my body and mind so far divided as, yourself shall judge, that melancholy (conceived by this unwonted absence) hath made myself forget myself. Your Mutton is black; scarcely will you know your own, so much hath this disease dashed me . . . I love yourself. I cannot lack you. I am taught to prove it by the wish and desire I find to be with you. Believe it, most gracious Lady, there is no *illud mitius*, you are the true felicity that in this world I know or find. God bless you for ever. The branch of the sweetest bush I will wear and bear to my life's end. God doth witness I feign not. It is a gracious favour, most dear and welcome unto me. Reserve it to the Sheep, he hath no tooth to bite; where the Boar's tush may both rase and tear. The branch of brass with your most noble word and sentence, I desire exceedingly to have . . . Humbly on the knees of my soul, I pray God bless you for ever. Your slave and EveR your own,

The signature is peculiar. First there is an elaborate 'CH' for Christopher, and this is followed by what is called a rebus on the surname, that is a sort of pictorial representation of it. Here we have a triangular hat crossed through with a capital X for 'ten', the whole being meant to represent 'Hatton'.

In this letter, Hatton, calling himself the Queen's Mutton, contrasts 'the Sheep' which has 'no tooth to bite' with 'the Boar' whose 'tush may both rase and tear'. By the latter phrase he seems to mean the Earl of Oxford, whose crest was a boar. Nicolas thinks that 'the branch of the sweetest bush' was a jewel that

Elizabeth had sent him. But it was possibly a sprig of rosemary, 'for remembrance'. It is contrasted with 'the branch of brass' which Hatton hoped Elizabeth would send him; and here he perhaps means a jewelled spray of gold, such as ladies wore in their hair, with a motto engraved on it. But his imagery is obscure, just as the precise meaning of his laborious sentences is not always clear.

Perhaps the earliest example that can be dated of Hatton's petname Mutton, belongs to the year 1579. The Earl of Warwick, Leicester's brother, had been enclosing some common ground in Northall Mimms in Hertfordshire. This action was resented by the inhabitants; there was a riot and some sheep were taken or maimed. Hatton was sent down to investigate, and as a result two men were burnt in the hand, two hanged and four others sent to gaol. Elizabeth, who seems to have been quite unmoved at these savage sentences (it has indeed and with some truth been charged against her that she only inclined to mercy towards those of gentle blood) was greatly pleased with the way Hatton had handled the business, but very solicitous for his safety. The 'outrage' upon the sheep being reported brought a jest from her: 'She feareth greatly her Mutton, lest he should take some harm amongst those disordered people', but though she was most anxious for his speedy return to Court, she wished him to rest for a day before travelling.

Sir Harris Nicolas made a diligent search for letters from Elizabeth to Hatton. He was not successful in his quest, though he found among the State Papers contemporary copies of two letters which he printed. They are endorsed, 'A couple of letters of the Queen, indited and written at one time'. Their subject is friendship, and they are in Elizabeth's most enigmatic vein. There is no occasion to print them here. For, in the first place, there is no internal evidence by which we can hazard a guess about the person or persons to whom they are addressed; and indeed Nicolas himself confesses that he does not think they formed part of Elizabeth's letters to Hatton. And, in the second place, Nicolas failed to notice that they had already been printed by Henry Harington in his *Nugae Antiquae*, the literary remains of Sir John Harington, the Queen's godson. In Harington's text it is said that 'The following letters were found in a MS. entitled "A precious Token of her Highness's great Wit and marvellous Understanding"', and it is explained that they were 'the Letters the Queen's Majesty wrote, whilst she gave instructions for the other that followeth, and hearing a tale which she had made answer unto'. It seems therefore that Elizabeth wrote the first while dictating the second, and it follows that they were not necessarily, nor even probably, written to the same person; while the circumstances of composition may explain an obscurity darker even than Elizabeth's wont.

Hatton's stay at Antwerp brought him a strange letter from one 'T.G.', which has already been briefly alluded to. Under cover of it was sent him a copy of a seditious book that had been published at Antwerp in January of that year, 1573. It was entitled *A Treatise of Treasons against Queen Elizabeth and the Crown of England.* It was anonymous, and was in two parts. The first was a refutation of 'the false and slanderous infamies' against Mary Queen of Scots, 'heir apparent of the Crown of England' and against the Duke of Norfolk. The second part was a bitter attack on Burghley and Sir Nicholas Bacon, the Lord Keeper, who were accused of plotting the death of Elizabeth and the Queen of Scots in the interest of the House of Suffolk, descended from Henry VIII's younger sister, Mary Tudor. It was sought to use Hatton to bring this book to Elizabeth's notice and to recommend it to her. Only a year had gone by since some of Hatton's relatives had thought that they might pit him against Burghley, and there is little doubt that the Catholic party still thought that they could exploit him.

'T.G.'s' letter to Hatton was addressed from Antwerp on June 25th, 1573. By seeking to play upon Hatton's supposed Catholic sympathies the writer reveals his own hand, that of a Catholic partisan of the Queen of Scots, and, despite his protestations, presumably no more a well-wisher of Elizabeth than he was of Burghley. The letter reminds Hatton:

> you were first baptized in the faith Catholic, your continuance for many years therein and the danger in forsaking the same, the weight whereof no worldy treasures or dignities can countervail, the one being eternal, the other temporal, brittle and frail, as over many of your condition have tried, finding their experience powdered with bitter repentance.

It goes on to deal with the succession to the English Crown, and presses Hatton, as one close in Elizabeth's confidence, to bring the book to her notice.

Mr. B. M. Ward has found a copy of this book in the Archbishop of Canterbury's Library at Lambeth Palace. With it are bound two items not found in either of the two copies in the British Museum. The first is a Table or summary of *The Treatise of Treasons* which is also mentioned in 'T.G.'s' letter to Hatton. It contains a dedication to Elizabeth urging her to read the Treatise or at any rate the Table, and saying that, as Burghley and Bacon will no doubt seek to prevent its coming to her hands, and indeed have had and concealed copies of it for months past, it has been addressed to a trusty servant of hers, Mr. Hatton (as well as to others) 'who of duty and allegiance hath been thought the most fit instrument to present you the same'. The dedication is signed, 'Your Highness's daily orator, G.T.' The second item is a copy of the letter sent to Hatton by 'T.G.', but here printed 'G.T.' The date is June 26th (not 25th), 1573, but otherwise except for a few minor differences, it is the same. It is headed, 'A copy of a letter addressed from Antwerp the xxvi of June to Mr. Hatton and delivered unto him at Spaw the 5 of July, 1573'.

Hatton apparently sent the letter not to the Queen, but to Burghley (it is among his papers at Hatfield), and it is unlikely that he sent her the book. A copy, however, was delivered by an unknown man at the house of Dr. Nowell, the Dean of St. Paul's, with a covering letter, signed 'Tom Truth' and dated at Calais, August 4th, 1573. The Dean, 'much troubled', handed it to Sir Ralph Sadler, who forwarded it to Bacon. Bacon sent it to Burghley asking him to show it to the Queen. Burghley seems to have consulted the Archbishop of Canterbury about printing a reply, but the Archbishop returned it saying that it was not worthy of an answer. On September 28th the Queen issued a proclamation:

> Certain traitors, unable to openly harm their country, are printing books in English, Latin and other strange languages, wherein, under cover of promoting the Queen's safety, they make charge of treason against two of her most devoted subjects. No persons are to regard these seditious slanders, but the books should be handed over to the Privy Council.

The whole episode bears a curious resemblance to that of *Leycester's Commonwealth*, published eleven years later. Both books were Catholic productions written in the interest of Mary Queen of Scots, but whereas the earlier books attacked Burghley and Bacon for putting forward the claims of the House of Suffolk to the succession, *Leycester's Commonwealth* attacked Leicester for his support of the claims of his brother-in-law, the Earl of Huntingdon. The author of the earlier book invoked the aid of Hatton; that of the latter praised Hatton at the expense of Leicester. In each case, by proclamation, the Queen condemned the book and defended her Ministers.

Another communication of a different kind was made to Hatton while he was abroad. The survivors of the Northern Rebellion, who had fled to the Netherlands, were looking forward to the day of the 'Enterprise' when a coalition of Pope and Catholic powers would invade England, depose Elizabeth and set Mary Queen of Scots in her place. Schemes were formulating in the year that Hatton was at Spa, and some details were communicated to an English gentleman there. The information, which was eventually sent to Burghley, probably told him no more than he already knew. It was the usual rather nebulous plan of which the English *émigrés* dreamed, nursing their illusions until the defeat of the Armada shattered them for ever. It appears that a certain English 'baron', perhaps Charles Neville, Earl of Westmorland, one of the Northern Earls, then in exile at Louvain, had spoken of the matter to Bertrand de la Tour, a French nobleman. But de la Tour was a Protestant, an enthusiastic admirer of Elizabeth as Protestant champion of Europe, and not at all the sort of person likely to be sympathetic. 'Hearing that a certain noble knight, a Captain of the Queen's Guards, was in the Spaw, he thought it his duty to certify the said officer, being a person very devoted to her Majesty', of these matters. No more is said of Hatton — for he, of course, was the Captain of the Guard — in this document, which was perhaps drawn up by him and sent to England where it was placed among Burghley's papers.

CHAPTER X

'A HUNDRETH SUNDRIE FLOWRES'

AFTER Hatton's letter to Elizabeth of August 10th, 1573, we lose sight of him until October 11th, when a student of the Inner Temple, a Puritan fanatic named Peter Burchet, planned to assassinate him because he considered him 'a wilful Papist', who 'hindereth the glory of God so much as in him lieth'. However, he mistook Sir John Hawkins, the celebrated sailor, for Hatton, and struck him with his dagger as he was riding with Sir William Winter, one of Elizabeth's admirals, near Temple Bar. Hawkins was badly, but not fatally, wounded; and Burchet, being sent to the Tower, murdered there one of the keepers, knocking him on the head with a billet which he snatched from the chimney.

Elizabeth was so agitated by the danger to which her favourite had been exposed that she ordered a commission to be issued for executing Burchet by martial law, and was only with difficulty dissuaded from so illegal a course. The man, as Francis Bacon reflected years later, was evidently insane but, in Lord Campbell's words, 'in those days they did not stand on such a nicety as criminal responsibility'. He was condemned to death; and his right hand being first cut off and nailed to the gallows, was hanged, 'discovering a silent reluctancy', in Campden's neat if insensitive phrase.

That Hatton was actually in London when Burchet conceived the idea of putting him out of the way is proved by a letter from the Secretary of State, Sir Thomas Smith, to Burghley. Writing on October 12th, he says, 'it is said here that divers times within this fortnight, both by words and writings Mr. Hatton hath been admonished to take hold of himself, for his life was laid in wait for'. Hatton was probably at home, therefore, by the beginning of October at latest.

His absence on the Continent in the summer of 1573 is one of the points in the argument advanced by Mr. B. M. Ward for assigning to Hatton a share in the authorship of the anthology called *A Hundreth Sundrie Flowres*, which Mr. Ward reprinted with a long introduction in 1926. His arguments have not been generally accepted; but the matter is so interesting, from its possible connection with an episode in Hatton's life, that it cannot be omitted here.

Mr. Ward's contention is briefly that *A Hundreth Sundrie Flowres*, which has generally been assigned in its entirety to the poet, George Gascoigne, was in reality a collection, of which Gascoigne was only one of the authors. There were, he argues, several others indicated by the 'posies' or Latin mottoes with which the poems are signed. One of these, *Si fortunatus infoelix*, is, he holds, Christopher Hatton, and he claims further that 'Master F.I.', whose adventures are chronicled in prose and verse is to be identified with *Si fortunatus infoelix*, that is, with Hatton.

For Mr. Ward's argument something turns on the precise date of the book's publication. It was published in 1573, according to Mr. Ward, in the summer, from which he concludes that it was issued while Hatton, on his theory one of the authors, was abroad, and without his knowledge. But the best opinion seems to be that the book was actually issued in the early spring of that year which, if accepted, would upset some of the argument, though not all of it; and in any case it is possible to suggest a connection between Hatton and the book, without accepting a good deal of that argument.

The book is on the face of it an anthology of pieces by different writers; and an ordinary reader, coming to it as it was published in 1573, would unquestionably so accept it. None the less he would notice an air of mystification. There are three prefatory letters, seemingly simple and above board but likely on reflection to arouse suspicion. One of these is from 'G.T.' to his friend 'H.W.', sending him a copy of these collected pieces which he describes as 'the works of your friend and mine, Master F.I., and divers others', and asking him to read them and to return them, 'for otherwise I shall . . . provoke all the authors to be offended with me'. The other letters are to much the same effect; and the device of multiple authorship is kept up in the arrangement of the contents. 'G.T.' prefaces the first section by saying that he had 'with no small entreaty obtained of Master F.I. and sundry other toward young gentlemen the sundry copies of these matters . . . ' He begins with 'The Adventures of Master F.I.', in prose and verse, and follows with

> sundry verses written by sundry gentlemen, adding nothing of mine own only a title to every Poem, whereby the cause of writing the same may the more evidently appear. Neither can I declare

unto you who wrote the greatest part of them, for they are unto me but a posy presented out of sundry gardens, neither have I any other names of the flowers, but such short notes as the authors themselves have delivered; thereby, if you can guess them, it shall no way offend me.

There follows a section consisting of poems each subscribed *Si fortunatus infoelix*. New sections are headed, 'Now to begin with another man . . . '; 'A strange passion of another Author'; 'Now I must desire you with patience to hearken unto the works of another writer . . . ', each section being subscribed with a Latin 'posy' or motto. Finally, comes this heading, 'I will now deliver unto you so many more of Master Gascoigne's poems as have come into my hands, who hath never been dainty of his doings, and therefore I conceal not his name; but his word or posy he hath often changed and therefore I will deliver his verses with sundry posies as I received them'.

Such are the contents of this collection. Whatever conclusions we may draw are complicated by the fact that two years later the book was reissued as 'The Posies of George Gascoigne, Esq., Corrected, perfected, and augmented by the author'. It is in fact a reissue of *A Hundreth Sundrie Flowres* with omissions, additions, and rearrangements. This volume contains not only the poems originally attributed to Gascoigne, but also nearly all those ascribed in the *Flowres* to other men; but the original sections are broken up, and the poems they contain scattered throughout the book. The whole is now ascribed to Gascoigne, who explains in the Preface that many of the poems were written for others.

This new edition makes us look at the problem of authorship in a different light. For whereas a reader of *A Hundreth Sundrie Flowres* in 1573 would naturally take it to be an anthology, one who came to 'The Posies of George Gascoigne' in 1575 would accept the whole as Gascoigne's work. What are we to believe? Were all these poems Gascoigne's? And if so, why were they originally assigned to other authors? Or were they the work of different men, and, in that case, why did Gascoigne later claim them as his own?

The accepted view is that Gascoigne was the sole author; that the elaborate mystification in the first presentation of the work was a literary artifice; and that Gascoigne gives us the true explanation of the reissue under his name in 1575. That is that many of the pieces were suspected of attacking well-known persons under fictitious names; there was an outcry at so scandalous an offence, and hence it was necessary for Gascoigne to acknowledge authorship, at the same time claiming that all the people and incidents named were fictitious: the modern formula, in fact that accompanies most works of fiction.

Mr. Ward, however, puts forward an elaborate argument for the other view, that the *Flowres* was really an anthology; that it made use of the unpublished work of well-known men about the Court; that this publication was unauthorized by Gascoigne; and that, in consequence of the ensuing scandal, he was forced to father the whole. Moreover, he has attempted to identify the authors. In particular, he equates 'Master F.I.' with *Si fortunatus infoelix* and identifies him as Christopher Hatton.

This identification rests upon two almost contemporary statements of Gabriel Harvey's. In his copy (now in the Bodleian Library) of the 1575 edition, Harvey wrote against the motto, *Si fortunatus infoelix*, 'lately the posie of Sir Christopher Hatton'. Harvey entered in his copy the date September 1st, 1577, presumably the date when he acquired the volume, and his annotation must have been made after December 1st, 1577, when Hatton was knighted. The second piece of evidence from Gabriel Harvey is the heading of one of the Latin poems in his own *Gratulationes Valdinenses* of 1578. These were congratulatory verses to the Queen and her principal ministers and courtiers Burghley, Leicester, Oxford, Hatton and Sir Philip Sidney, celebrating Elizabeth's progress at Audley End in July, 1578. The poem addressed to Hatton is headed, in Latin, 'concerning his symbol *Foelix Infortunatus*'. This is not quite the same as *Si fortunatus infoelix*, but it is close enough. It is certain therefore that Hatton used the former motto in 1578, and it is not unreasonable to suppose that by the latter motto, of five years earlier, Hatton was intended.

Mr. Ward then proceeds to another identification. The fictitious editor of the volume, 'G.T.', says that he obtained the manuscripts of the poems from 'Master F.I. and sundry other toward young gentlemen', that he 'did with more labour gather them into some order', and that 'as near as I could guess I have set in the first places those which Master F.I. did compile, and to begin with this his history that ensueth'. This last sentence must mean, he argues reasonably enough, that 'The Adventures of Master F.I.'

are by the author of the seventeen poems that immediately follow; and, as these are subscribed *Si fortunatus infoelix*, it follows that 'F.I.' stands for *fortunatus infoelix*, i.e. Christopher Hatton. Now the story of Master F.I. is that he 'chanced once in the northern parts of this realm to fall in company of a very fair gentlewoman, whose name was Mistress Elinor'. The course of their love-making and the extravagant letters and verses they exchanged are the subject of the story. Mr. Ward argues that this love affair, real or imaginary, of Hatton's, would be very distasteful to the Queen, and (on the theory that they were published when he was abroad) that Hatton would naturally be intensely indignant when, on his return from Spa, he found the verses in print.

Wherever Hatton may have been at the date of the publication of the *Flowres*, it is certain that Gascoigne was abroad. He had embarked for the Low Countries in March, 1573, served as a soldier there; was taken prisoner, and not released until November, 1574. The *Flowres* was published in 1573, probably in the late spring, and the new edition in 1575. The ostensible reason for this second edition is given in a prefatory epistle 'To the Reverend Divines', in which Gascoigne says:

> I understand that sundry well-disposed minds have taken offence at certain wanton words and phrases passed in the *Fable of Ferdinando Jeronimi and the Lady Elionora de Valasco*, the which in the first edition was termed *The Adventures of Master F.I.* And that also therewith some busy conjecturers have presumed to think that the same was indeed written to the scandalizing of some worthy personages, whom they would know thereby.

Certainly the scene and characters of the story have been changed out of all recognition. As Mr. Ward sums up, 'The "Adventures of Master F.I." were carefully and minutely altered in such a way that all the topical character of the story was destroyed, London became Venice, "the north parts of the realm" Lombardy, while the Lady Elinor became Leonora de Valasco'. He concludes that the man behind these changes was Christopher Hatton. And he argues that Hatton contrived to dissociate himself from the part authorship by arranging for Gascoigne to claim the whole as his, as he did in the second edition.

A reasonable theory is, as already suggested, that the *Flowres* is entirely the work of Gascoigne, and that the original ascription of the verses to different authors is a literary artifice. But that does not exclude the possibility that some of the verses were intended to indicate prominent people by the thin disguise of mottoes which would be understood by the initiated. Hence the scandal which Gascoigne admits. If this be accepted, there is a possibility that *Si fortunatus infoelix* and 'Master F.I.' were indeed intended for Christopher Hatton; and some additional evidence of this, not indeed conclusive but suggestive, may be given.

For it is possible to point out an episode in Hatton's life that would to some extent fit the story of Master F.I. When Mary Queen of Scots wrote to Elizabeth in 1584 to repeat the Court scandal with which Lady Shrewsbury had regaled her, she quoted her as saying that she had sought to marry her daughter, the late Countess of Lennox, to Hatton, but that for fear of Queen Elizabeth he had not dared to proceed with his suit. Elizabeth Cavendish, daughter of Lady Shrewsbury by her former husband, Sir William Cavendish, was born in March, 1555, and married in 1574 to Charles Stuart, Earl of Lennox, brother of Mary's husband Darnley. She had died in 1582. Before her marriage her mother had hawked her round the marriage market, and had sought in particular to marry her to Peregrine Bertie, son of the Duchess of Suffolk. And in a letter from Lord Shrewsbury to Burghley, excusing himself for the Lennox marriage, so disliked by the Queen, he says, 'there is few noblemen's sons in England that she [his wife] hath not prayed me to deal for at one time or other; so I did for my Lord Rutland, with my Lord Sussex, for my Lord Wharton, and sundry others'. There can be little doubt, in the light of the Queen of Scots' letter, that Hatton, one of the rising men in England, was another on whom Bess of Hardwick had cast her matchmaking eye.

At the time of her marriage to the Earl of Lennox in 1574 Elizabeth Cavendish was not yet nineteen. In 1572 when Hatton may have been at Sheffield Castle in connection with the affairs of the Queen of Scots, she would have been but seventeen. If Sheffield Castle was the scene of Hatton's brief wooing, it would fit the passage in the story that Master F.I. met his lady in the north parts of the realm. There is, however, the difficulty that the lady in the story was married. The name Elinor need not have any significance. If this story was really a hit at Hatton, the name would almost certainly be altered. It was bad enough to parade in a thin disguise the love affairs of the Queen's favourite; it would be intolerable if the names of the chief actors were not concealed.

For those who may be interested in such riddles it may be added that Elinor in the story has a sister Frances and that Elizabeth Cavendish had a sister Frances Pierrepont. Another character in one of Gascoigne's poems, whose story resembles Elinor's at certain points, is called 'Ferenda Natura'. She is a lady of the Court, and her playfellows are the Cavendish sisters, Frances Pierrepont and Elizabeth, Countess of Lennox. But it would be foolish to press such slight clues too far, and many of Gascoigne's riddles are confessedly mysteries, not to be understood 'but by the author himself'. However that may be, if we believe the Scots Queen's story that Elizabeth Cavendish was in fact courted by Hatton, it may not be entirely fanciful to suggest that we may have a record of a letter from her to Hatton. Some of the letters in the Hatton Letter Book are without signature or date. They present puzzles that cannot always be resolved, that are in many cases, perhaps, not worth resolving. But there are instances where one would be glad of a clue to the writer. Such is this interesting letter from a lady, who shows that she is out of favour with the Queen, and hopes that Hatton may stay her friend:

> Nevertheless, when I remember your courtesy offered even then when Fortune most showed her despite against me, I am persuaded a certain planet reigned that then assured me, and so doeth still, that I should receive some good of you, though the storms of my ill-fortune have shed since many drops untimely for me to gather fruit of your favour.

She signs herself 'Yours, as ever vowed during life, Elizabeth . . .'; and adds a remarkable postscript, 'I hope, Sir, that if a poor pilgrim wandering in the Park with a long bow, shoot at rovers, and hit a buck where the sign is, and die of it, you will not make it a pretended murder'. Altogether she sounds like one who knows or had known Hatton well, making private allusions which she knows will be taken. We may, if we like, think of her as Hatton's one-time love, Elizabeth Cavendish, who, with all the Lennox family, was out of favour at Court.

CHAPTER XI

CORFE CASTLE

MR. THOMAS BOND, in his History of Corfe Castle, says that Queen
Elizabeth in the fourteenth year of her reign (1571-2) granted, or
rather sold for £4761 18s. 7½d. Corfe Castle, with its lordship,
demesne lands, liberties and privileges to Christopher Hatton
Esquire, Gentleman Pensioner. He gives no source for his statement. A grant to Hatton of the castle, demesne or manor of
Corfe is entered on the Patent Roll of the year 1576, but this
possibly was in the nature of a confirmation of a previous sale.

Corfe Castle is in the county of Dorset and is situated in the
so-called Isle of Purbeck, a peninsula measuring twelve miles by
nine, bounded by the sea on the south and by a line of hills on
the north. The castle occupies an extremely strong position in the
gap or gate which here divides this line of hills. From its position
in this gap comes the original name Corvesgate. Corfe was one
of the strongest fortresses in the kingdom, a royal castle dating
from the early days of the Norman period, perhaps even from the
time of the Conquest. Frequently used as a prison, especially by
the tyrannical King John, it was granted from time to time to
members of the royal family or to great nobles, and had come into
the hands of the Crown on the attainder of Edward Seymour,
Duke of Somerset, to whom his nephew Edward VI had given it.

Considerable privileges attached to the tenure of the castle and
manor. Among these liberties, which may be studied in detail in
Mr. Bond's book, was the right to wreck of the sea and to prisage
of wine of every ship carrying wine and coming to the coast of
Purbeck. The Constable of the castle had also the power to array
the militia and to summon men to defend the castle in times of
disturbance. Hatton, as keeper of the castle, had the title of Lord
Lieutenant and Admiral or Vice-Admiral of the Isle of Purbeck,
and this title passed to successive holders after him. Lists of the
customs and privileges of Corfe were drawn up from time to time,
and one such list, which seems to have belonged to Hatton, exists
in a manuscript in a sixteenth-century handwriting. In this are
enumerated the various courts held by the lord of the manor, and
the regulations for such matters as fishing and the taking of conies.

III

Another important privilege was the right of hunting red deer in the Isle of Purbeck. Game in medieval England was a royal preserve; and even up to Tudor and Stuart times no one was entitled to hunt unless he had been granted the royal licence of free warren. Corfe Castle, being crown property, possessed of course these rights, which were transferred by Queen Elizabeth to Christopher Hatton.

There is among the records of the Court of Star Chamber a suit brought by Hatton in 1583 against certain persons whom he accused of poaching on his preserves, killing his deer, breaking them up, and taking away the carcasses. He complained particularly of John Haviland, John Uvedale and Thomas Eyres, gentlemen, as well as fifteen others, yeomen and countrymen, who with crossbows, guns, greyhounds, etc., had hunted and killed his deer. Haviland, Uvedale and Eyres, who was Hatton's ranger, of course denied the charges, as did two men who for the past eight years had been his under-foresters and keepers of the game of red deer in the east walk of the Isle of Purbeck. But one witness was found to swear to various occasions when deer had been poached. He spoke of gifts of deer being made for neighbouring wedding feasts and also of a present of three venison pies which Haviland had sent to his son at Oxford. We can identify the son, whom he regaled with Hatton's venison pasties, as Thomas Haviland, a scholar of New College.

There is preserved with this file of proceedings the usual list of questions to be put to witnesses. The last of these may be quoted as a picturesque illustration of the customs of Corfe Castle. 'How many of the said deer, or any other, have been brought to the barbican of Corfe Castle, and there viewed by the coroners according to the ancient usage of the Island, and to whom hath the flesh been distributed?' As with so many Star Chamber cases, the Court's decision is not forthcoming, and we do not know what redress, if any, Hatton obtained for the damage to his property.

Corfe Castle had been put in repair by Henry VII for the residence of his mother, the Countess of Richmond, and £2000 was granted by Parliament for that purpose. Hatton, according to Coker's *Survey of Dorsetshire*, 'much repaired it and amended it, being almost overcome by time'. But, however that may be — and Hatton made a similar claim in the Court of Star Chamber — in his day the castle stood intact, and its appearance may be gathered from the birds'-eye view and plan prepared for him in 1588, which Mr. Bond has reproduced. It was executed by his steward Ralph Treswell, who also drew the beautiful estate maps of Holdenby, referred to in a later chapter. Lists of costly hangings and rich furniture, given in an inventory made about a hundred years after Hatton's time, show how handsomely the castle was equipped. On Hatton's death Corfe passed to his nephew, Sir William Hatton, whose widow sold it to Sir John Banks. Banks lived there during the Civil War when it was almost destroyed by order of the Parliament. The ruins still stand, but to-day Corfe is only a shadow of its former magnificence.

To the north of the Isle of Purbeck lies the magnificent natural harbour of Poole, on the northern shore of which stands the ancient town of that name. In the middle of the harbour is the island of Brancksea, now Brownsea, with a castle built by Henry VIII. The town of Poole possessed the right of keeping this castle for the king, and exercised some sort of jurisdiction over the waters of Poole Harbour. In the year 1574 a ship was taken from Brancksea Castle by the men of Poole. Later documents, concerned apparently with the same incident, indicate that she was a pirate ship, all too common on that corsair-infested coast. Hatton, who was jealous of his privileges as Keeper of Corfe Castle and Admiral of the Isle of Purbeck, claimed it. At any rate that seems to be the meaning of some of Walsingham's letters, one of which says that his 'very good friend Mr. Hatton', the owner of Corfe Castle, had asked him to write to the effect that, in settling the dispute, due regard should be had to the liberties and privileges which he claimed, and that for his part he had no wish to interfere with those of Poole.

As this dispute turned on the privileges that Poole possessed as keeper of the Castle of Brancksea, Hatton proceeded to strengthen his position by obtaining possession of that castle. In 1576 its keeping was granted to him, and the Privy Council wrote to the townsmen of Poole saying that, whereas they had formerly had its keeping during the Crown's pleasure, the Queen had now by letters patent granted this custody to Mr. Hatton. The men of Poole were accordingly required to deliver to him the castle with its ordnance and munitions.

Hatton's position as Admiral of the Isle of Purbeck, involving a responsibility for dealing with pirates off the neighbouring coasts, and his powers of jurisdiction over pirate vessels taken in the vicinity of Poole and Weymouth have appeared incidentally in the records quoted above. But his precise relations with a pirate named John Callis, in connection with whom Burghley seems to have charged him with some irregularity, are obscure. Callis finds no place in such a work as the *Dictionary of National Biography*; but he appears in many entries in the State Papers, and despite the neglect of modern biographers (with the exception of Mr. C. L'Estrange Ewen) who may fairly be excused their indifference to such unimportant, if notorious characters, must have been an exceedingly familiar figure to the Elizabethan public of the years 1576 and 1577. In December of the former year he was off Newport; in January, 1577, he was haunting the neighbourhood of Haverford West. Sir John Perrot, later to be Hatton's enemy, was busy trying to round him up. He writes that he has arrested six pirates of Callis's company and sent them to Pembroke gaol; and offers to scour the seas and clear them of pirates, and so increase the customs dues by £2000 a year. Mr. L'Estrange Ewen tells us that Callis was arrested in that year. Some of his accomplices were hanged, but he petitioned Walsingham, and was eventually set free to serve the Queen, as so many pirates had done. This was the year of Burghley's dispute with Hatton, perhaps connected with Callis's wirepulling for his release. Callis renamed one of his ships the *Golden Chalice* no doubt after the precedent of Drake's *Golden Hind*, which again suggests a connection with Hatton.

As always, the seafaring folk of those coasts were not unwilling to traffic with the marauders, who no doubt added smuggling to their other activities. In April, 1577, there were extensive examinations at Cardiff of upwards of sixty aiders and abettors of pirates; and in May a similar series of depositions was taken at Lulworth in Dorset. These documents, which are extremely interesting, refer not only to Callis, but also to other notorious pirates, such as William Chick of Ipswich, John Morgan, William Gascoigne, Simon Ferdinando, a Portuguese, and two servants of Sir Edward Horsey, the Governor of the Isle of Wight. The witnesses were mostly men of Weymouth and Melcombe Regis, places where Hatton seems to have claimed jurisdiction; and it is from this circumstance, presumably, that Hatton's interest, whatever it was, in the activities of Callis arose.

This brief account of a matter that concerns Hatton only

slightly, so far as we can see, throws a little light on the ways of the Elizabethan pirates and the attitude of the public towards them. Men like Drake and Hawkins were of course technically pirates, though they were a good deal else also, great captains and navigators. But besides these national figures, whose piracy was confined in theory at any rate to the far seas, taking as their motto, 'no peace beyond the line', there were scores of lesser men, petty though brutal corsairs, who combined the looting of helpless ships with the business of smuggling. The inhabitants of the ports and maritime places, as these depositions show, were hand in glove with the marauders, victualling them, helping them in various ways and taking their stolen goods. And not only these humble townsmen but men of good family, such as Henry Knollys, probably the brother of that name of Lettice Knollys, Leicester's wife, even those in responsible positions, like Horsey, the Governor of the Isle of Wight, were often owners or part owners of pirate craft. It is not inconceivable, therefore, that Hatton, who was a shareholder in Drake's larger ventures, might have had a financial interest in John Callis, the pirate. But it is more likely that his concern, if any, for Callis, arose from his position as Admiral of the Isle of Purbeck, and that it was a question of jurisdiction over some pirate ship that drew forth Burghley's strictures.

At any rate, in 1577 Burghley made some comments on Hatton's relations with Callis in a speech or conversation of which we have no details. Hatton answered that he might conceive himself greatly defamed by Burghley's severe speeches; but, after conferring with Leicester and with John Stanhope, one of his friends, afterwards Lord Stanhope, he blames himself for being too ready to believe ill reports. Hatton at this time seems to have been still inclined to resent the superior position and influence of Burghley. Perhaps he had not quite forgotten the days when it was confidently predicted by his relatives that he would give the elder statesman 'the glike'. But appearances must be kept up, so he wishes Burghley godspeed in his journey. The gouty old Minister was visiting Buxton, and Elizabeth had asked him to send her some of its medicinal waters, though 'mistrusting it will not be of the goodness here it is there'.

In the following year Callis turns up again as Captain of one of Henry Knollys's ships which belonged to Sir Humphrey Gilbert's expedition of 1578 to the Atlantic Coast of North America, but which, on quarrels breaking out, had refused to follow him; and it is significant that of another of Knollys's ships, the *Francis*, the lieutenant Walter Spindola is described as 'Sir Christopher Hatton's man'.

Jealousies of the town of Poole were not the only matters that exercised Hatton as Keeper of Corfe Castle and Admiral of Purbeck. He felt it necessary also to keep an eye on affairs in Weymouth and Melcombe Regis. The older of these towns, Melcombe Regis, is now swallowed up in Weymouth, but they were originally twin boroughs, lying some twenty miles west of Corfe. In 1571 they had been united by Act of Parliament, but there was considerable friction between the two places. Hatton's interest in Weymouth affairs is illustrated by a letter from Lord Thomas Howard to William Pitt, the Mayor, written probably about the year 1581. Howard was a younger son of Thomas Duke of Norfolk; at the time of this letter he was one of the two bailiffs of the united towns. The letter gives 'Mr. Pyt' Howard's opinion that it is impossible to do anything in Parliament

> for when I should have bestowed chargeable sums of money in framing Bills, in rewarding them that should speak favourably in them, in gratifying the Speaker and other men of authority, then should I look for a hard passage of the Bill by reason that Sir Christopher Hatton's countenance and credit would work much against it, and surely would overthrow it when it should come to her Majesty's hands, and therefore would not cast away your money at this time in so [word illegible] affairs. Worse than this, these wicked men are so favoured and petted, as they had by Parliament clean overthrown your former decree and quietness for ever, if I had not thoroughly laboured all my friends and the Council also for the stopping of the same.

It does not appear what the Bill in question was. But the letter makes abundantly clear the corrupt methods to which promoters of private Bills had recourse, while it shows how strong was Hatton's influence with the Queen when it was confidently believed that he would be able to cause the royal assent to such a Bill to be withheld.

Hatton was, of course, too busy at Court to perform in person the duties of Admiral of the Isle of Purbeck. It is probable, indeed, that he spent little time, if any, at Corfe Castle. He kept an official there, Francis Hawley, whom he calls his servant, and who later is styled Vice-Admiral of the Island. As with others of his followers, Hatton secured Hawley's election to Parliament. He sat as one of the Members for Corfe Castle in the Parliaments of 1572, 1586 and 1588. In 1594, three years after Hatton's death, he was one of the commissioners appointed to inquire into the celebrated case of Ralegh's alleged atheism and other heresies in the county of Dorset. From one of his sons were descended the Barons Hawley. The name of another, Hatton Hawley, who matriculated at Oxford in 1600 and later became a barrister of the Middle Temple, suggests that Hatton was his godfather. This young man was one of a number who contributed poems to an Oxford collection of verse on the death of Queen Elizabeth.

CHAPTER XII

THE QUEEN'S PROGRESSES

QUEEN ELIZABETH was a mistress of the arts of popular government. She delighted in declaring that, under God, she placed her 'chiefest strength and safeguard' in the loyal affections of her people. In London, at Court, the keeping of Christmas and of such festivals as the anniversary of her accession, November 17th, gave opportunity for popular rejoicing, the entertainments including the acting of masks and the tilting in which Christopher Hatton distinguished himself. And the royal countenance was shown also throughout the country. The Court was ever on the move between the Queen's palaces of Greenwich, Whitehall, Richmond, Hampton Court and Windsor.

Farther afield there were the royal progresses, the most characteristic social function of Elizabeth's reign. Some prominent courtier's house was chosen for the Queen's visit, which was regarded as a great honour, however ruefully the host might contemplate the considerable expenditure involved. For, although the cost of food for the sovereign's retinue was in theory provided by the royal establishment, it had become customary to feed the Queen as well as to lodge her. And, though the furnishings were provided by the royal household, and hundreds of carts, carrying baggage, preceded the Queen's *cortège*, more or less extravagant preparations were expected from the master of the house. It is said that each of Elizabeth's twelve visits to Lord Burghley's house cost him two or three thousand pounds. There is evidence of occasional reluctance to play the part of host. The Hatton Letter Book contains, in fact, a letter on the point, addressed to him, presumably as Vice-Chamberlain and in charge of the preparations. Such reluctance was probably shared by many, though not all were brave enough to risk offending the Queen's Majesty.

But, if the entertainment of the Queen at her destination was ceremonious, the progress thither was delightfully informal. Elizabeth either rode on horseback or was carried in a litter, so that she could be seen by the people who thronged the route; and the procession stopped to receive addresses and petitions, or for the Queen to make gracious acknowledgments and exchange compliments and homely wit with the spectators. A happy example of such informality is the impromptu of a certain Serjeant Bendlowes who, coming to salute her Majesty during a progress, called out to her coachman, 'Stay thy cart good fellow, stay thy cart, that I may speak to the Queen'.

Elizabeth's principal ministers and officers of the Household accompanied her; and Hatton, as a Gentleman Pensioner, later as Captain of the Guard and later still as Vice-Chamberlain, must have taken part in most of the royal progresses throughout the middle part of the reign. Particulars of these progresses, some detailed, some meagre enough, but in their accounts of entertainments, speeches and incidents forming a bulky collection, have come down to us; and over a hundred years ago were collected in three massive volumes by a devoted antiquary, who has described himself as one to whom labour was ever delightful. To the toil of John Nichols all writers on this aspect of the Elizabethan social scene must acknowledge their debt.

The first mention of Hatton at a progress is in July, 1572, when the Queen visited Lord Burghley's house at Theobalds in Hertfordshire. In a note about the rooms allotted to members of her suite we read that Leicester had the lodgings over the parlour at the lower end of the Hall, while Mr. Hatton was given the Tower Chamber over Leicester's rooms. In 1573 the Queen made her progress to Canterbury, Archbishop Parker being her host. The Archbishop wrote to Burghley about his preparations. He said he had a convenient room for her Majesty, if she would please to remain in his house. He was able, 'for a progress time' to place Burghley, Sussex, the Lord Chamberlain, Leicester and Mr. Hatton, the Master of the Horse (really Captain of the Guard), 'thinking that your Lordships will furnish the place with your own stuff'. Deprecatingly, he went on to say that his house was 'of an evil air, hanging upon the Church, and having no prospect to look on the people', yet he trusted the convenience of the building would serve. But the Queen, if she chose, could stay in her own Palace of St. Austen's; and their Lordships in the house of the Dean and Prebendaries. He hopes, however, that the Queen and her train would dine in his bigger Hall. The account that follows of the entertainment, in its elaborate detail, shows the scale of the preparations, which, reported by the Archbishop to his brother of

York, drew the comment, 'I think it shall be hard for any of our coat to do the like for one hundred years'.

In May of the same year Gilbert Talbot had written to his father, Lord Shrewsbury, that there was talk of a progress to Bristol. In June the Queen began her journey, but she does not seem to have gone to Bristol then, and the Bristol progress was postponed until the following year. It is in these letters that Talbot reported Hatton's illness and his plans to go to Spa. Hatton was well again and back in England when the Queen visited Bristol in August, 1574. A full description of her entertainment there was published in the following year by the minor poet and miscellaneous writer, Thomas Churchyard, in his book called *The First Part of Churchyard's Chips*, which he dedicated to Hatton, the first occasion in which Hatton figures as a patron of literature. In Churchyard's dedication he calls Hatton 'his tried and worthy friend' and declares:

> the long liking and good will with the fast friendship I find in you (good Master Hatton) procures my pen presently to perform that I promised, no small time since, touching a book of all my English verses in metre. The offer whereof came from myself, not for the goodness of the matter, but for the parfitnesse of the person to whom I meant to dedicate my work.

He goes on to say that by his title he wishes to indicate that his works are to be regarded as trifles; and indeed the *Chips*, his entertainment of the Queen in verse, is rather dry matter. It follows the customary allegorical plan of such affairs. Elizabeth is met at the High Cross by Fame, who recites Churchyard's verses and flings up a great garland. At the next gate stand three boys: Salutation, Gratulation and Obedient Goodwill, who say their lines, concluding rather pleasantly:

> But since the time is short, and Prince to lodging goes,
> I say, God bless our Queen, that gives [i.e. bears, as of a coat of arms] the White and fair Red Rose.

Mock fighting against a fortress and symbolical scenes conclude the Bristol pageant, which, as entertainment, cannot match in brilliance the more famous spectacles at Kenilworth in 1575, of which the speeches were written by George Gascoigne, or at Woodstock later in the same year from the same hand. In the latter

Gascoigne addressed the Queen in English, Latin, Italian and French verse.

The barbarous custom of bear-baiting was a favourite sport with Elizabethans, and that the Queen patronized it may be gathered from the fact that it was one of the 'princely pleasures' provided by Leicester for the pageant on the occasion of the Kenilworth visit, when thirteen great bears were worried by ban-dogs. Elizabeth and many members of the nobility had their own bearwards, and it is possible that, like the companies of players attached to royalty and various noblemen, they and their bears were accustomed to give shows throughout the country. That seems to be the explanation of the frequent payments by the Corporation of Leicester to various noblemen's bearwards, for entertainments at the Mayor's annual feast. Hatton was in the fashion, as we learn from an entry of the year 1582 of payments to the bearward of the Earl of Huntingdon and 'to one other, being Sir Christopher Hatton's man and a bearward, at Mr. Mayor's Dinner'.

In 1577 when Hatton became Vice-Chamberlain, some of the detail connected with the royal progresses fell to him. The Vice-Chamberlain was a regular assistant to the Lord Chamberlain, among whose duties were the distribution of lodgings in the Palace, the arranging of the progresses and the reception of ambassadors and others having audience of the Queen. He planned the Revels and kept order in the Banqueting Hall. Hatton, as Vice-Chamberlain, was now partly responsible, whether as assistant or deputy, for these miscellaneous duties. Thus in 1582, at the reception of a Lord Mayor, 'some young gentlemen, being more bold than well-mannered, did stand upon the carpet of the cloth of estate, and did almost lean upon the cushions. Her Highness found fault with my Lord Chamberlain and with Mr. Vice-Chamberlain, and with the Gentlemen Ushers for suffering such disorders'. During Hatton's period of office as Vice-Chamberlain, 1577 to 1587, his chief, the Lord Chamberlain, was Thomas Radcliffe, Earl of Sussex, to 1583; Charles, Lord Howard of Effingham, 1583 to 1585; and Henry Carey, Lord Hunsdon, 1585 to 1587.

In July, 1578, came the celebrated visit to Audley End. The University of Cambridge proposed to wait upon the Queen there, and Burghley, as Chancellor, advised them what presents they should bring. They proposed to offer the Queen a book. Burghley agreed, 'that the present to her Majesty be allowed of, but that they must have regard that the book had no savour of spyke, which commonly bookbinders did seek to add, to make their books savour well, for that her Majesty could not abide such strong scent'. He suggested that they should provide gloves for the Earl of Leicester, for Sussex, the Lord Chamberlain, and for the Earl of Oxford, 'with a few verses in a paper joined to them, proper to every of their degrees, so that in number they exceeded not above eight verses'. He added dryly, 'that for himself he could spare them, so that others might have them'. Mr. Vice-Chamberlain (Hatton) he thought might have a pair of gloves also, with some verses: 'it should do well', he said, 'to conciliate his good-will, being a lover of learned men'. The entertainment given at Audley End was afterwards set forth in print by Gabriel Harvey in his *Gratulationes Valdinenses,* which contains the verses addressed to each of these dignitaries, and symbolizes Hatton as *Foelix infortunatus.*

In September, 1582, the Queen contemplated a visit to Lord and Lady Norris at Rycote in Oxfordshire. Lady Norris was a daughter of Lord Williams of Thame, who had befriended Elizabeth during her captivity in her sister's reign. The Queen felt a genuine affection for this mother of Elizabethan soldiers, and on the death of one of them, Sir John Norris, wrote her the well-known letter in which she addressed her as 'my dear Crow'. The affection was returned, to judge from Lady Norris's indignation with Leicester and Hatton for preventing one of those visits from Elizabeth which so many courtiers were only too anxious to escape. Leicester reports to Hatton his 'piece of cold entertainment', at her hands because they were 'the chief hinderers of her Majesty's coming hither, which they [Lord and Lady Norris] took more unkindly than there was cause indeed'. He had urged as an excuse 'the foul and ragged way' and the wintry aspect of Rycote in September. However, he succeeded in making his peace, though Lady Norris declared that she could not be quiet until Hatton had had 'part of her little stomach too'. Leicester concludes by saying of the Norrises, 'a hearty noble couple are they as ever I saw towards her Highness'.

In August, 1583, the Queen paid a visit, her third, to Sir William More at Losely. More was warned of her coming by Hatton in a letter directing him to see everything well ordered, and to have the house 'sweet and clean'. There had been a 'bruit' of infection, which had however turned out to be 'a misinformation'. Later in the month Hatton wrote again that More should 'avoid', that is remove, his family, and make everything ready 'as to your own discretion shall seem needful for her Majesty's good contentation'.

After Hatton had secured Ely House in Holborn from the Bishop of Ely, Elizabeth paid him several visits there, sometimes regular progresses, sometimes brief calls. She was at Ely House from November 21st to December 6th, 1587, as we learn from a letter from Philip Gawdy to his father: 'Upon Tuesday at night she came to my Lord Chancellor's, where she hath been ever since. Her entertainment hath been very great there both for herself and all her train, which a number of us hath very well tasted of.' Elizabeth again visited Ely House on August 19th, 1588, and dined there with Hatton in May, 1589. She made a longer visit at the end of May, 1590, staying till June 6th; and about November, 1590, 'secretly, as she thought, to meet the French Ambassador, Viscount Turenne'. A year later, in November, 1591, when Hatton was dying, she visited him for the last time, comforted him and fed him with her own hands.

CHAPTER XIII

'A LOVER OF LEARNED MEN'

THE story of the Queen's progresses has introduced us to one writer who owed something to Hatton, and who dedicated part of his works to him. Thomas Churchyard was the earliest of Hatton's literary dependants. There were others. All Elizabethans in high position were to a certain extent patrons of literature. Some were actively such, as lovers and fosterers of letters; others perforce because it was the fashion to patronize authors, and their way of life demanded it. Though Hatton was no great figure in the literary world, no patron to whose encouragement English letters owes any debt of importance, it is probably safe to conclude that he was not a mere figure-head whose name was sought to adorn a title-page, simply because he was Vice-Chamberlain or Lord Chancellor, one of the great men of his world. He does not rank with Leicester, or even with Burghley, as a literary patron. He was no inspiration, as was Philip Sidney, to men of letters. But Burghley called him 'a lover of learned men'. That was in 1578. Some ten years later, a very different witness, Father Crichton the Jesuit, gave testimony to his own learning. Learned in a technical sense he was not; and Burghley's description of him is probably the more accurate of the two.

'Of singular bounty to men of learning,' Camden says of Hatton, and Robert Greene in an elegy on his death makes the scholars lament his passing. Hatton has a continuous record as a literary patron, but how far he may have financed or helped those who dedicated books to him is for the most part unknown. The precise function of the literary patron in Elizabeth's time is a question that calls for further investigation. It may be assumed that poor men like Thomas Churchyard received some help from Hatton from time to time. There is, in fact, the evidence of Churchyard himself that Hatton procured him some royal grants. Yet Churchyard complains of his poverty and the uncharitableness of his friends. Barnabe Rich was in a sense a dependant of Hatton's, did him some service in Ireland and was his guest at Holdenby. He too probably got some monetary benefit from the connection.

The impecunious Dr. Dee may also have enjoyed Hatton's bounty. But there is no direct evidence; we have to fall back on the general statements of Camden and Greene.

Churchyard, Rich and Dee are the three literary men who had the most continuous relationship with Hatton, and their records are worth looking at from that point of view. Hatton's other literary connections can be more briefly dismissed. But they too are of interest in his life, and his contacts with them help to complete the picture of the man.

Thomas Churchyard had a chequered and adventurous life, the details of which can be pieced together from his various writings. Poet and soldier, he saw much service in the wars in France, Flanders, Scotland and Ireland. At home and abroad he was nearly always in poverty, and his writings, hurriedly thrown off in the hope of helping to meet expenses, suffer accordingly. His military life and various adventures are full of curious detail. His topographical account of Wales, *The Worthiness of Wales*, is of value and interest, and his knowledge of Irish affairs, based on his service there, has given us several quaint pieces such as *The Death of Rory Oge* and another about a Rover, composed at the request of Master Peter Carew, Captain of Leighlin, the same Carew who had set all Ireland in an uproar by his preposterous but successful claims to his supposed ancestors' estates.

In 1574, when Churchyard wrote the pageant for Elizabeth's visit to Bristol, his military service was nearly over. But in England the stout old soldier-poet had by no means come to an end of his adventures. He tried his hand at the secret service. His association with Hatton, which seems to have included some such work, points perhaps to kind-heartedness on Hatton's part, for he appeals to his generosity; but the evidence suggests that he may have sometimes appealed in vain. If he chose Hatton in 1575 for the dedication of his *Chips* it was because Hatton was an important personage and a likely patron, besides being no doubt a prominent figure in the Queen's entourage at Bristol. But it is possible that it was Hatton who chose him. Another of Churchyard's patrons, Philip Sidney's father, Sir Henry Sidney, then Lord President of the Council of the Marches, had sent Churchyard to prepare the contemplated pageant of the year 1574 at Shrewsbury, which did not take place. Hatton may perhaps have been busy helping to arrange the festivities at Bristol, and looking round for a likely writer, lit on Churchyard, of whose work for the Shrewsbury spectacle he would have been aware.

In 1578 Churchyard dedicated his translation of Ovid, *De Tristibus*, to 'his most assured and tried friend, Master Christopher Hatton, Esquire', and apologized again for the title, *Churchyard's Chips*. In the same year was published his *Lamentable and Pitiful Description of the Woful Wars in Flanders*, the first of a series of autobiographical works, dedicated to Walsingham. In 1579 appeared the second part of *Churchyard's Chips*, inscribed to 'the Right Honourable Sir Christopher Hatton, knight, Vice-Chamberlain, Captain of the Guard and one of the Queen's Majesty's Privy Council'. The running title of the work is *Churchyard's Choice*. It is mostly a prose narrative of English wars both by land and sea and in Ireland, from the reign of Henry VIII to the early part of that of Elizabeth, and is full of interesting matter, including the piece already referred to, composed at the request of Sir Peter Carew. He wrote numerous other books, including pageants for the Queen's visits to Norwich and Woodstock, but this was the last work he dedicated to Hatton. The Queen, Oxford, Ralegh, Lord Norris and others were to be the recipients of his future addresses. But several letters from him to Hatton are preserved in the Hatton Letter Book.

Towards the end of the year 1580 Churchyard got into trouble, and sought shelter in Scotland. His subsequent letters to Hatton show that his offence was that of killing a man, a case of manslaughter apparently, for he speaks of the deed as committed by chance and against his will. But the widow was proceeding against him, and he thought it best to fly. He took advantage of his exile in Scotland to undertake some intelligence work for the French Ambassador in London, Mauvissière de Castelnau, but he kept Hatton informed of his doings and seems to have been really acting as Hatton's agent. We know that he was ostensibly working for de Castelnau from a passage in a letter he wrote to Hatton, just after leaving Scotland, and more explicitly from a marginal note in the Letter Book. That he was acting with Hatton's approval appears from his reference to a promise he made Hatton: 'for a piece of service that I meant with hazard of my life to discover for the discharge of my duty to my Prince and Country'.

It was the year of the 'Enterprise' against England, busily

manœuvred by Catholic exiles negotiating with the Pope, Philip of Spain and the Duke of Guise, intriguing with the Scots for the invasion of England by way of Scotland, and Mary Stuart all the time actively in communication from her English prison with the conspirators. Her son, the future James I of England, was now King of Scotland in her place; and his cousin Esmé Stuart, Seigneur d'Aubigny, the head of the French branch of the Lennoxes, was in Scotland and the mainspring of the Enterprise there. He had quickly gained an ascendancy over James, who created him Duke of Lennox. He worked for the overthrow of Morton, the former Regent and leader of the Protestant party, whom Mary hated as the instrument of her fall. Elizabeth, though it was to her interest to support Morton, made but a half-hearted effort to save him. Lord Hunsdon, Elizabeth's cousin, the Governor of Berwick, was ordered to remonstrate with James, and Thomas Randolph, former English Ambassador in Scotland, now grown old, was sent to Edinburgh to try what words that were not meant to be backed by deeds would do. In the end, outwitted by Lennox, the English Queen suffered Morton to be executed.

It was in these circumstances that Churchyard went to Scotland towards the end of 1580 or beginning of 1581, six months before Morton's execution. Whatever the business he was undertaking for de Castelnau, he prudently kept Hatton informed of what he was doing. One needed to be careful, for the times were difficult, and it was not easy to forecast how events would fall in the drama of the imprisoned Queen of Scots, heir, in the event of Elizabeth's death, to the English crown. Hatton, if some notes made by Nau, Mary's secretary, can be trusted, was like most English statesmen at this anxious juncture, something of a trimmer. Though loyal to Elizabeth and prepared to put Mary to death if the English Queen would agree, yet at the same time he assured Mary that if Elizabeth should die he would come with the Guard to release her. In a wish to keep in touch with the obscure events that were taking place in Scotland, we can perhaps see the reason for Churchyard's presence there in de Castelnau's supposed and Hatton's real interest.

Posing as an exile and as the French Ambassador's agent, Churchyard was at first in some favour at the Scottish Court. James treated him well and indeed stood his friend, if he did not actually save his life. For soon matters began to take an ugly turn. Shots fired at him, first 'with a strong bow and a leaden pellet', twice in one day, and the next day 'with a harquebus and missed very narrowly'. Nor was Randolph, the English Ambassador, hoodwinked by Esmé Stuart, helpful. He resented Churchyard's presence, not knowing what to make of him, and believing presumably that he was what he professed to be, an agent of de Castelnau's. Churchyard could not take Randolph into his confidence: 'it had been present death to me, and besides he disgraced me all he could'. To Hatton he laments that he was 'stuck fast in the stocks among many wild wolves and cruel tigers in the shape of men', from whom he was only preserved by King James's good offices. He asked for leave to go, which was readily granted; but he stayed in Edinburgh long enough to see Morton beheaded. He chronicled that event in 'The Earl of Morton's Tragedy' in *Churchyard's Challenge*, published twelve years later.

Poor Churchyard. Events seem to have entirely outmanœuvred him. He was not of the stuff of which successful secret agents are made; nor had Hatton Walsingham's genius to choose and employ such men. Within three weeks Churchyard was in London and in prison for his misdemeanour. From gaol, where he remained for two or three years, he wrote to Hatton at intervals, begging for his intercession. And it may be that Hatton exerted himself to secure his release. But there is no evidence that he did so, and indeed, a letter to him from Churchyard, which from its position in the Letter Book seems to belong to 1582 or early in 1583, is couched in a tone of reproach. Nor does Churchyard exempt Hatton from the strictures he makes in his *Charge*, published in 1580, that for his honest labours as an author he had scarce received thanks. The only exception he makes is Sir Thomas Bromley, the Lord Chancellor, to whom he dedicated *Churchyard's Chance*. But he is not quite consistent in these complaints, which he seems to have pointed for the particular occasion. Renewing them eight years later to Ralegh, to whom he dedicated his *Spark of Friendship and Warm Goodwill*, while excepting his new patron from his general condemnation, he makes amends to Hatton: 'saving one, a most honourable personage, that I dedicated my book of Choice [*Churchyard's Choice*, 1579], who got me two Great Seals [i.e. grants under the Great Seal] besides common courtesies many, to shift withal a season.'

The last letter in the Letter Book from Churchyard to Hatton is undated, but must refer to the year 1585, when Leicester led his expedition to the Low Countries. Churchyard was with him, serving in the English army. The old soldier's martial feelings are reawakened:

> Now I have betaken myself to this course of service, my desire is to leave my bones, the rather because I see my country hath no grave for a Churchyard. In furtherance of my intention therein, I must entreat boldly, as I am wont, the mediation of your goodness by writing a word or two to my Lord of Leicester, to prefer me to the battle, to the breach . . . I seek no farm, I sue for no pension, nor I love not to live as an almsman: I covet to die like a soldier and a true subject, as loth to live any longer in misery, when I see the world waxeth weary of my well-doing.

Here Churchyard takes leave of Hatton and we of him. He did not die in this campaign, but lived to return to England, where the literary fruit of his last adventure appeared years later in his *True Discourse Historical of the Successive Governors of the Netherlands and the Civil Wars there* . . . with a section devoted to Leicester, among the commanders. The book was published in 1602; Churchyard died two years later.

Barnabe Rich, whom we shall meet again as one of Hatton's agents in Ireland was, like Churchyard, a voluminous writer. He served with Churchyard, Gascoigne and other literary adventurers in the Netherlands. He went later to Ireland, where he spent a great part of his life and about which he wrote much. He dedicated three books to Hatton. The first, published in 1578, *Alarm to England, foreshowing what perils are procured where the people live without regard of Martial Law,* was written in Ireland, the wretched state of which is described. In 1581 he was sent by Sir Henry Wallop, Treasurer of the Wars in Ireland, to Hatton to intercede for the Earl of Kildare, who was charged with disaffection. His mission resulted in a visit to Holdenby House, which he described in *Riche his Farewell to Military Profession,* published in the same year. This book was not dedicated to Hatton, though it has a fine tribute to his magnificence and the hospitality of Holdenby. Perhaps in naming his book, Rich thought that, secure in the friendship of his patron, he had left campaigning behind for ever. But this was not to be, and he returned to

Ireland. The book is famous for the fact that from one of its tales Shakespeare borrowed the plot of *Twelfth Night*. The other two books that Rich dedicated to Hatton are *The Strange and Wonderful Adventures of Don Simonides, a Gentleman Spaniard* (1581) and *The Second Tome of the Travels and Adventures of Don Simonides* (1584).

Better known than Churchyard or Rich to all but literary students is Dr. Dee, who dedicated one of his works to Hatton. John Dee, mathematician and chemist, astrologer and spiritist, cartographer and writer on naval affairs, came in contact with Hatton on several occasions, and it is tempting to fancy that he may even have cast a horoscope for the Queen's favourite. But the acquaintance was not perhaps very close, though it is certain that the two men were in touch. Hatton, as will be more fully recorded in the chapter on Drake's voyage round the world, was greatly interested in the Elizabethan voyages of exploration, and was a promoter of Drake's and other enterprises. And, as has been shown by students of these affairs, Dee had his share in these matters. He had an immense knowledge of medieval geography, and the Elizabethan sailors sought his advice on such subjects as the North-West Passage and the way to the land of Cathay, the objectives of so many of them. Sir Edward Dyer, Hatton's friend, was closely in Dee's confidence, and there is evidence that he acted as a medium of communication between them.

With Elizabeth and Leicester, Hatton, we learn from Dee's Diary, was one of those to congratulate him on his marriage in 1575. In August, 1576, Dee dedicated to him his *British Monarchy or Hexameron Brytannicum*, the first volume of a projected series, *General and Rare Memorials pertaining to the Perfect Art of Navigation*. It was an appropriate moment, for the book appeared in the midst of Drake's preparations for his famous voyage. There can be no doubt that Dee was intensely interested in Drake's schemes and almost certainly cognizant of his purpose. Hatton was one of Drake's most influential backers; hence the book and the dedication, which takes the form of an address, prosy though in verse, beginning:

> If private wealth be leaf and deere
> To any wight on British soyl,
> Ought public weale have any peere?
> To that is due all wealth and toyle.

Whereof such lore as I of late
Have lern'd, and for security,
By godly means to garde this state,
To you I now send carefully.

But though we may smile at Dee's poetry, there can be no doubt
of the importance of his work. This book contains also a fine
reproduction of Hatton's coat of arms of ten quarterings, surmounted by the hind, his cognizance.

On December 1st, 1577, Dee notes in his Diary: 'I spoke with
Sir Christopher Hatton; he was made knight that day.' Later
Richard Hickman and his nephew, Bartholomew, came with one
Mr. Flower to visit Dee, being commended to him by Hatton.
Francis Flower, one of Hatton's men, we have already met.
Bartholomew Hickman was to be Dee's medium years later in the
philosopher's old age, after Edward Kelley, his most famous
disciple, had died or been murdered in a European prison during
Dee's prolonged tour on the Continent. The Hickmans came from
Shuckburgh in Warwickshire, close to the Northamptonshire
border, about ten miles from Holdenby, and were thus Hatton's
neighbours.

A comical incident seems further to link Hatton and Dee together in an enterprise, delicate if not heroic. In April, 1578, the
Queen was suffering from toothache. No one apparently could
summon up the courage to tell Elizabeth that the tooth must come
out. The Court physicians declined the unenviable task of being
messengers of such cruel comfort to aching and irascible Majesty;
and Burghley pitched on Mr. Vice-Chamberlain, Sir Christopher
Hatton, as the fittest person to bell the cat. He has heard, he says,
in a letter to Hatton, of her Majesty's indisposition 'by some pain
in her head'. 'If my coming thither', continues the cautious
Minister, 'might either diminish her pain, or be thought convenient, I would not be absent; although in grief I am present.' He
does not doubt that Hatton is 'careful by her physician to provide
the remedy, which is said to be only the withdrawing of some one
tooth that is touched with some humorous cause'.

Dee next was called in, among other 'best experimented
physicians' and by the Queen's command had 'a diligent conference' with Dr. Bayly, Elizabeth's medical attendant, about 'her
Majesty's grievous pangs and pains by reason of toothache and

the rheum &c.' Draconian methods seem to have been eschewed on this occasion, for Dee undertook 'a very painful and dangerous winter journey, about fifteen hundred miles by sea and land' to consult with 'learned physicians and philosophers beyond the seas for her Majesty's health, recovery and preservation'. He was given but a hundred days to go and come again, while the Queen's toothache raged unabated.

At length, however, in December, as Strype tells us in his life of Bishop Aylmer, Elizabeth submitted to extraction, after enduring many sleepless nights. The advice of John Anthony Fenotus, 'an out-landish physician of some note' had been sought by the Privy Council. He recommended that the tooth should be filled with the juice of *Chelidonius major* (that is the greater celandine, a plant of the poppy family) and stopped with wax; after a time, he declared it would become so loose that it could be pulled out with the fingers. But the course he preferred was immediate extraction, if her Majesty would 'submit to such chirurgical instruments (which it seems he had heard something of the Queen's abhorrence of)'. Then it was that Aylmer showed that, whatever else he lacked, he was not wanting in courage. He persuaded the Queen that the pain she dreaded was not really so great; and to prove his point offered, although he was an old man and had not many to spare, to sacrifice one of his own teeth as an example. He ordered the surgeon, in the Queen's presence, to pull out the tooth, 'perhaps a decayed one', Strype thoughtfully adds, and so she was encouraged to follow suit.

In March, 1582, a foreigner who was to be responsible for a momentous event in Dee's life, a prolonged visit to the Continent, arrived at Harwich. He was Albertus Alasco, Free Baron of Lasco, Palatine of Saradia in Poland, a man deeply interested in alchemy; and his visit to England was probably undertaken largely with a view to making Dee's acquaintance. He is described as being of amiable appearance, studious and learned, speaking several languages. His most remarkable feature, of which he was very proud, was a magnificent white beard of such length and breadth that, lying in bed and parting it with his hands, it overspread his breast and shoulders. The news of his approaching arrival caused no little flutter at Court. Burghley, whose business it was to have an encyclopaedic knowledge of foreign affairs and who took the keenest interest in notabilities, wrote to Hatton, on whose shoulders as Vice-Chamberlain the duty of seeing to the reception and entertainment of a distinguished foreign guest would largely fall. Burghley writes:

> I perceive that a Count of Polonia, named the Palatine Laschi, is either arrived or shortly will arrive at Harwich to come to her Majesty; and if he be the very Count Palatine of that House of Laschi, he is a personage of great estimation, such as few are subjects to any Monarch in Christendom, few in the Empire of the greatest exceeding him in sovereignty and power; and he is also one, that, as I find by late observations since this King Stephanus's reign, hath carried great authority; and before his time in the interreign, none that had greater than he, but only the great Palatine of Lineland.

Hatton replied, thanking Burghley for notifying him of the coming of 'this great Personage'. He echoed Burghley's caution, intimating that there was some doubt in the Queen's mind concerning the Palatine's rank and political status:

> Her Majesty deferreth all her direction for order to receive him, until she be more fully informed both of his quality and occasion of access. She seemeth to doubt [i.e. think] that he departeth from his Prince as a man in displeasure, because in one sentence of his letter to her Majesty he calleth her the refuge of the disconsolate and afflicted.

The Queen indeed thought that he might be out of favour with the King of Poland.

The Count settled at Winchester House in Southwark, where he mostly resided while in England. He was splendidly entertained, and, in turn, spent lavishly; while Dee vigorously consulted with his familiar spirits about the Polish potentate, and from them learned to his satisfaction that Laschi (another variant of his name) was related to the English noble house of Lacy!

Dee returned with the Count to Poland in September, 1583, taking with him his wife and children and his medium, Edward Kelley and Kelley's wife. He was away for fifteen years, not returning to England until 1598. All through that long period the experiments for transmuting base metals into gold proceeded. Kelley, who was a thorough-paced rascal, fooled the aged philosopher to the top of his bent, fooled him all the time, and the Emperor Rudolph, their new patron, part of the time, until

Rudolph turned against him and sent him to prison, where he died in mysterious circumstances. But before Kelley's fall from Imperial favour marvellous stories began to be circulated and believed in England. Even the sceptical Anthony Wood, writing a hundred years later, reports that gold was so plentiful in Bohemia that the young Arthur Dee played with gold quoits made by projection, the transmuters' process. Burghley was anxious to secure Kelley's secret. He sent Sir Edward Dyer, Hatton's old friend, to urge Sir Edward Kelley — he had been ennobled by the Emperor — to come home, and 'honour her Majesty with the fruits of such knowledge as God has given him'. Burghley, indeed, modestly suggests that Kelley 'should send her Majesty as a token a good round sum of money, say enough to defray the charges of the navy for this season'.

But these events, in whose beginnings Hatton had been interested, no longer concerned him. When Dee returned in 1598 his former patron had been dead for seven years, and during the old philosopher's long exile the face of England had changed. Mary Stuart had gone to the block; the Armada had been defeated; all the great statesmen of the reign had passed away. The Elizabethan age was nearly over.

CHAPTER XIV

OTHER BOOKS AND AUTHORS

Of the authors who dedicated books to Hatton, Churchyard, Rich and Dee alone seem to have had any close relations with him. At any rate, of the numerous others who inscribed their works to him, there is no record of any particular contact, except in the case of George Best, the historian of Frobisher's voyages, and, in the absence of evidence, we must take it that Hatton's name figured on their title-pages not from any special reason of association, but merely as a compliment to one of the great figures of his world.

One of the most interesting of these works is the fourth part of Gabriel Harvey's *Gratulationes Valdinenses*, containing the verses written by him for the Queen's progress, already mentioned, to Audley End in 1578. It was printed by Hatton's 'servant', Henry Bynneman, the well-known printer, though his name appears only on the third and fourth parts. The first part is dedicated to the Queen, the second to Leicester, the third to Burghley, and the fourth in three sections to Oxford, Hatton and Sir Philip Sidney. The verses to Leicester, Burghley and Hatton are in each case preceded by a page bearing a fine coat of arms, Hatton's being his usual achievement of eleven quarterings, surmounted by a helm and above it the Hatton hind. On the title-page to the fourth part is Bynneman's neat device, Hatton's cognizance, the hind standing in an oval with the motto, *Cerva charissima et gratissimus hinnulus*, *Pro*. 5 [i.e. Proverbs v]. Hatton's section is dedicated *Ad Honoratissimum, fortissimum virum, Christophorum Hattonum, Equitem Auratum, atque Regiae Maiestatis Consiliarum, de suo Symbolo Foelix Infortunatus*. The section dedicated to Oxford is introduced in a similar manner with an allusion to Oxford's symbol, *Vero nihil verius*. There can be no doubt from all this that, as mentioned in the chapter on *A Hundreth Sundrie Flowres*, *Foelix infortunatus* was a symbol, posy or motto adopted by Hatton. The Latin poem that follows is a play throughout on the words *foelix, infoelix, fortunatus, infortunatus*, calling Hatton happy and fortunate because of the Queen's favour, and containing such sentences as 'Wherein then, happy one, art thou unfortunate? In arms? Whence thine emblem? Happy Hatton', etc. Sidney's pages and gentlemen in the tilt-yard wore, we are told, a scroll or band of silver on their coats, with 'a posy or sentence' written upon it, *Sic nos non nobis*. And we may guess, as perhaps Harvey's words imply, that Hatton used his symbol for the same occasions.

James Sandford was next in point of time after Churchyard to dedicate a book to Hatton. As in Churchyard's case, the circumstances throw some light on the obscure subject of literary patronage. Sandford, who was well-read in classical and later literature and a diligent translator, had in 1573 dedicated to Leicester *The Garden of Pleasure*, an anthology of 'pleasant tales, worthy deeds and witty sayings of noble princes and learned philosophers'. It was printed by Henry Bynneman, later the dependant or follower of Hatton. It seems likely that Leicester did not reward Sandford as he expected; for in 1576 he produced what was virtually a second edition of the book, and dedicated it to Hatton. The new title was *Hours of Recreation or After-dinners*, which may aptly be called 'Garden of Pleasure'. It too was printed by Bynneman; and it is possible that the change in dedication was due to Bynneman's suggestion, as by this time he had become Hatton's man. In his dedication Sandford repeats some dire prognostications for the year 1588. Alas! for the prophecies of publicists. It was the year of the Armada.

Another work printed by Bynneman and dedicated to Hatton was George Best's account of Frobisher's voyages. Best was a servant of Hatton's, who accompanied Frobisher and named a cape, north of Hudson's Bay, Hatton Headland in honour of his patron. The *True Discourse* was published in 1578, and in his imprint Bynneman calls himself Hatton's servant. Best's book is described in a later chapter.

Everard Digby, a Cambridge divine, also dedicated a couple of books to Hatton. He was a fellow of St. John's who was deprived of his fellowship by the Master of the College, his expulsion being confirmed through Leicester's influence, in spite of the efforts of Burghley and Whitgift on his behalf. He had attacked the Calvinists as schismatics and, evidently highly eccentric, was in the habit of blowing a horn and hallooing in the College. He also wrote a treatise on swimming, but is notable philosophically as a predecessor of Bacon. His *Theoria analytica . . . totius Philoso-*

phiae & reliquarum scientiarum was dedicated to Hatton and published by Henry Bynneman in 1580. A later work, also dedicated to Hatton, was his *Everard Digbie, his Dissuasive from taking away the Lyvings and goods of the Church*, 1589.

Another author who, though he did not dedicate anything to Hatton, pays a tribute to his wisdom and to his services to the State, is Christopher Ockland. In his Είρηναρχια, or *Elizabetha*, published in 1582, a work which contains characters of Elizabeth's chief Ministers, he names him 'Splendidus Hatton', and calls him the Maecenas of scholars:

> Splendidus Hatton,
> Ille Satelitii regalis ductor, ovanti
> Pectore, Maecenas studiosis, maximus altor
> Et fautor verae virtutis, munificusque.

By an Act of the Privy Council the study of this poem in schools was made compulsory. In a later work, his *Elizabetheis* (1589), a panegyric on the peaceful rule of the Queen, Ockland praises Hatton for his part in the detection of the Babington Plot. The story of that conspiracy will be told later, and it will be shown that, while the task of unravelling it fell mainly on Walsingham, Hatton was the most prominent figure at the trial of Babington and his companions. Hence in the public estimation it is probable that he was given a larger share of the credit than was his due. At any rate, for his discovery of the evil plot, hatched in the depths of night, Hatton, the poet declares, has won eternal honour.

In 1582, George Whetstone, a writer who had served in the Low Countries, like so many Elizabethan men of letters, and had been an eye-witness of the death of Philip Sidney at Zutphen, published his *Heptameron of Civil Discourses*. This purported to be a translation of 'the civil disputations and speeches of sundry well courted gentlemen and gentlewomen, his guests during the time of his entertainment with Signor Phylloxenus', a 'right noble Italian gentleman', by whom, it is conjectured, Geraldi Cinthio is intended. The book he dedicated to Hatton, and in his dedication referred to himself as the presenter of these tales, 'the trowchman of a stranger's tongue'. The truchman or trounchman we have already met as the introducer or announcer in the Elizabethan mask. The part was, of course, very familiar to Hatton as an actor in the Court masks.

One of a class of book with a long literary lineage, a satirical description of England in contrast with an imaginary Utopia, was dedicated to Hatton in 1587 by its author, Thomas Lupton, a miscellaneous writer of a strongly Puritanical temper. Though Hatton had scant sympathy with Puritanical ideas of Church Government, his sober and industrious life and the serious turn of his mind, to which John Harington testifies, perhaps moved Lupton to consider that this tirade against those whose principal occupations were 'bearbaitings, bullbaitings, players, vaulters and tumblers', forgetting that Hatton too kept a bearward, might appeal to the grave Vice-Chamberlain. Lupton's dedication runs in part: 'And though this is not the first book that hath been dedicated unto you; yet your Honour is the first man to whom I have dedicated any. Whose wisdom hath willed me, whose modesty hath moved me, whose clemency hath encouraged me, whose love of learning hath allured me, and whose common commendations hath enticed me to offer it unto you.'

The title of the book is *Siuqila, Too good to be true* . . . ' Like *Erewhon*, Mauqsun, the name of the Utopia described, when read backwards, equals 'nowhere' (*nusquam*). It tells of a man, Siuqila (*aliquis*) coming from an island named Ailgna (*Anglia*) who, wearied of the evils of his own country, travels in search of another. He meets with a man named Omen (*nemo*) who describes the Utopian conditions of Mauqsun. It must be confessed that the book is extremely tedious reading.

Like John Dee, Sir Anthony Ashley, Clerk of the Council, chose Hatton, on account of his interest in naval matters, for the dedication of a book. This was a translation from the Dutch of the first collection of sea charts for sailors, which had been published in Holland in 1584. The author was Lucas Janz Waghenaer, from whom such a book of charts came to be familiarly known as a 'Waggoner'. To Charles Howard of Effingham, Lord Admiral of England in the time of the Armada, belongs the credit of drawing the attention of the Privy Council to the importance of a work which was badly needed by English sailors. Being 'esteemed by the chief personages of the grave Council worthy to be translated and printed into a language familiar to all nations', the task of translation was committed to Ashley, who besides being the ancestor of the Earls of Shaftesbury, has a claim to fame as the introducer of cabbages into England. The title of the work is

The Mariner's Mirror . . . of Navigation. . . . It was published in the
year of the Armada, and the title-page contains references to the
defeat of the great Spanish fleet and to Drake's raid on Cadiz in
1587.

The most illustrious of those who looked to Hatton for literary
patronage is Edmund Spenser, who addressed him in one of the
introductory Sonnets to the *Faery Queen*. Spenser had been secretary to Arthur, Lord Grey of Wilton, while Grey was Lord
Deputy of Ireland. He was a great admirer of Grey's, and
warmly defended him against his traducers in the well-known
View of the Present State of Ireland. As Grey was on very friendly
terms with Hatton, to whom he was distantly related, and whom
in consequence he calls his cousin, it might have been expected
that Spenser would have had a closer connection with Hatton
than seems, in fact, to have been the case. Nevertheless, his
tribute to Hatton does suggest his recognition of an interest in the
Muses, not merely perfunctory, on the Lord Chancellor's part:

> Those prudent heads, that with their counsels wise,
>   Whilom the pillars of th'earth did sustain;
> And taught ambitious Rome to tyrranize,
>   And in the neck of all the world to reign.
> Oft from those grave affairs were wont abstain,
>   With the sweet lady-muses for to play.
> So Ennius, the elder Africain;
>   So Maro oft did Caesar's cares allay.
> So you, great Lord! that with your counsel sway
>   The burden of this kingdom mightily;
> With like delights sometimes may eke delay
>   The rugged brow of careful policy;
> And to these idle rhymes lend little space,
>   Which, for their title's sake, may find more grace.

Thomas Watson, the author of *Meliboeus Thomae Watsoni, sive
Ecloga . . .* , 1590, in honour of Sir Francis Walsingham, who died
in that year, did not dedicate that work to Hatton. But these
Eclogues, of which he gave also an English translation, contain
in addition to a flattering encomium of Elizabeth and an allusion
to Spenser, notices of some of the more important figures of the
reign, Burghley, Hatton and Howard of Effingham.

One other who dedicated one of his books to Hatton was
Arthur Golding, whose translation of Ovid is the source of some

of Shakespeare's classical allusions. The book that Golding inscribed to Hatton was his translation of *Seneca on Benefiting*, 1577. As is well known, the Queen also was a translator of Seneca, and a copy of some of her work which she gave to her godson, Sir John Harington, is printed in the *Nugae Antiquae*. Two years after Golding's dedication Sir Thomas Heneage refers to Elizabeth's versions in a letter addressed to Hatton: 'so as that shall be verified of her that Seneca wrote wisely, and her Majesty translated more sweetly — of adversity and virtue, *illustrat dum vexat*, it graces whom it grates.'

There was possibly an earlier connection between Golding and Hatton. In the year 1573 George Saunders, a citizen and merchant taylor of London, was murdered by his wife's lover. The Privy Council was very active in the matter, and the murderer was quickly caught and executed along with the erring wife before a great concourse of excited people. Golding wrote a pamphlet on the whole affair which was printed by Henry Bynneman and reissued in 1577. It is possible that he was moved or commissioned by Hatton to write this pamphlet. For George Saunders was first cousin of Hatton's mother, and was otherwise well connected, being first cousin also to Sir Edward Saunders, Chief Baron of the Exchequer, and half-brother of the celebrated Dr. Walter Haddon, the friend of Cheke and Ascham.

Perhaps the last work to be inscribed to Hatton was *The Book of Honour and Arms*, printed by Richard Jones in 1590. No author is named, but it is generally thought that it was the work of Sir William Segar, then Somerset Herald and later Garter King of Arms. On the reverse of the first title-page is Hatton's achievement, a coat of arms of twelve quarterings. Above is a helm and Hatton's cognizance, the hind; around is the motto of the Garter; and above all the words *Tandem si*, Hatton's motto at this time. The book debates questions of honour and explains such subjects as procedure at duels. It gives too the oaths taken by performers in the tilt-yard, quoted in a previous chapter. There is also a list of tilts in Elizabeth's reign, including those, already chronicled, in which Hatton took part.

John Norden wrote in Hatton's lifetime a *Delineation of Northamptonshire*, containing a description of Holdenby House. He had intended to dedicate this to Hatton, but the Lord Chancellor dying, he inscribed it instead to Sir William Hatton, his heir.

The foregoing list is probably not complete; and it is possible that further research would unearth other authors who looked to Hatton for patronage. There is some evidence also that Hatton, as 'a lover of learned men', to quote Burghley's phrase, had a closer contact with the world of books than such a string of names alone would indicate. His relations with Thomas Norton, Counsel to the Stationers' Company, and Licenser of Books, have already been glanced at, and something more will be said later about Norton and Hatton. Moreover, one of the most celebrated printers of Elizabeth's reign, Henry Bynneman, is, as noted above, described as Hatton's servant. Archbishop Parker had been Bynneman's patron, and when Parker died in 1575 he found another in Hatton. Among the ornaments he employed on his title-pages was the cognizance and motto of his patron, Hatton. This is the explanation of the device used in his later books, a hind passant on a half-wreath, with the motto *cerva charissima et gratissimus hinulus Pro.* 5, the loving hind and pleasant roe of Proverbs v.

It is of interest to notice the titles of some of Bynneman's books, as they have a connection, direct or indirect, with Hatton. Such are Thomas Norton's *Warning against the Dangerous Practices of Papists and specially of Partners in the late Rebellion*, 1569, that is the Revolt of the Northern Earls; *A Hundreth Sundrie Flowres*, 1573, and Gascoigne's *Poems*, 1575; Golding's *Brief Discourse of the late Murder of Master George Saunders*, Hatton's cousin, 1573 and 1577; and Gabriel Harvey's *Gratulationes Valdinenses*, 1578. Another of Bynneman's publications was one of Thomas Churchyard's compositions for the entertainment of the Queen during a progress in 1578 in Suffolk and Norfolk. The imprint is at London, 'for Henrie Bynneman, Servant to the Right Honourable Sir Christopher Hatton, Vice-Chamberlain'. And further evidence of Bynneman's connection with Hatton is supplied by a letter in the Letter Book from Norton to Hatton in 1583. From this it appears that Bynneman had infringed the privileges of the Stationers' Company, to which Norton was Counsel. In the course of this letter Norton calls Bynneman Hatton's servant and indicates that it was through Hatton that he had procured his licence for printing certain books.

Another of Hatton's dependants, Francis Flower, was, as already mentioned, granted in 1573 a licence to print books in

Latin, Greek and Hebrew, including school books. This right he farmed out to a group of printers for £100 a year; and he and his associates took an action in the Court of Star Chamber against a number of other printers, headed by Christopher Barker, later the Queen's printer, for printing 2000 copies of Lilye's Grammar.

Like all Elizabethans, Hatton was interested in music. The excellent concert with which Hatton entertained the Sieur de Champagny at the Palace of Eltham in 1576 has already been mentioned. William Byrd, the famous musician, dedicated one of his works to Hatton, *Psalms, Sonnets, and Songs of Sadness and Piety, made into Music of Five Parts*, by William Byrd, 'one of the Gentlemen of the Queen's Majesty's Chapel Royal', 1588. This book has a further interest, for like some of those printed by Bynneman, the title-page is adorned with Hatton's cognizance, the hind supported by Pallas and Minerva, with the motto from the Book of Proverbs. In his dedication Byrd speaks of the duty, honour and service due from him to the Lord Chancellor, and of Hatton's judgment and love of that art, which moved Byrd to dedicate to him his first printed work in English: 'I hoped that (by this occasion) these poor songs of mine might happily yield some sweetness, repose and recreation unto your Lordship's mind, after your daily pains and cares taken in the high affairs of the Commonwealth.' Without pressing the language of a dedication too far, it seems that Byrd owed something to Hatton, and that Hatton was a real lover of music.

As some further evidence of Hatton's musical tastes, one of Sir John Harington's anecdotes of him may be introduced here, as it shows him enjoying grave discourse and music, while more frivolous persons played cards. Harington is writing of moderation in play:

> But, because examples are more effectual often than persuasions, and to praise the dead is no flattery, I will allege one example, well known to many of us, and therefore not unfit for this purpose. Who was more magnificent in matters of true honour, more sumptuous in building, rich in furnishing, royal in entertaining, orderly in maintaining his house than Sir Christopher Hatton, late Lord Chancellor?, a man taught virtue, framed to wisdom, raised to honour, by her Majesty's special grace and choice; yet when some ambassadors lay at his house (knowing the general humour of the meaner sort to love to see great play) while he

himself entertained the chiefest of them with some grave discourse or some solemn music, he caused some of his friends to play cards, with £1,000 in fair gold of his money, rating it at their own pleasures at 12d the pound, or as themselves agreed on, that the sums played might seem great, the show bountiful, and the substance not unsupportable.

The drama too had a friend in Hatton. Again, as with literature, he cannot compare as a patron with Leicester who had his own company of players. But, as the regular assistant of the Lord Chamberlain, Hatton, the Vice-Chamberlain, took a part in helping to plan the Revels and, as we have seen, to arrange the Queen's progresses, with their masks and spectacles. These two officials were almost necessarily, therefore, patrons of the stage; and the Lord Chamberlain, as well as Leicester, had his company of players. They were often at loggerheads with the Puritans of the City of London. The Corporation had power to regulate plays, and under the influence of the Puritan preachers sought to suppress them. Thomas Norton, Hatton's Puritan acquaintance, as City Remembrancer, denounced the plays and players, writing of 'the unchaste, shameless and unnatural tumbling of the Italian women'. One of the arguments used was the danger of the spread of plague. In 1584 matters came to a head. At Whitsuntide disputes arose among the serving-men and apprentices who haunted the Theatre and the Curtain. The Corporation approached the Privy Council, and in spite of the opposition of Lord Howard of Effingham, then Lord Chamberlain and of Hatton, the Vice-Chamberlain, obtained permission to suppress both theatres. Serjeant Fleetwood, the Recorder of London, in a letter to Burghley says:

My Lord [apparently Lord Chief Justice Anderson] sent two Aldermen to the Court for the Suppressing and pulling down of the Theatre and Curtain; for all the Lords [of the Privy Council] agreed thereunto, saving my Lord Chamberlain and Mr. Vice-Chamberlain; but we obtained a letter to suppress them all. Upon the same night I sent for the Queen's players, and they all well nigh obeyed the Lords' letters. The chiefest of her Highness's players advised me to send for the owner of the Theatre [Burbage] who was a stubborn fellow, to bind him. I did so.

Hatton was also a patron of Cornelius Ketel, one of the most remarkable portrait-painters of his day. Ketel was a Dutchman who came to England in 1573 and worked in London for eight years. The contemporary Karel van Mander, who wrote of the Dutch painters, says that he was introduced to Hatton by a young English merchant, whom he calls Pieter Hachten. As he calls this man an Englishman and as he spells Hatton's name 'Hatten', we may perhaps read the merchant's name as Peter Hatton and identify him with one of the Cheshire family, in which Peter was a common Christian name. Hatton at this time was claiming these Cheshire folk as relatives, and no doubt they were willing to oblige so powerful a man. At any rate, the story goes that the young merchant presented Hatton with an allegorical painting of Ketel's, 'Force vanquished by Wisdom', and that through Hatton's influence Ketel thus obtained an introduction to Court circles. The Winchilsea portrait of Hatton is traditionally said to be Ketel's work, as is the Dillon portrait which seems to be a copy of it, or at any rate closely resembles it. If so, it must have been painted between 1573 and 1581. In it Hatton's costume appears to be that of a Gentleman Pensioner, and it is certainly the earliest portrait of him in existence.

CHAPTER XV

NABOTH'S VINEYARD

In the year 1576 Christopher Hatton, by methods which appear to us extremely high-handed, acquired from the Bishop of Ely a lease for twenty-one years, followed by another on terms that made it virtually perpetual, of the Bishop's town house in Holborn. The present Ely Place marks the site of the Bishop's palace, and Hatton's association with the neighbourhood persists to-day in the name Hatton Garden.

The connection of the Bishops of Ely with Holborn began with John de Kyrkeby, a powerful official of Edward I's. As Treasurer of England he bought property there, was made Bishop of Ely and, dying, left these premises to the See. Kirby Street preserves his name. His estate consisted of a messuage or house, and nine cottages. It was increased by his successors, one of whom built the chapel of St. Etheldreda, the patron saint of Ely, while another added a vineyard (where Vine Street is to-day), kitchen-garden and orchard. At the end of the Middle Ages the property consisted of a garden, a vineyard of seven acres, and five acres of arable land with a chapel and hall. It stretched from Leather Lane to the Holborn River. In old documents the principal buildings are described and their dimensions given. The hall in front was 72 feet by 32 and about 30 feet high, lighted by six Gothic windows, and roofed with oak. At the west end were the chief lodging rooms and other apartments. North-west was a square cloister, 95 feet by 73, built round a garden, and over it rooms and galleries. On the north side of the cloister, in a field of about an acre, walled and planted with trees, stood the chapel 91 feet by 39, with a large east window and a crypt, ten feet high, supported on eight chestnut posts.

The Bishop and his household did not occupy the whole of this large area. High officials and legal luminaries had suites of rooms there, and part was built over by shops. The Sutherland View (1543) shows the Palace with banqueting hall and chapel, and the large and handsome gate-house or front towards Holborn, built by Bishop Arundel. In Ralph Agas's map drawn in Elizabeth's reign, the vineyard, meadow, kitchen-garden and orchard are shown. Ely Place is the scene of the well-known passage in *Richard III*, where the King says to the Bishop:

> My lord of Ely, when I was last in Holborn
> I saw good strawberries in your garden there. . . .

The strawberries, like the vines, were witness to the amenities of the Bishop's gardens, which were also famous for their roses and saffron-crocuses.

The officials, who had suites of apartments in this pleasant spot, cast covetous eyes from time to time on the Bishop's lands. Thomas Wriothesley, Henry VIII's Chancellor, who seems to have been the Bishop's tenant at Ely House, sought to gain possession of it, but was unsuccessful. He exchanged houses with Dudley, Earl of Warwick, later Duke of Northumberland, who also made an effort to secure the Bishop's property. It was Richard Cox, Bishop of Ely, who was at length compelled to part with this estate, on the insistent demands of Elizabeth, to Christopher Hatton.

Hatton's filching of Ely House has been immortalized in the *Ingoldsby Legends*. 'The House Warming! A Legend of Bleeding-Heart Yard' tells picturesquely though with the inaccuracy of poetic licence the story of how the estate was wrested from the Bishop. It confuses Hatton with his name-sake and eventual heir, Sir Christopher Hatton, the husband of the Alice Fanshawe of the tale; and it makes Hatton Lord Chancellor at the time he acquired Ely House. He was not that. He was not Vice-Chamberlain even until a year or so later. But he was Captain of the Guard; and, for an important figure about the Court and the Queen's favourite, a commodious house not too far from Whitehall, was certainly desirable. So, as Ingoldsby has it:

> His course always had been,
> When he wanted a thing, to solicit the Queen,
> So now, in the hope of a fresh acquisition,
> He danced off to Court with his 'Humble Petition'.

It was apparently in the beginning of the year 1575 that Hatton first made a bid for the lease of the Bishop's property. In a letter dated in February, 1574, that is 1575 on our reckoning, Cox writes to Burghley that he has considered the request made by him on behalf of a nobleman for his house in Holborn. He excuses himself on the ground that other noblemen, his friends, had made suit to him for the house, but had been 'quietly and friendly stayed'. That he is speaking of a lease not of a sale (and a Bishop had only a life interest and could not sell if he would) appears from his statement that he would be loath to leave his house inhabited, so that 'when God shall call me, my successor shall be driven to make suit for his own house'. The place, he adds, is convenient for him when he visits London and Westminster on business, and he has furniture there which would be a nuisance to a tenant who would have to remove it.

The nobleman of this letter is unknown; but it is probable that Hatton is meant, and that this was the beginning of the effort to force the Bishop to lease to him. For, though not technically a noble, Hatton was a more powerful and splendid figure than many of the nobility. But, whether this letter refers to Hatton or not, there is evidence that during the year 1575 great pressure was put upon the Bishop to make a lease to him. There is no need to credit as genuine the famous letter which Elizabeth is supposed to have written to Bishop Cox:

> Proud Prelate! I understand you are backward in complying with your agreement, but I would have you know that I who made you what you are can unmake you; and if you do not forthwith fulfil your engagement, by God I will immediately unfrock you.

No original is known, and different versions of it are given; in some the Bishop is called Cox, in others his successor, Heaton, is named. The letter seems to be a hoax perpetrated by a writer in the Annual Register of 1761. But it was too good a story for Ingoldsby not to make use of. And, on Hatton's soliciting for a town house:

> The Queen, when she heard this petition preferred,
> Gave ear to Sir Christopher's suit at a word; —
> 'Odds Bobs, my good Lord!' was her gracious reply,
> 'I don't know, not I, Any good reason why
> A Lord-Keeper like you should not always be nigh
> To advise — and devise — and revise — our supply —
> A House! we're surprised that the thing did not strike
> Us before — Yes! — of course! — Pray whose House would you like?

When I *do* things of this kind, I do them genteelly,
A House? — let me see! there's the Bishop of Ely!
A capital mansion, I'm told, the proud knave is in,
Up there in Holborn, just opposite Thavies' Inn —
Where the strawberries grow so fine and so big,
Which our Grandmother's Uncle tucked in like a pig,
King Richard the Third, which you all must have read of —
The day — don't you know? — he cut Hastings' head off —
And mark me, proud Prelate! I'm speaking to you,
Bishop Heaton! you need not, my lord, look so blue —
Give it up on the instant! I don't mean to shock you,
Or else by ——! ——(The Bishop *was* shocked!) I'll unfrock you!'

There is indeed no doubt of Elizabeth's displeasure. A communication not less menacing than the apocryphal ultimatum was a long letter to the unfortunate Bishop Cox from Lord North, who was himself endeavouring to lay hands on some of Cox's manors and lands. Writing in November, 1575, North says:

You remember how tenderly and heartily her Majesty wrote this summer unto you for a lease of Somersham for herself, and she forgetteth not your answer. Being now in the Court, I understand her Majesty did very zealously recommend Mr. Hatton to be the Keeper of your house in Holborne, a man much favoured of her Highness, and much esteemed of the best and honest sort of England. Beside her Majesty's request was qualified with so reasonable conditions, both for your ease and honour, as it is more than marvellous to know with what face you could deny her. Well! this last denial being added to her former demands, hath moved her Highness to so great dislikeing as she purposeth presently to send for you, and to hear what account you can render for this strange dealing toward your gracious Sovereign.

There is some modest understatement here. Somersham Lord North really wanted for himself; while 'Keeper of your house in Holborn' is a too innocent description of an unwanted interloper.

North goes on to say that the Queen is aware that the Bishop has injured many of her subjects, and has asked him to prepare a statement of their complaints for the Privy Council. The Queen, he proceeds, has promoted Cox from nothing to the richest bishopric in the country, with £3000 a year; but he has shown no gratitude in return. There follows a eulogy of Elizabeth coupled with a warning not to trifle with her. The phrases become more and more menacing:

> My Lord, it will be no pleasure for you to have her Majesty and the Council know how wretchedly you live within and without your house, how extremely covetous, how great a grazier, how marvellous a dairyman, how rich a farmer, how great an owner. It will not like you that the world know of your decayed houses, of the lead and brick that you sell from them, of the leases that you pull violently from many, of the copyholds that you lawlessly enter into, of the free land which you wrongfully possess, of the tolls and imposts which you raise of God's good ministers which you ceaselessly displace. You suffer no man to live longer under you than you like him. And to be flat, you nourish the ill and discourage the good.

In the face of this terrific indictment and these blackmailing threats the Bishop was forced to yield. In March, 1576, Cox made to Hatton a twenty-one-year lease of the gate-house of the Palace, the first courtyard within the gate-house, the stables, the long gallery with the rooms above and below it, and other apartments, fourteen acres of ground and the keeping of the gardens and orchards. Hatton's rent was one red rose for the gate-house and garden, and ten loads of hay and £10 a year for the ground. The Bishop reserved to himself free access through the gate-house, and the right to walk in the garden and to gather yearly twenty bushels of roses. Hatton undertook to repair and make the gate-house a convenient dwelling.

But he was not satisfied. Almost immediately he began to demand that he should be allowed to acquire the freehold or what virtually amounted to a freehold. On August 20th — the year is not stated, but from the course of events it was presumably 1576 — the Bishop writes to the Queen in Latin. Her letters, he says, written on behalf of her Hatton (*in Hattoni tui gratiam*) have upset him not a little. His predecessors had been firmer; for not only had Henry VIII not been able to take the house for his Chancellor Wriothesley, but the Duke of Northumberland (Dudley) had also failed to wrest it from the Bishop of the day. Nor had he himself yielded to the Queen's request for the house for her servant, Master Parris. But, wearied by her supplications, and not wishing to appear ungrateful to her, he had leased part of his house to her Hatton for twenty-one years. And now it is required that he should grant it in perpetuity. He cannot, he says, leave his successors naked, with the house shorn of garden, orchard and walled pasture, a phrase that confirms the evidence that only part of the house had been leased.

However, the Bishop was again forced to yield. Some sort of legal fiction was raked up. Hatton, it seems, had bought up an old lease of Ely Place which had been made by Cox's predecessor, and under colour of this he instituted a suit against the Bishop. In the end Cox was compelled to convey a mortgage of Ely House to the Queen, who in turn conveyed it to Hatton. The amount of this mortgage was nearly £1900, the sum which the lavish Hatton claimed he had spent on repairing and rebuilding and on laying out the grounds. There is a letter among the State Papers to the Master of the Court of Requests, saying that his expenses had been certified by Commissioners in a document of which copies were in possession of the Court, the Bishop and himself.

In June, 1577, Hatton in a letter to Burghley speaks of 'my house in Ely Place', showing that he was then in occupation. A lawyer, one Arden Waferer, of whom some particulars will be given later, was busy on legal matters connected with the conveyance, and Hatton asks that he should not be detained before Burghley in the Exchequer Court, but should be given leave 'presently to attend my causes'. A year after this, in June, 1578, Hatton obtained a formal grant of Ely Place (presumably the Queen's mortgage) from the Crown.

Bishop Cox had from the first sought a way out of his difficulties by begging permission to resign his See. This request called forth a sneering remark from Lord North: 'it is, I confess, but a small matter to forego a bishopric, being so well provided as you are.' The poor Bishop was exceedingly sensitive about these reports of his wealth, and had written to Burghley that he hoped it was not true that he 'should conceive of him that he was rich, and had great heaps of money lying by him'. At length the Queen consented, in 1580, to let him go; but he was still Bishop when he died in 1581, and the conveyance of his lands to Hatton had not apparently been fully completed. No successor was appointed for eighteen years. During the vacancy the Queen took the revenues of the See, while Hatton for the ten more years that he lived remained in fact, if not in strict legal title, owner of Ely Place. From Ely Place he rode in state on May 3rd, 1587, to take the oath as Lord Chancellor. To Ely Place in the following year the Vice-Chancellor and Heads of Colleges came to offer Hatton the Chancellorship of Oxford University. It was at Ely Place that he entertained the Queen on several occasions. And it was at Ely Place that he died on November 20th, 1591.

After Hatton's death the premises in Holborn and his other lands were extended (the technical term for a Crown valuation) in connection with his debt to the Queen of £42,139 5s. It was found that his total rentals amounted to £717 2s. 11d., and this included Hatton Garden, valued at £10 a year. This small sum is presumably explained by the fact that the title to Hatton Garden was not clear, being not really a freehold and complicated by the claims of the Bishop of Ely.

In 1599, eight years after Hatton's death, a new Bishop of Ely, Martin Heaton, was at last appointed. He got possession of the house, but the grounds that Hatton had appropriated and beautified were withheld. Sir William Hatton, Sir Christopher's nephew and successor, had died in 1597. The Bishop was technically in the position of being able to reclaim his property by repaying the so-called mortgage of £1900. He sought to do this, but Sir William Hatton's widow, then the wife of Sir Edward Coke, the Attorney-General, clung to the property and, despite the efforts of succeeding Bishops, Hatton House on her death in 1646 passed to Lord Hatton, son of Sir Christopher's cousin, John Hatton. By that time the Bishop's property, according to a contemporary writer, was in a lamentable state. The gate-house and a great part of the dwelling-house had been taken down, and the Bishop had to enter the apartments reserved for him by the back way, while to get to Holborn he had to bring his horses through the great hall. 'One half of the crypt under the chapel, which had been used for interments, was then frequented as a drinking place, where liquor was retailed; and the intoxication of the people assembled often interrupted the offices of religion above them.'

Not till 1697 was the dispute between the Bishops of Ely and Hatton's heirs finally adjusted, when the Bishop of the day agreed to accept a settlement on the See of Ely of £100 a year in return for Hatton Garden. The Palace remained with the Bishops until it was sold to the Crown in 1772. The thirteenth-century chapel of St. Etheldreda still stands.

The affair of Ely Place was not the only instance of the Queen's intervention when the pampered Hatton did not get leases of lands that he coveted. In the same year that the Ely Place negotiations began, Hatton was 'a suitor' for leases belonging to the Dean and Chapter of Peterborough. In February, 1575, these officials were severely rated by the Privy Council, and the Bishop of Peterborough was commanded to examine the reasons why the Dean and Chapter pretended that they could not consent to the leases which Hatton demanded. What the upshot was does not appear, but it is likely that the Queen's favourite got his way.

CHAPTER XVI

THE PALACE OF HOLDENBY

THE outburst of magnificent building in the Elizabethan era was especially conspicuous in Northamptonshire. For it happened that some of the most important officials of the Court had hereditary connections with that county. The splendour of the age demanded that the new men, such as Burghley and Hatton, should build sumptuously, as if to emphasize the importance of the new times and new ways which they represented. As with their pedigrees, so with their mansions, there must be no suspicion that the men of Elizabeth's inner circle were not the equals, nay, the superiors, of the feudal barony they were supplanting. And with the fashion of royal progresses, the Queen's servants had to provide accommodation on a huge scale to house the sovereign's entourage, and in architectural splendour to secure a setting worthy of the lavish entertainment expected. The spirit that prompted the presents of rich jewels and other New Year's gifts to the Queen was the same that built a Theobalds or a Holdenby House, even though, as in Hatton's case, the builder were practically bankrupt. For build the Elizabethans would, though their Queen, in her cynical moods, might warn them of the precarious position of courtiers. Sometimes in mockery she would tell the Council that she would come back after her death to see the Queen of Scots make their heads fly. And she advised Hatton to buy no land and build no houses. When she was gone, she said, there would be no living for him in England.

Not all the great house-builders of Northamptonshire in the Elizabethan era were of the new nobility. The mansion at Kirby, for instance, was built for the Staffords, an ancient family of feudal origin. There is a close parallel between Kirby Hall and Holdenby House. For both were erected about the same time, Holdenby possibly by John Thorpe, the architect who designed Kirby; and both illustrated the careless spirit of their founders. Sir Humphrey Stafford, the builder of Kirby, already possessed a house in the county only eight or nine miles distant; and Sir Christopher Hatton, who bought Kirby from the Staffords, almost immediately began to rebuild on a lavish scale at Holdenby, his ancestral seat.

John Thorpe, architect and surveyor, was the author of a number of drawings of Northamptonshire houses, now preserved in the Soane Museum. It is a collection of great importance for the domestic architecture of the period. As a surveyor, Thorpe's services were probably in constant demand in that age of frequent transfers of property, involving accurate 'extents' or valuations and measurements of the areas to be conveyed, elaborate maps of demesnes and fields, and drawings and plans of buildings. As an architect he left his mark on Elizabethan Northamptonshire, though his precise contribution is disputed. He could not indeed have designed all the houses whose plans he reproduced in his portfolio. But he was probably concerned in the reconstruction of Burghley House; he certainly built Kirby, for on his plan he has written, 'Kerby whereof I laid the first stone, A.D. 1570'. It is possible that he designed Holdenby also, as he has left an elaborate plan of the house, but it may be that his concern with it was limited to making a survey at the time of its sale to James I.

Both Holdenby and Kirby were planned in the grand manner, but Holdenby was much the larger building. It was, in fact, if Hampton Court be excepted, the greatest mansion of its day. There is no occasion to say much of Kirby here. It was not built by Sir Christopher Hatton; he had no family connection with it, though it gave its name to his collateral descendants, the Lords Hatton of Kirby; and he does not seem to have lived there, his heart being naturally set on the ancestral home upon which he lavished so much of his fortune. Begun in 1570, Kirby was completed in 1575. Sir Humphrey Stafford, its builder, died just after it was finished, and his heir immediately sold it to Hatton.

Hatton does not seem to have been at Holdenby for any but the briefest of visits during those long, busy years when he was making his way in the world. In Ely Place he had just acquired a town residence, which was all that was necessary for an official whose business kept him so much in or near London. But his thoughts were turning to his native county. Kirby was in the market, and he bought it. With rising fortunes — socially, that is, for he was shockingly in debt and had just acknowledged to Burghley that he owed £10,000 — his mind began to exercise itself with the project of rebuilding Holdenby House on a scale fit to receive visits from the sovereign to whom he owed everything. He would rebuild his ancestors' homely manor-house on truly splendid lines and dedicate it to his Queen. In 1580, five years after he had bought Kirby, he wrote to Sir Thomas Heneage that he had not yet seen it, nor, he protested, had he seen his other shrine, that is Holdenby, nor would he see it until that holy saint (the Queen) might sit in it, as it was dedicated to her. The words need not be taken too literally; but it is obvious that he had not bothered about Kirby, since he had begun to rebuild at Holdenby, nor had he as yet had a house-warming at the latter place.

Though Holdenby was the hereditary possession of the Holdenbys, Hatton's ancestors, his tenure of it had been complicated by his financial arrangements with the Queen. In 1568 he passed this manor to her by fine, the final concord or recognized manner of conveying lands. The arrangement seems to have been nominal only, for the Patent Roll of the same year discloses the fact that Hatton's grant of Holdenby to the Queen was made in exchange for the site of the Abbey and demesne lands of Sulby in Northamptonshire; and on the same day Elizabeth leased Holdenby to him for forty years; two years later she reconveyed the property to him in fee. These arrangements were confirmed in 1576 by a charter agreeing to a proposal to assure to Hatton by Act of Parliament the lands of Holdenby and Church Brampton adjoining. Hatton's signature is appended to this instrument, with his seal showing the six quarterings which he used on his signet. There followed in February of that year 'An Act for the assurance of certain lands and tenements unto Christopher Hatton, Esquire, Gentleman of her Majesty's Privy Chamber and Captain of her Majesty's Guard', of which the title alone is given in the printed Statutes of the Realm. Holdenby was now settled on Hatton by all the forms of law.

In 1575 among other grants made to Hatton in several counties was included the manor of Chapel Brampton. It also adjoined Holdenby, and Hatton already had some land there as part of the estate he had inherited from the Holdenbys. But his financial difficulties were acute. In November of that year he writes from the Court at Windsor to Burghley about his affairs. In this, speaking of an exchange of lands with the Queen, he says he has procured a warrant in which he has 'joined both manors together'. The manors are perhaps Holdenby and Sulby; but it may be that Holdenby and Chapel Brampton beside it are meant. He goes on to bemoan his 'poor state', and tells Burghley that he is £10,000 in debt. There is expectation of an annuity from the Queen, but he hesitates to mention it because she is apparently annoyed with him for pressing for it: 'The annuity I dare not speak of, because it seemeth to me by her Highness that it should be delivered me before I looked for it', meaning presumably that he should not ask but wait till he got it. It was not long delayed, for in December Elizabeth settled £400 a year on him.

Three years later Hatton was granted the office of Receiver of Tenths and First Fruits, the date being determined from the fact that it is mentioned in the inquisition taken after his death. So it was presumably about the affairs of this office that he wrote to Burghley in December, 1578. Hatton, of course, had a fee as Receiver, and this was probably a proportion of the monies collected. The precise amount appears to have been in dispute, for he says:

> I offered her Majesty what I am able, to the advancement of her ordinary revenue. I did acknowledge my gain, through her goodness, for my comfortable relief. I made your Lordship privy, and you misliked not. But now this little is thought too much, and so do content myself with what shall please her I am most bound to.

Burghley had evidently questioned Hatton's claim as being too large. Hatton says he fully comprehends that Burghley was influenced by his duty to the Queen and not by any feelings against him. That being so, 'My poor case hath no defence: *demisso vultu dicendum, rogo*. I ask because I want: my reward is made less, but I confess my unworthiness. I do my service with diligence, pain and travail, according to God's gift in me'.

Hatton's tactful letter brought a handsome acknowledgment from Burghley: 'I find you readier to change offence taken than any with whom I have had like occasion.' But the office of Receiver of Tenths and First Fruits was to prove a thorn in Hatton's side. His debts in connection with it formed the greater part of the immense sum he owed the Queen when he died, an incubus which his earliest biographers believed hastened his end.

The new Holdenby was building in 1578, as can be gathered from a letter from John Stanhope to Hatton. Stanhope lived at Harrington in Northamptonshire, whence Hatton's mother's people came, and it may be that Hatton, who had a long lease of the manor from his uncle William Saunders, had sub-let Harrington to Stanhope, at that time a Gentleman of the Privy Chamber. In Stanhope's letter, written in August, he says that he has passed Hatton's house on his way home, that is to Harrington: 'in my journey from London I had a little sight afar off of your fair house, which I had then gone to view better, had I not been tied to such a charge as I could not well part from, till I came to my cousin Thomas Markham's house. . . .'

By August of the following year Hatton was preparing to welcome to Holdenby, though not in person, Burghley and Sir Walter Mildmay, the Chancellor of the Exchequer, albeit the house was not yet completely finished. On August 3rd a letter from the Privy Council, addressed to Burghley and Mildmay, intimated that, as they intended shortly to be at Mr. Vice-Chamberlain's house not far from Northampton, it would be an opportunity for them to investigate questions of religion there, and particularly the complaints of the Bishop of Peterborough 'that divers of the inhabitants of that town, refusing to conform themselves in matter of religion, do repair to Lillingstone to Mr. Wentworth's house, and there do and are admitted to receive the Sacraments after another sort . . . ' Peter Wentworth's Puritanism has already been discussed, and Hatton's connection with him mentioned. On August 9th Burghley writes from Althorp, the Northamptonshire seat of the Spencers, to Walsingham:

> I pray you, Sir, with my hearty commendations, tell Mr. Vice-Chamberlain that Mr. Chancellor and I, in our way to Northampton, mean to survey his house at Holdenby, and, when we have done, to fill our bellies with his meat, and sleep also, as the proverb is, our bellies-full all Monday at night; and on Tuesday in the morning we will be at Northampton where after noon we mean to hear the babbling matters of the town for the causes of religion.

Hatton, who was detained at Court, then at Greenwich, was not able to be at Holdenby to welcome them. He writes to Burghley, and his letter is of interest, as it shows that the house was not completely finished, and it is the authority for stating that Holdenby was built on the plan of Burghley's house of Theobalds:

> . . . I fear me that as your Lordship shall find my house unbuilt and very far from good order, so through the newness you shall

find it dampish and full of evil air; wherefore I pray God your health be not impeached . . . I humbly beseech you, my honourable Lord, for your opinion to the surveyor of such lacks and faults as shall appear to you in this rude building, for as the same is done hitherto in direct observation of your house and plot at Tyball's, so I earnestly pray your Lordship that by your good corrections at this time, it may prove as like to the same as it hath ever been meant to be . . . Your Lordship will pardon my lack of presence to attend you, because you know my leave cannot be gotten . . .

The following day Burghley acknowledged his host's kindness, and testified to the magnificence of Holdenby:

Sir, I may not pass out of this good house without thanks on your behalf to God and on mine to you, nor without memory of her Majesty, to whom it appeareth this godly, perfect, though not perfected work is consecrated . . . I came yesterday in the afternoon to your house with Sir Walter Mildmay, who came with very good will to visit this house. I was first met on the way with Mr. Colshill, and your good uncle Mr. Saunders, your cousin Mr. Tate, and others, and then with a great multitude of your gentlemen and servants, all showing themselves, as by your direction, glad of my coming. But approaching to the house, being led by a large, long, straight fair way, I found a great magnificence in the front or front pieces of the house, and so every part answerable to other, to allure liking. I found no one thing of greater grace than your stately ascent from your hall to your great chamber; and your chambers answerable with largeness and lightsomeness, that truly a Momus could find no fault. I visited all your rooms high and low, and only the contentation of mine eyes made me forget the infirmity of my legs. And where you were wont to say that it was a young Theobalds, truly Theobalds I like as my own; but I confess it is not so good as a model to a work, less than a pattern, and no otherwise worthy in any comparison than a foil. God send us both long life to enjoy Her, for whom we both meant to exceed our purses in these. And so I end with my prayer for her health, and thanks humbly for her Majesty's remembrance of me her weak Spirit. From a monument of her Majesty's bountifulness to a thankful servant, that is, from Holdenby Queen Elizabeth's memory, by Sir Christopher Hatton her faithful servant and counsellor . . .

Here Burghley informs us, as Hatton does in a later letter that Holdenby was 'dedicated' to Elizabeth. Hatton's uncle Saunders is William Saunders, his mother's brother. Tate, his cousin, is

one of the sons of his aunt Anne Saunders, who married Bartholomew Tate of Laxton, Northamptonshire.

Hatton was at Bedford in September, 1580. He writes from
there to the Queen a letter quoted in the next chapter, stating
that one of his servants was sick; and, writing to Sir Thomas
Heneage a few days later, he says that the illness was suspected to
be small-pox. On this account he had decided to disperse 'my
little company, and to take my way to Sir Ed. Bricknell's [sic. Sir
Edmund Brudenell's] to view my house of Kirby, which I yet
never surveyed; leaving my other shrine, I mean Holdenby,
still unseen until that holy saint may sit in it, to whom it is
dedicated....'

Holdenby, though not yet fully completed, had become one of
the show places of the county, both for its magnificence and for
the lavish hospitality held even in the absence of the owner which,
at this period of a busy Court life, was the rule rather than the
exception. Hatton's house has found a modest place in literature,
being described by Barnabe Rich in one of the introductory pieces
of *Riche his Farewell to Military Profession*. Rich was a soldier who
had fought in the Low Countries and in Ireland and had now
retired, like Thomas Churchyard, to write of his military life and
to devote himself to other branches of letters. He dedicated three
of his books to Hatton, and in his *Farewell* speaks of Hatton as
his patron. His description of Holdenby is meagre and conventional, but he gives a glowing account of Hatton's hospitality:

> ... and such worthy port and daily hospitality kept, that although
> the owner himself useth not to come there once in two years, yet I
> dare undertake there is daily provision to be found convenient
> to entertain any nobleman with his whole train, that should hap to
> call in of a sudden. And how many gentlemen and strangers that
> comes but to see the house are there daily welcomed, feasted and
> well lodged! From whence should he come, be he rich, be he
> poor, that should not there be entertained, if it please him to call
> in? To be short, Holdenby giveth daily relief to such as be in
> want for the space of six or seven miles' compass.

Rich's *Farewell* was published in 1581, and was probably composed shortly before then. At this time, he states, Holdenby was
not quite finished. It may be conjectured that 1583 was the date
when the last touches were given to the building, and Hatton's

heraldic achievement, bearing that date, was put up over the entrance gates.

In that year Sir Thomas Heneage writes in appreciation of Holdenby, that it is

> altogether even the best house that hath been built in this age; and it more showeth the good judgment and honour of the builder than all the charge that hath been bestowed upon stones by the greatest persons and the best purses that hath been in my time. Shortly, if the praise of a house consist in the seat, beauty and use, both within and without (howsoever it may be cavilled with), Holdenby shall hold the preeminence of all the modern houses I have known or heard of in England. That is all I will say of it saving, your outhouses make me remember my noble old master the Earl of Arundel, that made his garments most beautiful and rich where the common sort least looked for it. There is nothing better pleaseth me than your park, which you dispraised; your green and base-court, that you devised; and your garden, which is most rare; but all the steps of descent must be of stone, which it lacketh . . .

Burghley, Heneage, Barnabe Rich, all who visited Holdenby were agreed on its magnificence. And, in fact, the name became legendary, even before Holdenby was swept out of existence. Thus Ben Jonson in a mask played before Queen Anne at Althorp in 1603:

> They come to see, and to be seen,
> And though they dance afore the Queen,
> There's none of these doth hope to come by
> Wealth to build another Holmby.

According to a survey made in 1587 the area of the Holdenby estate was 1789 acres, of which 606 were laid out in park, the site of the house, gardens, orchards, and pastures. The dimensions given at other times vary a little from this. The modern measurement is stated by Baker, the historian of Northamptonshire, as about 1820 acres.

On the sale of Holdenby to James I in 1605 it was valued as worth £1596 13s. 11d. a year, while the timber was priced at £1922 3s. The agreed sum to be paid by the King was £9922 3s., i.e. £8000 and the value of the timber. At the same time James surrendered the interest he had in any lands of the late Lord

Chancellor Hatton in virtue of any extent issued for debts owing by him to Queen Elizabeth, with the proviso that the outstanding debt to the Crown should be redeemed at the rate of £1500 a year 'at the days appointed in an instrument made by the late Queen Elizabeth for securing payment thereof'. This is Hatton's bond to Elizabeth, so often mentioned by his biographers as hastening his death. The amount of his debt to her is recorded as £42,139 5s., though other slightly different sums are also given.

The later history of Holdenby does not concern us. Students of the life of Charles I will remember that Holdenby, generally known as Holmby, was the royal residence in which the King was imprisoned in 1647, and that there he lived most of the time until his execution in 1649. In 1650 it was sold by the trustees for the sale of Crown lands to a captain of the Parliamentary Army, Adam Baynes of Knowsthorp, Yorkshire. It was compulsorily relinquished to the Crown at the Restoration, but it is not known how much of the house was then standing. A great deal had been taken away or destroyed. In particular, part of the materials was removed to Northampton, where three houses built from them were pointed out in Baker's time, one of them named Little Holmby.

'The last and greatest monument of his youth.' So the noble mansion which Hatton built in his Queen's honour has been characterized, and such he perhaps himself called it. Besides Rich's account of Holdenby and the complimentary letters about it from Hatton's friends, there is an unilluminating line in Camden, the contemporary historian: 'Holdenby House, a fair pattern of stately and magnificent building, maketh a fair glorious show', and a long, though vague rhapsody from John Norden, which internal evidence shows was written in Hatton's lifetime.

A survey of Crown property made by Parliamentary commissioners after the execution of Charles I gives a good account of the general appearance of the house and grounds; and is of interest also as showing the enthusiasm which the magnificence of Hatton's palace aroused in the minds of men who, one imagines, were not by nature impressionable. They speak of the 'noble mansion-house', the 'beautiful gate-house or porter's lodge', the four 'magnificent towers or turrets' at each corner of the first court, the 'many costly and rare chimney-pieces' and the many 'spacious chambers and withdrawing-rooms'. South of the house they notice 'a pleasant, spacious and fair garden, adorned with several long walks, mounts, arbors and seats, with curious delightful knots' and planted with fruit-trees. They then go on to mention the orchards, fish-ponds, bowling-alley, and spinneys planted with ash, and with 'a variety of delightful walks'. The site of the house and garden is given as 38 acres and the dimensions of the park as 500. With upwards of 200 deer, and hundreds of timber trees, the value of the whole premises they estimate to be worth over £9000.

Though Hatton's great palace has almost completely disappeared, there is no difficulty in reconstructing the general lay-out of the house and grounds. This George Baker, the historian of Northamptonshire, writing between 1822 and 1830, was able to do from a careful inspection of the remains aided by the recollection of an old inhabitant, whose father and grandfather had lived nearby. But there is no need to quote Baker's account, for the setting of Holdenby House in its grounds is made clear from two beautiful maps preserved in a volume of plans of some of Hatton's estates, Holdenby, Kirby and others. This volume, was prepared for him by Ralph Treswell his steward, who also executed the plan of Corfe Castle, already referred to. It is a handsome book with a title-page giving Hatton's armorial achievement in colours; and the maps of the different estates, charmingly executed in wash, show the house in plan and elevation, and depict deer and rabbits running about in the park, with the keepers looking on. The volume forms part of the extensive Finch-Hatton collection of manuscripts relating to the Hatton family, which was deposited by the late Lord Winchilsea with the Northamptonshire Record Society.

There are two plans in this volume of the Holdenby estate, one of the year 1580, the other of 1587. The earlier of these is of particular interest, for it marks the site near the church of the old manor-house of the Holdenbys. The two courts round which the new house was built are shown in plan and in them is fitted a neatly-executed elevation of Holdenby House as it was. That part of these plans which shows the house and gardens has been redrawn and reproduced by Mr. J. Alfred Gotch in his *Early Renaissance Architecture in England* and also in his *Old Manor Houses and Halls of Northamptonshire*. For the architectural details we have to go to Thorpe's plan in his volume of drawings in the Soane

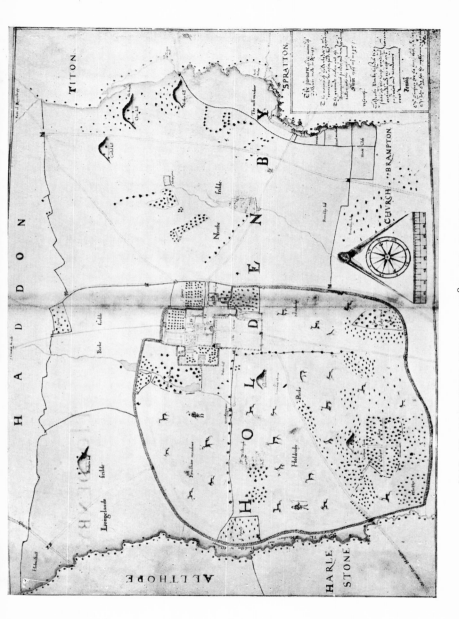

MAP OF HOLDENBY ESTATE, 1587, BY RALPH TRESWELL

From the Finch-Hatton Collection

Museum. This was reproduced by Emily Hartshorne in her *Memorials of Holdenby* (1868) and also by Mr. Gotch in his *Old English Houses*. Miss Hartshorne has also reproduced Thorpe's small plan of the gate-house or porter's lodge.

The house, as can be seen from the plan in Hatton's estate book, was approached by a long road leading through a large inclosure called The Green of nearly 17 acres in extent, flanked by the stables on the north. This is 'the large, long, straight fair way' of Burghley's letter. This road terminated at the porter's lodge, which was the entrance to a walled court, seventy yards square, called the Base Court. At the opposite side of the Base Court was the main entrance to the house. On the two other sides of the Base Court were two large archways, which still stand, giving access to the Base Court from the gardens. To the north of the house were two walled gardens of nearly an acre each, and beyond these were spinneys, or small woods, between which lay the little village with its inn. Beyond the gardens was the Park, stocked with deer.

The house itself was raised a few steps above the general level, and to the south the ground sloped steeply away in a series of terraces. The plan shows, as Mr. Gotch describes it, that at the top of these terraces and flanking the whole length of the Base Court, the house and the orchard beyond, ran a broad, straight path. In the midst of the terraces a great platform was run out at the level of this long path, containing a rosery laid out with paths in a simple geometrical pattern. At the extreme end of the long path was a cross path leading each way to a prospect mount, up at least one of which wound a spiral path, ending probably in a banqueting-house, such as Bacon describes in his essay 'Of Gardens'. The lay-out of the grounds corresponded in fact fairly closely to the 'prince-like' gardens such as Bacon designed. At the foot of the terraces lay fish-ponds amid orchard trees, and in a small inclosure of its own was the church with the old Holdenby manor-house beside it.

A full description of the architecture of the house will be found in Mr. Gotch's *Old English Houses*. It was built round two great courts, the first 128 feet by 104, the second 140 feet by 110, 'comparable in point of size with those of Hampton Court and a good deal more intricate in detail'. The first court of the house, round which the principal rooms were placed, was entered from an archway in the Base Court, which opened into a loggia or colonnade. This was the point at which Burghley found 'a great magnificence in the front or front pieces of the house, and so every part answerable to other, to allure liking'. At the far end of this first court was the actual entrance to the house, which opened into the screens, a wide passage characteristic of the houses of the period, cut off from the end of the Great Hall. In the middle of the Hall were three pyramidal pillars mentioned by Norden and shown on Thorpe's plan; in Buck's View (1729) one of these is still standing among other fragments. At the farther end the screens led to the second court of the house, one side of which was occupied by the kitchens. This court was larger than the first, but simpler in treatment. At its farther end was yet another archway leading to the gardens.

Other features of the mansion were a chapel, the screen from which is now in the church and is illustrated in Miss Hartshorne's book, and a long gallery, a characteristic feature of Elizabethan houses, 140 feet by 22. The building was full of windows, divided by bays, and at the corners of the first court were the magnificent towers or turrets which drew the admiration of the Parliamentary commissioners. Mr. Gotch sums up by saying, 'no façade on so fine a scale had been attempted before, but a number of great houses had led up to it. It must have been a master-piece of simple, effective design'.

Of all this splendour scarce anything remains. The great archways leading into the Base Court stand to-day forlorn, seventy yards apart, their purpose incomprehensible when all else has gone. They bear the date 1583 and Hatton's heraldic achievement. Portions of the walls of the second court which contained the kitchen buildings, also remain, and have been incorporated in the present house, which stands on part of the site.

One other detail we get from Bishop Corbet's *Iter Boreale*, written about the year 1620. He indicates that at Holdenby, presumably at the gate, stood two statues of giants or tutelar *lares*, whose memory would have perished but for the poet-Bishop. The traveller of the poem had just witnessed Nottingham Castle, in ruins despite the two giants that still stood at the gates, and he reproaches them with the fidelity of their brethren of Guildhall and Holdenby, who had carefully kept the respective buildings entrusted to them:

THE PALACE OF HOLDENBY

Oh, you that do Guildhall and Holmeby keep,
So carefully when both the founders sleep,
You are good giants, and partake no shame
With those two worthless trunks of Nottinghame.

When Hatton rebuilt Holdenby House, he turned his attention
also to the church. Laurence Bostock, his genealogical and
heraldic agent, had visited Holdenby Church in 1573, and found
there and listed various tombs and arms of the feudal Holdenbys.
He does not mention the Hatton tombs there. Two of these are
for Hatton's brothers Francis and Thomas, and so it is certain that
they were erected by Hatton himself. The similarity to these of
the others, each having a brass plate of four lines of Latin verse
and no date, is proof that they were all of Hatton's making, probably at the time of the building of Holdenby House. The tombs
are five in number. The first is for Elizabeth Holdenby, Christopher Hatton's great-grandmother. Its Latin verse may be
quoted as an example of the others:

> Hic Holdenbei castissima nominis heres
> Hattoni Conjux Elizabeth jacet.
> Legerat haec talem non inconsulta maritum
> Ut foret huic generis major origo sui.

which may be translated, 'the most chaste heir of the name of
Holdenby, Elizabeth the wife of Hatton, lies here. Not incon-
siderately she chose such a husband that she might give a greater
origin to her descendants'. The feudal race of Holdenby, sleeping
beneath their ancient quarterings, might have worded it differently.

The next tomb is for John Hatton, Christopher's grandfather;
the third for Francis, his elder brother; the fourth for Thomas,
his younger brother; and the fifth for Alice Saunders, his mother.
There was also a stone with an English inscription, no doubt
erected in fulfilment of his will by the widow of William, Christopher Hatton's father: 'Here lieth William Hatton, sonne of John
Hatton, sonne of Elizabeth Hatton, daughter and heire of William
Holdenbye, on whose soule Jesus have mercie.' Another stone
with a Latin inscription was for Dorothy, wife of George Belgrave
and daughter of Laurence Saunders, who died in 1536. She was
Christopher Hatton's aunt.

In the church also was a font, on which Baker found seven coats
of arms, six of them representing Holdenby and its alliances, and

165

the seventh Hatton impaling Holdenby. A purely Holdenby achievement, except for the last coat, we may surmise that it probably dates from the time of William Hatton, Christopher's father. Among the articles valued when King James bought Holdenby were six bells in the church steeple, 'made by Lord Chancellor Hatton, weighing seven thousandweight, worth £166 13s. 4d., which have been removed as private property, and two smaller ones substituted'.

CHAPTER XVII

THE FRENCH MARRIAGE PROPOSALS

IN September, 1577, it was known that Hatton was to be appointed Vice-Chamberlain and made a member of the Privy Council. On the 19th of that month a newsletter sent to Hatton's friend, William Davison, Ambassador to the Low Countries, announced that the Vice-Chamberlain, Dr. Wilson (one of the Secretaries of State) and Mr. Horsey, Captain of the Guard (he was not that but Governor of the Isle of Wight) are to be made councillors. 'Mr. Hatton and Wilson', the writer adds, 'were in the Council Chamber to be sworn, when there came a great let which I will tell you of when we meet.' What the hindrance was does not appear; perhaps it was some opposition from Burghley. At any rate, on November 11th, a few days before Drake sailed on his voyage of circumnavigation, Christopher Hatton was appointed Vice-Chamberlain and sworn of the Privy Council.

Soon afterwards, on December 1st, according to Dr. Dee's Diary, he was knighted, Walsingham, one of the Secretaries of State, and Thomas Heneage, Treasurer of the Chamber, receiving the same honour. The Vice-Chamberlain was the Lord Chamberlain's assistant; his was an office that had existed as far back as the fourteenth century and probably earlier. Some of his duties in connection with the royal progresses and ceremonies at Court have already been indicated. As Elizabeth's Vice-Chamberlain, Hatton was entitled to the statutory fee of £66 13s. 4d. a year and a table at Court. But the indirect emoluments, chances of securing grants of monopolies and of lands, gifts from suitors whose affairs he could promote, pickings in fact of all kinds, were much more substantial.

Hatton had now, save for the last and greatest step, reached the summit of his fortunes after thirteen years at Court. If, as Captain of the Guard, he had been a man of some prominence, his importance was increased enormously as a member of the Council. If he had been formerly an influence behind the Throne, a man who, having the Queen's ear, was worth cultivating by the needy suitors that hung around the Court, of weight in promoting a

Bishop or forwarding a petition, as a Privy Councillor he at once took his place as one of the small band of men responsible for the day to day government of the country and, as an adviser of the Queen, for influencing policy. We find Hatton henceforth taking an interest in foreign affairs, in Scotland and Ireland, being in receipt of frequent communications from ambassadors who send him newsletters and appreciations of conditions on the Continent. No Burghley or Walsingham, but working in general harmony with those directors of England's policy; at variance occasionally with the former, usually joined with the latter in a common outlook on affairs.

One of the first matters that engaged his attention, with that of the other councillors, was the French marriage proposal, or rather that phase of its long spun-out course which began in the year 1578. It stretched back indeed to 1570, when the Duke of Anjou had been Queen Elizabeth's suitor. Later, his brother, the Duke of Alençon was substituted for him, a youth twenty years Elizabeth's junior. These negotiations, to which the Queen bent all her powers of coquetry to the service of diplomacy, form part of the intricate history of the relations between England, France and Spain in the middle period of the reign. They marked the orientation of England's drift towards France and away from Spain. The change had begun with English dreams of overseas enterprise, which could only be fulfilled at the expense of the latter country. The raids of English sailors upon the Spanish treasure ships and the part that Philip of Spain had taken in the Ridolfi Plot were among the signs that relations were deteriorating. England began to turn to France, and in 1572, by the Treaty of Blois, became her ally. Elizabeth was looked upon as the champion of Protestantism in Europe, and Walsingham and Leicester began to work for the salvation of Protestant liberties, threatened by the campaign of the Spanish King against his revolted Netherlands. If the Massacre of St. Bartholomew was to prove a heavy strain on the alliance between England and France, the slaughter of the Huguenots was no argument for returning to good relations with Spain; and England could not afford to be isolated. Negotiations for the French marriage were resumed in 1572, this time with Alençon, Anjou's brother. They dragged on till 1576 and were revived in 1578, when Alençon in turn had become Duke of Anjou, his brother having succeeded to the French throne.

The new Duke of Anjou had few religious scruples, thus making him a more suitable match for the Protestant English Queen than his brother would have been. He could be won over to tolerance of the Protestants and, having himself ambitions in the Low Countries at the expense of Spain, had contrived to have himself declared Defender of the Liberties of the Netherlands. A proposal of marriage between him and Elizabeth could thus be used as a curb upon the Catholic policy of France, while on the other hand it could be viewed as a link between the two countries, a weapon directed against Spain. The negotiations for the French marriage therefore formed part of an intricate diplomatic game. They belong to the general history of the period and cannot be pursued here. All that need be attempted is an account of these events so far as Hatton was concerned in them.

It has been supposed that Hatton was all along averse from the French marriage. That is not the case. With Leicester he at first supported it. It was only when Elizabeth began to show too great a familiarity with the flirtatious Simier, the agent whom Anjou sent to England to support his interests, that Hatton evinced some of the resentment that Englishmen were feeling. And when she appeared to show a disposition to fall a victim to Anjou's blandishments and to treat as serious a proposal that had originally been part of a diplomatic fencing-match, Hatton joined with the other members of the Council in dissuading the Queen from the marriage for which she seemed to hanker.

In 1576 M. de Champagny, an envoy from the Spanish viceroy of the Netherlands, arrived in England to beg Elizabeth not to join with the French in an invasion of the Low Countries. The naive de Guaras, representing Spain in London, reports that Hatton entertained de Champagny 'like a prince', but adds 'lampoons greatly libelling Hatton have been circulated, of which de Champagny has a copy'. Hatton's entertainment of the Flemish agent with music and tilting has already been described. Going to visit de Champagny, he took de Guaras aside and told him how much the Queen and Council esteemed the visitor and commended his desire for peace and concord. 'Hatton', de Guaras writes, 'is very friendly and gracious to me.' On de Guaras uttering a warning against those who interfered with Spain in the Netherlands, Hatton 'replied laughingly that the Queen of England had incredibly great forces, but he hoped that, notwithstanding the present fears of trouble, all would turn out well. He is a gentleman of distinguished position and desires, above all things, harmony between the two crowns'.

On June 18th, 1578, Hatton wrote a remarkable letter from the Court at Hampton to Leicester. The original is in the possession of the Marquess of Bath, and only the second page of it has been reproduced by Miss Tenison in her *Elizabethan England*. The earlier part is of a more or less formal nature, and the interest lies in the portion which Miss Tenison has printed. It is as follows:

> . . . Since your Lordship's departure the Queen is found in continual and great melancholy: the cause thereof I can but guess at, notwithstanding that I bear and suffer the whole brunt of her mislike in generality. She dreameth of marriage that might seem injurious to her: making myself to be either the man or a pattern of the matter. I defend that no man can tie himself or be tied to such inconvenience as not to marry by law of God or man, except by mutual consents on both parts the man and woman vow to marry each to other, which I know she hath not done for any man, and therefore by any man's marriage she can receive no wrong, with many more arguments of the best weight I could gather. But, my Lord, I am not the man that should thus suddenly marry, for God knoweth I never meant it. By my next I think you shall hear more of this matter; I fear it will be found some evil practice . . .

The Queen 'dreameth of marriage'. It is unlikely that it is her own proposal of marriage to the Duke of Anjou which is here in question. That proposal had not been resurrected in June, 1578. It was not apparently till August that the first overtures were made. The marriage to which Elizabeth referred was presumably Leicester's to Lettice Knollys, the Queen's cousin, widow of Walter Devereux, Earl of Essex, who had died in Ireland in 1576. His death was not without suspicion, however unfounded, of poison administered on behalf of Leicester who is said to have carried on an intrigue with Essex's wife in his absence. Leicester did not openly marry Lettice Knollys until September, 1578, but it was believed that they had been secretly wedded some months before, and rumours of this, or at any rate of Leicester's intentions, may well have reached Elizabeth. It was not until the following year that Simier, Anjou's agent, revealed the marriage to her. And at the same time, according to a letter from Mary Queen of Scots to the Archbishop of Glasgow, her Ambassador in Paris, there were rumours put about that Hatton too was secretly married. The revelation of Leicester's intentions and the gossip about Hatton infuriated the Queen, and the two favourites were in disgrace.

With these facts in mind, Hatton's cryptic letter to Leicester becomes fairly clear. The marriage that might seem injurious to Elizabeth was Leicester's. Elizabeth was taxing Hatton with it, and insinuating that he was no better than his friend, making him 'to be either the man or a pattern of the matter'. 'But, my Lord', he protests to Leicester, 'I am not the man that should thus suddenly marry.' Hatton defended Leicester to Elizabeth, pointing out that for a man to be forbidden marriage was intolerable, unless he were bound by a promise to another and she to him, 'which I know she [the Queen] hath not done for any man, and therefore by any man's marriage she can receive no wrong'.

In January, 1579, Simier arrived in England on Anjou's behalf. He had come armed with twelve thousand crowns' worth of jewels as presents to be bestowed upon the Queen's advisers. Leicester entertained him at once, inviting him to supper and to the ball that followed, 'a very grand one', writes Bernardino de Mendoza, the new Spanish Ambassador, 'with an entertainment in imitation of a tournament between six ladies and a like number of gentlemen, who surrendered to them'. Hatton followed suit in March, entertaining Simier and the French Ambassador, Mauvissière de Castelnau, at a great banquet which he gave in honour of the Queen.

Camden describes Simier as 'a man of wit and parts, and one thoroughly versed in love-fancies, pleasant conceits and other gallantries'. Elizabeth delighted in the small, chattering, voluble, amusing creature, as Froude depicts him. Calling him her monkey, her *singe*, in punning allusion to his name, she was closeted with him almost daily in close and amorous conversation.

At this time Leicester and Hatton were in favour of the marriage. Mendoza reported to the King of Spain that they had become great friends, and that to forward the French alliance they had agreed to support the candidature of Sir Thomas Bromley as Lord Chancellor, so that the Council might be strengthened by a man of weight who would vote with them. Bromley, Mendoza wrote, had promised them both large pensions when he got the post. In the event, Bromley did indeed vote with Leicester and Hatton, but when the time came their vote was to be cast not for the marriage but against it. At this time, however, Mendoza thought that something more must be done to win these men to the Spanish side. He suggested a present of jewels to the value of 3000 crowns or more to Sussex and Burghley, and 2000 to the Comptroller of the Household, Sir James Crofts. 'Hatton', he adds, 'although he is attached to your Majesty's service, has joined Leicester in the French affair, so that, if your Majesty thinks fit, a jewel worth 500 may be sent and he may be entertained until we see how he goes on . . . If your Majesty thinks well it would be desirable to give something handsome to Leicester, just to make him think we have not found him out.' It is doubtful if the Spanish King got value for his money. Simier was also giving jewels to the courtiers; presents of this kind were indeed the order of the day, a courtesy which seems to have had very little influence on conduct. Crofts alone, 'who faithfully serves your Majesty', is said to have been frankly in Spanish pay. No presents, it is safe to say, could bribe such men as Burghley and Walsingham. And Hatton, for all his impecuniosity, was, judging by events, incorruptible. Though soon he and Leicester were to turn against the French marriage, later they were advocating it again. It was not Spanish or French jewels that influenced them, not primarily jealousy or pique, but the shifting currents of foreign affairs. But it was all very bewildering to the Spanish Ambassador, well informed about events but an indifferent judge of English character. 'These people', he writes, 'change so constantly in whatever they take in hand, that it is difficult to send your Majesty any definite information, because, although they may do a thing with all deliberation, they alter it in a moment.' A year or so later, writing of Leicester and Hatton, he reports, 'the Queen is completely in the hands of these two men'.

Meanwhile the flirtation between Elizabeth and Anjou's agent, partly conducted on behalf of his master and partly as an amorous entertainment, waxed fast and furious. The bounds of propriety were overstepped in speech and gesture. Simier expressed his admiration for the Queen's charms and his anxiety for the mating of Queen and Prince in terms of considerable freedom, so that even the manners of an outspoken age revolted from this foreign dalliance. Feeling ran high in the country. Leicester and Hatton grew jealous and sulked, and doubts began to form in the minds of other members of the Council. In May they discussed the matter at great length, and, led by the new Lord Chancellor, declared, unanimously save for Sussex, against the marriage.

In July a man named Appletree, a servant of Henry Carey (presumably some relative of Hunsdon, the Queen's cousin), fired a shot at a barge in which Elizabeth, Simier, the Earl of Lincoln and Hatton were rowing on the Thames. The shot struck one of the rowers, within six feet of the Queen, and passed through his arms. The man screamed out in agony, but Elizabeth, with presence of mind, bound the wounds with her scarf. Camden says that 'some buzzed' in the Queen's ears that the man was purposely set upon 'to mischief either her or Simier'. But Elizabeth, sure of her popularity, sensibly refused to regard the affair as anything but an accident; and Appletree, though sentenced to death, was pardoned. It seems indeed ridiculous to regard this stray shot, most clumsy, if intentional, as an attempt on Simier's life.

Simier seems, however, to have believed that he was the object of a plot, and struck back by informing the Queen (what everyone else knew) of Leicester's secret marriage the year before with the widow of the Earl of Essex. On this Camden reports that Leicester harboured thoughts of revenge, and says there were some who accused him of suborning 'a hackster' belonging to the Queen's Guard to assassinate Simier. Such a charge would perhaps involve Hatton also, as he was the Captain of the Guard and was acting with Leicester in opposing the marriage. But as Hatton could have had nothing to do with the shot that endangered his own life as a passenger in the Queen's barge, so we need not suppose he was cognizant of Leicester's attempt, if indeed it were made, to murder Simier by the hand of a man of his own corps.

Simier's disclosure had at any rate done something to draw the teeth of the opposition to Anjou's coming and wooing. He came in August and conquered. Short of stature and deeply pock-marked, he was yet an adept in the arts of love. The middle-aged Queen was enchanted. Her Frog (*grenouille*), as she named him from his hoarse croaking voice, seemed indeed to be carrying all before him with the fire of his wooing; and, though he stayed but three weeks in England, his success was such that the marriage seemed almost certain, if Elizabeth should have her way. But, never popular among the common people, the prospect of a French alliance was becoming more and more distasteful to all, both on religious and political grounds.

In September, just after Anjou's visit, John Stubbs or Stubbe, a gentleman of Lincoln's Inn, brother-in-law of Thomas Cartwright, the celebrated Puritan divine, published a pamphlet entitled 'The Discovery of a Gaping Gulf wherein England is like to be swallowed up by another French Marriage, if the Lord forbid not the Banns by letting her Majesty see the Sin and the Punishment thereof'. Whatever its patriotic intent, it overshot the mark by its gross abuse of the French prince and people. The Queen was furious at this interference in affairs that she believed herself so competent to manage, coming too at a moment when her Council was growing restive. A proclamation was issued condemning the pamphlet as 'a fiction of traitors to raise envy abroad and sedition at home'.

But opinion in the City of London was running strongly against the marriage, so much so that Elizabeth took steps to see that it was not further inflamed by the London preachers. Hatton undertook the task of securing that, through Bishop Aylmer, the City clergy was properly regimented. Aylmer who, it will be shown later, had been promoted to the See of London through Hatton's influence, was in close touch with him and took his orders on questions of Church discipline, about which Elizabeth held strong views. Instructions were accordingly given to a selected preacher to express the Government's condemnation of Stubbs's pamphlet. Hatton himself coached him; Aylmer reported how he discharged his task; and Samuel Cox, Hatton's secretary, was sent to listen to the sermon and see how it was taken by the populace.

These facts we learn from a letter from Aylmer to Hatton. He reports that Hatton's directions to the preacher had been zealously remembered and earnestly uttered by him, so that, as the Bishop believes, 'the heady' had been 'much stayed', the wise confirmed in their good opinion of the Queen, and 'the sparks of murmuring, misliking and misconstruing of matters of State wherewith the seditious libellers had kindled many of the busier sort' had been 'somewhat quenched'. The preacher, after sharply reprimanding Stubbs, went on to praise the Queen for 'twenty sweet, peaceable years' of good government. This part of the address was well received: 'the people seemed, even as it were with a shout, to give God thanks'. But the Bishop gathered they were not so pleased with the attack on Stubbs: 'to say plainly, they utterly bent their brows at the sharp and bitter speeches which he gave against the author of the book; of whom they conceive and report that he is one that feareth God [and] dearly loveth her Majesty.'

Author, publisher and printer were indicted under an Act of Parliament of the previous reign 'against seditious words and rumours', an Act of doubtful application in this case. They were condemned to lose their right hands. The printer was pardoned but the others suffered in the market-place of Westminster. Camden, who was present, says 'their right hands were cut off with a cleaver driven through the wrist with the force of a beetle', whereupon Stubbs who had bravely jested, 'my calamity is at hand', took off his hat with his remaining hand and, waving it in the air, exclaimed in a loud voice, 'God save the Queen'. The publisher, equally courageous, lifted his bloody stump: 'I have left there a true Englishman's hand,' he cried. Camden records also the silence of the watching crowd, horrified at this new and barbarous punishment, and hating the marriage and its feared consequences for the Protestant religion of England.

Stubbs, in addition to savage mutilation, was sent to prison. A letter from him to Hatton, written in December, shows that Hatton had taken a leading part in his examination. The wretched prisoner begins: 'the round dealing which your Honour used at my first examination, and your severe sifting out of that fault which bred me all my woe, doth not for all that affray me from coming to your Honour with some hope of pitying me, now fallen into the extremity of affliction'. He goes on to ask Hatton to intercede with the Queen for him and for his wife and small child: 'I humbly beseech your Honour to say for me that you found me no perverse examinate. For albeit upon the first examination the terror of a Prince's wrath made me tremble to accuse myself, yet did I without any accuser, after a while lay myself open.' He confirms Camden's story: 'notwithstanding the bitter pain and doleful loss of my hand immediately before chopped off, I was able by God's mercy to say with heart and tongue before I left the block these words, "God save the Queen".'

Stubbs was to languish in prison for eighteen months before he was released to find shelter and employment in the house of Lord Willoughby de Eresby, Oxford's son-in-law. He eventually retired to France, and died in the same year as Hatton, at Havre, where a pitying friend buried him at high-water mark in the spot nearest the shores of England. Perhaps Hatton did indeed intercede for him, but it is probable that he found his course in the affair of the French marriage so difficult that he hesitated to approach the indignant Queen, who had so far forgotten the claims of mercy.

To this period, September, 1580, belong three of Hatton's letters, two of them addressed to the Queen and the third concerning her, which may be inserted here, especially as two of them refer to the French marriage. The first two, read together, show Hatton at Bedford, struggling with an outbreak of sickness in his household. They seem to imply that the Queen had been in his company, but not much else can be gathered from them except that he was in low spirits on account of his enforced absence from his sovereign.

The first letter, headed by two triangles, a variant of the usual cipher, is in Hatton's most abject vein:

I most humbly, with all dutiful reverence, beseech your sacred Majesty to pardon my presumption in writing to your Highness. Your kingly benefits, together with your most rare regard of your simple and poor slave, hath put this passion into me to imagine that for so exceeding and infinite parts of unspeakable goodness I can use no other means of thankfulness than by bowing the knees of my own heart with all humility to look upon your singular graces with love and faith perdurable.

I should sin, most gracious Sovereign, against a holy ghost most damnably, if towards your Highness I should be found unthankful . . .

The poor wretch, my sick servant, receiveth again his life, being as in the physician's opinion more than half dead, through your most princely love of his poor Master, and holy charitable care, without respect of your own danger, of the poor wretch . . .

I should not dissemble, my dear Sovereign, if I wrote how unpleasant and froward a countenance is grown in me through my absence from your most amiable and royal presence, but I dare not presume to trouble your Highness with my not estimable griefs, but in my country I dare avow this fashion will full evil become me. I hope your Highness will pardon my unsatisfied humour, that knoweth not how to end such complaints as are in my thoughts ever new to begin; but duty shall do me leave off to cumber your heaven-like eyes with my vain babblings . . .

Your bounden slave, Chr. Hatton.

The next letter, written within a few days and referring also to the sickness within his domestic circle, was probably written to Sir Thomas Heneage, but it bears no superscription. Heneage was Hatton's close friend, and the bearer on occasion of most tender messages between Queen and subject. Hatton's intimate references to Elizabeth are therefore the less surprising. There is here also a comparison between his love and that of the Duke of Anjou for her:

> My good Sir Thomas, I thank you much for your happy letters, assuring our dear Mistress her present health unto me; pray God continue it for EveR. I have one servant yet free of infection, which I trust I may use to deliver my care and duty, to my singular comfort and satisfaction. I have presumed to send him, that I may daily know either by my own or yours, the true state of our Mistress, whom through choice I love no less than he that by the greatness of a kingly birth and fortune is most fit to have her. I am likewise bold to commend my most humble duty by this letter and ring, which hath the virtue to expel infectious airs, and is, as is telled to me, to be wearen between the sweet dugs — the chaste nest of most pure constancy. I trust, Sir, when the virtue is known, it shall not be refused for the value . . .

The rest of the letter has been already quoted. In it he states his intention 'to view my house of Kirby, which I never yet surveyed; leaving my other shrine, I mean Holdenby, still unseen until that holy saint may sit in it, to whom it is dedicated'.

The last of these letters is addressed to the Queen. It is headed with two triangles, and in tone recalls the ardent epistle from Spa of seven years before. This extraordinary letter is in the most enigmatical Elizabethan vein. The remark about frogs is obscure enough; it refers, of course, to Anjou, and seems to be an apology for Hatton's attitude to the royal suitor. Later he refers, in a characteristically dark passage, to the marriage. Disentangling its circumlocutions, it is seen to be a counsel in favour of it. Hatton's reference to the Queen's cipher is most interesting, for it seems to show that she used a cipher in writing to him, just as he had the three triangles for his letters to her:

> . . . The cunning of your Highness's style of writing, with the conveyance of your rare sentence and matter, is exceedingly to be liked of; but the subject which it hath pleased your Majesty to endite for my particular, exceedeth all the eloquence of the

world. Your words are sweet; your heart is full of rare and royal faith; the writing of your fair hand, directed by your constant and sacred heart, do raise in me joy unspeakable . . .

I crave most humbly your gracious favour and pardon for the offence I have made you. Frogs, near the fens where I then was, are much more plentiful, and of less value than their fish is: and because I knew that poor beast seasonable in your sight, I therefore blindly entered into that presumption, but *Misericordia tua super omnia opera tua* . . .

Against love and ambition your Highness hath holden a long war; they are the violent affections that encumber the hearts of men: but now, my most dear Sovereign, it is more than time to yield, or else this love will leave you in war and disquietness of yourself and estate, and the ambition of the world will be most maliciously bent to encumber your sweet quiet and the happy peace of this most blessed Realm. I pray God bless your kingly resolutions whatEveR. I trust your Highness will pardon this part of my presumption, because your little $ *siphere* hath the occasion. And so your Highness's most humble Lydds, a thousand times more happy in that you vouchsafe them yours, than in that they cover and conserve the poor eyes, mostly lowly do leave you in your kingly seat in God's most holy protection . . . Your Majesty's sheep and most bound vassal,

Chr. Hatton.

A week later in a weighty letter to Walsingham, that sets forth Hatton's considered judgment on current affairs, he says a few words about the marriage which shows that he had no wish to interfere, but urges the need of a decision:

. . . With the disposition of France, which lieth now in her Majesty's arbitrament, I dare not meddle, for she only knoweth what shall become thereof; and so her judgment therein must needs be most sound, which in truth maketh much to all these matters before mentioned. But if her Highness mean to marry, I wonder she so delayeth it. If she do but temporize, and will leave it at the last, what may we look for then, but that the Pope, with Spain and France, will yoke themselves in all ireful revenge, according to their solemn combination so long concluded on against us? . . .

That was in September. By October Hatton, with the majority of the Council, had come into open opposition to marriage. It is probable that the influence of Walsingham, the uncompromising

Protestant, and of Leicester possibly also, was decisive. When the Council, ordered by Elizabeth to advise her, met in that month, Burghley was found to be almost the only member of prominence in favour of the alliance. Having for months, as was his habit, drawn up innumerable memoranda pro and con, he had finally come to the conclusion that the marriage would be best. In particular he felt that it would greatly strengthen Elizabeth's position against the assassination which the adherents of the Scots Queen advised and the Pope seemed to favour, if she could be married and have an heir. After a discussion lasting several days, on one of which they are said to have sat from eight in the morning till seven at night, seven councillors, including Leicester and Hatton, carried the day against the five who favoured the marriage. A deputation of four waited on the Queen. She broke down and in tears bitterly reproached them for denying her marriage and the prospect of a child to carry on the line of Henry VIII. Though they promised support if she continued in her wish, the marriage project was virtually dead. Walsingham, who had not been present at the Council meeting, and Leicester were banished from Court for a couple of months, and Elizabeth, in the words of the Spanish Ambassador, had a 'squabble' with Hatton, who had to go a week without seeing her.

The feelings of the chief actor in the drama can only be guessed at. Elizabeth seemed to waver between make-believe and earnest. By the end of the year she appeared to have quite cooled in her desire, but the farce had to be played to the end in the interests of her diplomacy. Early in 1581 the project was revived again. Anjou sent another envoy, de Marchaumont, Count de Beaumont, and in April Elizabeth showed her favour to her lover and her contempt for Spain by choosing de Marchaumont to give Drake the accolade when he was knighted at Deptford. She jokingly told the great sailor that she had a gilded sword with which to strike off his head, and, turning to de Marchaumont, handed the sword to him. It was on this occasion that her purple and gold garter slipped off, and de Marchaumont, seizing it, only consented to part with it if she promised to send it to Anjou. She gave the promise and kept it.

In the same month Anjou's ambassadors crossed to England for the final arrangements for the marriage, to which Elizabeth had now pledged herself, though with no intention of fulfilment. The embassy, consisting of some five hundred persons, arrived in great splendour, and elaborate preparations were made to receive it. Holinshed described at length the jousts, balls and other enter-tainments in its honour, but their magnificence, though impressing the visitors, was no substitute for a decision. The envoys pressed the Queen to get down to business and to appoint commissioners to work out the terms of the alliance. Burghley, Bedford, Leicester, Sussex, Hatton and Walsingham were chosen. As before, Burgh-ley supported the marriage; Leicester as strenuously opposed it. But it is not necessary to follow here the interminable moves in the Queen's game. She was not in earnest now, though Leicester and Hatton feared at times that her amorous nature would sweep her off her feet. In November they had the greatest fright of all, when Elizabeth kissed Anjou in public, and, taking a ring from her finger, placed it on his. Hatton went to her and in tears re-monstrated, saying that she ought to consider the griefs she was bringing upon the country, and urging the danger of such a union without her people's good wishes, since the security of her throne depended upon their affection. It was a bold speech for the suave Hatton to make, but the Queen, confident of her diplomatic abilities, suffered him, as Mendoza reports, to speak his mind, and answered him 'very tenderly'. And Hatton was chosen to support Elizabeth at an interview with Anjou, and state the objec-tions to the marriage which the Council regarded as insuperable.

The end came early in 1582, when Elizabeth finally got rid of Anjou by granting him a subsidy, and Leicester was sent to see him safe out of the country on an expedition to the Low Countries. But Elizabeth had no intention of helping in a French conquest of the Netherlands, and her support was nicely calculated as just sufficient to make of Anjou a thorn in the side of Spain. Leicester left him, as he said, stranded like an old hulk on the sandbanks of the Netherlands, and Elizabeth sent an apology to the Prince of Orange for having shot so much rubbish on his land. At other times, keeping up the farce, she declared that she could not bear to think of her poor Frog suffering in those stagnant marshes, and that she would give a million to have him swimming in the Thames again.

Mendoza reports that Hatton received an acknowledgment of his services in the matter of the French marriage. Elizabeth told him with many endearments how much she was indebted to him as, had it not been for his great faithfulness and prudence, she would have found herself linked to that evil beast Anjou, who now only thought of his devilish plans of vengeance upon her, after she had rescued him from his enemies and lent him money. She said she would be her own enemy if she did not before the year was out reward Hatton as he deserved. But Hatton's reward was not yet. He was to wait four years before his final promotion came to him.

Whether Mendoza was reporting accurately or not, the speech he puts in the mouth of Elizabeth sums up her final opinion of Anjou and the proposed marriage. The mask, which had concealed so much dissimulation, mixed at intervals with what seemed to be real affection, was off at last. The long-drawn-out game was finished. Elizabeth had fought with the weapons she understood, however undignified they may seem to our eyes. She had, in the words of Professor Pollard, 'devoted her wiles to the purpose for which most English battles in Europe were fought from Crécy to Waterloo'.

CHAPTER XVIII

THE *GOLDEN HIND*

THE name that Drake gave to his famous ship serves to remind us that Hatton was one of the promoters of the celebrated voyage of circumnavigation. His association with the greatest of Elizabethan sea captains is indeed one of his best claims to remembrance. We may forget the Captain of the Queen's Guard, the Vice-Chamberlain, the Lord Chancellor of England, but we should remember the friend and patron of Drake. If Hatton's fourteen quarterings are forgotten, his cognizance, the *Golden Hind* is immortal.

Of all the splendours of the Elizabethan age, the growth of English sea-power is second only to the blossoming of its astonishing literature. Begun with the challenge of England's intrepid sailor pirates to the pomp of Spain, it ended with the overthrow by the same men of the mighty Armada. Men of action led by men of genius gave the British Navy birth. But if Hawkins and Drake were its creators and interpreters, the whole nation were its sponsors. From the Queen down to the humblest of her subjects, all were committed in word and thought to the Empire beyond the seas to which Drake and his associates pointed the way. Many, including the Queen, had a financial interest in the ventures that brought to English shores the treasures garnered by Spain in the Indies. All approved, after the full-blooded fashion of the age, in which moral scruples and niceties of international law found no place.

Or nearly all. There were a few who felt this organized plunder of the ships of a nation nominally at peace with her to be a blot on England's fame. Their leader, Burghley, endeavouring to play the diplomatic game in more orthodox fashion, found himself hampered at all points by what he deemed to be a scandalous policy, that privately comforted while officially frowning on the pirate leaders of the English Navy in being. His Queen even was secretly in the business, a shareholder in these shady ventures. Leicester and Walsingham were openly for singeing the King of Spain's beard, as a preliminary skirmish in training for the conflict they held to be inevitable.

Hatton was one of those who chafed at the caution of the elder statesmen. Though a Catholic by upbringing, he had been drawn by inclination and circumstances to favour the views of Leicester and Walsingham, who were coming to see in Continental Catholicism the enemy of England. And as one chronically in debt he would naturally be attracted by the prospect of large returns for money ventured in the Spanish game, the course too that his Queen's cupidity favoured. He was already a patron of letters; in that age of splendid patronage, he would be a patron of explorers too. Sir Ralph Lane, afterwards to be the first Governor of Virginia, a man full of restless projects of commerce and travel, was of his circle, a distant connection by marriage, who called Hatton his cousin.

More important in his influence on Hatton was his friend Sir Edward Dyer, ever active in assisting schemes for overseas expansion. And through Dyer Hatton was brought into contact with John Dee. Professor E. G. R. Taylor has shown that Dee's writings contain many mysterious hints and guarded statements which there is strong reason to believe refer to Drake's projected voyage of circumnavigation in 1577-80. That Dee was aware of Drake's objectives, if he did not actually suggest them, is argued by Dr. Taylor from the entries in his Diary, which show the Queen, Leicester, Hatton and Dyer visiting him at the time when Drake's voyage was preparing. On December 1st, 1577, for instance, comes the entry, 'I spake with Sir Christopher Hatton. He was made Knight that day. I went from the Court at Windsor'.

In the same year, as already mentioned, Dee dedicated to Hatton the first volume of his work on the British Empire, entitled *General and Rare Memorials pertaining to the Perfect Art of Navigation*. From this book we learn that Dyer, 'that ready friend, E.D. Esq.' as he calls him, acted as a constant link between Dee and Hatton. It is from the fourth volume, never printed but existing among the Cotton MSS., though badly damaged by fire, *The Great Volume of Famous and Rich Discoveries*, that we learn of Dee's interest in the land of Beach, Marco Polo's Locach, the 'land rich in gold', which lay to the south of Java, 'and most apt for the British wisdom, manhood and travail to be bestowed upon henceforwards'. Dee indicates that he was aware that this objective was to be 'a worthy attempt at discovery, faithfully intended by a true British subject', who 'hath secretly offered up to God and his natural sovereign and country the employing of all his skill and talent and the patient enduring of the great toil of his body' in that attempt. These words, written in the spring and early summer of 1577, must refer to Drake's projected voyage. And the Draft Project of Drake's Voyage, which Dr. Taylor has discovered, confirms the view that his objective was to be the land of Beach or Locach. His instructions were to go and return by the Straits of Magellan. From the Straits in 52° S. he was to proceed along the coast as far as latitude 30° S. and to prospect for treasure. Dr. Taylor interprets these instructions as meaning not that Drake was to sail up the coast of South America, but that he was to proceed along the coast of the unknown Terra Australia, which was supposed to run north-west from the Straits to the Beach of Dee's dreams.

Here then is evidence that Drake's original objective was that proposed by Dee in the book that he dedicated to Hatton. And Hatton was a principal shareholder in the venture and, of course, fully cognizant of Drake's plans. Subsequently the objectives of the voyage were extended, and it was agreed that Drake was to go on to the Moluccas.

In Hatton's position at Court, it was inevitable that he must come in contact with Drake, returning triumphant from his first voyage to the Indies. The precise manner of their meeting is unknown. It could have come about in a score of ways: in that small circle nothing could keep apart two such prominent men as the Queen's favourite and the greatest captain of his age. Dyer, the friend of Dee, and Dee, the expert adviser of the British School of oversea explorers and in touch with all the Elizabethan navigators, are the most likely links between Drake and Hatton. But let us accept, for the moment, Thomas Doughty's statement that it was he who brought the two men together, and so signed his own death warrant. The story of Drake and Doughty has been often told. It concerns us here, because Hatton was Drake's patron, and Doughty, according to his own tale, had been Hatton's servant.

When Drake returned from his raid on the Spanish Main in 1575, he came at a moment unpropitious for him and for all that he stood for. He was caught in the shifting currents of English foreign policy. He had left England on the verge of war with Spain. He returned when the two countries, after the disturbance of the Ridolfi Plot, were settling down again and seeking peace.

It was impolitic for the arch-pirate, as Spain regarded him, to remain in England. He went to Ireland, almost certainly on Government orders, at once to be put out of the way and to keep an eye on Spanish movements. At Drake's Pool, near Queenstown, he is supposed to have lurked, ready to sally forth in search of Spanish ships. He comes into daylight again, later in the year, when he joined Essex's punitive expedition into Ulster and was in charge of the ships that landed Norris's army to do its dreadful work of massacre on Rathlin Island. It was in this campaign that he met Thomas Doughty. Doughty had been in Essex's employment in Ireland. Having reported to him, falsely as Essex believed, that Leicester was working in England against the success of his operations in Ireland, he fell into disgrace with his master, and seems to have been dismissed from his service before Drake joined Essex's expedition in the summer of 1575.

The documents that have come down to us are not unprejudiced. They are written by partisans on both sides; and it is not always easy to know what to believe. But it seems that Doughty used to boast that it was he who introduced Drake to Essex. Drake denied this, affirming that he owed his employment with Essex to Hawkins.

Doughty's character has been sketched by Drake's chaplain, Fletcher, an adherent whom he had won over to his side:

> He feared God, he loved His word, and was always desirous to edify others and confirm himself in the faith of Christ. For his qualities in a man of this time they were rare and his gift very excellent for his age, a sweet orator, a pregnant philosopher, a good gift for the Greek tongue and a reasonable taste of Hebrew; a sufficient secretary to a noble personage of great place and in Ireland an approved Soldier, and not behind many in the study of the law for his time.

In the light of what we can learn of the events that were to lead to Doughty's death we can dismiss a good deal of this. We may even suspect that the quick-witted Doughty had rubbed up, if he had not picked up, his Greek and Hebrew in conversation with the credulous chaplain. Yet his will made in September, 1577, on the eve of undertaking 'a long and dangerous travail by the seas', reveals that he was a gentleman entitled to bear arms and a member of the Inner Temple. But he was vain and boastful, an intriguer skilled in the double-dealing so characteristic of the least pleasant side of Elizabethan life, an ardent though not too successful player on the passions of men. He undoubtedly strove to stir up discontent in Drake's fleet; but his cleverness stopped short of any searching knowledge of character. In pitting himself against Drake he mistook his man. Still, when all allowances have been made for Drake's position, so far as we can judge the evidence, weighing partisan against partisan, we shall probably conclude that his conduct was harsh and arbitrary. His best defence is that he sincerely believed that the expedition, which was dearer to him than life, could not succeed while Doughty lived. And he was probably right.

A more sinister report about Doughty was that Leicester had contrived the poisoning of Essex, who had died suddenly at the conclusion of his Irish campaign, and had employed either Thomas Doughty or his brother John, to remove his rival. For Leicester was in love with Essex's wife, and married her after her husband's death. She was the Queen's cousin, Lettice Knollys, mother of the young Earl of Essex, Elizabeth's favourite in her old age, but was herself detested by the Queen for her marriage with Leicester and the circumstances attending it.

There was, apparently, no truth in these rumours about Essex's death; he seems to have died from natural causes. But Leicester's reputation was bad. His first wife, Amy Robsart, had expired in tragic circumstances, not without suspicion, probably unfounded, of her husband's complicity. He was a friend and patron of the Queen's physician, Dr. Julio, said to have an Italianate talent for poisoning. Hence rumour easily connected together Leicester and Essex, Doughty and Drake, who had served with Essex in Ireland; and in Drake's execution of Doughty it saw Leicester's hand. Leicester, it was said, had persuaded Drake to take Doughty with him and to see to it that so dangerous a witness to his crimes should not return. Drake either believed, or affected to believe, that Doughty had been the agent by whom Essex had met his death. But that was later, when the two men had quarrelled. At this time, when they met in Ireland, they quickly became friends; and, Essex's campaign over, left for England to push their fortunes.

In England Drake formulated his project for a voyage to the Pacific by way of the Straits of Magellan, and so to raid the rich trade of Spain on the west coast of South America. This trade was carried overland through Panama to the Atlantic, for the route by the Magellan Straits was regarded as impracticable. It was a project so daring and unheard of that, though Spanish agents got wind of preparations which could scarcely be concealed, they had only the vaguest suspicions of Drake's true designs. To organize and carry through such a scheme, not only was Government permission necessary, but it was essential to secure powerful backing to finance it. Burghley naturally held aloof, and the most influential support came from Leicester, Walsingham and Hatton. The Queen too approved, and was a shareholder. The names of the shareholders, formerly only partially known and then but a matter of inference, have now been determined, thanks to Dr. Taylor's discovery of the draft project of the voyage. The Queen was to contribute a ship, a proportion of the value which represented her investment. The others were the Earl of Lincoln, Lord High Admiral, Leicester, Walsingham, Hatton, Sir William Winter, one of Elizabeth's admirals, George Winter his brother, John Hawkins and Drake himself. The investments of the last four only are given. They are £750, £500, £500 and £1000. Those of the others are not stated, and probably, as we know was the case with other voyages, the sums were subsequently revised. Drake himself claimed that his own share was equal to any three. And Hatton was certainly a considerable shareholder. His nominees accompanied the expedition, and the name of the *Golden Hind* with which Drake, in his honour, rechristened his ship the *Pelican*, sufficiently testifies to his position as a patron of the voyage.

Doughty claimed that it was he who had introduced Drake to Hatton, just as he claimed the introduction to Essex. He and Drake, he is reported to have said, conferred about the voyage when they were in Ireland, and he proposed to sink a thousand pounds in the venture. Elsewhere the figure is put at a thousand marks, but whatever the sum, it seems certain that he had a financial interest in the scheme. After thinking over the matter in England, Doughty

> considering within himself that this voyage was more meet for a prince than a subject, continently went to Mr. Secretary Walsingham and to Mr. Hatton, and like a true subject brake the matter to them, and they brake it to the Queen's Majesty, who had a great good liking of it, and caused our Captain to be sent for and commanded this voyage to go forwards: and joined the said T.D. and our Captain together and gave them as large a commission as ever went out of England.

It is difficult to know how far Doughty, or the witness who reports him, is telling the truth. It is possible that he did introduce Drake to Hatton, and induced Hatton to take an interest in the project, for Doughty also claimed that he was Hatton's secretary, and Chaplain Fletcher, in the passage quoted above, seems to hint the same. This, if true, must have been the interval between Doughty's leaving Ireland in 1575 and his sailing with Drake in 1577. There is nothing against the dates, for Samuel Cox, to whom we owe the Hatton Letter Book, did not become Hatton's secretary before 1577 or 1578, the period in which the transcripts of Hatton's letters begin. But Doughty's claims are difficult to assess. He boasted too that Burghley had also invited him on different occasions to be his secretary. This is almost certainly untrue. As Sir Julian Corbett sums up, Doughty, from what we know of him, would not have refused such a position, and Burghley, with the rumours flying about of the supposed poisoning of Essex, would not have employed such a man. This reasoning probably applies to Hatton also.

Drake himself swept aside all this talk of patrons and influence. He held his commission he averred, from the Queen, to whom Walsingham had presented him on an introduction from Essex, to whom in turn he had been recommended by Sir John Hawkins. Just before Doughty's execution Drake opened a bundle of letters and documents:

> But here he showed forth the first letters that were written (as he said) by Master Hawkins to my lord of Essex for his entertainment, secondly he showed letters of thanks from my lord of Essex unto Master Hawkins for the preferring so good a servitor unto him and how much he had pleasured him, then read the letters that passed from my lord of Essex unto Secretary Walsingham in his great commendation, then showed he letters of Master Hatton's unto himself, tending for the acceptance of his men John Thomas and John Brewer, and their well usage in this voyage, and lastly he read a bill of her Majesty's adventure of a thousand crowns.

But we may believe that Doughty, as Drake's friend and associate, canvassed for him in London; met all the notables, including Burghley, Walsingham, Leicester and Hatton; influenced men where he could and claimed to influence where he could not. He may have been, or considered himself to have been, one of Hatton's representatives of the voyage. There is no evidence, however, that he associated with Hatton's known nominees, John Thomas, the Captain of the *Marigold*, and John Brewer, Drake's trumpeter. On the contrary the truth seems to be, as Doughty himself blurted out at his trial, that he held some sort of a watching commission from Burghley. When the Queen gave Drake permission to undertake the voyage she made, according to Drake's statement, a 'special commandment that of all men my Lord treasurer [Burghley] should not know of it'. The reference is presumably to Drake's intention of raiding Spanish ships and the settlements on the west coast of South America. But Burghley must have suspected what was afoot, and it is possible that, disliking such enterprises and believing them fatal to the policy of peace he was pursuing, he tampered with Doughty and sought to use his presence on the voyage to hamper Drake.

Drake's precise plans, which were to be kept secret from so well-informed a man as Burghley, naturally puzzled the Spaniards. His movements could not be concealed: the fitting out of ships, the recruitment of the men. They were enlisted for a voyage to Alexandria. De Guaras, the Spanish Ambassador, reported in May, 1575, that three ships had sailed from London to join three more at Plymouth, and were destined, as he believed, for a plundering expedition to the Indies. The enterprise, he learned, had been helped by Hawkins and the ships were partly owned by Hatton. But he had confidence in the latter, whom he believed friendly to him: Hatton 'is such a good gentleman that they will certainly do no harm with his consent'. In May, 1576, he still held the same opinion. On the eve of Drake's sailing he believed he was going to Scotland to kidnap the infant son of Mary Queen of Scots. When, on November 15th, 1577, Drake weighed anchor, his secret was still unguessed.

Drake's fleet consisted of the *Pelican*, admiral: Captain-general Francis Drake; the *Elizabeth*, vice-admiral: Captain John Winter son of George Winter, a brother of Admiral Sir William Winter; the *Marigold*, bark: Captain John Thomas; the *Swan*, a fly-boat or store-ship, in charge of John Chester; and the *Benedict*, pinnace, in charge of Thomas Moone. John Thomas, the captain of the *Elizabeth*, was one of Hatton's nominees, as was John Brewer, Drake's trumpeter. For Drake, who kept great state at sea, was 'served with the sound of trumpets and other instruments at his meals'. Thomas Doughty and his brother John were among the gentlemen adventurers, having no command, who accompanied the expedition.

Before striking out for South America, Drake made for the coast of Morocco, picking up a few prizes by the way. One of these he exchanged for the *Benedict*, putting the crew of that pinnace on board the new ship, which he rechristened the *Christopher*, perhaps in honour of Hatton.

As the voyage proceeded, first a suspicion, then a certainty came to Drake that some agency was working against him. It was a sentiment that need not surprise us in an age of spy and counter-spy, crossing and double-crossing. Instinctively Drake became aware that Doughty wished no good to the expedition. And filled with the superstition of his time, he believed, when fearful storms arose, that Doughty was the cause, ascribing to him powers of witchcraft. When, later, testimony was collected on the point, a witness deposed:

> John Doughty told me and John Deane that he and his brother could conjure as well as any man, and that they could raise the devil and make him to meet any man in the likeness of a bear, a lion or a man in harness. More, John Doughty told me and John Deane that he the said John Doughty could poison as well as any man, and that he could poison a man with a diamond that he should be twelve months after or [i.e. before] he should die.

Poison again! Drake recalled and now believed the story of the manner of Essex's death. And John Winter in his narrative, lately discovered by Dr. Taylor, says that Drake commanded the Doughtys, when he first became suspicious of them, 'on pain of death neither to write nor read but in English'. He would have none of the conning over of astrological and alchemical symbols in strange tongues.

Later, evidence came to light of Doughty's endeavours to tamper with the men, and when Drake finally put him on his trial and procured depositions from various members of the crews, Doughty blurted out that Burghley had a 'plot' of the route, that is precise details of Drake's plans. ' "No, that he hath not", quoth Master Drake. "He had it from me", quoth Master Doughty.' Here to Drake was the explanation of his subconscious suspicions. The nature of the secret influence that he had sensed became clear.

The command with which the Queen had particularly charged him, to keep the objects of the voyage at any rate the plans for raiding the Spaniards, from Burghley, had been betrayed by the man whom he had thought his friend.

From that moment Drake was resolved on Doughty's death. There is no need to repeat the charges and counter-charges of the two men; or when his fate was settled, the blessings which the now penitent Doughty invoked on Queen, Captain and ship; to tell of the solemn taking of the communion together, after the good Elizabethan manner, by the two friends, lately enemies, now reconciled for the moment in the presence of death; of the final ghastly scene when Drake picked up the bleeding head with 'Lo, this is the end of traitors'.

Psychologically, Thomas Doughty is the main human interest of the story of Drake's voyage. Of Hatton's other men, John Thomas, and John Brewer, there is little to say. Brewer, the trumpeter, twice informed Drake of Doughty's machinations, and once had to complain of a coarse familiarity from Doughty, which he seems to have resented only because he was not friendly with him. Captain Thomas showed his courage in standing inshore with the *Marigold*, in great danger from fog and storm, to save Drake who had ventured on a survey with a small boat off the coast of Patagonia. He was the assessor, Drake being the judge, at Doughty's trial. Shortly after the passage of the Straits, the *Marigold* with Thomas in charge disappeared and was never heard of again. And a little later, Winter, with the *Elizabeth*, lost sight of Drake's ship and, failing to get into touch with her again, returned to England. The documents discovered by Dr. Taylor clear Winter, after three and a half centuries, of the charge of desertion that has been laid against him. It seems indeed that Drake made little effort to find him, and was perhaps only too glad to shake off those who were not whole-heartedly with him in his plans for raiding the Spaniards.

A few weeks after Doughty's death, Drake on August 20th, 1578, reaching Cape Virgins at the entrance of the Magellan Straits, caused the fleet to strike their topsails in honour of the Queen and 'in remembrance of his honourable friend and favourer, Sir Christopher Hatton, he changed the name of the ship which himself went in from the *Pelican* to be called the *Golden Hind*'. Hatton's cognizance was 'a hind statant Or'.

There is no occasion here to follow the voyage to Peru and across the Pacific, then by way of the East Indies to the Cape of Good Hope and so home. Winter had reached England in June, 1578. The execution of Doughty was reported, but inquiry was shelved for the moment, indeed for ever. A year later, when Drake was in mid-Pacific, the Spanish Ambassador received a report of his exploits and of the stolen treasure he was bringing home from the South Seas. 'The adventurers', he wrote, 'are beside themselves with joy'; and he had learned that some of the Privy Council were among those interested in the result. In September, 1580, Drake entered Plymouth Sound, nearly three years after the immortal voyage had begun. He sent Brewer, his trumpeter and Hatton's man, to the Queen and wrote to others at Court, Hatton no doubt among them. The Queen's answer was a summons to her presence, while instructions were given for the treasure to be bestowed in safety. Burghley summoned the Council, Drake's supporters, Leicester, Walsingham and Hatton being absent; and it was decided that the treasure was to be registered and sent to the Tower, pending restitution.

Leicester and Hatton gave it as their opinion that, although privateers ventured to the Americas at their own risk and might be sent to the bottom if the Spaniards could catch them, yet, if they returned safe the Spanish Government had no case against the Queen, either for their punishment or for the restitution of their spoils. But Burghley had not changed his views. When, therefore, the order of the Council was brought to the three absent Privy Councillors who were members of Drake's syndicate, they refused their signatures. Mendoza, the new Spanish Ambassador, reported in October on this refusal of Leicester, Hatton and Walsingham, and added that they were 'the principal owners in the venture'. He noted also that 'they are very particular not to divulge the route by which Drake returned, and although . . . Hatton's trumpeter had said that the road home had been by the Portuguese Indies, Drake himself signifies to the contrary . . .' The three impenitent Councillors took the matter to the Queen, and she, a partner also, directed the order to be suspended. Drake was privately allowed to take ten thousand pounds' worth of the plunder for himself, and more for his crew. While the battle for restitution raged, the treasure gradually disappeared among the partners, who are said to have received 4700 per cent upon their capital. On this basis, the Queen's share of her investment on 1000 crowns was £11,750. Leicester and Walsingham were apportioned by royal warrant £4000 each, and Hatton £2300. On the basis of a dividend of 4700 per cent, it would appear that Hatton invested £50 in Drake's venture. These sums would have, of course, to be multiplied considerably to arrive at present-day values. Hatton's £2300 would probably be represented by £15,000 to £20,000 to-day.

The remainder of Drake's career may be studied in Sir Julian Corbett's brilliant pages, and in a later account by Dr. James A. Williamson who gathers together all the new evidence that has come to light since Corbett wrote over forty years ago. It does not concern us here. But a few words must be said of other voyages of discovery in which Hatton was interested. He was a shareholder in the voyages of Martin Frobisher to discover the North-West Passage. As in the case of Drake, he had a representative on the expedition, George Best, who was the captain of one of the ships, the *Anne Frances*, and wrote an account of Frobisher's three voyages of 1576, 1577 and 1578, dedicating the work to Hatton. Best named after Hatton the place still known as Hatton Headland on Resolution Island, south of Frobisher Bay. He records, 'and the rather for the honour the said Captain [i.e. himself] doth owe to that honourable name which himself gave thereunto the last year [1577] in the highest part of this Headland he caused his company to make a column or cross of stone, in token of Christian possession'.

George Best's account of Frobisher's voyages was published in 1578: *A True Discourse of the late Voyages of Discovery for the finding of a passage to Cathaya, by the North-West* . . . It was printed in London by Henry Bynneman, Servant to the Right Honourable Sir Christopher Hatton, Vice-Chamberlain, whose connections with his patron have already been discussed. In Best's dedication he calls Hatton 'my singular good master'.

A marginal note in Hatton's Letter Book informs us that George Best, described as a man of Hatton's, was slain in a fight by Oliver St. John (later Viscount Grandison). Hatton, we are told, was vexed because the Queen was unwilling that he should prosecute St. John for his act. On this account and 'some other hard measure offered by the Queen, very unkindly', he withdrew to Holdenby where 'he remained in great sorrow and perplexity many days'. From Holdenby he writes a letter to Elizabeth in April, 1584, in which he apologizes for withdrawing his attendance, speaks of his grief which makes him unfit to be seen by her, and acknowledges his faults. More boldly than is his wont, he adds, 'But, Madam, towards yourself leave not the causes of my presumptiousness unremembered . . . though you find them as unfit for me as unworthy of you . . . ' The marginal note informs us that at length the Queen 'was pleased to take some pity of his grief, and to send for him'.

The sums of money ventured in Frobisher's second voyage of 1577 are on record. The Queen heads the list with £500, and is followed by Burghley and Leicester, £100 each, Hatton, Sir Thomas Heneage and Edward Horsey, £50 each. In another record Hatton's contribution is given as £25.

In 1579 there is a reference to a voyage 'for the discovery of certain islands not yet trafficked in'. One of the participators, Thomas Baylye, is described as 'Servant to Sir Christopher Hatton'. He and Edward Elliott were granted letters patent in that year to discover strange islands and foreign countries. Nothing more is known of him, unless he is the Thomas Bailiff, one of Hatton's men, who in 1585 was put in charge of the Earl of Northumberland in the Tower, as narrated in a later chapter.

In June, 1578, Sir Humphrey Gilbert, Walter Ralegh's half-brother, obtained a patent empowering him to plant a colony on the Atlantic coast of North America; and under colour of this he proposed to carry out attacks on Spanish shipping and possessions, if circumstances favoured. He was ready to sail with a strong fleet in November. The expedition had little chance of success, the three months before it started having been consumed in quarrels between its leaders. Three ships under Henry Knollys refused to follow Gilbert. With the others, including one commanded by Walter Ralegh, he set forth on a voyage of which little is known. Most of the ships were back by February, 1579. Some of the particulars of the dissensions above referred to may be found in the Hakluyt Society volume of the voyages of Sir Humphrey Gilbert. Knollys was accused of piracies, and Gilbert complained of him that he had 'a store of notorious evil men about him, as Loveless and Callice'. This was John Callis, the pirate, whom we have met before. On this occasion he was in charge of the *Elephant*, one of the expedition's ships which was later Knollys's flagship, Callis being then apparently transferred to the *Swallow*. In another deposition concerning the piracies committed by Henry Knollys and Miles Morgan, it is stated that the 'pirate ship *Ermyn* otherwise the *Swallow*, appertaining to Mr. Harry Knowles', had for captain Edward Fenton, a well-known voyager, and for lieutenant Walter Spindola, and it was added that Spindola was 'Sir Christopher Hatton's man'.

In Edward Fenton's voyage to the East Indies and Cathay in 1581 Hatton was also an adventurer. There are two lists of subscribers. In the first Leicester is put down for £2200, Drake £666 13s. 4d., Hatton £250, Burghley and Walsingham £200 each; in the second Leicester's share has increased to £3000.

In 1584 there was a project to found a company to enter the lucrative Eastern trade, and Burghley drew up a memorandum of 'the charge of the Navy to the Moluccas'. The Queen is given as venturing £2000 in shipping and £10,000 in capital. Leicester contributed £3000, John Hawkins £2500, Drake and Hatton £1000 each and Ralegh £400. Hatton also subscribed towards the expedition of Essex, Drake and Norris to Cadiz in 1589, part naval operation, part marauding expedition. Hatton was now Lord Chancellor, and with Walsingham and Burghley is said to have favoured the scheme against the objections of Howard, the Lord Admiral, Ralegh and others. Of a total of nearly £52,000 said to have been subscribed, the Queen was responsible for the lion's share of £15,800. The Lord Chancellor's £1000 seems modest beside it.

That is the last we hear of Hatton's subscriptions to naval or piratical adventures. With it his connection with Drake comes to an end. But it may be permissible, if fanciful, to speculate if he concerned himself with the fate of the famous ship with which his name had been associated. In 1581, the year following Drake's return from the voyage of circumnavigation, the tall spire of St. Paul's, round which the luck of London was supposed to cling, fell in a storm. The Privy Council entrusted to Sir Christopher Hatton and Sir Walter Mildmay the duty of seeing to its re-edification. The *Golden Hind* had now become one of the sights of London, and it was agreed that she must be preserved as a memorial. From one enthusiast came the proposal that she should be set up on the broken tower of St. Paul's. It would be pleasant to hear Hatton's views on the proposed association of the metropolitan church, the famous ship and the cognizance of the Hattons. However, the visionary scheme was stillborn. The *Golden Hind* was hauled ashore and laid up in a shed at Deptford, with some Latin verses inscribed by the scholars of Winchester in Drake's memory; and St. Paul's, denied the visible emblem with which Drake had honoured his patron, had to be contented with his bones: Hatton was buried there ten years later.

CHAPTER XIX

CHURCH AND STATE

FROM the year 1577, when Hatton became a member of the Privy Council, thus adding to his former offices a direct share of responsibility for the government of the realm, he began to take an active part in public affairs. Besides his interest in foreign policy, in which his influence was naturally not comparable to that of Walsingham, the Secretary of State, he had a definite and important part to play in domestic affairs. His principal role was that of the Queen's spokesman in the Commons. In addition, he was at this time active in endeavouring to keep ecclesiastical affairs in line with Elizabeth's moderate inclinations.

To sustain his dignity as a Privy Councillor, Hatton had got possession of a suitable London residence in Ely Place, and had begun to build and improve on a large scale. To keep his accumulating papers in order, he engaged a secretary. It may be that, as he claimed, Thomas Doughty, Drake's associate, served Hatton in that capacity. That would have been at some time between 1575 and 1577. There is no doubt that Samuel Cox became his secretary in 1577 or early in 1578, and remained in that position until Hatton became Lord Chancellor in 1587. It was he who compiled Hatton's Letter Book, the foundation upon which Sir Harris Nicolas built up his life of Hatton. Something more of him will be said later.

Perhaps Hatton's first exercise of the power that office brings was his exertions on behalf of John Aylmer, who owed to him his elevation to the See of London. This fact, which was unknown to Aylmer's biographer, Strype, can be inferred from one of his letters to Hatton. It is also stated explicitly in a fragment of a damaged State Paper in the Public Record Office. The circumstances are interesting, because they raise again the question of Hatton's religion; while the development of his relations with Aylmer illustrates the ecclesiastical policy of the Queen at this time. To this policy, whatever his early religious beliefs, Hatton conformed, passing from Catholic to Protestant, though inclined to be intolerant, as his mistress was, of the Puritans. By the time of the Armada we find him voicing a full-blooded hatred and contempt of the Pope and all his works.

John Aylmer, a man of great learning, had for early patron Henry Grey, Duke of Suffolk, and was tutor to his daughter, the ill-starred Lady Jane Grey. In 1577 he was Archdeacon of Lincoln, and in March of that year was chosen for the See of London. He proved himself a bitter enemy of the Puritans. The fragmentary document, referred to above, is the deposition of April 24th, 1578, of Zachary Jones, Bachelor of Arts, a Cambridge man, who had had a conversation with one Gifford, a Cornishman, no doubt a member of one of the well-known Catholic families of that name. Gifford had recently been in touch with some Catholics imprisoned for religious offences. He remarked that, though these men were in prison, there were greater favourers of the Catholic cause at large, important personages, 'almost second in the realm', among them Sir Christopher Hatton who, he said, had made Mr. Aylmer Bishop of London in the expectation that he would persecute the Pr[esbyterians?] and Puritans. 'But', he concluded, 'the Bishop had turned his sword and power' against the papists, and when he preached before the Queen at Easter (1578) had persuaded her to give him an audience, presumably (for here the document breaks off) to ask her sanction for his policy of persecution of Puritan and Catholic alike.

Elizabeth's own inclination was towards toleration in religious matters. She would have no 'opening of windows into men's souls'; all she asked was a reasonable measure of outward conformity and loyalty to the Throne. Burghley and the other Protestant Ministers who surrounded her might press for firmer measures against the Catholics; but Elizabeth wished to make things as easy as possible for old-fashioned people, adherents of the old faith, so long as they were loyal. If Hatton were in truth a Catholic, it was certainly not counted against him in the eyes of the tolerant Queen. On the other hand she had no patience with the Puritans. She disliked their programme of a self-governing Church which would cast off the royal authority; their democratic spirit seemed to her incompatible with monarchy; and there was some justification for the complaint that she favoured the Catholics at the expense of the Puritans.

Hatton's expectation that the Bishop of London, whom he had helped to his mitre, would deal rigorously with the Puritans, was

probably more or less in line with the Queen's private wishes; at
any rate, it was not likely to be strenuously opposed by her. A
letter from the Bishop to Hatton, written in May, 1578, bears out
precisely the general tenor of Gifford's remarks quoted above.
Aylmer gives it at his opinion that it is 'safest and profitablest' to
correct offenders on both sides, Papist and Puritan. When he had
had the audience of the Queen mentioned by Gifford, he had
presumably enunciated this policy, for his letter states that 'it was
her Majesty's pleasure that I should understand her mind by you
in these things'. This passage is extremely interesting, for it shows
the important position that Hatton had attained in so weighty
a matter as the conduct of ecclesiastical policy, at any rate so far
as concerned the large and vital diocese of the powerful Bishop
whom he had sponsored. Aylmer accordingly begs Hatton for
'some direction, in a word or two, how you think good I should
deal in these matters, and then you shall see that I shall so guide
the helm as the ship shall keep the best and safest course'.

It would have been better for Aylmer if he had consulted
Hatton before he gave rein to his persecuting spirit. For it
appears from the opening of his letter that he had offended him
by the way he had dealt with friends, perhaps Catholic relations
of Hatton's, thus bearing out Gifford's statement. After rendering
him, in fulsome terms, 'most hearty thanks for that mild and calm
manner of expostulation which you used with me at our last
conference', he goes on to say, 'I will not forget to commend, both
to God in my prayers and to all men in speech, that rare conquest
that by great wisdom you have had over your affections, which
by the motions of flesh and blood must needs have been set on
fire marvellously against me, had not a natural instinct of heavenly
and Christian philosophy and wisdom quenched the flame thereof'. We may read between the lines and conclude that Hatton
had been seriously annoyed that the weapon he had prepared
against the Puritans was being turned against his Catholic friends
and relatives. And this inference is confirmed by Aylmer's next
letter to him, written in the following month. Here he shows
himself in an abject state of misery on account of Elizabeth's
displeasure: 'I study with my eyes on my book, and my mind is
in the Court; I preach without spirit; I trust not of God, but of
my Sovereign, which is God's lieutenant, and so another God
unto me — for of such it is said *Vos estis dii*; I eat without stomach,

I sleep without rest, I company without comfort, and live as one dead.' He prays also for Hatton's forgiveness, acknowledging that it was Hatton's influence that had promoted him to the See of London: 'you labour daily to your great commendation to cherish other Bishops set up by others, and will you throw down him whom you have set up yourself?'

A few days later the Bishop is excusing himself for his action against one of Hatton's Catholic friends, a certain John Roper, probably a relative of William Roper of Eltham, Kent (where Hatton was keeper of the Royal park), who married Sir Thomas More's daughter, and presumably identical with a man of that name who served under Hatton in the Queen's Guard. It appears that, by the Bishop's authority, Roper's house had been searched, and 'vestments, albes and such trumpery' found in it. Aylmer denies that he was concerned in the raid on Roper's premises: 'I was so free from the rifling of his house that, upon the receipt of your letters, I dispatched a pursuivant at midnight to call them [his officers] back.' It is evident that Hatton had been very angry with him, for he says, 'I was blamed in the hottest time of the paroxysm between you and me'.

The last letter in the Letter Book from Aylmer to Hatton reminds him of his promise to the writer, 'that I may likewise perform mine unto you; where if you should show any remissness, it may haply hurt us more than either of us is like to gain by the bargain'. The Bishop's promise to Hatton is not disclosed; it may have had some reference to his treatment of Hatton's recusant friends. But there is no doubt of what Aylmer expected. It was preferment to a See about to become vacant. He urges his patron to forward the matter with the Queen, using such arguments as:

> the crookedness of the old tired father, whom, if her Majesty do not soon ease him of this place of service, she must shortly lose him, either by death, where she can have but the bones, or by unableness of service; in which case she shall be sure deceived, and I by weariness compelled not, as the common saying is, to hang up my hatchet but, as infirmity and not lack of duty will force me, to yield up my rochet. Sir, if you will have her Majesty well served, your own creature somewhat in life preserved, and your credit kept uncracked for commending me first, and now retaining me still in state of reputation by this increase of advancement, put to your hand resolutely . . .

A marginal note in the Letter Book says that 'the old tired father', whom Aylmer wished to 'ease of his place', was Richard Cox, Bishop of Ely, the same Bishop whom Hatton had despoiled of his house in Holborn. It was certainly Ely that Aylmer wanted. There could be few bishoprics which he would consider preferment; but Ely, the richest see in the kingdom, was one of them. Cox had been agitating to retire; he died in July, 1581. But this marginal note is a misapprehension. The context shows plainly enough that 'the old tired father' was Aylmer himself. Strype's *Life* proves that Aylmer was at this time petitioning for the Bishopric of Ely, and advancing his age and feeble health as an argument for transfer to a less arduous post than London. His letter, moreover, is dated March 20th, 1581; that is March, 1582 by our reckoning, or eight months after Cox's death. It is agreeable to record that Aylmer was disappointed, for Elizabeth did not fill the vacancy at Ely for eighteen years, long after both Hatton and Aylmer were dead.

Two years before this date, when Aylmer, wearied with his turbulent years in the See of London (so turbulent that he calls London, with wry humour, not a 'see' but a 'sea') was asking for a change, the two famous Jesuits, Campion and Parsons, landed in England, the pioneers of the Counter-Reformation. These events added greatly to Aylmer's perplexities, and, it must be added, to his opportunities to display that persecuting spirit that his letters to Hatton reveal. They involved Hatton also in some degree, as well as Thomas Norton, whose fortunes touched Hatton's at several points. Norton goes down to posterity for the odious part he played in the martyrdom of the saintly Campion.

At this time the English Catholics fell into two groups. There were those who, while privately keeping their faith, frequented the Protestant churches; there were others who preferred to go to prison rather than conform. The more severe forms of persecution came later, and were directed against the Catholics, not for their religion, but for their political activities. That is, in theory; in practice things might be different. It became increasingly evident as the years passed that it was in many cases exceedingly difficult to draw the line.

The papal excommunication of Elizabeth, depriving her of her pretended title to her kingdom, releasing her subjects from their allegiance, and forbidding obedience to her laws, had placed the

English Catholics in an impossible position. As Englishmen their duty was to obey the Queen; as Catholics the Pope. Campion, who had been consulted in Rome about the effect of this Bull, declared that it had brought great evils to the Catholics, and was told that it could doubtless be mitigated so as to allow them to obey the Queen without censure. He procured an interpretation of it as in no way binding Catholics, 'while things remain as they are'; in other words, it was conditional on the existing state of affairs, but envisaged a change such as might be brought about by the endless series of plots to dethrone Elizabeth and set Mary Queen of Scots in her place. For the moment, however, the lot of the Catholics, while not easy, was not desperate. Though uncompromising Catholics were in prison they enjoyed a certain amount of indulgence. The law seems to have been loosely administered; and the lax methods of such authorities as could be influenced or bribed, provided a number of loopholes. The Catholics had a kind of club in the city of London, a 'Catholic Association', founded by George Gilbert, a wealthy young man, with headquarters at the house of Norris, the chief pursuivant of the Bishop of London. Here priests and Catholic gentlemen seem to have been able to meet together unmolested, for Norris was in Gilbert's pay, and at Lambeth, in his pay also, was Dr. Adam Squire, the unsavoury son-in-law of the Bishop himself. Such Catholics as were in prison seem to have had little difficulty in receiving visitors. Gifford's gossip with Catholic prisoners, regarding the relations of Hatton with Aylmer, illustrates this.

But however true all this might be, the time chosen for the mission of Campion and Parsons to England was, from their point of view, unfortunate. Leicester and Hatton and those other advisers of the Queen who had at first been inclined to favour the Catholics at the expense of the Puritans, were being driven by the pressure of events, such as the Northern Rebellion and its aftermath in the Ridolfi and other plots centring round the Queen of Scots, to see the logic of the position, that it was not possible to make a clear-cut distinction between Catholic religious and political activities. By 1579 Elizabeth was led to enforce a general obedience to the Act of Uniformity, and this resulted in increased imprisonment of Catholics. The French marriage proposals were unpopular with the people, who feared that the marriage would bring with it a great increase in Catholic influence, and the arrival of Campion and Parsons added to the difficulties of the French Ambassador. About the same time a joint Spanish and Papal expedition landed in Ireland, where the Deputy, Hatton's relative, Lord Grey, defeated it and put the garrison of Smerwick to the sword, a dreadful massacre (though legal according to the laws of war) at which the poet Spenser was present.

Robert Parsons arrived in England on June 11th, 1580, a fortnight before Campion. He went immediately to London to get in touch with the imprisoned Catholics there. At the Marshalsea Prison in Southwark he inquired for Thomas Pound, a Catholic who had been in confinement for many years. Pound was a man of birth. He was a nephew of Thomas Wriothesley, first Earl of Southampton; and Honora, the daughter of his brother Anthony, was married to Henry Radcliffe, fourth Earl of Sussex. He was interested in literature and the drama; and in the year 1566, when Elizabeth was present at the marriage of two of Pound's relations, Henry, Earl of Southampton to Mary Browne, daughter of Anthony, Lord Montague, and Thomas Mildmay to Frances, sister of Thomas, Earl of Sussex, two masks were performed in each of which was an oration 'spoken and pronounced' by Mr. Pound of Lincoln's Inn. He played a prominent part in the drama of Edmund Campion. He had contacts also with Hatton, with whom he had been a student at the Inns of Court. A letter from him to Hatton, which will be quoted below, shows that he had taken part in the Revels of Kenilworth during one of the Queen's progresses there, probably, in Sir Edmund Chambers's opinion, that of 1568.

Some idea of the looseness of the supervision of the imprisoned Catholics at this time may be gathered from the fact that Pound took Parsons to his room, and told him that he and the other Catholics had been praying for many days for the safe arrival of the two Jesuits. Parsons then dined with the Catholic prisoners, and visited the Catholic Club, where the plans were discussed. A fortnight later Campion arrived, and, after he had joined Parsons in London, it was decided to set forth on a mission to the shires. They agreed to meet at Hogsdon, and then to part and proceed on their several ways. Hogsdon has not apparently been identified. Simpson, in his *Life of Campion*, thought that it might be a house of Sir William Catesby in Northamptonshire. But there seems to be little doubt that it was Hoxton, near London, which, spelled Hogsdon in those days, was a manor belonging to Sir Thomas Tresham, a Northamptonshire Catholic friend and neighbour of Hatton's, whom we shall meet again. In this year 1580, Tresham with Lord Vaux, Catesby and others was arraigned before the Court of Star Chamber on a charge of contempt in refusing to swear that he had not sheltered Campion. Tresham was brother-in-law of Sir William Catesby, from whom Hatton had bought the manor of Gretton.

Just before Parsons and Campion left Hoxton, Pound came to them in hot haste. He had found means to absent himself temporarily from prison, and hastened to urge on the two Jesuit Fathers the need to do something to counter the rumours, which he declared the Council was encouraging, that their mission was a political one. He pressed them to write a declaration of the true causes of their coming to England. Hence Campion's famous tract, known familiarly as his 'Brag' or 'Challenge'. In nine points or articles he announced his mission to England to preach the Gospel and to forward the Catholic faith, and disclaimed any political intention. He went on to beg permission to argue on religion before the Privy Council; to challenge the doctors and masters of the universities to a disputation at which he invited the Queen to attend; and to justify himself also before the lawyers, spiritual and temporal. He concluded with a profession of faith and an announcement of his readiness for martyrdom. He kept a copy of this declaration and gave another to Pound, desiring that it might be kept until the need arose, but omitted to seal it, as the more businesslike Parsons had done with the declaration that he had also drawn up.

Pound, going back to London, read Campion's declaration and, in his enthusiasm, issued a challenge to two Puritan ministers, Tripp and Crowley, who used to visit the prison with a view to converting the Catholic prisoners. He wrote also petitions to the Council and to Aylmer, Bishop of London, asking for an opportunity for public debate. Pound's activities had their part in helping to persuade the authorities that there was a Catholic conspiracy on foot. He had challenged the Puritan ministers on September 8th. It was not long before he felt the heavy hand of authority. On September 18th the Bishop of London removed him to his episcopal manor of Bishop's Stortford, a half-ruined castle where he was heavily ironed and placed in solitary confinement. From his prison he sent a petition to Hatton, whom he had known in happier days, at the Inns of Court, at the Queen's Court and on royal progress at Kenilworth. Before leaving the Marshalsea, Pound, determined that Campion's Challenge should not be suppressed, had communicated it to a fellow prisoner. The Challenge passed from hand to hand and eventually came to the notice of the authorities. Hence it is that there is a file of documents preserved to-day in the London Public Record Office, which contains Pound's petitions and a copy of the Challenge.

Of all the papers in this file perhaps the most moving is Pound's letter to Hatton. It begins:

> Your noble courtesy towards me, already showed in writing so exceeding friendly to my L[ord] of London as you did of late for some favour at least towards me for your sake, although it were but for a few days respite, to have some of my debts cleared before my removing, which yet would not be granted, terming me, as you vouchsafed, your old acquaintance and companion both in Court and before in Inns of Court, doth embolden me eftsoons to beseech your honour that you will not be denied the obtaining of so much favour towards me as that my man or boy may be admitted to me in this miserable and desolate place, to bring my diet or for any other servile service for necessity of nature.

This beginning is of interest, for it illustrates Hatton's efforts to alleviate the lot of this unfortunate Catholic, and the Bishop's refusal to grant his request. It is exactly in harmony with the attitudes of Hatton and Aylmer to the Catholics, as deduced from the correspondence of the two men. It is evidence, too, of Hatton's real kindness of heart. For, although like other public figures, he was in frequent receipt of petitions of all kinds, there is a general testimony, which cannot lightly be set aside, to his generosity, in the letters of men so different as the Duke of Norfolk, John Stubbs, Thomas Churchyard and Thomas Pound, as well as of many others who approached him in matters unconnected with high affairs of State.

After this opening poor Pound breaks out, somewhat incoherently:

> Oh, God, Sir Christopher, I would you saw the spectacle of it, what a place I am brought into; here is nothing but a huge, vast room, cold water, bare walls, no windows but loopholes too high to look out at; nor bed, nor bedstead, nor place very fit for any,

nor chimney, nor table, nor light almost for any but the homeliest things; in the midst of the house a huge pair of stocks, such a pair of virginals as made my poor boy to see, although far too big either for his fingering or footing all athwart my cold harbour; and nothing else but chains enough which yet I am not worthy of. And if there were neither meat nor drink, neither for love nor money, then the end would be but short.

He concludes:

... well hoping if your honour will vouchsafe to present my petition that her Highness will not be so vanquished by her vassal [i.e. the Bishop] but that even for her poetical presents sake, which her Majesty disdained not to take at poor Mercury's hand, if you remember it, at Killingeworth Castle, she will now vouchsafe of her princely good nature to give me as good a gift again for double requital thereof as this suit comes to, especially knowing as her Highness well doth, what is written, that it is a blesseder thing to give than to take, wherein I humbly beseech your honour, at your wisdom and discretion, to try once more what stead you can stand me in, according to your goodwill, whereby for ever you shall bind me more and more unto. At Starford, before my entering, the 18th of September, 1580. Your servant to God in daily prayer, Thomas Poundes.

Alarmed by the successes of the Jesuits, Parliament met in January, 1581, to pass an 'Act to retain the Queen's Majesty's subjects in their due obedience'. Thomas Norton seconded the moving of the Bill. We have met this gloomy Puritan before as the part author of *Gorboduc,* in which Hatton probably acted before the Queen in his student days. As Counsel for the Stationers' Company, Norton was an expert of the *provenance* of religious and seditious books and tracts which were being circulated at this time; he played a more unfavourable part in endeavouring to extract confessions by torture from the captive Catholics. In the endeavour to find where Parsons printed his books, a priest named Alexander Briant was racked. When later Norton was called to account, as one of the commission of inquiry which had caused Briant and Campion to be racked, he admitted the charge which Parsons had made against him of saying to Briant that, if he would not for his duty to God and the Queen tell the truth, 'he should be made a foot longer than God had made him'. If in general Norton was doing no more than he had been ordered to do and was made a scapegoat after the Elizabethan fashion, he cannot be forgiven for the cruel, persecuting spirit which earned him the name of the 'rackmaster'.

The history of Edmund Campion does not belong to these pages, and it cannot be pursued here farther than it touches Hatton. That contact did not, apparently, amount to a great deal, at any rate so far as Hatton as a private individual is concerned, though as a member of the Privy Council he shared responsibility for the Government's attitude towards the Jesuits. When Campion was finally taken in 1581 and sent to the Tower, Norton was one of the commission appointed to examine him, being ordered by the Privy Council to proceed to racking him if he refused to answer concerning his relations with other Catholics and the places where he had been harboured and had celebrated Mass.

Before Campion suffered, he had his wish, a public disputation in which, whatever faith we profess, we must realize that the scales were heavily tipped against him. Pound, to his delight, was present to hear his beloved master, denied resort to books or authorities, 'worn with the rack, his memory destroyed, and his force of mind almost extinguished', debate with a number of learned adversaries. The ardent Pound, for his 'odious interpellations' and his 'most scornful looks through his fingers' at Dean Nowell, called forth from that dignitary the angry ejaculation, *os impudens*, at one that dared to cock a snook at him.

Hatton cannot be held to have had any special responsibility for the trial and martyrdom of Campion. He has the responsibility that attaches to a member of the Privy Council, no more, no less. It is a perfectly good defence of the general Elizabethan treatment of the Catholics that harshness was forced on the authorities by the policy of the Pope, bent upon converting Catholics to traitors, and by the determination of the Jesuits to make martyrs. Such an argument Burghley advanced in a tract which he published after Campion's death. This defence historians have labelled despicable or just, according to their proclivities. Yet it is impossible to justify the torture and execution of Campion; and the passages which Burghley transcribed from Norton's letters defending his methods with the rack, do not add to the strength of the Government's case. And on the general subject of torture, it may be said that, clever as they were, the Elizabethans did not appreciate that the rack was no infallible discoverer of truth. It might and often did succeed in extorting from reluctant lips the details of a plot; as often may it not have persuaded its victim to declare what authority demanded of him?

> Ay, but I fear you speak upon the rack,
> Where men enforcèd do speak anything.

Burghley, though he connived at making scapegoats of Norton, 'the Rackmaster', and of Hopton, the Lieutenant of the Tower, saw to it that Norton did not suffer too much. Hatton too stayed his friend. By April, 1582, he was out of prison. In a letter of thanks to Hatton he shows that it was due to him and Burghley that the Queen had been moved to release him. Hatton, in fact, had probably the greater part in securing his release, and there is again evidence of his sense of justice and kindness of heart in his dealings with Norton. For, however odious Norton's conduct was, he was obeying commands, though willingly enough. He writes to say that since his release from prison he has learnt of Hatton's 'great pity' towards him and of 'the comfort that my poor wife received of your gracious speeches in my heavy extremity'.

But, if Hatton showed compassion in his dealings with Norton, that is not to say that he personally approved the racking of Catholics for their religion. The rack, in theory at any rate, was not used against Catholics as Catholics, but only against such as were proved or were held to be traitors. For the distinction between Catholicism as a faith and Catholicism as a department of politics, though wearing thin, was still recognized. Men like Sir Thomas Tresham suffered heavily for their faith, but their loyalty being as unimpeachable as their Catholicism, their sufferings were limited to fines, unbearably heavy it is true, and imprisonment or confinement in their homes. Hatton drew the distinction when he laid down the rule quoted by Camden as his, that in the cause of religion 'neither searing nor cutting was to be used'. His Catholic sympathies were undeniable, and though his position as a statesman of a country threatened by enemies fostered by Rome, forced him to say many hard things of the Pope, there is no evidence that he felt any of that prejudice towards Catholicism that Walsingham and Leicester had. It is difficult to find any example of hostility on Hatton's part to a Catholic because of his faith; on the contrary, up to the date of

Mary's execution, if not later, there are numerous records of Catholics who were Hatton's friends.

At any rate there is nothing in Hatton's attitude towards Catholics at all analogous to the real animus that he, in company with the Queen and Archbishop Whitgift, felt against the Puritans. Yet it seems undeniable that the passage of the years and the development of the political situation gradually weaned him from any Catholicism, even in name, that he had once held. He had, indeed, as Father Crichton wittily put it, been deflected from his orbit by the more powerful motion of the Elizabethan heavens of which he formed part. David Lloyd, though not a contemporary witness, writing eighty years after his death, probably sums up accurately his religious outlook when he says that he stood for the Church against the enemies of both sides. He stood in fact for the Elizabethan settlement.

CHAPTER XX

THE TRESHAMS AND OTHER CATHOLICS

HATTON's Catholic upbringing and the sympathies with the old faith, which remained with him throughout the greater part of his life, explain his many friendships with individual Catholics. And his tolerant nature allowed him to retain such friendships even when the Catholics were under a cloud and held in the greatest suspicion.

A Catholic friend, with whom he had close dealings, was Sir Thomas Tresham, a member of an ancient Northamptonshire house. Neighbours in the county, the two families were very intimate, and may indeed have been related. Sir Thomas's great-great-grandfather, another Sir Thomas Tresham, Speaker of the House of Commons, who died in 1471, married Margaret, daughter of William, Lord Zouch of Harringworth; and Hatton's ancestors the Holdenbys quartered the arms of Zouch. But he and Tresham in their letters do not recognize any relationship.

Sir Thomas Tresham, whose mother was a Catesby, a family mostly Catholic, was nevertheless brought up as a Protestant. He is said to have been converted to Catholicism in 1580 by Robert Parsons, the Jesuit; and in 1581, as before related, was summoned before the Council and committed to the Fleet, for harbouring Parsons' fellow Jesuit, Edmund Campion. He was tried before the Star Chamber, and as a result remained in custody for seven years. After this he was constantly in prison for recusancy, but though a staunch Catholic, there seems to have been no question of his loyalty.

Tresham is best remembered to-day for his extensive building operations, which brought him on one occasion into an interesting relationship with Hatton. Rushton Hall in Northamptonshire was the Tresham family seat; and here over a hundred years ago, in pulling down a very thick partition wall in the passage leading from the Great Hall, was discovered in a large recess an enormous bundle containing manuscripts and some theological books wrapped in a large sheet. These papers were probably walled up at the time of the Gunpowder Plot in 1605, when Francis, Sir Thomas Tresham's eldest son, was arrested for the part he had played in it. They were calendared by Mrs. Lomas for the Historical Manuscripts Commission. They contain some interesting letters which concern Hatton and relate to circumstances which are alluded to also in the Hatton Letter Book.

The first letter addressed to Hatton in this collection was written from prison by Sir Thomas Tresham in February, 1582, Hatton being then in attendance on the Queen at Canterbury. It concerns the affairs of his younger brother William Tresham. The writer acknowledges the great kindness which this brother had received from Hatton, 'his dear good friend', and recalls how Hatton had befriended him, in prison and at liberty, in the country and at Court, in his youth and in his maturity; how he had contrived to free him from imprisonment for an offence not specified; how, when disgraced, he had restored him to the Queen's favour and helped him to a position at Court, securing for him at his own charges the post of Gentleman Pensioner. It appears from this letter that William Tresham had suddenly left England a month before, without applying for the customary permission from the Queen for leave to travel abroad. Sir Thomas is consequently full of apologies for his brother's misconduct and want of proper gratitude to his benefactors, the Queen and Hatton, while on his own account he laments the fact that the runaway owes him no less than £600.

In letters addressed to Sir Thomas Tresham's wife, to the Queen, the Privy Council and to Hatton, William Tresham gives as the principal reason for his sudden decision to leave England the enmity towards him of the Earl of Leicester. For years, he says, he has sought to gain Leicester's good opinion, or even to learn what his offence is, but without avail. Now he fears that there is nothing left for him but to go abroad. Also he feels that the presence of one out of favour at Court is prejudicial to his brother; but Sir Thomas, in relating all this to Burghley, feels that his brother has done him a worse injury by going away in debt to him.

The letter that William Tresham wrote to Hatton survives in the Hatton Letter Book. It is without place or date, but internal evidence shows that it was written after his flight and before a most interesting interview between Sir Thomas and Samuel Cox,

Hatton's secretary, in March, 1582, for Cox quotes some of the phrases of that letter. It is full of reproaches for unkindness shown by Hatton to the writer, who protests that he has not deserved such treatment. No man, he says, ever bore more perfect affection to another man than William Tresham to Sir Christopher Hatton, 'long and faithful before he was a Counsellor', that is, before 1577, 'and never ceased (oh that I am enforced to declare it!) until so strangely I was rejected'. This change in Hatton's attitude he ascribes to Leicester's influence. If Tresham knew no reason for Leicester's ill will, we can do no more than guess at it. He had been a member of Gilbert's Catholic Association and was an ardent Catholic, to whom the ultra-Protestant Leicester was an object of dislike, and it is probable that Leicester returned that dislike. A man so slandered by the Catholics (*Leycester's Commonwealth* was published two years later) could scarcely be expected to look with favour on the more politically minded members of that Church.

Proceeding, William Tresham goes on to warn Hatton against Leicester. Hatton, he says, knows that 'he affecteth you only to serve his own turn'. 'Take heed of him in time!' he continues. 'I speak it for goodwill; and all the harm I wish you is that you will, with the eyes of wisdom, look into him thoroughly; and then you shall find that he knoweth only to gain friends, and hath not the good regard or grace to keep them.' He asks little for himself, he protests, but begs that Hatton may incline favourably towards his 'poor brother, detained now in prison for the remorse and liberty of conscience'.

Then comes a passage worth quoting for its echoes of the euphuistic phrases of the time (Lyly's *Euphues* had been published four years before):

> I pray you, Sir, remember that the bee gathereth honey of every flower, and of many travails frameth a sweet and comfortable being for herself and young ones all the cold winter; but the grasshopper all the summer-time joyeth with gallantry in the pleasant meadows, and dieth commonly with the cold dew of Bartholomew. You know that the high cedar-trees on the tops of huge mountains are most subject to the danger of storms, and therefore have most need of many and sure roots. We are all in God's hands, to be raised or pulled down as it shall please Him; and there is none so high now, but may one day, through affliction, stand in as great

need of comfort as now my poor brother and your dear friend doth.
I beseech you to think of him, and vouchsafe to bind us and our
posterity unto you by the goodness that you may now afford him
in furthering his enlargement. The day may come that you may
find either him or his better able than now they are to acknowledge in all good sort, and thankfully to requite your kindness. . .

This homily gave great offence to Hatton, as is shown by a
memorandum which Thomas Tresham kept of his conversation
with Samuel Cox, Hatton's secretary, whom he had sent to discuss
with Sir Thomas the behaviour of his brother. Tresham had just
risen from table, where he was dining in the Fleet, when 'Mr.
Cox, secretary to Mr. Vice-Chamberlain' arrived, saying he had
a message from his master. Sir Thomas took him aside into a
cupboard behind the portal, and Cox began, saying that Hatton
was right sorrowful that he must add to Sir Thomas's many
crosses, but knew he would endure all patiently, and in time
'wear them all out'.

What Cox had to say could not, he intimated, be put into a
few words; and so Tresham took him into his chamber and gave
him a stool, while (stools being somewhat scarce) he himself sat
at the foot of his bed. Being seated, Mr. Cox very courteously
began in the pompous and sententious manner of which other
specimens may be found in the chapter which it has been thought
fitting to devote to that worthy man:

> I shall not need particularly to ransack the error that your brother
> hath lately committed by his unadvised departure from the Court,
> from her Majesty's service, yea, and from his native country, or to
> say how unkindly my master did take it, or how offensively her
> Majesty was therewith displeased. . . .

A graver fault of William Tresham's, Cox intimated, was the tone
of his letters to the Queen, the Privy Council and Hatton. He
had greatly annoyed the Queen by his letter to her, and to
Hatton his message was such 'that had I not well known his hand,
I would never have thought Mr. William Tresame, with whom I
was so specially acquainted withal, would have written such a one
to my master, his dear good friend and always lover'. So peevish,
despiteful and false was it that, in Cox's words, Hatton scarce had
patience to listen to it.

The charges against Hatton of ingratitude, the claim that he was beholden to the Tresham family and had done little for them, and the reflection that perhaps they would one day be in a position to do more for him than he had done for them, upset Hatton considerably: 'my master much wondereth to be threatened with that family which he always hath so loved'. Cox went on to say that Tresham untruly accused Hatton of calling him a papist galliard. 'Galliard' is a gay fellow, a man of fashion, and the phrase perhaps means a Catholic *poseur*. But this accusation is not made in the letter from which extracts have been given above, though the next count of Cox's indictment is taken directly from it, 'he offereth my master very unseemly and proud speeches; that he is like a grasshopper, who flourisheth in the summer's heat, and yet is killed with the first Bartlemew dew'. Hatton took all this unkindly, saying to Cox, 'to whom can I think to deserve well when William Tresham, whom I reputed to be my faithful good friend, doth challenge me of discourtesy and ingratitude, and withal that he should threaten me with some adversity in short time, and that I was but like a grasshopper'. If adversity should come to him, Hatton protested, the world should find him 'no such fainting thing' as a grasshopper. But he bore no lasting resentment, and told Cox to assure Sir Thomas that he was anxious to restore his brother to the Queen's favour, and that he had written to the culprit urging him to return, apologizing for any oversight he had committed.

That is all we hear in this correspondence of William Tresham. In the State Papers and accounts of Catholic refugees abroad there are many notices of him. He did not return to England until 1603, when Elizabeth was dead. Meanwhile, a year after the interview with Cox, Sir Thomas Tresham wrote again from the Fleet to Hatton, saying he had paid all his fines and served the uttermost legal sentence for his recusancy, and begging Hatton's intercession with the Queen for his release, protesting the loyalty of himself and his ancestors during hundreds of years.

Shortly after the date of this letter Sir Thomas was released on bond not to come within four miles of London, but as a result of his wife's intercession, he was eventually allowed to live in his own house at Hoxton, and from there a number of his letters were written. One of these in the year 1583 is addressed to Hatton, whom with Leicester and others of the Privy Council he petitioned that he might remove to his house at Westminster. To the letter to Hatton he adds thanks for past kindnesses, 'and especially for that to which the very stones bear witness', Hatton's gift of a pit of freestone in his quarry at Weldon for the finishing of Rothwell Cross, which stands in the highway midway between Hatton's 'two stately edifices, as a witness of the bounty of happy Holdenby to ruinous Rushton'. Hatton's two houses are Kirby and Holdenby. Weldon is near the former, and Rothwell, to the south of Rushton, lies between the two Hatton estates.

This letter is of considerable interest. Sir Thomas Tresham was famous for his building operations, of which a good deal can be read in Mrs. Lomas's introduction to the Tresham Papers, already referred to, and in Mr. J. Alfred Gotch's book, *The Buildings of Sir Thomas Tresham*. The first building he took in hand was Rothwell Market House, otherwise called Rothwell Cross. It was built in 1578 and, as this letter shows, some of the stone for it was given to Tresham by Sir Christopher Hatton from his quarry at Weldon.

Six years after Hatton's death Tresham was still building away. Several notable buildings had been completed, and he was now busy on the New Building at Lyveden. In 1597 he wrote a long, detailed letter to his head man there about the building and the laying out of the beautiful gardens. All the stone possible, he directed, was to be got from Pilton and Weldon, which shows that he was still making use of Hatton's quarry. He draws a distinction between the freestone of Weldon and the 'perfect hard stone of Pilton pits', which is stronger and able to carry a better polish. We have no means of knowing of what stone Holdenby was built, but it seems probable that it was of Weldon stone; and this distinction is interesting. The directions for laying out the gardens at Lyveden are also of interest, as they show the minute control of detail which Tresham exercised, and his knowledge of horticulture and landscape gardening. More roses are to be grown, both damask and red; the birch arbour is to be repaired, and he remembers that one of his ditchers is an expert in setting birches; and there are other directions concerning the gardens and orchards, the staking of trees, the grafting of stocks and nuts and the planting of arbours. On this last point he says that if his men cannot well manage the arbours, his sister [Lady Vaux of Harrowden, about ten miles from Holdenby] has a gardener who was bred up under the priest (who lately died and excelled in gardening work) in Holdenby works, and that they may do well to use him, as he is accounted a very honest man. This priest can almost certainly be identified with Hugh Hall, who was involved in Somerville's plot to kill the Queen, as described in a later chapter. For *Leycester's Commonwealth* calls him Hatton's priest; and that he was the priest who excelled in gardening work at Holdenby and trained a gardener there is practically proved by Hall's own statement. He said, under examination, that he had resided fourteen years with Mr. John Talbot, Sir John Throckmorton, Lord Windsor and Mr. Ralph Sheldon. John Talbot was of Grafton, Worcestershire, and the Grafton Estate Book for the years 1568-9 mentions Mr. Hall's chamber there, and, most significant, that he was twice paid 40s. by Talbot 'for his pains taken in the garden at Grafton'. In 1580, Hugh Hall, priest, was a visitor to Rheims, according to the Douai Diaries. He presumably then went to Holdenby to lay out the gardens. Holdenby was finished in 1583, the year when Hall was busy in the Somerville Plot. He was in prison for this treason in 1585, according to the prison lists, and may well have died there, being lately dead in Tresham's letter dated 1597. But whatever the priest's identity, this letter throws a welcome light both on Hatton's gardening tastes and his Catholic sympathies.

Ralph Dutton of Hatton in Cheshire had a certain Catholic connection through his wife's family, the Townsends. We have already met one of Dutton's brothers-in-law, Henry Townsend, who persuaded Dutton to take an interest in Hatton's search for a pedigree and to assist his genealogical agent, Laurence Bostock, in his investigations. Another brother-in-law, Robert Townsend of Ludlow, together with Ralph Dutton himself, got into trouble in the year 1581 over their relations with Campion. It appears that Townsend's sister was the mother of George Gilbert, the young Catholic gentleman who with Thomas Pound had founded the 'Catholic Association' for assisting Campion and Parsons on their arrival in England. Gilbert had been on the Continent in 1579, when he was reconciled to the Catholic Church by Parsons, and it may be that Parsons suggested to him the idea of the Association. At any rate, on his return to England, Gilbert founded it. It was blessed by the Pope, and was in being when the two Jesuits landed in 1580. Its members were young men of family and property, unencumbered by wives or office, and so free to devote themselves to fostering the Jesuits' campaign. In the list of its members, as Froude notes, may be read the names of Charles Arundel, Francis Throckmorton, Anthony Babington, Chidiock Tichbourne, Charles Tilney, Edward Habington, Thomas Salusbury and William Tresham. The story of Tresham, the Gentleman Pensioner and Hatton's protégé, has been told above; Arundel, extensively mixed up with the Catholic plots, we shall meet later; as we shall the others, who were all conspirators in the Babington Plot.

It was alleged that Robert Townsend had brought both Campion and Gilbert to the house of his brother-in-law Ralph Dutton of Hatton. Commissioners were sent to Hatton in March, 1581, to inquire. Both Townsend and Dutton denied any knowledge of the matter. Townsend admitted that he had seen his nephew for three days in the previous summer, but did not know that he was acquainted with Campion, whom he had never met. The records tell us no more, but it may be surmised that he protested a little too much. He may have been completely innocent, but he could scarcely have been quite unaware of his nephew's notorious activities. Gilbert had withdrawn to Rheims, and died two years later. He is remembered for the frescoes of English martyrs which he caused to be made at great expense for the walls of the English College in Rome.

When Christopher Hatton 'called cousins' with Ralph Dutton of Hatton, he also embraced the elder branch of the family, Duttons of Dutton. They too were Catholics. Both John Dutton of Dutton and Rowland Dutton of Hatton are included (in a State paper of date? 1580) among thirteen people in Cheshire 'whose houses are greatly infected with Popery'. It appears that Christopher Hatton had taken Peter, the son of John Dutton of Dutton, into his service. In a graceful letter written to John Dutton from the Court of St. James's in 1583, Hatton thanks his correspondent for placing his son in his service. Peter Dutton had been travelling abroad at Hatton's wish and with the Queen's approval, with a view probably of acquiring a knowledge of foreign affairs and fitting himself for public life. Hatton speaks of the experience Peter had gained and doubts not 'he will perform honestly in every point to his own credit and commendation, and in time do much honour and reputation to the House he cometh of'. Perhaps the father had some misgivings about his son's absence from home, for Hatton is at pains to recommend Peter to his father and to beg a continuance of his favour. He concludes:

> After he hath been with you for a while, and discharged some part of his duty by presence towards you, in case I may perceive in him any desire to follow the life of a courtier yet for a time, he shall have my best furtherance for his preferment, doubt you not, as occasion shall be offered; accounting that whatsoever I shall do for him I shall do for one of my best friends and kinsmen. I pray you, Sir, once again, cherish him and make much of him for my sake. . . .

That there may have been an estrangement between father and son seems the more likely from the fact that Dutton and his wife were at odds. In the following year Hatton writes to the Bishop of Chester about the suit pending before the Bishop between 'my very good friends, Mr. John Dutton of Dutton and Mrs. Eleanor his wife, upon certain complaints which she hath lately exhibited against him'. For the sake of his alliance and good friendship he begs the Bishop to see if something may not be done to reconcile them: 'Your Lordship knoweth how ungodly a course of proceeding this is between man and wife, like to breed utter discredit to them both if it should go forward as it hath begun.' But if the suit must proceed, he requests that steps may be taken to secure that there may be no obloquy 'to touch the name of Mr. Dutton, which otherwise would leave too great a scar in his credit and reputation, being a principal gentleman of the Shire, who may hardly endure any such disgrace. . . .'

Here we may leave the Duttons of Hatton and those of Dutton, with whom Hatton claimed alliance across the centuries, and whom he certainly seems to have befriended to the best of his ability.

Another instance of Hatton's tenderness for Catholics and of his kindly nature is his letter to the Earl of Derby and the Bishop of Chester on behalf of Lady Egerton of Ridley, who is to appear before the Bishop on account of her religion. Hatton says he is credibly given to understand that 'upon a certain preciseness of conscience incident to divers of her sex', she has not always conformed as she should have done, but in other respects is very dutiful and of good behaviour, and is deserving of compassion as she is very old and in bad health. And here may be added another of the numerous letters from desolate and oppressed persons which testify directly or indirectly to his kindly nature. Margaret Countess of Derby, was a granddaughter of Mary Tudor, sister of Henry VIII. She was thus the Queen's first cousin once removed. Like others of her relations, she was looked upon with some suspicion by Elizabeth and had been kept under surveillance. About the year 1580 she wrote to the Queen and to Walsingham, and also sent three letters to Hatton. It appears that, through Hatton's mediation, this unfortunate lady had been allowed some liberty. In gratitude she writes to him:

> You are the sole person in Court that hath taken compassion on me, and hath given comfort unto my careful heart and, under God, kept life itself within my breast. All these noble kindnesses are derived from your virtue and good favour towards me, a poor, wretched, abandoned lady, no way able to yield you thankfulness worthy thereof. You are the rock I build on.

CHAPTER XXI

MONOPOLIES: TIPPER'S PATENT

THE granting of monopolies to private individuals was one of the most characteristic features and, it may be added, one of the scandals of Elizabethan life. Courtiers, as such, naturally received no salaries. But most courtiers held positions about the Queen's person or in the various offices of State; and such people, if they got anything at all, were paid at the rates which, fixed in medieval times, had become quite inadequate. There is an amusing story told of Dr. Valentine Dale, who was appointed Ambassador in France at a salary of a pound a day. He pretended to be overwhelmed with gratitude; he could not spend, he said, above nineteen shillings daily, and he would be able to send home the remaining shilling for the support of his wife and family. Froude sums up the financial position of Elizabeth's Ministers, and shows plainly that their emoluments were very far from commensurate with the expenditure expected of them:

> Walsingham spent his private fortune in his office, and ruined himself. Sir Henry Sidney declined a peerage, his viceroyalty in Ireland having left him crippled with debt. Sir James Crofts excused his accepting a pension from Spain, on the ground that the Queen allowed him nothing as Controller of her Household. Lord Burghley has left on record in his own hand-writing that the grants which he had received from his mistress had not covered his expenses in attending upon her: that he had sold lands of his own to maintain his state at Court, and that the fees of his Treasurership did not equal the cost of his stable.

And the historian goes on to contrast Elizabeth's parsimony where her Ministers were concerned with the largess which she lavished upon her favourites and flatterers, such as Leicester and Hatton: grants of lands, high places about the Court and the bestowal of monopolies.

Froude is no admirer of Hatton, whose career he had not studied with either care or sympathy. The balance has been redressed in recent years by less prejudiced writers, such as Dr. Conyers Read and Professor Neale, who recognize Hatton's abilities and his devotion to duty. Here it is enough to point out that Hatton was an official as well as a courtier; and that his fees as Vice-Chamberlain, £66 13s. 4d. a year, perhaps representing £500 of our money, were absurdly inadequate to the establishment he was compelled to keep. The life led by the courtier was an expensive one, and the higher he climbed the more elaborate had to be his way of living. Men of no private wealth, like Hatton or his friend Edward Dyer, men who held but a hereditary manor or two, were chronically in debt; and if, like Hatton, they added building on a large scale to their other extravagances, might easily go the way of insolvency. The Queen might make a loan here and there, but the loan had to be repaid; and such obligations were a constant embarrassment. Hatton, who had to cut a special figure in his various employments about Elizabeth's person, could not be expected to manage on his salary as Vice-Chamberlain, supplemented by the rents of his one manor. Hence, to enable him to live up to his position, the Queen made him frequent grants of lands and keeperships of royal parks and, more remarkable still, an annuity of £400 a year, quite a comfortable income for the period. And yet he was £10,000 in debt in 1575, and died sixteen years later owing the Queen £42,000.

For, whatever grants the more favoured courtiers might receive, the need for ready money was insistent, and Elizabeth, recognizing this, and having no fund from which the demands of her impecunious officials might be met, had recourse to the granting of monopolies, a method developed by the Tudors and carried by her to its climax. Just as many countries to-day raise money by making certain commodities State monopolies, so in Elizabethan times a monopoly of the manufacture or sale of some article, or of a tax or privilege, was conferred upon a private individual. Trade and commerce were so regimented during the Middle Ages that there was no difficulty in the Tudor period, which inherited these regulations, in tapping an industry for the benefit of any selected individual. The grantee of the monopoly levied a toll on the commodity concerned. Usually he did this by farming out his monopoly for a lump sum to an agent who reimbursed himself by levying such a toll. Or a man might be given a patent which placed him in virtual control of an industry, enabling him to grant licences for following it, and to relax for a consideration some of the hampering medieval regulations with which such a craft was hedged about. So Dyer had a patent for the tanning of leather, with power to license tanners and remit restrictions. Again, a Government tax, such as the customs duties, might be farmed to an official, Walsingham in this case, who paid the Crown a fixed sum and made what profit he could from the taxes levied.

Hatton was in possession of some grants of this kind. The earliest that has been traced was a licence to import a certain amount of yarn from Ireland. This expired about the year 1576, and was not apparently renewed. The Irish Deputy, Sir Henry Sidney, set his face against such transactions. He had been responsible for placing upon the Irish Statute Book a law to keep the manufacture of cloth in that country; and when Hatton's licence, 'the granting whereof was thought to be of no benefit', to Ireland, lapsed, he was reluctant to see it resurrected. Another grant which Hatton had was the impost or customs dues on wines, all wines apparently. Essex and Ralegh after him, towards the end of the reign, had a similar patent for sweet wines. Hatton's grant was for a term of years only, for he writes to Burghley in July, 1580, to say that his term in the impost of wines is due to expire at the end of the year, and to pray Burghley's intercession with the Queen for its renewal, thanking him for his great goodness and favour, and acknowledging that the recovery of his fortunes, 'in effect all entirely ruined', was due to him.

There seems to be no record other than these of the possession of a monopoly by Hatton. But he was behind the efforts of a man named William Tipper, a merchant and citizen of London, to obtain a grant of an unusual kind; and we may, with some confidence, believe that for the time that Tipper's patent was in operation Hatton enjoyed a commission for his backing in securing it. Hatton, in spite of his immense debts, was launching out on new commitments; his building schemes at Holdenby and Ely Place, and his share in financing Drake's and other voyages. His need for money was imperative; and Tipper's scheme, backed by the City of London and needing only the influence which Hatton could bring to bear, seemed to promise large profits.

William Tipper, according to a statement he made as a witness in a lawsuit of the year 1578, was a London grocer, then aged thirty-five. He had other connections with the Grocers' Company. He had been a servant to Lady Laxton, widow of Sir

William Laxton of Oundle, Northamptonshire, the founder of the famous school. Lady Laxton's daughter by a former marriage was the third wife of Sir Thomas Lodge, the father of the dramatist. So that Tipper, presumably, had some influence in the City of London, while his Northamptonshire connections may possibly have brought him to Hatton's notice. It was two years before this time that he approached Hatton and the City authorities.

His proposal was to revive the ancient laws of 'hosting', or 'hostage' of merchant strangers, which had long fallen into disuse. By hosting was meant the obligation of a foreign merchant coming to England to lodge with an English merchant who was called his host. In this way the trading communities of London and the other cities could ensure that foreign merchants did not infringe the laws by which English trade and industry were regulated, and could also keep a check on the foreigners' activities. These laws of hosting were made in the interest of the great City Companies, in which commerce and industry were vested as a close preserve; but, though embodied in successive Acts of Parliament, they had not been in operation for years, perhaps for centuries. But, if the Government had ceased to enforce them, they remained a part of the law and custom of the City of London, which endeavoured from time to time to revive them; and, according to Tipper, they were actually in operation in the City of Newcastle-on-Tyne.

There is in the London Public Record Office a neat manuscript book, in which the details of Tipper's case are set forth: his arguments for the justice and expediency of the grant he sought; the terms of the patent he was given on the recommendation of Hatton, whose dependant he was; the protests against the grant made by English companies, such as the Merchant Adventurers and the Company of Merchants trading to Spain and Portugal; the remonstrances of the rulers of the Netherlands, whose merchants were especially affected by the proposed regulations; the opinions of the Judge of the Admiralty and other advisers of the Crown, and of Sir Thomas Smith, one of the Queen's Principal Secretaries. The whole forms a most curious chapter in the story of Elizabethan commercial policy, and is well worth the attention of economic historians.

This file of papers shows that it was through the influence of Hatton, at that time Captain of the Guard, that Tipper in the year 1576 secured a grant from the Crown of the privilege of hosting merchant strangers throughout England, except Italian merchants and those of the Hanseatic League or Steelyard. Later, Spanish merchants were also excluded. At the same time he secured a grant from the City of London, which claimed the privilege of issuing such licences within its liberties. It appears that the City had previously given a grant of hostage to one Hunte, a fishmonger and citizen of London, but nothing more is known of this, and it may be presumed that it was never enforced. The file of papers opens with a statement that Tipper had petitioned the Mayor and Aldermen of London, whereupon they wrote to Hatton to say that Tipper had approached them, that they were well disposed to make the grant to him, 'and the rather for your Worship's sake, whose goodness towards him he most thankfully reporteth'.

There follows a reasoned statement of the causes which moved the Mayor and Aldermen to desire a renewal of these laws, 'and now finding the time convenient and the matter most needful to be executed, we most earnestly requested the Right Worshipful Mr. Christopher Hatton to deal with Her Majesty for the same', that she might make a grant of hostage throughout England to William Tipper of London, merchant, as the Mayor and Aldermen had done for London. It appears therefore that Hatton, Tipper and the City were working together in the matter, and we may presume that Hatton expected to reap some of the benefits of Tipper's patent. The reasons set forth by the City are of the familiar kind, arising from jealousy of the foreign merchants. In particular, it was alleged that these merchants had not confined themselves to the role of wholesale importers and exporters, but had sought a share of the retail trade which was the prerogative of the freemen of the City. They were also accused of raising prices and evading customs dues.

For the privilege of having this patent, Tipper paid the Crown forty shillings a year. His own remuneration was that laid down in the ancient statutes, twopence in every pound's worth of goods bought or sold by the foreign merchants. Apart from the imposition of this tax, the arrangement seemed to the foreigner, and especially to the merchants from the Netherlands, to whom the exemption of others practically confined it, a monstrous interference with their trade and liberty; and they argued, not without justice, that it was contrary to the provisions of various commercial treaties, dating back to the Treaty of the Intercourse of 1495, the famous *Intercursus Magnus*.

When Tipper's patent came for sealing before Sir Thomas Smith, the Secretary, that experienced official not unnaturally took the view that it was illegal. 'This office' [of hostager], he writes, 'seemeth new and strange to me and contrary to our leagues made with the Low Countries and with France . . . How would we like that one man should lodge all Englishmen throughout all France or Spain?' He held the grant to be contrary to Magna Carta and to all humanity. 'Indeed, I like not monopolies', he adds, 'for they be to the monopolyer tyrannical, to all other servitude and bondage.' This letter seems to have been written to Hatton, for he says he had deferred sealing the patent 'until I had advertised you of it, which now I send you herewith, if you think so good to move her Majesty in it, or else to cause it to be sealed'. For his part, his conscience will not suffer him to seal it until he is better persuaded of its legality.

To this, as to other objections, Tipper replied to the effect that the laws of hosting had never been repealed and that, though they might have fallen into disuse, they could be enforced at any time at the will of the Crown; and that his patent did not infringe any commercial treaty, for those treaties only reaffirmed the arrangements already in force, which included these unrepealed laws. He affirmed also that similar laws of hosting were in force in Spain, Denmark, Hamburg and partly in Flanders. Petitions from the English Company of Merchants trading to Spain and Portugal and from the merchants of the Netherlands followed. Tipper obtained a favourable judgment from the Judge of the Admiralty, Dr. David Lewes and from Dr. William Aubrey, a cousin of John Dee the astrologer and grandfather of John Aubrey the biographer, to the effect that no article of the *Intercursus Magnus*, the treaty with the Netherlands concluded in 1495, was infringed by his patent.

The Netherlands Government then took action, and their Ambassador in London made representations. Dr. Lewes and Dr. Aubrey were ordered by the Council to answer him. They advanced their interpretation of the *Intercursus*, as before; but the Ambassador remained unsatisfied, principally because the merchants of the Steelyard or Hanseatic League, the Italians and the

Spaniards were excepted from the scope of Tipper's patent. To this the two lawyers replied that the Hanse merchants had had from ancient times a house of their own in London, while the Italians and Spaniards were so few in number that there was no need to deal with them in that way.

But, in spite of this favourable legal opinion, Tipper found great difficulty in enforcing the terms of his patent. Having complained to Bacon, the Lord Keeper, that he could not enjoy his grant although he had used 'courteous entreaty' towards the merchant strangers and had even begun suits of law, the Privy Council directed the Lord Mayor and Alderman of London to grant him a legal commission to execute his patent against certain merchants. In consequence of this order, Tipper summoned before the Mayor and Aldermen three Dutch merchants living in London. This action brought a remonstrance from Archduke Matthias, the Emperor's brother, who had arrived in the Netherlands in 1578 to take over the government at the invitation of the Catholic party there.

The three Dutch merchants were Emanuel Demetrius, Martyn de la Fayle and John Vanderbeck or Papote. Complaining of Tipper's action against them and of the order made that they were to leave their houses and lodge with an English host appointed by him, they protested that it was intolerable to put them, their wives and children, their merchandise and books, and even their lives into the hands of an Englishman arbitrarily selected, which 'neither the Jews nor Turks do at any time offer to the Christians, nor the Christians to the Turks or any other nation, be they ever so barbarous'. Of these men Emanuel Demetrius (a Latinized form of Van Meteren) is a well-known figure. He was a Flemish merchant and historian, born in Antwerp in 1535, who spent the greater part of his life in London and died there in 1612. He was a cousin of Ortelius, the famous Flemish cartographer, and was intimate with the younger Hakluyt. He is known also as the author of a substantial *History of the Low Countries*.

The privy Council supported Tipper, and announced their intention to 'make such answer unto the Archduke as they trust he will rest satisfied withal'. But Tipper was getting into trouble. He had backed a bill for a man who owed money to a person named Munsloe; and, failing to pay, Munsloe clapped him into prison. While in prison he mortgaged to Munsloe his patent for hosting, and Munsloe sold it to Thomas Wilford, President of the Company of Merchant Adventurers trading to Spain and Portugal. Tipper, hearing of this, 'made his honorable master privy thereof, who took it in very evil part'. His master was, of course, Hatton. The Privy Council, no doubt on Hatton's representations, took the matter up and directed an inquiry to be made. The commissioners appointed for this purpose went into the circumstances, 'finding the matter to be very foul' against Munsloe, who confessed that Wilford and other merchants had at different times urged him to convey the patent to them. Munsloe pretended that he had only sold it for Tipper's benefit, and Wilford said that his company had bought it in order 'to bridle Tipper in some other matter which was then depending before the Lords of the Council, to be determined between them'. The matter in question was an agreement between Tipper and the Company regarding procedure under the patent. It is of some interest to note that Wilford's sister Elizabeth was the mother of Robert Gage, one of the Babington conspirators.

In February, 1580, William Davison, the Queen's agent at Antwerp, best known as the man who was made a scapegoat for the execution of Mary Queen of Scots, and an old friend of Hatton's who stood godfather to one of his sons, wrote to Hatton from Antwerp. He informed him that his Highness, that is the Archduke Matthias, had sent two commissioners to him to complain about the patent of 'one Typper', which was offensive to the Netherlands merchants trading to England, 'though I knew not then that the matter did in any way touch your Honour'. He urged Hatton to withdraw from the business. In March followed a letter in Latin from the Archduke, the last letter in the Record Office file.

Notwithstanding all this, Tipper managed to retain possession of his patent for some years, as is shown by an undated memorandum from Robert Ardern, customer, that is customs officer, of Berwick-on-Tweed, addressed to Walsingham who was farmer of the customs. It is probably to be dated in 1585, the year when Walsingham obtained a patent for this. In this memorandum various considerations are submitted, particularly in regard to aliens and hostage regulations. 'One William Tipper of London', the writer says, 'hath a grant of hostage from her Highness in all ports within England for certain years, procured by Mr. Vice-

Chamberlain [Hatton], and it were very requisite that your Honour had the directing thereof, although the fourth part of the issues growing in the same office were yielded to him in regard to his grant.' This is important, as proving again that Tipper's patent was procured by Hatton's influence, and showing that by this date, though it was still in operation, Tipper was only getting a quarter of the fees originally granted to him. Ardern recommends further that there should be four officers at each port, the customer, hostager, packer and weigher, the last two seeing to the unpacking and weighing of the merchandise landed. We may surmise that an application from Hatton to the City of London in 1580 for the office of packer for his secretary, Samuel Cox, was made with an eye to Tipper's patent.

Eventually, on pressure from his 'honourable master, Hatton', Tipper waived his rights so far as the Spanish and Portuguese merchants were concerned. This we learn from a petition from him to the Council, which suggests indeed that he had surrendered his patent, on which, for the 'defence of her Majesty's right and prerogative and for the encouragement of the Mayor and Aldermen of London' he has spent, 'his poor substance and means of living', being now £800 in debt. In recompense apparently he had been granted a monopoly for the importation of cochineal. But here again he found himself balked by his enemies, the Company of Merchants trading to Spain and Portugal, the importers of that commodity.

The restless Tipper, like a typical Elizabethan, now looked around for fresh sources of income. His new venture was the business of 'discovering concealed lands', that is investigating imperfections in title. One Edward Stafford, who seems to have been identical with Edward, later Sir Edward Stafford, English Ambassador in Paris, had a patent for this, challenging titles to estates in the interest of the Crown, in return for a fee or percentage of the profits. As the system developed, it became customary to offer terms of composition to the threatened landlords. But Stafford seems to have worked it at a loss. He was heavily in debt, and so was Tipper when in 1582 he began negotiations with Stafford for the purchase of his patent.

That Hatton was concerned in Tipper's new scheme appears from correspondence preserved in the Remembrancia Rolls of the City of London, a letter to him from the Lord Mayor, Sir James

Harvey, about some lands, said to be concealed, belonging to the City Companies, against whom an action was being brought in the Court of Exchequer, and 'praying your favour according to your accustomed goodness to this City, before any suit made to any other of the most honourable Council'. Hatton meanwhile had written to Serjeant Fleetwood, the Recorder of London, suggesting the submission of the question to arbiters. The patentees who claimed an interest in the concealed lands were, of course, Stafford and Tipper who was negotiating with him; and Hatton, as before, was presumably at Tipper's back. In October, Fleetwood informed Hatton that he had communicated to the Companies a speech of Hatton's on the subject. It must have been conciliatory for, after hearing it, the Companies 'acknowledged with one consent his accustomed goodness to the City'. A year later the Lord Mayor wrote to Burghley, saying that the matter had been submitted to Bromley, the Lord Chancellor, and Sir Walter Mildmay, the Chancellor of the Exchequer, who had directed that the two Chief Justices should give their opinion in certain cases which would govern the others. Pending this, all suits, both those of Sir James Mervyn and those of 'the patentees depending upon the Vice-Chamberlain' [Hatton] should be postponed. But Mervyn, contrary to this order, had instituted proceedings against the Haberdashers' Company.

This Sir James Mervyn had a patent for these concealed lands; and there is in the Public Record Office a large file of papers concerning an agreement entered into between him and Edward Stafford, the other patentee, for whose patent Tipper was negotiating. These last are 'the patentees depending upon the Vice-Chamberlain'. But these further documents do not concern us for, whatever his precise connection, Hatton scarcely appears in the matter again. But it may be noted that a Mr. Moody, a servant of Edward Stafford, was concerned in the negotiations on behalf of his master. This is, no doubt, Michael Moody who with William Stafford was later concerned in an obscure conspiracy to plant on the French Ambassador's secretary a bogus plot for murdering the Queen. Moody was then stated to be a servant of Sir Edward Stafford, the English Ambassador in France, who was William Stafford's brother. There seems therefore to be no doubt that the patentee whom Tipper was buying out was later Ambassador to France.

Eventually, in 1588, Hatton's friend Sir Edward Dyer secured the patent, with the obligation of acquiring Stafford's interest. He appointed Tipper his agent, and in the end Tipper made a good competence, though Dyer did not fare so well. But it is not necessary to follow Tipper's fortunes farther, diverting as they are, save to notice that in 1599 Hatton's secretary, Samuel Cox, was threatened by him in respect of the title to his estate in Oxfordshire.

CHAPTER XXII

THE PARRY PLOT

THAT Hatton took an active part in the proceedings against William Parry, who was supposed to have contemplated the assassination of Queen Elizabeth, and against the Babington conspirators is plain from the volumes of State Trials. While it is true that the unravelling of the Babington Plot and the collection of evidence against Babington and his fellows and against the Queen of Scots was the work of Walsingham and his spies, there is no doubt about Hatton's prominence in the sequel. In the case of Parry, as in that of Babington and his associates, he was one of those commissioned to examine the prisoners, and he was the Queen's representative at their trials. As such he took the leading part, even though high legal luminaries were nominally in charge. On the other hand, he was not much concerned in the details of Mary's trial, his role being confined to an important intervention at its beginning. But, for her trial as for that of Babington, as well as for his speeches in Parliament on Mary's case, he prepared himself by a close study of the documents.

Those who hold that Hatton was no more than a Royal favourite, who took little or no share in national affairs, cannot be aware of the evidence contained in such a collection of documents as the Bardon Papers, the significance of which was not fully appreciated until Dr. Conyers Read edited them nearly forty years ago. The Bardon papers are a special collection concerning the Queen of Scots, put together for Hatton's information. They will be described more particularly in the chapter on Mary's trial. They have no reference to William Parry, and for the part Hatton played in his prosecution it is necessary to go to the published volume of State Trials. Parry's trial he dominated as effectually as he did the Babington Trial a year later.

The so-called Parry plot to assassinate Queen Elizabeth, like its successor the Babington conspiracy, was largely the fruit of the schemes of Thomas Morgan, one of the agents in Paris of the Queen of Scots. William Parry, or William ap Harry, was a son of Harry ap David, a gentleman of good family in Flintshire. He had in his youth been apprenticed to a lawyer in Chester; in 1583 he tells Walsingham, he took a degree in law in Paris, and in his indictment is accordingly styled Doctor of Laws. In 1570 he had received a small appointment at Court, being sworn, as he says in his confession, her Majesty's servant. But he was a disreputable character, a broken courtier who had run through the fortunes of two wives and had incurred sentence of death for a violent assault of a creditor. He had been pardoned and allowed to go abroad, on condition of supplying information about exiled Catholics. For he was taken into the Government's secret service, and as early as 1580 was sending Burghley reports about English Catholics in France. But, as is so often the case with spies, it is not easy to be sure what his real designs were. It has been argued that Parry throughout was nothing but an agent of the English Government, and that his so-called plot was purely imaginary, invented by the Government for some obscure purpose, that is scarcely made manifest by such apologists. On such a theory Parry's conversations with other Catholics and the oath he took to kill the Queen were but the actions of an *agent provocateur*, designed to entrap victims. It is a plausible hypothesis, up to a point. There were certainly such *agents provocateurs* in the Babington plot, as Gilbert Gifford, Robert Poley, perhaps Barnard Maude and the mysterious Captain Jaques. But in Parry's case, no completely satisfactory explanation is, on this theory, forthcoming why the Government should throw him over, try him and execute him.

It seems simpler to take Parry's own account of his activities, see where it leads us and whether it makes a consistent story. Having been reconciled to the Roman Church in September, 1582 (according to his own statement, but his conversion seems to have taken place earlier), he met in October Thomas Morgan, who urged him to make an attempt on Elizabeth's life. Parry professed himself willing, provided the deed were lawful, that is from the Catholic point of view, but on the case being put (the names suppressed) to a priest, it was pronounced unlawful. Nevertheless, Parry resolved upon the murder of Elizabeth, and Morgan began to make arrangements for a Scottish force to enter England in Mary's defence, when news should come of Elizabeth's death; but Mary herself, Parry declared, was not a party to his schemes. After nearly eighteen months abroad Parry returned to England, landing at Rye in January, 1584. He began to put it about that he had important news for Elizabeth's ear; and contrived to have audience of her at Whitehall, where he spoke to her of plots against her life, which news she took 'doubtfully'.

At this point one asks oneself the question, why did Parry desire this interview with Elizabeth? His own story seems to give a reasonable explanation. Parry was a boastful man, an exhibitionist, who loved the limelight, and yet, like many of his type, irresolute. His conduct at his trial and some of the passages in his confession seem to point to the conclusion that he was a little mad. He had the symptoms of derangement, the exaltation, the grandiose conception of himself, and with it a good deal of faltering. He was urged by the one impulse to push his way into the Queen's presence. At the same time his apprehensions impelled him to seek some means of withdrawing from the desperate enterprise to which he had pledged himself. He thought that if he could move Elizabeth to less rigour against the Catholics he would have accomplished enough to deserve the applause for which his nature craved, without having to proceed to his terrible purpose. He says himself that he was 'fully resolved never to touch her . . . if by any device, persuasions or policy she might be brought to deal more graciously with the Catholics than she doth . . .' He wanted to have it both ways, he wished to pose to himself and his circle as a man committed to a desperate enterprise, while frantically seeking a way out of the tangle into which his feet had strayed. It was this inconsistency of boasting of the crime he contemplated, while passionately protesting that he never meant to kill the Queen, that puzzled the commissioners at his trial, including Hatton. It is fairly certain that Parry would never have screwed up his courage to the fatal point.

Up to this stage the Government, Burghley in particular, seem to have accepted Parry as one of their agents, and to have had no doubt that he was engaged in work for them which might be useful. Elizabeth seems to have been impressed by his hints of plots against her life. Parry had shown to friends the letter he had received from the Cardinal of Como, commending his enterprise in the Pope's name, and through them it had been communicated to the Queen. She was, of course, given to understand that Parry was acting as an *agent provocateur*; but it was a dangerous game he was playing. Elizabeth, however, seems to have believed him, unless indeed she was but giving him rope. She showed him some favour, and Parry was given a seat — Queenborough in Kent — in the Parliament of 1584, which met in November.

That Parliament had been elected in a fever of resentment and alarm, following the discovery of the latest plots against Elizabeth's throne and life, the Throckmorton Plot and the conspiracies organized by the Duke of Guise and Cardinal Allen to have her assassinated. In connection with these conspiracies the Earl of Northumberland and the Earl of Arundel, son of the late Duke of Norfolk, had been sent to the Tower. It was a critical moment, and Sir Walter Mildmay, the Chancellor of the Exchequer, and Sir Christopher Hatton took occasion to speak of the sudden calling of Parliament at such an unseasonable time of the year, declaring it to be for very urgent and necessary causes. Their speeches, which lasted more than two hours, have not been preserved. But Fleetwood, the Recorder of London, writing to Burghley, says of Hatton, 'his speech tended to particularities and special actions, and concluded upon the Queen's Majesty's safety. Before this time I never heard in Parliament the like things uttered; and especially the things contained in the latter [i.e. Hatton's] speech. They were *magnalia regni*'.

Parliament's first Bill, for the Safety and Preservation of the Queen's Royal Person, was a measure to legalize the Bond of Association, a voluntary pledge by which Englishmen had bound themselves to 'withstand and revenge to the uttermost all such malicious actions and attempts against her Majesty's most royal personage'. The Bill was, of course, directed against Mary Queen of Scots, in whose interest any attempt to murder Elizabeth would be made. Participants in any plot or effort at invasion were to be excluded from the succession and exposed to the vengeance of private citizens (which last provision Elizabeth vetoed), and anyone in whose interest the Queen might be killed was deemed incapable of inheriting the Crown. It was Hatton, who, for the Government, brought forward this Bill. His speech has not come down to us but, as Dr. Conyers Read points out, what seems to be his rough notes for it are among the Bardon Papers, discussed in another chapter. They are brief jottings of arguments for the duty of citizens to take special care for preserving the Queen's life.

A second Bill proposed to banish all Jesuits and seminary priests who would not submit and take the oath. On its introduction,

SIR CHRISTOPHER HATTON
AS CHANCELLOR OF THE UNIVERSITY OF OXFORD
From the portrait in the National Portrait Gallery

Parry whom Camden somewhat inadequately describes as 'a man passing proud, neat and spruce', made a scene. It is probable that while he was willing to intrigue against the leaders of his Church, he was genuine in his endeavours to oppose the persecution of the Catholics as such. At any rate, he delivered a violent attack on the Bill, 'affirming it to savour of treasons, to be full of blood, danger, despair and terror or dread to the English subjects of this realm, our brethren, uncles and kinsfolks; and also full of confiscations', characteristically adding that he would reserve for her Majesty's ear the reasons for his saying so. He was committed for contempt to the custody of the Serjeant, but was released the next day on making his humble submission and dutifully acknowledging his fault, Hatton communicating to the House the Queen's wishes to this effect.

Two days later, Hatton moved the adjournment, and the House resolved to send their humble and dutiful thanks to the Queen for her gracious acceptance of their care in providing for her safety. To this address Hatton returned answer, conveying Elizabeth's grateful appreciation of their labours, with some pious reflections on the goodness of Providence, an admonition against wasting time, and a suggestion that they would be best employed in improving the laws so as to expedite and cheapen the course of justice. Throughout Hatton appears here in his familiar role of the Queen's mouthpiece, but the following little scene, when Parliament adjourned on December 21st until February, was perhaps impromptu. Hatton moved:

> that besides the rendering of our most humble and loyal thanks unto her Highness, we do, being assembled together, join our hearts and minds together in most humble and earnest prayer unto Almighty God for the long continuance of the most prosperous preservation of her Majesty, with most due and thankful acknowledgment of His infinite benefits and blessings poured upon this whole realm, through the mediation of her Highness's ministry under Him. And he said he had a paper in writing in his hand, devised and set down by an honest, godly and learned man, and which, albeit it was not very well written, yet he would willingly read it as well as he could, if it pleased to follow them and say after him, as he should begin and say before them. Which being assented unto most willingly of all the whole House, and everyone kneeling upon his knees, the said Mr. Vice-Chamberlain begun the said prayer.

We are not given the text of the prayer so modestly introduced, but this specimen of Hatton's pulpit manner has a certain humour.

To resume Parry's own narrative. In the previous March (1584) he had received the letter, referred to above, from the Cardinal of Como, the Papal Secretary of State. Parry described it as commending his enterprise, absolving him in the Pope's name of all his sins, and willing him to go forward in the name of God. And although the letter merely expresses a general approval of Parry's intentions, it seems fairly clear that it was intended to have reference to his project for the murder of Elizabeth. However that may be, Parry stated that it confirmed his resolution to kill the Queen, his conscience being clear that the deed was lawful and meritorious. Yet, when he remembered Elizabeth's many excellencies, he was greatly troubled. Whenever he came near her he left his dagger at home, 'determined never to do it, if either policy, practice, persuasion or motion in Parliament would prevail'. In July, Cardinal Allen's book, maintaining that it was not only lawful but honourable to kill princes excommunicate, was sent to him from France, and his wavering mind was again moved to the deed he contemplated.

In August he fell in with Edmund Neville, and discussed his designs with him. Neville, whom Parry calls his cousin, was distantly related to him through Parry's mother, a daughter of Peter Conway, Archdeacon of St. Asaph. On his mother's side, he was a nephew of Edward Arden, father-in-law of that Somerville who in October, 1583, had conceived the idea of shooting Queen Elizabeth, hoping 'to see her head set upon a pole, for she was a serpent and a viper'. On his father's side Neville was great-grandson of John Neville, third Baron Latymer, and so distantly related to Charles Neville, Earl of Westmorland, one of the leaders of the Northern Rebellion of 1569 and now living in exile on the Continent. Charles Neville did not die until 1601, but, according to Parry, Edmund Neville had heard of his death at this time, and hoped to establish his claim to the earldom. It was, however, the Barony of Latymer that Neville was claiming in 1584, though in 1601 he laid claim to the Earldom of Westmorland also. At any rate he was eager to keep in with the authorities, and betrayed Parry to them. Probably each was willing to give away the other, but Neville laid his information first. Parry stated in his confession that Neville was quite prepared to murder Elizabeth, and had said that 'though he would not lay hand on her in a corner, his heart moved him to strike off her head in the field'.

For in this hysterical way they had got so far as to discuss plans, and had finally decided on the manner of the assassination, 'to be on horseback, with eight or ten horses when she should ride abroad about St. James's or some other like place'. The meaning of this sentence — it is Parry's, and like all his phrases grandiloquent — is not too clear. Another version which was told to Lupold von Wedel, while it may not be strictly accurate, contains some of the proper ingredients — Parry's dagger, his fellow conspirator and his interviews with the Queen which, so far as they illustrate her vanity, have a certain verisimilitude. Von Wedel was a German traveller, who was in England in 1584 and 1585, the time of the Parry Plot. Incidentally, he repeats the gossip about Leicester and Hatton having been Elizabeth's lovers. He describes them both as being 'fine old gentlemen'; Hatton was then 45. This is his story of Parry's plot:

> At last he found a person whom he made a partner of the plot, charging him to give his assistance in the effecting his plan. The day having been fixed, the doctor [Parry] entered the Queen's chamber, where she was by herself, with a knife hidden in his sleeve, intending to stab her. The Queen, however, when she observed him, asked 'Doctor, do you know what dream I had this night?' On his replying 'No', she remarked, 'I dreamed I had a vein opened, and lost much blood'. The doctor, on hearing this, got frightened, thinking she had discovered the plot, and fainted, upon which the Queen, who was much attached to him, called for medical help. For she was of opinion that the dream had frightened him so much because he loved her, and for this she esteemed him the more. Having recovered himself, he sought his companion, telling him what had happened, encouraging him at the same time to try whether he could bring the affair to an end. The other promised to do so, but when on entering he saw the Queen, he, struck by fear, fell down upon his knees begging forgiveness, and made a full confession.

On Neville's information, laid early in February, 1585, Parry was immediately arrested by order of Elizabeth and brought to Walsingham's house. Walsingham examined him and told him, without mentioning Neville's name, that the Queen had been informed of plots against her person, and asked if he had gleaned any information about them among his Catholic acquaintance. Parry said he knew nothing. Walsingham then asked him whether he himself had 'let fall any speech unto any person (though with an intent only to have discovered his disposition) that might draw him in suspicion as though he himself had any such wicked intent'; or, cutting through the intolerable verbiage of the sixteenth century, whether he had acted as an *agent provocateur*.

Dr. Conyers Read, pointing out that whatever status Parry had enjoyed as a spy had lapsed since he had ceased to be a Government agent and had become a Member of Parliament, and that he had no warrant of any kind to talk treason with Neville, says, 'here was Parry's chance to reveal his dealings with Neville and perhaps clear himself of the charge of treason. Upon his answer to this question of Walsingham's his fate in large manner hung'. But he denied vehemently that he had so spoken. Walsingham then pressed him more closely, and told him there was a gentleman of very good quality prepared to accuse him to his face. Parry persisted in his denial, but the following morning professed to have called to mind a conversation with Neville about a statement in a recent Catholic book (Allen's) that it was lawful to kill a prince in the cause of religion. But he still denied that he had spoken about any attempt to murder the Queen. That night he was taken to Leicester's house, examined before Leicester, Hatton and Walsingham, and confronted with Neville. Once more he denied Neville's accusations, and was sent to the Tower. On February 11th he was again examined by Walsingham, Hatton and Lord Hunsdon. He then made the confession from which extracts have been quoted.

In the House of Commons on February 24th, Hatton made a 'very exact and elaborate speech' on behalf of the Government on the whole circumstances of Parry's plot. He said that Neville and Parry had resolved to murder the Queen at St. James's or else to set upon her when she was in her coach in the Fields, each of them being accompanied by five or six men with pistols. He concluded by setting forth at length the details of Parry's career. The next day Parry was brought to trial at Westminster for high treason, the commissioners including Lord Hunsdon, Sir Christopher Hatton and Hatton's friend Sir Thomas Heneage, as well as the legal officers of the Crown. Parry having pleaded guilty, the Court was about to proceed to judgment, when Hatton inter-

posed saying that, as the matter was of great importance, the
Government had decided that it should be made as public as
possible.

With the consent of the commissioners, counsel and prisoner,
it was agreed that Parry's confession should be read, and with it
his letters to the Queen, to Burghley and Leicester, and the letter
of the Cardinal of Como to him. Parry eagerly offered to read
these documents himself, but was told they must be read by the
Clerk of the Crown. Before this was done, Hatton asked him to
say if his confession was true and if it was made freely and willingly, 'or was there any extort means used to draw it from you?'
Parry agreed that it was true, and had been made freely and
without constraint. The reading of these documents concluded,
Parry begged leave to speak. Hatton answered, 'if you will say
anything for the better opening to the world of those your foul
and horrible facts [i.e. acts], speak on; but if you mean to make
any excuse for that which you have confessed, which else would
have been and do stand proved against you, for my part I will not
sit to hear you'.

Parry then began in that mood of exaltation which seems to
hint at a disordered intellect:

> My cause is rare, singular and unnatural, conceived at Venice,
> presented in general words to the Pope, undertaken at Paris,
> commended and allowed of by his Holiness, and was to have been
> executed in England if it had not been prevented. Yea, I have
> committed many treasons, for I have committed treason in being
> reconciled, and treason in taking the absolution. . . .

But he denied that he had ever intended to kill the Queen, and
appealed to her own knowledge of the facts, and that of Burghley
and Walsingham. At this Hunsdon, one of the commissioners,
caught him up. Was he going back on his confession? and Hatton
burst out, 'This is absurd . . . all this thou hast plainly confessed;
and I protest before this great assembly thou hast confessed it
more plainly and in better sort than my memory will serve me
to utter. And sayest thou now that thou never meanest it?'

The desperate man then began to protest that his confession
had been obtained by torture. 'Ah', he said, 'your honours know
how my confession, upon my examination, was extorted.' Hunsdon and Hatton objected that no torture, no threatening words

had been offered him. To which Parry replied that they had told him that if he would not confess willingly he should have torture. Hunsdon and Hatton denied that they had spoken of torture. 'You said', answered Parry, 'that you would proceed with rigour against me, if I would not confess it of myself.' This was also denied; 'but I will tell thee', said Hatton, 'what we said. I spake these words: "if you will willingly utter the truth of yourself, it may do you good, I wish you to do so; if you will not, we must then proceed in ordinary course to take your examination." Whereunto you answered that you would tell the truth of yourself. Was not this true?' Parry assented.

Hatton then made a rather curious speech. He said that 'it was a wonder to see the magnanimity of her Majesty which, after that thou hadst opened these traitorous practices [i.e. with Morgan] in sort as thou hast laid it down in thy confession, was nevertheless such and so far from all fear as that she would not so much as acquaint anyone of her Highness's Privy Council with it, to his knowledge, no not until after this thine enterprise [i.e. with Neville] discovered and made manifest'. Father J. H. Pollen, who has written at length on the Catholic plots of the reign and who holds that Parry had no serious intention of killing the Queen, which is probably true enough, claims also that the Government had no real belief in the Parry plot. He interprets this speech as the Government's explanation why, having made use of Parry's services, they were now throwing him over. Hatton's speech, he thinks, was an attempt to meet this difficulty, that Parry had lately been rewarded for the very same 'treasons' for which he was now to be executed. The Government, he holds, were sacrificing Parry to the Puritan clamour, to which the legislation passed by the Parliament of 1584 bears witness. It may even be, he conjectures, that the real reason for Parry's death was the conflict between Walsingham and the extremists on the one side and Burghley and the moderates on the other. Parry's concluding speech, discussed below, shows that he at least believed that his fate had been determined by Leicester and the Puritan party.

Whatever the facts, we may agree that it was necessary for the Government to explain how it was that Parry was now to be executed for plots for which he had been previously rewarded. It was absurd to allege that Neville had revealed something that had been unknown before: Parry's statement of his intention to kill the Queen. For Parry had all along posed as an *agent provocateur*, one who had discussed this very question with others in order to entrap them. And so much, he hints, he had told the Queen. He had even shown his letter from the Cardinal of Como to friends, who had told Elizabeth about it. And for this he had been rewarded with a seat in Parliament.

How to explain these things? Dr. Conyers Read holds that Parry's government service having come to an end, he was technically guilty of high treason in discussing with Neville the killing of the Queen. But he does not explain what was the Government's object in turning against him after using his services. The question of Parry's guilt or innocence is really, as he says, a question of motive. There is little doubt of the general truth of his confession or of the fact that he was technically guilty. He had frequently discussed plans for the killing of Elizabeth. Was it as an *agent provocateur* or did he intend them? The view has been set forth above that he was not quite sane; he posed as a potential slayer of the oppressor of the Catholics; he toyed with treason, but would probably have done no more than toy with it. As for what the Government believed, Father Pollen is probably right in thinking that Parry was differently regarded by the two rival parties in the Council, and that Neville's information turned the scale, and strengthened the Walsingham-Hatton party to proceed against him. But the Government could scarcely say that Parry had acted for them as an *agent provocateur* up to but not including the time he met Neville. They had to find a different excuse. The method adopted was to make a distinction between the Queen and the Privy Council, a ruse which was also employed two years later when William Davison was made the scapegoat for the execution of the Queen of Scots. In Parry's case the argument was that his revelations had been made to the Queen only, and that her magnanimity and courage had kept them from the knowledge of the Council, which was ignorant of them until Neville made his accusations.

Such seem to have been the reasons at the back of Hatton's reference to the Queen's action. The remainder of his speech adds some details which do not appear in Parry's confession, pointing to statements made by him which were not incorporated in it. Parry, Hatton said, had confessed that he had prepared two

Scottish daggers for stabbing the Queen. And in a remarkable passage, he reminded him, 'Parry didst thou not also confess before us how wonderfully thou wert appalled and perplexed upon a sudden at the presence of her Majesty at Hampton Court this last summer, saying that thou didst think thou then sawest in her the very likeness and image of King Henry VIII? And that therewith and upon some speeches used by her Majesty, thou didst turn about and weep bitterly to thyself?' So greatly had the memory of Henry VIII the power to awe men nearly forty years after his death.

Hunsdon then again took up the point that Parry was now denying that he meant to kill the Queen. On this, the prisoner cried out in a furious manner, 'I never meant to kill her: I will lay my blood upon Queen Elizabeth and you, before God and the world'. On which Hunsdon accused him of trying to pretend that he died for his religion and not for his treason. Parry was then asked what he could say why judgment of death should not be awarded against him. He replied that he saw that he must die, because he was not settled. Hatton was, or pretended to be, puzzled by this remark. He asked him what he meant. Parry answered, 'Look into your study and into your new books, and you shall find what I mean'. But Hatton professed not to understand: 'I protest', he said, 'I know not what thou meanest; thou dost not well to use such dark speeches, unless thou wouldst plainly utter what thou meanest thereby.' Parry's use of the word 'settled' is explained by a passage in *Leycester's Commonwealth*. There Leicester's Puritan party is described as conspiring against Catholics and Protestants alike, and against the claims of Mary Queen of Scots to the succession to the Throne, and in support of the claims of Leicester's brother-in-law, the Earl of Huntingdon. The watchword of this party is said to be 'Whether you be settled or no, and if you answer Yea, and seem to understand the meaning thereof, then you are known to be of that faction'. So, when Parry said he was not 'settled', he meant that he was to be condemned because he was a Catholic, and that his death would be due to the influence of Leicester and the Puritan party. And his allusion to 'your new books' was clearly to *Leycester's Commonwealth*, published in the previous summer.

The Lord Chief Justice then summed up, delivering a short homily before passing the terrible sentence of death for high treason with its disgusting formula of cruelty and mutilation. And Parry, persisting still in his rage and passion, cried out, 'I here summon Queen Elizabeth to answer for my blood before God'. On March 2nd, 1585, he suffered on Tower Hill, protesting to the last that he had never any intention of assassinating the Queen.

CHAPTER XXIII

THE DEATH OF NORTHUMBERLAND

ABOUT the time that Hatton was engaged in the examination and trial of William Parry, he was also concerned with special investigations regarding the treasons of Henry Percy, eighth Earl of Northumberland; and when Northumberland committed suicide in the Tower in June, 1585, there were rumours that Hatton had somehow contrived his death. That he had been murdered at the instigation of the Government was widely held by the Catholics; that Hatton was believed to be specially concerned in the alleged murder there is slight but fairly definite evidence. Camden refers cautiously to these rumours when he says, 'what the suspicious fugitives [i.e. the Catholic refugees] muttered of one Bailiff that was one of Hatton's men and was a little before appointed to be the Earl's keeper, I omit, as being a matter altogether unknown unto me, and I think it not meet to insert anything upon vain heresays'.

The charges against Hatton find their most famous expression in the well-known letter concerning the Earl of Essex which Ralegh wrote to Sir Robert Cecil sixteen years later, when he advised him not to relent towards Essex from any fear of consequences to himself, saying:

> For after-revenges, fear them not; for your own father, that was esteemed to be a contriver of Norfolk's ruin, yet his son followeth your father's son, and loveth him. Humours of men succeed not [i.e. are not followed up or remembered], but grow by occasions and accidents of time and power. Somerset made no revenge on the Duke of Northumberland's heirs. Northumberland that now is, thinks not of Hatton's issue. Kelloway lives that murdered the brother of Horsey, and Horsey let him go by all his life-time.

On this passage, writers from Nicolas in his life of Hatton (1847) to Edward Thompson in his life of Ralegh (1935) have pointed out that Ralegh is not here advocating the death of Essex, but his disgrace and banishment from Court. He first names men whose ruin, not murder, had been contrived by political enemies, and there is no more reason to believe that he meant it to be inferred that Hatton had contrived the assassination of Northumberland, than that he meant to say that Burghley had murdered Norfolk, or that Dudley had killed Protector Somerset. When Ralegh did really allude to murder, he expressly said so in a separate sentence. That may be granted, but there can be no doubt that he insinuates that Hatton was in some special sense responsible for Northumberland's overthrow. It seems clear that, while he is not to be understood as definitely charging Hatton with Northumberland's murder, he is voicing the rumour or tradition that Hatton in some way brought about his death. It has been pointed out that Ralegh is in any case a biased witness, as he was Hatton's rival, if not his enemy. But that is really immaterial; there would be no point in Ralegh's mentioning the matter unless the story were familiar to all.

There seems to be no doubt therefore that there was gossip, however unfounded, that connected Hatton with Northumberland's death. There is no doubt at all that there were rumours that Northumberland had been murdered, whoever the criminal. Immediately after his death there was published at Cologne a tract entitled *Crudelitatis Calvinianae Exempla duo recentissima ex Anglia*, charging the English Government with the Earl's murder as well as with the enforcement of the penal statutes against Catholics which had been passed in the previous year. It was translated into French, German, English, Italian and Spanish. But even before its appearance, public excitement was so great that it was decided to hold an investigation; and accordingly two days after Northumberland's death a Court of Inquiry met in the Star Chamber.

Henry Percy, eighth Earl of Northumberland, succeeded his brother Thomas, one of the leaders of the Northern Rebellion who had been executed for his share in that rising. For Henry Percy had been loyal on that occasion. He had, in fact, borne arms against his brother, and was reputed to be a Protestant. But his family traditions proved too strong for him. He had no sooner stepped into the shoes of the brother whom he had helped to crush than he, in his turn, entered into schemes for the release of the Queen of Scots. He was arrested in November, 1571, sent to the Tower, tried for treason, and got off lightly with a fine of 5000 marks (never paid), being released in 1573. Ten years passed till, in November, 1583, Francis Throckmorton was arrested, racked by Thomas Norton the rackmaster, who played so odious a role in the torturing of Campion and his associates, and revealed the existence of the plot that is known by his name. This was the Duke of Guise's plan for the invasion of England and Scotland in the Catholic interest, and the liberation of Guise's cousin, the Queen of Scots. With Throckmorton's papers was found a list of Catholic noblemen favourable to Mary's cause. Among them was the Earl of Northumberland, who was further incriminated by Throckmorton's confession; and in September, 1584, the Government chanced to fall upon full particulars of the designs of Guise and Cardinal Allen. Father Crichton, the Scottish Jesuit, had been captured at sea, and some documents which he had torn up and thrown overboard had been blown back on the deck of the ship and pieced together. They proved to be a history in Italian of the proposed invasion of England from the time of the arrival of the Duke of Lennox in Scotland. As a result of the new information, thus gradually collected, Northumberland was again committed to the Tower in December.

It appeared that in September of the previous year Charles Paget, one of Mary's principal agents in France, had come to Petworth, Northumberland's place in Sussex, and there with Paget's brother, Lord Paget, had discussed with the Earl schemes for the invasion. William Shelley of Michelgrove, a Sussex neighbour, had been present at the interview. Later, on being racked, he revealed what had taken place. But for the moment Northumberland thought he was safe. He had contrived, with Shelley's help, to send out of the country Lord Paget, the principal witness to his interview with Charles Paget, who had returned to France. Hatton now comes into the story.

In all the Catholic conspiracies of the reign, from the time when Walsingham became Secretary, the work of directing the secret service that brought the plots to light was his. But, as in the case of Norfolk in 1572, William Parry in the same year as Northumberland, and Babington a year later, Hatton had a special duty laid upon him by the Queen. This was the interviewing and examining of prisoners and, in Parry's and Babington's cases, as in that of the Queen of Scots, of taking part as a commissioner in their trials. He was sent by Elizabeth to see the Earl before his committal to the Tower, and interviewed him accordingly. His business was to remind Northumberland of the Queen's many past favours and clemencies, and to advise him to tell the truth, either privately by letter to her or in speech to Hatton. If he would do so, Hatton promised that he would not be sent to the Tower, but would receive such mitigation as the Queen could contrive of whatever punishment the law might decree. Northumberland, however, believing that no evidence could be brought against him, elected to go to the Tower and abide the consequences.

While the Earl was in the Tower he contrived to communicate with his fellow-prisoner, William Shelley; and from him and others sought to learn the extent of Shelley's confessions. The Government got wind of this, changed the keeper whom they had evidence that he had corrupted, and removed the groom of Northumberland's chamber and another of his servants who had been the means of bringing him the information of what was going on outside. Thomas Bailiff, who, Camden tells us, was one of Hatton's men, was put in charge of the prisoner; and this circumstance no doubt helped to strengthen the rumour, if it did not indeed originate it, that Hatton was concerned in the Earl's death.

Meanwhile Northumberland had had word from Shelley that he could hold out no longer against the horrors of the rack, and must confess all. In despair Northumberland resolved to commit suicide. A dag, or pistol, was procured by James Price, one of his servants, smuggled into his room, and concealed within the mattress of his bed. Northumberland then bolted the door and, lying on his back in bed, put the dag to his breast and fired it. So, at any rate, the court of inquiry reconstructed the tragedy. He was found dead with his heart torn to pieces and the backbone broken. Three bullets were discovered by Lord Hunsdon in the body within an inch of each other, and were cut out by the surgeon.

Northumberland's death took place on June 21st, 1585. On the 23rd the court of inquiry assembled in the Star Chamber. It included the Lord Chancellor, Attorney-General, Solicitor-General, the Lord Chief Baron and Sir Christopher Hatton, Vice-Chamberlain. The Lord Chancellor, Sir Thomas Bromley, briefly expounded the Government case that the Earl, growing desperate, as he learned by 'corrupting his keepers and other like devices' that his treasons were known, had committed suicide.

He said that the Privy Council had directed this inquiry to be
made lest 'through the sinister means of such persons as be evil-
affected to the present estate of her Majesty's Government, some
bad and untrue conceits might be had, as well as of the cause
of the Earl's detainment as of the manner of his death'. The
Attorney-General then gave an account of Northumberland's
treasons. He was followed by the Solicitor-General who detailed
his communications with Shelley and described his despair on
learning that Shelley had confessed.

Sir Roger Manwood, Lord Chief Baron of the Exchequer, then
repeated the circumstances of Northumberland's death, as revealed by the coroner's inquest. He told of the removal of
Palmer, the Earl's 'corrupt keeper', and of his men James Price
and Jaques Pantins and the substitution for them of Thomas
Bailiff. The night before Northumberland's death Bailiff served
him with supper, attended him to his bed and then left him. In
the middle of the night the prisoner got up and bolted his chamber
door, saying he could not sleep unless it was fast. Presently
Bailiff was awakened from his slumber by a great noise. It was
the dag exploding. The Lieutenant of the Tower, Sir Owen
Hopton, was hastily summoned, broke down the door, and found
the dead body. Hopton and his servant and four warders gave
evidence to that effect.

The Lord Chief Baron then argued how impossible it was for
the prisoner to have been murdered in a locked room with no
passage out of it except to a closet. Without expressly mentioning
it, he met the charge that the Government had been concerned
in a murder, by saying that had the Earl stood his trial and been
condemned, his lands and goods would have been forfeit to the
Crown, which stood to take nothing if he were murdered. It was
the Crown's view that he had committed suicide to save himself
from attainder, and so prevent 'the honour and state of his house
and posterity' from being 'utterly overthrown'. The Lord Chief
Baron was at pains also to point out that the prisoner had not
been narrowly or oppressively confined, but had had the use
during the day of five large rooms and three entries (or passages).
Three of the rooms and one of the passages, he said, 'lay upon
two fair gardens within the Tower wall and upon the Tower
wharf, with a pleasant prospect of the Thames and to the country
more than five miles beyond. The windows were of a large

proportion, yielding so much air and light as more cannot be desired in any house'. Almost too seductive a description of the amenities of the grim Tower. Finally, Hatton described his interview with Northumberland before the Earl's committal.

Hatton's connection with the Earl of Northumberland is therefore confined, according to the official account, to his interview with him at the Queen's direction. The fact that it was his man Thomas Bailiff who was in attendance on the Earl on the eve of his death was no doubt the principal point on which public suspicion fastened. One can imagine that the change of keepers must have appeared to many as highly significant. The argument would certainly run that the Earl's own servants had been removed to make way for a complaisant official, if not the actual murderer. Such a man would be able to kill the prisoner and then relock the door. Or perhaps the Lieutenant of the Tower and the warders had been suborned to swear that an unfastened door was locked and had had to be broken in. Wild rumours would be flying about. And it was the memory of such rumours that Ralegh revived sixteen years later.

Perhaps the most suspicious circumstance of the affair is the absence of some of the principals as witnesses at the coroner's inquest. It is true that Jaques Pantins, the Earl's groom, was called, but only to give evidence that James Price had procured the dag, and that Pantins had suspected that his master 'meant mischief to himself, and did all that he could to persuade the Earl to send away the dag, but could not prevail', useful evidence for the Crown's case for suicide. But neither James Price nor Hatton's man, Thomas Bailiff, appears among the witnesses, though Camden says that Price was examined. Nicolas's argument that the record of the inquest does not give the names of all the witnesses, and that Bailiff, at least, must certainly have been called, merely begs the question. Lingard, the Catholic historian, is the most fervent champion of the view that Hatton was responsible for Northumberland's death. But other authorities have not accepted it. Ralegh's famous letter proves little or nothing. There is a strong argument for the innocence of the Government in the absence of motive for the crime; and Hatton who, so far as we can see, stood to gain nothing from Northumberland's death, had probably no other concern in the affair than the exercise of his legitimate duty.

Nicolas reminds us that, in a later generation, an Earl of Essex, who had married Northumberland's granddaughter and was a prisoner in the Tower on account of the Rye House Plot, committed suicide in the same chamber in which Northumberland killed himself. He quotes Bishop Kennett about two traditions in the Percy family, which show that they at any rate did not believe in the assassination of their ancestor. The Bishop says:

> I have heard a tradition from some of the family that the dag, or pistol, was sent to him inclosed in a cold pie, carried to his table without suspicion. I have heard Dr. Mapletoft, who travelled with the last Earl of Northumberland, say that it helped much to confirm him in a belief of the Earl of Essex murdering himself in the Tower, because he had seen him pointing at the picture of this Henry Earl of Northumberland, and telling the then heir of the family, 'you owe more to that brave man than to any of your ancestors; he had the courage to save your estate for you'.

For, by his suicide, Henry Percy had preserved his lands from forfeiture.

CHAPTER XXIV

ECHOES OF THE THROCKMORTON PLOT

A GREAT part of the history of Elizabeth's reign is concerned with the position of the Catholics and with the various plots which had for object the overthrow of the Queen and her Government, the placing of Mary Stuart on the throne and the restoration of the Catholic religion. The Northern Rebellion of 1569, the Ridolfi Plot of 1571, for complicity in which the Duke of Norfolk was executed, the Parry Plot of 1584 have already been noticed. The Throckmorton Plot of 1583 involved the Earl of Northumberland, whose imprisonment in the Tower was followed, as narrated in the last chapter, by his death there, probably by suicide, though some suspected the hand of Hatton. Finally, the Babington Plot, the unravelling of which brought matters to a head and led to Mary's execution, was a matter in the investigation of which Hatton was closely involved.

But these plots, some of them of extraordinary intricacy, are part of the general history of the time, and only concern Hatton as an individual in a comparatively small degree. They may be studied in broad outline in the histories of Elizabeth's reign, and in detail in the works of such writers as Father Pollen in his articles in *The Month* and in his *Mary Queen of Scots and the Babington Plot*, and Dr. Conyers Read in his great life of Walsingham. In a biography of Hatton only those conspiracies with which he was specially concerned can be mentioned, and they can be no more than summarized except when they possess details of special importance for the story of his life.

Besides the Duke of Northumberland, others concerned in varying degrees in the Throckmorton Plot, with whom Hatton was brought into close contact, were Lord Henry Howard, brother of the executed Duke of Norfolk, the Earl of Arundel, the Duke's son, and Charles Arundel, a brother of Sir Matthew Arundel of Wardour. Hatton's connection with these people must be examined.

In 1573, ten years before this, the Howards had been in communication with the Queen of Scots. Henry Howard had been examined when these proceedings came to light in 1575, but nothing more could be proved than that they and Mary had exchanged some messages which amounted to little more than mutual expressions of goodwill. In January, 1581, the French Ambassador, Mauvissière de Castelnau, reported to the King of France that Lord Oxford had just confessed to the Queen that about four and a half years before he and some of his friends, Lord Henry Howard, Francis Southwell and Charles Arundel, had secretly professed the Catholic faith, and vowed to do all they could for its advancement. Oxford had now recanted, and accused his former friends of conspiracy against the State. The Queen, the Ambassador reported, was very upset. Mendoza, the Spanish Ambassador, made a similar communication to the King of Spain, and stated that Howard kept him informed of all he heard, that is presumably of news of movements in the interest of the Queen of Scots. Charles Arundel had been a member of George Gilbert's Catholic Association, founded to help the Jesuits Campion and Parsons in their mission. But though these people were known to be Catholics or of Catholic sympathies, Oxford found it difficult to substantiate his accusation that they had conspired against the State. He appealed to de Castelnau for confirmation of his charges; the Queen added that de Castelnau well knew her favourable attitude towards Catholics who did not place their consciences in antagonism to the State, and entreated him to tell her the truth. But he prudently denied all knowledge of the matter, and Oxford found himself out of favour with Elizabeth in consequence.

Nevertheless, the three men whom he had accused were put under restraint, Lord Henry Howard being committed to the charge of Sir Christopher Hatton and Southwell to that of Sir Francis Walsingham. Charles Arundel appears to have been kept at Sutton in Surrey, in whose charge does not transpire. From Sutton he wrote to Hatton in May, 1581. The letter does not reveal much of his circumstances, but it is evidently concerned with these troubles, for he begs that 'your virtue may in this time of distress both plead and promise for your poor friend'. In July he writes again to Hatton, asking that he should be brought to trial and claiming that he would be able to confound his enemies, no doubt a reference to Oxford's charges:

only craving of charity and justice that my trial which hath been long promised, may not be any longer deferred: for then shall my enemies sink with shame, and I depart out of the field with honour; and whatsoever either malice hath unjustly built, or a fool devised upon a false ground, must play castle-come-down, and dissolve to nothing. . . .

Four more letters from Charles Arundel to Hatton occur in the Hatton Letter Book. They are without date or place, but evidently belong to this period, as they continue to press that he should be brought to trial. The first of these can be dated approximately in September, 1581, for he says that he has now suffered eight months' imprisonment. Hatton who, whenever his position would allow him, was, as other instances prove, willing to act kindly and considerately towards those in trouble for political reasons, had evidently held out some hopes to Arundel of an improvement in his situation. Arundel writes that he has 'conceived such comfort of your last message'. Hatton's sympathy had apparently taken the practical form of helping the prisoner materially, for Arundel speaks of 'the due respects I owe you, by whose aid only I have been enabled to live the better'. And from these letters too we learn that, as in the case of other political prisoners, Hatton had been employed in Arundel's examination, for Arundel says, 'I have most plainly unfolded before you my knowledge in all points, not concealing anything to excuse myself, nor adding more than is truth to harm others'.

To return to Lord Henry Howard, another of those accused by Oxford of heresy and treasonable correspondence with the Queen of Scots. On that occasion he had been committed to Hatton's charge, but he was almost immediately transferred to the custody of Sir Ralph Sadler. An earlier letter from him occurs in the Hatton Letter Book, dated from Whitehall, May 1st, 1579. The name of the person to whom it is addressed is not given. Not all the letters in the Letter Book are to or from Hatton; Howard here calls his correspondent his dear cousin, and as he and Hatton were not related it is certain that it was not written to Hatton. It is probable that it was addressed to Oxford, Henry Howard's first cousin, with whom he was on friendly terms at the time. It is a curious letter, full of strange conceits, which laments the departure of Elizabeth from Whitehall where she had held Court, and is worth reading as an expression of the language of the time, which reached such heights of extravagance where Elizabeth was concerned. Hatton himself might be more ardent, but even he could not reach such heights of delicate flattery. Speaking of the Queen's departure, Howard says:

> ... for men's minds are never more inclined to contemplate than while the senses are suspended from their chief felicity. There is no bush nor flower in this garden which yieldeth not a comfort or a corrysine. Violets are gathered to make conserve. Rosemary begins to bloom, but it is too common. Primroses seem more pleasant for their season than sweet by their favour. Eglantine hath ten delights for every other's one, if it had no prickles; and heartsease is so raised upon the tops of the walls as I cannot reach it. The grace which cometh from the windows is most welcome, for by this mean I can say what was, though wiser men that I can hardly tell what shall be. Every favour brings a thirst, but the streams retire; and every fancy putteth us in hope of fruit, but Tantalus is famished. This sharp sauce to my sweet conceits enforceth me to write and seek that comfort, by assurance of her Majesty's good health, which cannot be conceived by my deepest meditations in her absence. ...

The influence of Lyly's *Euphues*, published in the previous year, is evident here; and it would not be worth while, perhaps, to inquire too closely the precise meaning of these elaborate tropes. But all this has little or no connection with Hatton, and the letter is only quoted as an example of the curious things which one may find scattered throughout the Letter Book.

Howard was not long in custody, but on his release, having written a learned attack on judicial astrology which was suspected to contain heresy and treason, he was sent to the Fleet in 1583. But it was not easy to prove anything against him. From prison he wrote to Hatton in April, 1584, complaining that for six months he had endured all kinds of sifting and examining; but, contrary to what we have found in other cases, Hatton, as he expressly states, had not been one of his examiners. He denied that he had ever spoken to Throckmorton save once, and then only by chance and of unimportant matters. One of the charges against him was that the Queen of Scots had sent him a ring with a message that she 'did repute him as her brother'. Such a message was sufficiently incriminating, as his brother Norfolk had lost his head for Ridolfi's conspiracy, which included in its programme a marriage between him and Mary; and Camden records that Henry Howard was, in fact, suspected of a similar design: marriage with the Scots Queen and election by the English Catholics to the throne of England. In this letter to Hatton, Howard flatly denies this story of the ring. He complains that 'this long and close endurance hath already brought me to that extremity of the stone . . .', and he begs Hatton to use his influence to procure his release, speaking of 'the pity and compassion which is engrafted in your honourable mind'. Merely diplomatic words, perhaps, prudent for a person in his situation; but the testimony to Hatton's kindness of heart is too general to be dismissed as nothing but flattery from the distressed. There is in the Hatton Letter Book another letter from Howard, which appears to have been written a month later; and with it Howard disappears from Hatton's history. Towards the end of Elizabeth's life he was restored to favour, and received a pension of £200 a year from the lands of his nephew, the late Earl of Arundel. In James's reign he advanced farther in the royal regard, and was created Earl of Northampton.

The discovery of the Throckmorton Plot in 1583 sent flying to the Continent Charles Arundel and Lord Paget, brother of Charles Paget, one of the Queen of Scots' agents in France. In Paris the three men formed a centre around which the Catholic refugees gathered and plots revolved. It is not necessary to follow Arundel's career further. He had no more dealings with Hatton, and died a pensioner of the King of Spain in 1587. Nor do the Pagets at any time come into the story of Hatton's life.

An attempt was made to implicate Philip Howard, Earl of Arundel in the Throckmorton Plot. He was sent to the Tower, released and attempted to fly the realm. He left behind a dignified letter to the Queen, protesting his innocence and saying that he had had to choose between the 'certain destruction of his body' and the 'manifest endangering of his soul'. But he had scarce taken sail when he was overtaken by two ships under the command of one Kelloway, a pretended pirate. The coup had, of course, been arranged by his enemies; and Arundel was brought home and committed again to the Tower. That was in 1585. In May of that year Walsingham writes to Hatton, complaining of Arundel's haughty demeanour in imprisonment, and saying that his courage is to be 'abated', adding, 'it cannot be but that he receiveth some comfort, and that not from mean persons, that putteth him in this courage'. Walsingham therefore recommends that a change should be made in the lieutenancy of the Tower. It looks as if he were thinking of what was happening in the case of the Earl of Northumberland, who at that moment was receiving information smuggled into the Tower from outside. It is possible that the conduct of Sir Owen Hopton, the Lieutenant of the Tower, had come under criticism in consequence. At any rate, Walsingham adds: 'It suffereth not for him that shall hold that place to be only faithful, but he ought to be wise. I know it now to be the corruptest prison in England.' Hopton continued in his post, but Arundel was put specially in the charge of Henry MacWilliam, and Walsingham asks Hatton to advise MacWilliam to look well to his charge. Henry MacWilliam, about whom something has been said in a previous chapter, is the Gentleman Pensioner who was a fairly close associate of Hatton's.

A letter from Arundel to Hatton, written from the Tower in May, 1585, occurs in the Letter Book. It is known that Hatton had been one of those charged with his examination, and had specially pressed him to confess all, as he loved his life. Arundel's letter, therefore, says that he has been trying to call to mind anything else he ought to have disclosed. He does not deny that he has been both absolved and confessed, but protests that he was moved by religion only, and not by any hostile intention towards Queen or State. He admits, however, that he had offered to be at the direction of Dr. Allen, that is Cardinal Allen, notoriously Elizabeth's bitter traducer, and that in that respect he had 'offended against her Majesty'. His letter to Allen has in fact been intercepted, apparently by means of Henry Dunne, one of Hatton's servants, a Catholic later executed as one of the Babington conspirators. Arundel has done no more, he protests, and has not been privy to any plot: 'I must confess I was slipping, but not fallen. I call God to witness she hath raised many that hath slipped more, and therefore I cannot despair but that she can raise me . . .' And so he asks for mercy. He was not brought to trial until 1589, when he was sentenced to death. But the sentence was not executed; he was fined instead £10,000, and imprisoned during pleasure. He died in 1595.

These records are sufficient to show how closely Hatton was concerned in the affairs of Catholic conspirators accused of treason. His was often the task of examining them, and for that purpose it sometimes happened that they were entrusted to his custody for a time. This phase of his life is illustrated by an amusing message that the Queen sent him about a Catholic priest named Isaac Higgins who was in his charge. The message was that 'her Highness thinketh your house will shortly be like [a] Gravesend barge, never without a knave, a priest or a thief &c'.

A minor design to assassinate the Queen was that of John Somerville, a Warwickshire gentleman. Somerville was a son-in-law of Edward Arden, another Warwickshire squire, who is remembered as a cousin of Shakespeare's mother. The Ardens were distantly connected with Francis Throckmorton, the conspirator, and all were Catholics. Edward Arden lodged a priest in his house, Hugh Hall, who lived with him disguised as a gardener. To Hall's influence was due the plan of Somerville, a weak-minded man, to murder Elizabeth. He seems indeed to have become quite insane. Declaring that he would go to Court to shoot the Queen, and hoping to see 'her head set upon a pole, for she was a serpent and a viper', he took the road to London, threatening and assaulting those whom he met by the way. He and his wife, Arden and his wife, and Hall were apprehended, and all were sentenced to death. Hall and the two women were reprieved; Somerville was found strangled in his cell, presumably by his own hand; and Arden was executed.

Camden is the authority for the statement that Arden's prosecution was largely due to the influence of Leicester, whose livery he had declined to wear and whom he had enraged by reflections on his conduct with Lady Essex while her first husband was alive and before her marriage with Leicester. This intrigue, which was supposed to have played its part in the events that led to Doughty's execution by Drake, here crops up again. And just as the notorious *Leycester's Commonwealth* lends colour to the Doughty story, so it has a word to say of Hall the priest and of Edward Arden, in a tale that concerns Hatton.

Leycester's Commonwealth cannot, of course, be relied upon for accuracy; it is so obviously inspired by malevolence that historians have generally ignored it. But it was written in 1583-4, close to the events which it chronicles; and it is probable that there is some foundation, however twisted, for many of its statements. Purely imaginary tales are worthless as propaganda; there must be some element of truth in them if they are to be in any way effective.

The Hatton story occurs in an attack on Leicester for his practice of 'driving men to attempt somewhat whereby they may incur danger, or remain in perpetual suspicion and disgrace'. After instancing, as a case in point, Leicester's collusion with Norfolk in his plan for marrying the Queen of Scots, and his subsequent abandonment of the Duke, the narrative proceeds:

> As, for example, what say you to the device he had of late to entrap his well deserving friend, Sir Christopher Hatton, in the matter of Hall his priest, whom he would have sent away and hid, being touched and detected in the case of Ardent [Arden], thereby to have drawn in Sir Christopher himself (as Sir Charles Candish can well declare, if it please him) being accessory to this plot, for the overthrow of Sir Christopher. To which intent the most devilish drift pertaineth (I doubt not) if the matter were duly examined, of the late intercession of letters at Paris from one Aldred of Lyous [Lyons], then in Rome to Henry Umpton [Unton], servant to Sir Christopher, [in] which letters, Sir Christopher is reported to be of such credit and especial favour at Rome, as if he were the greatest Papist in England.

All this is incoherent enough. But the intention, as in the two other passages in *Leycester's Commonwealth* where Hatton is named, is to praise Hatton at the expense of Leicester, presumably with the hope of making mischief between them. Leicester, as the spokesman of the Puritans, was detested by the Catholics, who were aware of Hatton's inclination to Catholicism and had not abandoned hope of reclaiming him to the fold. And the characters in the story are, of course, real people. Hall and Arden were involved in Somerville's mad project to murder Elizabeth; and it is possible that Hatton endeavoured to save the priest, if so successfully, since Hall was pardoned, or, at any rate, not executed. Froude says he was spared, 'having paid, it is easy to see, the only price by which he could have saved himself, and undertaken to be a spy'. But there is no evidence that Hall was ever so employed. He was still in prison in 1585, two years after this, and may have died there. In a previous chapter it has been suggested that he may have been the priest-gardener who laid out the gardens at Holdenby. If so, he was lately dead in 1597, when Sir Thomas Tresham referred to his recent death. That Leicester tried to implicate Hatton in responsibility for the Arden-Somerville plot is most unlikely.

Sir Henry Unton, the English Ambassador in Paris, was a follower of Hatton's. At this time he writes to Walsingham, concerning 'one Aldred, the player of my brother's tragedy'. This is the Aldred of *Leycester's Commonwealth*, who had been involved in the imprisonment in Milan of Unton's elder brother, Edward. He was Solomon Aldred, an agent of the Pope, who afterwards deserted to Walsingham, becoming an English spy. He has another interest, since his widow married Thomas Lodge, the dramatist. The statement in *Leycester's Commonwealth* that Aldred had written to Unton that Hatton was regarded in Rome as an active Catholic, is put in such a way as to insinuate that the letter reflected the inspiration of Leicester.

CHAPTER XXV

PRELUDE TO THE BABINGTON PLOT

THE Babington Plot concerns a biographer of Sir Francis Walsingham more closely than that of any other Elizabethan statesman. Walsingham's was the hand that unravelled it; his opponents would say that he was its fomenter, if not its begetter. The credit, or discredit according to the point of view, that attaches to a successful police coup which sent nigh a score of young Catholic gentlemen to the gallows and Mary Stuart to the block, belongs to Walsingham alone. Hatton, however, played a prominent part in the trial of the conspirators, and the history of the plot is therefore an important chapter in his life. In the lengthy list of its *dramatis personae* there are a number of characters who had more or less intimate dealings with him. In order not to interrupt the story of the conspiracy, it is proposed to consider here separately two figures who played minor parts in these events. They are not of much moment, men of reckless character and evil lives. But Hatton had his share in dealing with the crimes of the one; and the other, a violent and somewhat enigmatic person, was one of those many men who are described as his servants, a term that may mean actual members of his household or, as in this case, men to whom he posed as patron and who looked to him for support. The stories of Barnard Maude and Jacomo di Francisci bring us into the Elizabethan underworld, and illustrate the rich, if sordid variety of the teeming life of the great Queen's reign.

In the Babington drama Barnard Maude and Jacomo di Francisci figure as spies and *agents provocateurs*. We do not know very much of Maude in his role as *agent provocateur*. But we do know something of his previous history; and it is so dramatic, though unsavoury, that it is worth setting out in some detail as illustrating the kind of agent upon whom Walsingham, unavoidably, no doubt, had to rely for much of his information.

Barnard Maude is presumably the man of that name who was a scholar of Trinity College, Oxford, in 1561, and took his B.A. degree in 1566. If so, he would have been in the early forties at the time of the Babington Plot. Presumably also he belonged to the well-known Yorkshire family of Maude; at any rate, he shows a knowledge of its traditions, since he sometimes went by the alias of Montalto, a reference to the Latinized form, de Monte Alto, of Mohaut or Monthalt, the early spelling of his family name. He first steps on the stage of history, minor, it is true, as a gentleman in the household of Edwin Sandys, Archbishop of York, whom he treated in a singularly scurvy fashion. There is a certain scandalous interest in the story, and it may be told here in illustration of the varied background of the Babington Plot, and because Hatton had a connection with it.

Sir Robert Stapleton, of Wighill in Yorkshire, belonged to an old and wealthy family, and was apparently well thought of. There is, for instance, a letter in the Hatton Letter Book from Sir Walter Mildmay, Walsingham's brother-in-law and Chancellor of the Exchequer, addressed to Hatton, commending to him Stapleton's suit to marry an heiress. Mildmay writes of him as 'a gentleman whom I have and do love and like of as well as any in the North parties', while Sir Harris Nicolas quotes a contemporary as speaking of him as 'a man well spoken; properly seen in languages; a comely and good personage; had scarce an equal and, next to Sir Philip Sidney, no superior in England'. Singularly indiscriminating eulogies both, for Stapleton in May, 1582, entered into the basest conspiracy against the unfortunate Archbishop of York. One day that month the Archbishop was lodging at the Bull Inn, Doncaster, where Stapleton arrived accompanied by John Mallory, Barnard Maude and three or four other retainers. Stapleton and Sandys were not on good terms; and on Stapleton asking to be employed by the Archbishop on some business in London, Sandys flew out at him in 'very ill terms', and there was a scene. Stapleton, going to supper with William Sisson the innkeeper, and his wife, and speaking of the quarrel, the innkeeper, who might have stepped out of the pages of *Tom Jones*, made a villainous proposal, for:

> after supper Sisson drew Sir Robert aside into a window, where very privately he told Sir Robert that he might well be even with the Bishop for his hard usuage, for that the Bishop had entreated his wife to lie with him that night, and that the hour was appointed about eleven in the night. Sir Robert did very hardly believe this. 'Well', said Sisson, 'ask my wife, for she can tell you a whole story

of it.' 'Truly,' quod Sir Robert, 'I don't think it possible, considering the time and place'. 'So God shall save me, Sir Robert', said Sisson, 'it is most true, and take this for one note, while my wife were at supper set with you, the Bishop sent his man Kyrrell twice for her, and the latter time she went and found him in his bed. Then he would needs have her stay with him, but she excused herself for business she had to do.'

It appeared later that Maude contrived the plot, and bent to his purpose the needy Sisson, scenting blackmail, and Stapleton, full of spleen against the Archbishop. Sisson sent his wife into the Archbishop's bedroom, and presently with one of his men and Maude 'who had been the Archbishop's servant', followed with a dagger in his hand. Placing his dagger against the Archbishop's breast, he shouted, 'God's precious life, I will mark a whore and a thief'. Stapleton then made his appearance and proceeded to blackmail the Archbishop. No less than £800 was demanded from the terrified prelate, who eventually agreed to surrender £600 and a lease of some lands. But further demands for lands and money being made, Sandys plucked up his courage to refuse, and informed Burghley of the whole business.

It is not easy to imagine how the Archbishop can be completely cleared of misconduct. There seems to be little doubt that the innkeeper's wife was found in his bedroom; and, although he protested that she was not there with his consent, it is fairly evident that he fell into the trap set for him. As Froude sums up the story, 'a letter from Walsingham to the Archbishop, with which the records of inquiry close, is not exactly what would have been written to a wholly innocent man. But the Archbishop was old, and had probably only been foolish'.

An investigation was ordered, and the Queen took a close interest in the matter. She stood the Archbishop's friend, and left the tactful handling of the case to Burghley, Hatton keeping her informed of what was being done. There are thus a number of letters in the Hatton Letter Book concerning this affair. Burghley, after sifting it to the bottom, interceded with the Queen through Hatton to have Stapleton leniently dealt with on account of his position and previous good conduct. He writes to Hatton, saying that after Sisson had confessed to the plot he examined Stapleton, who at first denied Sisson's charges against him and relied on the testimony of Mallory and Maude to clear him. But, being pressed, he confessed, saying that Sisson and his wife had concocted the plot, and he had joined in it as he was displeased with Sandys and wished to have him 'under his girdle'. Burghley is inclined to be merciful. At the end of the letter he notes that Sisson confessed that 'his speeches of looking in at the keyhole were false, and of the Bishop kissing of his wife'.

To this letter Hatton replied, conveying the Queen's thanks for Burghley's 'grave and wise handling of this great cause'. But she was dissatisfied with the treatment of Stapleton and thought that he should be 'more strictly looked unto', and ordered the Master of the Rolls to have him in safe keeping. Stapleton and the rest were found guilty. It seems that Hatton had a hand in their trial, as he had in most trials in which the Queen was specially interested. The evidence for this is a letter from Dr. Toby Mathew, thanking him on behalf of the Archbishop

> specially for that excellent oration of yours (for it was no less) in his purgation and punishment of his accusers, to the glory of God, the honour of her Majesty, the credit of our calling, the further-ance of the Gospel, the confusion of our adversaries, the comfort of all true professors, and perpetual testimony of your zeal to religion, justice and innocency.

What happiness, he proceeds, had the Archbishop 'to light upon so gracious a Prince as is our Sovereign, so sacred a Senate as is that board, so plain, so dear, so honourable a friend as was your Honour'. And amid his congratulations, Toby Mathew does not omit to enter a plea for himself for the Deanery of Durham.

Of Maude the court of inquiry found that he had lately served the said Archbishop, and upon sundry misbehaviours

> and abuses by him committed, was put out of his services, in respect whereof he was become a malicious enemy against the said Archbishop

and had been the prime mover in concocting the slander. He was ordered to give back to Sandys all the money he had fraudu-lently obtained from him and pay the Queen £300, and he was sentenced to be imprisoned in the Fleet for three years. Had he not 'humbly submitted and confessed his offence', his ears would have been slit, 'as he had well deserved'. He turns up next as a Government spy in the Babington drama.

Jacomo di Francisci, commonly called Captain Jaques, was a much more important person than Maude. A violent and dangerous man, his connection with Hatton is tantalizingly obscure. According to a report on English fugitives in the Netherlands among the papers of the Elizabethan statesman Sir Ralph Sadler, he was born in Antwerp of Italian parents, but was brought up in England from his infancy, 'and in many duties tied both to the nation and to sundry gentlemen of the same, for many their loves and liberalities towards him, especially to the late Lord Chancellor [Hatton], whom he served and who had always been his especial good friend and favourer'. The earliest reference to him is in Babington's confession. Babington says he met him in France about September, 1583. He calls him a soldier of Ireland; and this agrees with the next mention of him that has been found. For the Irish State Papers show that he was in Ireland in 1585, where he was Lieutenant to Sir William Stanley. Stanley, after serving with Alva in the Netherlands, had spent fifteen years of fighting in Ireland where he rendered good service to the Deputy, Lord Grey, Hatton's friend and distant relative, before joining in Leicester's campaign in the Netherlands, where he gained an odious notoriety by his treacherous surrender of Deventer to the Spaniards.

At this date Captain Jaques, among his other activities, seems to have acted as some sort of an agent for Hatton in Ireland. For in June of that year, 1585, he was about to return to England armed with a letter of introduction to Burghley from Archbishop Loftus, who commends 'the bearer, Mr. Jacomo di Francesqui, servant to Mr. Vice-Chamberlain [Hatton], a forward and valiant gentleman'. It is Loftus who tells us that Jaques was Stanley's Lieutenant, adding that he had gallantly fought in Ulster and Munster, 'sundry times lost his blood, and very hardly escaped with life; his behaviour otherwise such as may become a civil, honest gentleman'. But the Archbishop's ideas of honesty are not, perhaps, ours. Loftus was busy at this time intriguing against Sir John Perrot, Hatton's enemy, who had succeeded Grey as Irish Deputy; and in a later chapter it will be shown that he was also employing Hatton's chaplain, Richard Bancroft, afterwards Archbishop of Canterbury, to frustrate Perrot's scheme for founding a University in Dublin. It is possible that Jaques was of use to Hatton in various Irish affairs, such as keeping an eye on Perrot and looking after Hatton's interests in the forfeited Desmond estates.

Jaques next appears in the confessions of a priest, Anthony Tyrrell, who accompanied Ballard, one of the Babington conspirators, on three long circuits among the Catholics of England in 1585. In the last of these, apparently towards the end of the year, Ballard, Tyrrell says, became acquainted with Babington, Tilney, another of the conspirators, Jaques, 'Sir Christopher Hatton's man', and others. This therefore was the service to which Hatton, no doubt with Walsingham's approval, put Jaques on his arrival from Ireland — to spy on Ballard, as Maude was also doing. Jaques seems to have returned to Ireland in the following year, for Babington in his confession of September, 1596, says he last saw him a little before he went into Ireland, 'which was about the last term', that is presumably about June. Jaques boasted to Edward Windsor, whose most interesting letter to Hatton will be quoted in the next chapter, that he would raise insurrection in Ireland, while Maude, as a Yorkshire man, similarly undertook to foment rebellion in the North.

How did Hatton come to be the patron of a man whose record is so enigmatic, one who posed as a Government agent, yet whose subsequent career proves that he was a potential if not actual enemy of the State he professed to serve? For in the end we meet him in the pay of Parma, serving under the traitor Sir William Stanley, and using violent speech against Queen Elizabeth. It was a critical time in the history of the revolted Netherlands; and Elizabeth, while professing to help them, was through underground channels endeavouring to reach a peace with Spain at their expense. Hatton, who trimmed his sails so closely to the inconstant breezes of his Queen's policy, may have thought that Captain Jaques, with his connections in Ireland and the Netherlands, might prove a useful political agent.

Amidst so much that is obscure, one can only conjecture. It would be unjust to suggest that Hatton did anything more in the Netherlands affair than keep an eye on events and fly a few peace kites, as his mistress was doing. There is no need to suppose that he was actively intriguing against his friend Leicester, who had been dispatched by the reluctant Queen to attempt or pretend to attempt some help for the revolting Provinces; or that he was trying to balk the efforts steadily made in their behalf by Walsingham, with whose views he was in general agreement. On the contrary, his nephew William Hatton took part in the campaign; and his old follower Thomas Churchyard, a straightforward soldier innocent of any gift for intrigue, was with Leicester's army and keeping Hatton informed of events. Moreover, there is ample evidence that Hatton and Walsingham did all they could to help Leicester, whose actions in the Low Countries had enraged the Queen. A little must be said about the campaign here, for not only does it furnish a characteristic anecdote of Hatton, but it concerns the subsequent career of Captain Jaques.

Elizabeth's dislike of this overseas enterprise was inflamed by Leicester's action in assuming the title of Governor of the Netherlands. That appeared to derogate from her authority; perhaps it sounded too much as if the English really intended business, for her liking. And there were rumours that Leicester's wife, whom she loathed, Lettice Knollys, widow of the Earl of Essex, was preparing to join her husband in the Low Countries with a great suite, to keep semi-regal state there.

From Thomas Dudley, a member of Leicester's household, we learn something of these reactions. He wrote to the Earl to say how much the Queen disliked his assuming the Netherlands government, and his intention of having his wife with him to share his honours. Dudley denied that Lady Leicester was going to her husband, and on Burghley and Hatton telling Elizabeth this, it 'did greatly pacify her stomach'. But she prepared to send Sir Thomas Heneage, the Treasurer of the Chamber, to Leicester with a message, presumably one of three devastating royal letters which followed him to the Netherlands, for Hatton and Walsingham were delaying its dispatch as long as they could and, with Burghley's help, were hopeful of softening it. Meanwhile Leicester had written to Hatton. Hatton wondered if he should show the letter to the Queen, but on Walsingham's advice suppressed it, as Elizabeth was angry because Leicester had not written to her. However, 'they conferred of the letter again, and blotting out some things which they thought would be offensive, and mending some other parts as they thought best', Hatton showed it to the Queen, hoping to pacify her. 'Mr. Vice-Chamberlain', writes Thomas Dudley to Leicester, 'thinketh that your Honour's own letters to her Majesty will do more good and better satisfy her Majesty in all things than all that they can or do say; and wisheth withal that you would bestow some two or three hundred crowns in some rare thing for a token to her Majesty.'

Hatton's advice to Leicester to make Elizabeth a costly present in order to appease her has often been quoted as an illustration of her vanity, and of Hatton's cynical view of a courtier's way with his Queen. It was practices of this kind that Bacon no doubt had in mind when, five years after Hatton's death, he wrote his celebrated letter of worldly advice to the hot-headed Essex, Lettice Knollys's son. Scorning the faults he professed to find in Hatton, he yet recommended them to his pupil's imitation:

> Next, whereas I have noted you to fly and avoid (in some respect justly) the resemblance or imitation of my Lord of Leicester and my Lord Chancellor Hatton, yet I am persuaded (howsoever I wish your Lordship as distant as you are from them in points of favour, integrity, magnanimity and merit) that it will do you much good between the Queen and you, to allege them (as oft as you find occasion) for authors and patterns. For I do not know a readier mean to make her Majesty think you are in the right way.

Begun thus inauspiciously, Leicester's campaign came to nothing, and is almost forgotten to-day except as the occasion of the death of the incomparable Philip Sidney at Zutphen. And besides suffering his Queen's annoyance, he was surrounded by spies and traitors, such as Robert Poley, whom we shall meet again in the story of the Babington Plot. And soon came Sir William Stanley from Ireland, with his army of Irish kernes. Stanley meditated treachery from the outset. He was in the confidence of the Jesuits, knew of the activities of Babington, and corresponded with Arundel in the Tower and with Mendoza. He wrote to Captain Jaques in Ireland to join him; a witness to these events afterwards deposed that his reason for asking Jaques to come to him was that Jaques had vowed that he would never serve against the King of Spain.

That was in the latter part of the year 1586. Jaques did not join Stanley's army in the Netherlands on that occasion; he was detained at home by his duties as spy and *agent provocateur*. But how far he really acted as a Government agent is doubtful. His subsequent career proves that his sympathies were really with the Catholic party, and he spent the rest of his life in reviling Queen Elizabeth. It is likely that he was a mere adventurer, willing to play any part that promised him advantage.

In the following January, Stanley surrendered the town of Deventer to the Spaniards; and Cardinal Allen defended his action on the ground that Deventer belonged to the King of Spain. Thereupon the Lords of the Council wrote to the Irish Deputy to keep a watchful eye on all those known to be Stanley's secret friends and dependants, especially one 'Jaques de Francesco his lieutenant, of whom both in respect he is a stranger ill-affected in religion, and noted to have had some intelligence with Ballard, lately executed here for the conspiracy against her Majesty's life, we think fit to be removed out of his charge and sent hither before this fact [i.e. act] of his captain be divulged'. Jaques appears to have been sent to the Fleet for a year, partly on account of his friendship with Stanley and partly for the sake of appearances, to keep up the pretence that the Government spy was one of the Babington conspirators. From prison Jaques got into correspondence with Florence McCarthy, whom he had known in Ireland, and counselled him to take a step which greatly agitated the Government.

Florence McCarthy, a young Irishman of noble birth, was closely allied to the head of his house and had been at Court and made a good impression there. He aspired to marry the daughter and heiress of his kinsman McCarthy Mor, Earl of Clancarty and representative of the ancient Irish Kings of Desmond. He was also a nephew of Sir James FitzMaurice, who had been a thorn in the English side. His powerful Irish and Anglo-Irish connections, crowned by his marriage to McCarthy's daughter, must result as the Deputy and the President of Munster pointed out to the Government, in McCarthy growing 'greater in Munster than ever the Earl of Desmond was, and no less dangerous'. In the year 1588 the marriage took place, and Sir Thomas Norris, the President of Munster, reported that Jaques had been one of Florence McCarthy's counsellors, urging him to go through with the marriage out of hand and assuring him that he would work with his friends to obtain the Queen's consent to it. Norris recommends that the details of his complicity should be 'boulted out of the said Jaques'. McCarthy was arrested and sent to the Tower, where we need not follow his fortunes further; but the incident gives a strong indication of the capacity for intrigue of Sir Christopher Hatton's favourite.

In 1589 Jaques went to the Low Countries, to join his friend

Sir William Stanley, who made him Lieutenant-Colonel of his regiment. But Stanley was no longer in much credit with Alva and the Spaniards. 'Jaques, I suppose', runs the statement of Anthony Copley, an imprisoned Catholic informer, 'wisheth himself in Ireland again, seeing how much his hope of advancement in Flanders by Sir William Stanley is come to nothing'; and, after mentioning the favour he enjoyed from his friends at Court, 'courtesies which for ever would have tied a thankful mind', the account of him in the State Papers concludes, 'he was suffered to depart the realm; all which, notwithstanding, it is reported that there is not any beyond the sea that doth run a more violent and unreverent course against the person of her Majesty than he doth'. He was fond too of asking English Catholic refugees whether it would not be a good thing to attempt Elizabeth's life; and his reckless speeches were a constant source of danger to them, beset as they were on every side by informers. We catch a last vivid glimpse of him in the deposition of an English Catholic, who met him in Antwerp in 1592:

> One day a Mr. Jaques came to dinner, whom I never saw before that time. He was attired in black satin, with a man attending on him. He uttered these, or the like words, at the table: 'By God, they say in England I would have killed the Queen, but, by God, belie me.' What he was I am not able to say; he was slender and reasonably tall of stature, and had a black beard; and had been, as he said, a follower of the deceased Lord Chancellor [Hatton].

CHAPTER XXVI

THE BABINGTON PLOT

THE Babington Plot is the most important Catholic conspiracy
of Elizabeth's reign. Not that there is any certainty, or even
perhaps reasonable likelihood that, if left to themselves, any of
the rather amateurish conspirators would have summoned up the
resolution to murder the Queen. Of all the plots directed against
Elizabeth's life, it is difficult to point to one that passed the stage
of aimless confabulations, hints, threats and boasts, and approached that of matured plans, let alone a real attempt to put
them into execution. Assassination does not come easily to
Englishmen. In this case the impetus came from abroad. The
idea of killing the Queen first took shape after the murder of the
Prince of Orange in 1584. That deed can be traced to the Ban
placed on the Prince four years before; and the horror it aroused
in England called into being a 'Bond of Association for the
Safety of the Queen', by which private citizens bound themselves
to take vengeance on anyone making an attempt on Elizabeth's
person, or on anyone in whose favour such an attempt should be
made.

The formulation and condemnation in advance of an apprehended crime may indeed in unbalanced minds, avid for notoriety,
act as an incentive to it; and it is possible that the formation of the
Association actually encouraged the idea of the crime against
which it was directed. But the seed scattered by foreign enemies
of the Queen seems to have fallen in England on singularly
unstable ground. The potential assassins of Elizabeth were either
semi-lunatics like Somerville and Parry, wandering priests such
as Ballard, who had picked up in their peregrinations abroad
something of the foreign insensitiveness to political assassination,
or groups of Catholic youths, Babington and Tichbourne and their
associates, hare-brained enthusiasts, posturing in speech and
letter, and posing for the portrait painter as men dedicated to a
fatal purpose, though they lacked the resolution to bring matters
to an issue.

But though one may doubt, not the fact of a conspiracy among

270

Babington and his fellows, but the urgency of any real danger to Elizabeth's person, the plot that takes its name from Anthony Babington was of great political importance. For its discovery and its collapse in the execution of the conspirators were the prelude to bringing Mary Queen of Scots to the block. The exposure — his enemies aver even its fostering, if not its actual contrivance — was the work of Walsingham. But the members of the Privy Council and the Queen herself were, of course, aware of what Walsingham was doing, and followed developments as the implications of the plot were unfolded.

In addition to this general interest, Hatton was concerned in the Babington Plot in other ways. One of the spies, or *agents provocateurs* whom Walsingham employed, Jacomo di Francisci, otherwise Captain Jaques, was, as shown in the last chapter, a member of Hatton's retinue. And two of the conspirators, Chidiock Tichbourne and Henry Dunne had also been his followers. More important than these personal contacts, was the part Hatton played at the trial of the plotters. He was the most prominent of the commissioners present. Then, as on other occasions, we may take it that he was in a special sense a representative of the Queen. He had prepared himself carefully for his task for, as already pointed out, the Bardon Papers are to a large extent Hatton's 'brief' for his speeches at the trials of the conspirators and of Mary Queen of Scots, and for his speeches in Parliament later.

From more than one point of view, therefore, the Babington Plot is of importance in the story of Hatton's life. But it cannot be dealt with in full detail here. To unravel all its ramifications would demand a book in itself, which would look backwards to the Duke of Guise's plan for assassinating Elizabeth three years before, while forwards its implications, in the person of Robert Poley, one of Walsingham's spies, might be conceivably prolonged to the violent and mysterious death in 1593 of Christopher Marlowe. A book which surveys nearly all the scene has indeed been written by Father J. H. Pollen in his *Mary Queen of Scots and the Babington Plot*, and to that work and to Dr. Conyers Read's more impersonal study in the third volume of his life of Walsingham, the reader must be referred for a full narrative. As in the case of other national events touched upon here, our account must be limited to what closely concerns Hatton.

The foregoing remarks indicate the difficulty of selecting a point at which to begin. The Babington Plot was not a single conspiracy complete in itself. There were plots within plots, and portions of old plots incorporated in the new. As far back as 1583 the Duke of Guise, Mary Stuart's cousin, had offered a reward for the murder of Elizabeth. A candidate appeared in the person of George Gifford. He is the first member of this family, so intimately connected with the Babington Plot, to come upon the scene. He was the head of the ancient Catholic clan of Gifford of Itchell, Hampshire, and Weston-under-Hill, Gloucestershire. In 1578 he was a Gentleman Pensioner, and therefore must have known Hatton. Indeed it seems certain that he knew him well. He was Hatton's neighbour, having a house at Eltham where Hatton was Keeper of the royal palace. A man of shady character, he had been party to the escape from prison of a noted highwayman named Nix, and had endeavoured, unsuccessfully, to secure Hatton's influence on Nix's behalf.

Under a cloud, therefore, Gifford crossed to the Continent, and offered himself to the Duke of Guise for the prize for murdering Elizabeth. Nothing came of his plans. He was judged untrustworthy, if not treacherous; and returned to England, to his post of Gentleman Pensioner. He was still a Pensioner when he was arrested in 1586 for suspicion of complicity in the Babington Plot, and lodged in the Beauchamp Tower, where he whiled away the time carving his name and arms. But he denied the charges against him, and escaped with his life. His name was carefully kept out of the proceedings at the trial of the conspirators; and the lenient attitude of the Government towards him, no less than the mistrust he inspired abroad, suggests that he may in reality have been a Government agent, playing a double part throughout. Like many rogues — he was accused also of a whole series of crimes, such as assisting burglars and receiving stolen goods — he prospered in the world, retained the royal favour, turned Protestant, married a Cecil, and was finally knighted by James I.

Guise's plan had probably been suggested by the Ban placed on the Prince of Orange in 1580. In 1584 Orange was assassinated, and another zealous Catholic came forward to carry the torch of murder into England. This was John Savage. Savage had left England in 1581, and had been a soldier in the Low Countries under the Duke of Parma. In 1585, as he afterwards confessed, he had taken at Rheims, where he seems to have been studying for the priesthood, the resolve to assassinate Elizabeth. His resolution was made after conference with three friends, Christopher Hodgson, a priest Dr. William Gifford, afterwards Archbishop of Rheims, a brother of George Gifford, and Gilbert Gifford a distant cousin of George and William, who will afterwards come on the scene in person. William Gifford, according to Savage, was the chief contriver of the plan, but Gilbert Gifford certainly had a good deal to do with it. In August of that year Savage went to England to execute his purpose, but he lacked the necessary resolution, found no suitable opportunity, and did nothing.

Meanwhile, Thomas Morgan, agent in Paris of Mary Queen of Scots, was striving to open up a channel of communication with her. He approached a former pupil of Cardinal Allen's, Christopher Blount a Catholic gentleman in the Earl of Leicester's retinue. Blount was a distant kinsman of Leicester's and his master of the horse, and on Leicester's death in 1588 married his widow, whose first husband had been that Earl of Essex under whom Drake had served in Ulster and whom Leicester had been accused of poisoning with the help of Thomas Doughty, Drake's enemy and victim. Blount thus became the stepfather of Robert Devereux, Earl of Essex, the favourite of Elizabeth in her old age. He was a wild and reckless man, who proved an ill counsellor to his stepson. He was prominent in Essex's rebellion, was specially accused by the unstable Essex in the confession he made before his execution, and suffered with him in 1601. But in 1585 the tragedy of Tower Hill was sixteen years distant, and Christopher Blount was a trusted official of Leicester's household. It appears that Morgan had at one time saved Blount's life, and he therefore thought he could count on his assistance. He asked Blount to help him in his scheme to open up communication with Mary. Blount's answer, probably with Leicester's approval and Walsingham's knowledge, was to send to Morgan a messenger, his relative Robert Poley.

Robert Poley is perhaps the most sinister figure in the Babington Plot. It is some twenty years since the researches of Dr. Leslie Hotson disclosed the part which he played in 1593 in the death of Christopher Marlowe. That tragic happening has not yet been probed to the bottom; all we can guess is that the quarrel, whether

contrived or not, that led to the poet's death, had some connection
with Marlowe's career in the secret service which had brought
him into contact with Walsingham's spy. But even before Dr.
Hotson's discoveries, enough was known of Poley to recognize him
as a singularly unsavoury character. There was obviously something shifty about the man, for Morgan, having made his acquaintance, began by distrusting him and in recommending him
to Mary warned her to test him before reposing faith in him. But
he was plausible, and on his return to England in July, 1585,
gradually won the complete confidence of Mary's friends. His
principal part in the plot was to spy upon Babington and his
associates, into whose friendship he had insinuated himself, and
to keep them at hand until Walsingham was ready to strike. He
is the 'Sweet Robin' of Babington's last letter, a poignant message
which shows that at the eleventh hour Babington began to feel
doubts of his friend's faith.

A few months passed, and Morgan made another effort to open
up communication with Mary Stuart. In December, Gilbert
Gifford who with his kinsman, William, had helped to persuade
Savage to take his oath of murder, came to England with a letter
of recommendation from Morgan to Mary. His ostensible reason
for the journey was to oppose the Jesuits in England, a mission
which would commend itself to Walsingham who was busy trying
to foment dissension between them and the secular Catholic
party, to which Mary's agents, Morgan and Charles Paget, belonged. Gifford landed at Rye and was sent by the port searcher
straight to Walsingham. Certainly then, perhaps earlier, he
entered Walsingham's service and consented to play the part of
spy.

With the aid of Gilbert Gifford and of Thomas Phelippes, a man
deep in his confidence, Walsingham contrived a system by which
Mary would be led to imagine that her friends had opened up a
safe channel of communication with the outside world, while in
reality all her letters were passing through Walsingham's hands.
Morgan was thus brought to believe that he had at length succeeded in his endeavours to find a way by which Mary could write
freely to her friends and receive letters from them, a privilege
denied her since her more strict imprisonment at Chartley under
the stern Puritan, Sir Amyas Paulet, so different from the easy-
going Shrewsbury, with whom she had spent so many long years

at Sheffield Castle. But, owing to the treachery of Gilbert Gifford, Morgan's channel of communication was to be controlled by her enemies.

Thomas Phelippes, a pock-marked, short-sighted fellow, with dark yellow hair and light yellow beard (Mary Queen of Scots' description), was a shrewd and double-faced man who, however, seems to have been consistently faithful to Walsingham. He is best known for his skill in deciphering letters in code — Latin, French and Italian; and his name is in consequence writ large on the State Papers of the day. Walsingham sent him to Chartley to arrange the method of correspondence. It was contrived with the assistance of a Burton brewer who delivered the beer. His name has not come down to us, and Paulet, with unconscious humour, calls him 'the honest man'. Honest he was in a sense, though as Froude puts it, 'like a true English scoundrel, he used the possession of a State secret to exact a higher price for his beer'. Briefly, the arrangement was that letters to and from Mary were inclosed in a receptacle which fitted through the bung-hole of the cask in which the beer was delivered.

By January, 1586, Phelippes had made all arrangements at Chartley with Paulet and the brewer. Meanwhile, Gilbert Gifford, armed with Thomas Morgan's recommendations, was ingratiating himself with the French Ambassador, de Castelnau, who was friendly to Mary's cause; and on the completion of Phelippes's plans went to de Castelnau and told him that he had contrived a way to communicate with the Queen of Scots. A non-committal letter was accordingly sent by the ambassador through Gifford to the brewer and thence to the imprisoned Queen. Mary was delighted; she soon threw all caution to the winds, and asked for her correspondence which had been lying at the French embassy since the discovery of the Throckmorton Plot. She received a substantial bundle, the accumulation of two years, not however before Walsingham had perused the lot — letters of all sorts, many of them relating in especial to Spanish plans for the invasion of England.

In May Mary wrote to Charles Paget, urging him to press forward with these plans. Her letter crossed one from Paget; telling her that a priest named Ballard had just come to France from England, bringing messages from English Catholics that they were ready to rise if they could be assured of some help from abroad. John Ballard thus comes on the scene. He is perhaps the most important figure in the Babington Plot. For it seems that it was he, more than anyone else, who added to the normal plan of the many plots that contemplated invasion and rebellion, the special ingredient of Elizabeth's murder. He appears to have thought of assassination about the same time that Savage took his resolution in 1584 for, according to the confession of Anthony Tyrrell, who is not however a very reliable witness, Ballard had gone to Rome in that year to obtain endorsement from the highest members of the Church for his murder plan. When he was admitted to the councils of Morgan and Paget, he seems to have thought first of Savage, already dedicated to the murder of Elizabeth, as the prime instrument. Afterwards, as he came to know the group of young Catholic gentlemen who centred round Anthony Babington, he passed on to them the task of assassination, and Savage was admitted to the circle because of his vow.

Ballard was a Cambridge graduate who had fled from England in 1579 for his religion, and had wandered about the Continent. As has been related above, he had been in England again in 1586, and in April of that year had just arrived in Paris from that country. Unknown to him, Walsingham, as we shall see in a moment, had already set Barnard Maude to spy upon him. Maude dined with him in London in March, and accompanied him to France. Ballard was a boastful man, given to rash speeches. He told Morgan, Paget and Mendoza, lately Spanish Ambassador in London and now in Paris, of the enthusiastic attitude of the English Catholics towards Mary's cause and towards plans for invasion and rebellion. They existed mostly in his imagination. Mendoza was sceptical, asked for details, and gave him minute instructions how to set about accomplishing these aims. Morgan and Paget were more credulous; and it was through their recommendations to Mary that Ballard was put in a position to wield an influence within the Babington group. His tendency to wild statements is illustrated by his assuring Babington and Savage that he had a promise of an army of 60,000 men. But, if he inflamed these rash young men and, through faults of temperament, misled them on the possibility of accomplishing their designs, his actions were in good faith. He was undoubtedly an ardent believer in the cause of assassination, rebellion and invasion.

Not so two other figures who now emerge, spies and *agents provocateurs*, Barnard Maude and Jacomo di Francisci. We left Maude undergoing three years' imprisonment for his blackmailing attempt on the Archbishop of York. Before his sentence had expired he was at liberty. He had entered Walsingham's service as a spy, and in March of this year (1586) when he should have been in prison, he was in the company of Ballard, Babington, Tichbourne and others of the conspirators at the Plough Inn, Temple Bar. In April, Ballard, as we have seen, arrived in France, bringing letters to Morgan and Paget about the strength of Catholic feeling in England. According to Camden, Maude accompanied him as a spy. There can be little doubt that Maude was released from prison for just that purpose. Camden calls him a shrewd fellow, who accompanied Ballard on his journey to France and wrung from him all his secrets. And Babington reported to Poley that Maude and Ballard went to France together.

Ballard, whether or not he suspected Maude at this time, contrived to give him the slip, and returned to London armed with Morgan's letters of recommendation. Maude wrote to Walsingham at the beginning of August, confessing that he had no news; and a few days later Walsingham wrote to the Queen, saying that Maude had never got thoroughly into Ballard's confidence, and that it was useless to employ him further. He was clearly of no great assistance to the Government.

Maude turns up again in 1592 in Flanders, where he was spying, and was arrested by the Spanish authorities at the instance of John Pauncefote, a Catholic exile who had married a sister of Edward Windsor, one of the Babington conspirators. Pauncefote said that Montalto, or Maude, posed as a Catholic, and later accused him of betraying Ballard and his associates to their deaths. Maude made his escape on this occasion, and the last we hear of him is in a report from Flanders in 1596 of an English spy, who declared that if he or Poley returned to that country they would be executed.

Bearing in mind all this history of espionage, it is not remarkable that Maude was not produced as a witness at the Babington Trial. The Government relied for their case on the confessions of the prisoners. They would not damage it by bringing such a shady character into Court. The same remark applies to Jacomo di Francisci or Captain Jaques. The testimony of Edward Windsor goes to show that Maude and Jaques were particularly active as *agents provocateurs*. And as with Maude, Jaques was not produced at the Babington Trial. But he was arrested, no doubt as a blind, and got a year's imprisonment in the Fleet. It was this concealment of the part that Maude and Jaques had played that moved Edward Windsor to indignation.

Edward Windsor was brother to Lord Windsor, a nobleman with whom Ballard had been in communication and who was strongly suspected of sympathy with Catholic plots. Edward Windsor was closely in touch with the Babington conspirators. He avoided capture in the first instance, but was tried later, condemned, and escaped death through the intercession of his mother. While in the Tower in May, 1587, he wrote to Hatton. His is a long, rambling letter, but one that contains matter of great interest.

Windsor, who begins by declaring that there is no evidence against him save what is contained in his own confession of his faults, goes on to remind Hatton of the course of Hatton's examination of him. Here, as in other cases, we see Hatton employed in examining prisoners. His suave methods are illustrated by Windsor's remarks:

> Your Honour knoweth that I did not deny anything at the first, that your Honour when ye did but ask me I did as plainly as I could declare unto your Honour, whereupon your Lordship said to me that if your Honour should not examine me straitly concerning these causes I might think that your Honour should not discharge the part of careful servant to the Queen's most excellent Majesty, which was both an honourable speech and wrought that effect in me as myself plainly and truly in all things did discharge the part of a subject in the best manner I could.

Burghley also had urged him, he says, to confess everything, so that he, Hatton and the rest of the Privy Council might be in a favourable position to intercede with the Queen for him. But his candour, he complains, had not availed him anything; and he had been condemned, principally on his own confession that he was to have been present 'at the taking away of the Queen of Scots, and then for being acquainted with the rest of such things as I did confess'.

The main theme of his letter, however, is the scandalous injustice of the Government in taking no measures against Barnard Maude and Captain Jaques, 'whom I did accuse in Westminster Hall to be the chief workers of this conspiracy and to be wholly employed by Ballard to be ready in anything they could do for the assistance of the invasion, the one in the North, the other in

Ireland'. When Windsor wished to withdraw from the whole business, Maude persuaded him to remain; and when his mother's servant warned him that Ballard was a dangerous man, Jaques urged that he should not alter his good opinion of him, as a man of judgment and wisdom.

There follows a passionate and almost incoherent denunciation of Jaques. Windsor had demanded to be confronted with him, yet he was surprised when, sent for by the Lieutenant of the Tower, he found himself face to face with Jaques, whom he expected to see 'no more than the Grand Turk'. The Attorney-General and Solicitor-General were present to ask him of what he accused Jaques, as the Queen desired no man's blood without justice. But Jaques 'most damnably' swore to his innocence of all Windsor's charges, standing 'so stiffly to it before me, to save his scurvy body in damning his soul, and laughing at me, and saying I was drunk, and that I had a devil within me, and how I was a dead man'. One can well believe that the subtle Italian was more than a match for the well-nigh hysterical Englishman.

Windsor then makes his most specific charges:

> For I know (and so will stake it upon my death) that by means of Jackhous and Maude these treasons hath been wrought, and one other [? Gilbert Gifford or Poley] who shall at this time be name-less. Then, considering they have been the chief cause of the loss of so many young gentlemen's blood, and those too the chief persuader of myself to frequent Ballard's company. . . . If it be justice that these men shall live, offending so monstrously as by the laws they have, and be chief workers of such disturbation in the realm, and the chiefs and causers of the shedding of so much blood, I must say, as I did in Westminster Hall that the King's Bench should be a place where justice should be executed. . . . But, my Lord, there is none of ye but knowth that this that I say in the accusation of these men, that they have been the chief workers in these causes. . . .

The letter, rambling, incoherent in places, is poured forth in a torrent, defying grammar and punctuation. But it has the ring of truth; and it is no wonder that the Government did not produce Maude and Jaques at the trial. There was enough sense of fairness left to ensure Windsor's release. Jaques went to the Fleet for a year, no doubt, as already suggested, to give the impression of justice done. His master's favour, says Thomas Barnes the spy, saved Jaques, from trial. The 'master' is presumably Hatton. Jaques' subsequent career has been noticed in the previous chapter.

We have now brought on the scene most of the characters of this complicated plot, some of them hovering on the circumference, some deep at the centre. We have made the acquaintance of Morgan and Paget, Mary's agents in Paris; of George Gifford, Gentleman Pensioner and so colleague, if not friend of Hatton's, posing as a potential murderer of Elizabeth, in truth perhaps a double agent; of the more serious candidates for the role of assassin, John Savage and John Ballard; of Robert Poley, Gilbert Gifford, Barnard Maude and Captain Jaques, Walsingham's spies. It is time to turn to the group of young Catholic gentlemen who belonged to the circle of the man after whom the plot has been called, Anthony Babington.

Anthony Babington of Dethick, Derbyshire, was a Catholic gentleman of good family and considerable estate. He had been a page to the Earl of Shrewsbury when Mary Queen of Scots had been in Shrewsbury's keeping, and had been the means of conveying several letters to her at that time. He was now aged about twenty-five, moved in Court circles and was the leader of a group of Catholics, many of whom had been members of George Gilbert's Catholic Association founded in 1580 to help the mission of the Jesuits Campion and Parsons. They included Charles Tilney, a Gentleman Pensioner, cousin of Edmund Tilney, Master of the Revels; Edward Abington or Habington, son of Elizabeth's Under-Treasurer, elder brother of Thomas Habington the Worcestershire antiquary, and uncle of William Habington the poet; Thomas Salusbury, heir of a great Denbighshire family, at one time a ward and follower of Leicester's; Chidiock Tichbourne, a Hampshire gentleman, described as a servant of Hatton's; Edward Jones, Salusbury's bosom friend, son of the Master of the Wardrobe; Henry Dunne described as a servant of Sir Christopher Hatton's and called by Mendoza 'a secretary of Hatton's' — he was of the First Fruits Office, an office of which Hatton was Receiver;[1]

---

[1] In a list of the Babington conspirators (Cal. Hatfield Papers, iii, n. 444) he appears as 'Hen. Dune, sometime servant to Mr. Dodge', and Father Pollen glosses, 'probably enough a blind to hide the name of Hatton' (*Life of Philip Howard, Earl of Arundel*, p. 116, n.). But Dodge was a real person. Francis Flower and Edward Dodge write to Sir William Catesby in 1581 regarding a fine, probably in connection with Hatton's purchase from Catesby in that year of the manor of Gretton (Cal. State Papers Dom.). Flower was Hatton's man, and so presumably was Dodge.

Robert Gage, son of a Surrey squire who had been M.P. for
Lewes, and nephew of Thomas Wilford, Treasurer of London and
President of the Company of Merchant Adventurers trading to
Spain and Portugal; and Robert Barnewall, an Irishman on a
visit to the Court, presumably a member of the well-known Irish
family of Barnewall, Lords Trimlestown, with whom Campion
had found refuge during his visit to Dublin. An alarmingly large
number of these men thus belonged to Court circles in intimate
contact with the Queen. The vainglorious spirit in which they
approached their enterprise, posing as deliverers of their country,
is illustrated by the fact that they had their portraits painted in a
group, with Babington in the midst of them. Someone contrived
to show it to Elizabeth. She recognized Barnewall, the Irishman,
and when she next saw him at the Court she looked at him, to
quote Froude, 'with a steadiness that would have alarmed a wiser
man'. This seems to have been a different portrait group from that
mentioned at the trial, as described below.

To his ardent Catholicism Babington added a trustful nature;
he was not particularly brave, somewhat vainglorious and theatri-
cal, fond of debating matters at great length, posing alternative
courses of action and not easily coming to a decision. His havering
speeches and wavering deeds make it difficult to decide whether
he ever really contemplated proceeding to extremities.

Ballard returned to London in May, and began to cultivate
Babington, whose acquaintance he had made before his trip to
France. He unfolded to him his grandiose schemes of foreign
invasion, which existed mostly in his imagination. Babington
raised doubts about the help that might be expected from abroad.
Even should the promise of assistance from Continental powers be
genuine, he thought it hopeless to expect much result while the
Queen of England lived, head of a powerful and settled State.
Ballard answered that 'that difficulty would be taken away by
means already laid: and that her life would be no hindrance
therein. He told me the instrument was Savage, and some others
whose names he told not'. And so Babington was won over to
dally with thoughts of plotting and the still more agreeable long
discourses with his associates that they afforded.

He posed a dilemma to his friends, Tichbourne and the rest.
He saw no remedy for the oppressed state of the Catholics of England; on the other hand, he disliked the idea of a foreign invasion.

Would it not be best for men who thought as he did to leave the country? He made an effort to do so, and applied for a licence through Robert Poley to travel abroad. Poley we have met before, a relative of Christopher Blount, Leicester's Master of Horse, whom Blount sent, presumably with Government approval, to Thomas Morgan to endeavour to hoodwink that arch-plotter and gain his confidence, and with it that of Mary Queen of Scots. Poley was now in the service of Lady Sidney, wife of Sir Philip Sidney and Walsingham's daughter. The French Ambassador, de Castelnau, regarded this arrangement as a master stroke, an agent of Mary's cause successfully planted in the household of Walsingham's daughter. He little guessed that Poley was in reality Walsingham's creature.

We have a picture of Poley at this time, keeping open house, hail-fellow-well-met with all, pretending Catholicism, eager to give what seemed like disinterested advice, really egging on these shallow men to their destruction. Babington held one of his characteristic debates with Poley. Should he and his friends dedi-cate themselves to upholding Queen and State, preserving them from all dangerous practices, as he conceived he would be able to do by reason of his influence with Catholics? Should they on the other hand seek to overthrow the regime? Or, eschewing both courses, should they give themselves over to the contemplative life? For his part, he preferred such a life, and thought to seek it abroad. Poley agreed that might be the best, if one thought only of one's own good, but he hinted that it was unworthy of Babing-ton. So, sincerely by Ballard, treacherously by Poley, the tempting went on.

On Babington's application to travel abroad, Poley brought him to Walsingham. Babington, torn between his three courses, made an offer of service. Walsingham cross-examined him, but was disappointed that he did not reveal all he knew. There was no question of travelling abroad; Walsingham wanted Babington in England, where he could watch the development of his inter-course with Ballard. It was eventually to lead Walsingham to Mary Stuart. Already Savage had been introduced by Ballard to Babington. Gilbert Gifford was flitting to and fro between England and France. And, while the irresolute Babington was applying for leave to go abroad and making offers of service to Walsingham, he was also toying with the idea of revolution — to murder Elizabeth and to set Mary free and put her on the throne. The assassination plan did not get farther than paper. Six of the band were to undertake the murder, but the six were, according to Babington, never actually chosen, though Savage named them as Salusbury, Tichbourne, Barnewall, Habington, Tilney and himself.

Almost immediately after his first meeting with Walsingham Babington was writing to Mary. Morgan had been seeking to persuade him to enter her service and help to keep her supplied with news. Mary wrote to him in June, asking him to forward to her letters which he had from Morgan. In reply, though perhaps his letter was composed before he heard from her, Babington sent her a long epistle, beginning: 'Most mighty, most excellent, my dread sovereign Lady and Queen, unto whom I owe all fidelity and obedience.' It went on to tell of Ballard's activities and of arrangements made for rebellion and invasion. And then came two clauses committing himself and his friends to Mary's rescue and Elizabeth's murder:

> Myself, with ten gentlemen and a hundred our followers, will undertake the delivery of your royal person from the hands of your enemies. For the dispatch of the usurper from the obedience of whom we are by the excommunication of her made free, there be six noble gentlemen, all my private friends, who, for the zeal they bear to the Catholic cause and your Majesty's service, will undertake that tragical execution.

This letter, written in the first week of July, was of course intercepted and read, by means of Walsingham's elaborate arrangements with Phelippes, Paulet and the brewer. Here was something of importance at last. What would be Mary's answer to this revelation? No wonder Phelippes wrote, 'we attend her very heart at the next', decorating the envelope of his letter with the representation of a gallows, which however had no more sinister implication than that it was the usual official sign of urgent haste. Walsingham indeed knew all that was going on; Poley was watching Babington and taking him to see Walsingham; Maude was accompanying Ballard on his tours through England to sound Catholic feeling; and when Maude's treachery was suspected by the conspirators, Gilbert Gifford took his place, to keep an eye on Ballard while urging him on.

The plotters began to take fright. The Catholic rising they had looked for was obviously coming to nothing; Ballard had grossly over-estimated the possibilities of revolution and the insurrectionary feeling of his co-religionists. Nor was the help from abroad, promised by Morgan, forthcoming. Ballard thought of going to France and reporting to Mendoza. He procured through one Knight, a gentleman of Hatton's, a licence to travel abroad under the name of Mr. Thoroughgood of the Temple who, it was pretended, was 'touched by the death of Best' and wanted to escape Hatton's wrath. George Best, the historian of Frobisher's voyages, was another of Hatton's men who had been killed, as related in a previous chapter, by Oliver St. John in obscure circumstances two years before.

Ballard however changed his mind about going abroad, and meanwhile Babington was in agony and confusion, toying with the idea of confessing everything, and alternately commissioning Gilbert Gifford to undertake one more journey to the Continent to ascertain finally if every part of the action they contemplated was considered lawful by the ecclesiastical authorities, a pitiable reopening of discussion on a principle that ought to have been settled once for all at the start. Gifford was only too glad to go before the storm broke. True, he was a Government agent, but it was doubtful how far his actions would be covered by the official mantle. For it seems to have been the rule that the *agent provocateur* must seek sanction for each fresh act of treason undertaken in pursuance of his unsavoury calling. Neglect of this precaution had led Parry to his doom.

Babington had seen Walsingham for the third and last time on July 13th, when Walsingham already knew the contents of his fatal letter to Mary. Walsingham urged him to tell all he knew, and, returning from the interview much frightened, Babington thought of making a full confession. Poley tried to head him off. Babington had perhaps begun to have doubts of his friend's sincerity; he had come in from a walk one day to find Poley making a copy of a second letter he had written to Mary. At any rate, he was resolved on confession. He sent Poley to Walsingham, but Walsingham refused to see him; he said he would not see Babington again until he was a prisoner. Ballard also wrote to Walsingham offering to turn Queen's evidence. He too was refused a hearing.

When Walsingham denied himself to Babington on August 3rd, he had been acquainted for nearly a fortnight with Mary's reply to Babington's proposals. The reply was, in general terms, an acceptance of the services offered. Commentators are not agreed how far it endorsed Babington's plans for murdering Elizabeth, nor is it necessary for our present purpose to argue the point. Most readers would see in Mary's letter an endorsement of all Babington's implications. But Walsingham wanted some more definite information, and had a forged postscript added to Mary's answer, asking for the names of the six men who had been chosen to kill Elizabeth. The evidence for this forgery is overwhelming; its purpose, however, was not to incriminate Mary further, but to induce Babington to supply the names of the proposed assassins and so to pile up further proof of the guilt of the men of his circle. The precise degree of Mary's complicity in the plot must be judged from her letter alone, and not from the postscript. There we may leave it.

On August 3rd, the day that Walsingham refused to see him again, Babington wrote a second letter to Mary, the one that he found Poley copying. It was to say that Maude's treachery was discovered, that there was extreme danger of the plot being revealed, but that they were taking steps to put matters right. The plot had, however, been discovered not through Maude but through Walsingham's access to Babington's correspondence with Mary. Meanwhile, the warrants were out for the conspirators' arrest. Phelippes and his associates were hunting for Babington at his lodgings, dismayed not to find him there. Walsingham was anxious also because Gilbert Gifford had disappeared, having bolted to France; he was afraid his forged postscript had put the plotters on their guard. But Babington and Ballard were in Poley's house, where their host held them, unsuspecting, in safe keeping. And there Ballard was arrested on August 4th. Babington was allowed a little more rope, probably in the hope of his incriminating others. The volume of State Trials gives us a characteristic glimpse of him at this moment. On Ballard's arrest he went to Tichbourne's lodgings, and not finding him there, proceeded to a barber's shop outside Bishopsgate, no doubt a meeting place, where were his own, Tichbourne's and Savage's portraits. On Babington's was written: *Hi mihi sunt comites, quos ipsa pericula jungunt* ('my comrades these, whom very peril draws').

But not altogether liking this, he had added: *Quorsum haec alio properantibus* ('to what purpose these things to those hastening hence?'). To what purpose indeed? But Babington must have his gesture before he goes down in the darkness of the tomb.

Poley was arrested at this time, probably as a blind, for, after being kept a while in the Tower, he was set at liberty. Babington with four of his associates, Gage and Charnock, Dunne and Barnewall, managed to give the pursuers the slip, hid in the forest about St. John's Wood, and were not taken for ten days. Tilney, Savage and Tichbourne were arrested in the south London suburbs. Salusbury got away to the west, but was finally captured with Jones in Cheshire. Habington, in Worcestershire, avoided capture for a month; Edward Windsor eluded pursuit for six. Babington and the others, after being examined, were sent to the Tower. As for Gilbert Gifford, who had escaped to France, he was arrested the following year in a brothel in Paris and, when found to be a priest, was sent to the Bishop's prison, where he lay till his death.

There is in the Hatton Letter Book a copy of a letter from Babington to a man whom he addresses as 'Robyn'. Sir Harris Nicolas supposed that the recipient was probably one of the conspirators, either Barnewall or Gage, each of whom had the Christian name Robert. It is now known that the man to whom Babington wrote this moving letter was Robert Poley. It shows Babington trying to persuade himself of Poley's good faith, though shaken by the suspicions that were crowding thick and fast upon him.

The original of this letter is unknown. Father Pollen prints it from a contemporary copy in the Lansdowne MSS. in the British Museum. This copy has several careless readings, especially *rati* for *araeni* in the Latin quotation in the first line. This reading also occurs in the Hatton Letter Book; but there are several minor differences between the two versions, so that it is unlikely that one was copied from the other. The most probable explanation is that a copy was made from the original by an ignorant scribe, confronted with a difficult handwriting, who copied Babington's *araeni* incorrectly as *rati*; and that the copies in the Letter Book and in the Lansdowne MSS. were both made independently from this version or from copies of it that were circulating. For it is scarcely likely that Babington would have made the mistake; and the same mistake, occurring in the Letter Book, shows that it was not made by Samuel Cox, Hatton's secretary. Cox was a good scholar. But though he would notice the error he would not correct the text before him; for all he knew it was as Babington wrote it.

The version given here is that copied into the Letter Book with the principal variations printed by Father Pollen in his *Mary Queen of Scots and the Babington Plot*:

> *Robyn, Non solicitae possunt curae mutare rati stamina fusi*[1] I am ready to endure what shall be inflicted: *et facere et pati magna, Romanum*[2] What my courses have been towards Mr. Secretary [Walsingham] you can witness; what my love towards you, yourself will confess. Their procedinegs at my lodging have been strange. Look to your own part, lest of these my infortunes you bear the blame. I am the same I pretended. I pray God you have been and ever remain so towards me. *Est exilium inter malos vivere*[3] Farewell, my sweet Robyn, if (as I take thee) true to me; if not, adieu, *omnium bipedum iniquissimus*[4]. Return thine answer for my satisfaction, and my diamond, and what else you wilt. The furnace is made wherein thy faith must now be tried. Farewell till we meet, which God knows when. Yours, you know how far, Anthony Babington.

A few last words of Poley. He was in prison for a year, and there he was supposed to have poisoned Richard Creagh, Archbishop of Armagh; afterwards he was sent to the Tower for suspected treason — he had been in touch with Sir Thomas Stukeley, for instance, the man who had plotted an invasion of Ireland ten years before. Poley was then set free and sent on a mission to Denmark. In 1589 he was in prison again, charged with 'lewd words' against Walsingham, and then with seducing his gaoler's wife. In 1583 he was a spy in Flanders and again in 1595. In the meantime he was one of those involved in the tragic death of Marlowe. But that does not belong to our story.

---

[1] Father Pollen translates: 'Nor care nor cautel ever mends of spider's threads the broken ends.'
[2] In the Lansdowne version: *et facere et pati Romanorum est*: both to do and to dare, is this worthy of Romans.
[3] To live amidst the wicked, what an exile!
[4] Nequissimus in Lansdowne: of all two-footed things the wickedest.

CHAPTER XXVII

THE BABINGTON TRIAL

BALLARD, Savage and Tichbourne were the first of the conspirators to be captured, and their confessions were taken down on August 8th, 10th and 11th respectively. Babington's first examination was made a week later at Ely House, Hatton's London residence, and his confession also put in writing. His examiners were the Lord Chancellor, Sir Thomas Bromley, Burghley, Walsingham and Hatton. Of these Hatton, as usual, represented the Queen. Elizabeth took the greatest interest in details of plots and espionage; in the present case she was in addition thoroughly alarmed. Many of the conspirators, as already noticed, were closely connected with the Court; there seemed to be traitors very near the Throne, and it is not to be wondered at that the Queen, usually so brave, was frightened. Her alarm was to lead her into depths of cruelty foreign to her nature.

Babington was subjected to nine examinations in all between August 18th and September 8th. Before the eighth examination (September 2nd) Hatton had left London for Holdenby, apparently seeking leisure to study the documents. He left under the impression that the trial was to take place earlier than it actually did; and when he heard of the change of plans he thought its postponement a mistake. It seems to have been arranged that Burghley was to join him at Holdenby, presumably for a conference. Just before leaving for the country Hatton, by the Queen's command, wrote to Burghley thanking him for his services. The reference apparently is to his examination of Babington which was conducted after the masterly but unscrupulous fashion of Tudor times — cross-examination; confession taken down; new points put to jog the memory, after comparison with other prisoners' statements; a second confession; more points suggested; and so on.

Burghley acknowledged Hatton's letter, writing on September 4th from his house at Westminster where he was ill in bed with gout. He says that since Hatton's departure Henry Dunne, one of the conspirators, had confessed, and that Edward Habington and his brother Thomas had been captured. He adds a sentence, often quoted:

> I think Nau and Curle [Queen Mary's secretaries] will yield in their writing somewhat to confirm their mistress's crimes, but if they were persuaded that themselves might scape and the blow fall upon their mistress betwixt her head and her shoulders, surely we should have the whole from them.

He expects Hatton back by the 12th, the day before the trial, to meet him at the Lord Chancellor's where, no doubt, they were to make final arrangements. Burghley's letter crossed Hatton's, written on the 2nd, which shows that Hatton had been taken suddenly ill and did not think he would be well enough to keep this appointment:

> Assuredly, my good Lord, I find myself much bound to you for your oft and most honourable letters. I find thereby the time is deferred, and I fear the cause in this course will receive some prejudice. Is it not possible that, with the eye of her Majesty's wisdom, these most horrible and dangerous practices may be thoroughly looked into? Surely, Sir, if she did, there would be no days given to the prevention of them. God hath mightily defended us. He is all and EveR one. I beseech Him that these our negligences may not tempt Him.
>
> I am come sick to my poor house, full of a fever, with stitches, spitting of blood and other bad accidents. I must commit myself to God and the physician for a while; and though your access hither be further off than before, yet, Sir, by reason of my sickness I cannot return. . . .

But when the 12th came Hatton was evidently better and back in London, for a letter from Burghley to him written to him on that day from Windsor where he was with the Queen, indicates as much, and indeed we know that he was present at the trial on the following day. Burghley allows it to be seen that Elizabeth was badly frightened. She particularly wished that during the proceedings nothing should be said to incriminate Mary, for she feared violence against herself if Mary's friends should believe the Scots Queen's life was in danger. Burghley thought these fears absurd and, in any case, he argued, Mary's guilt appeared from the prisoners' indictment. But Elizabeth's recollection was that there was nothing about it in the indictment, which she called for.

Burghley therefore asks Hatton to procure it with all speed from the Attorney-General.

Elizabeth's agitation bred in her a cruelty quite at variance with her usual merciful nature. She shows a savage desire that the accused men, whose condemnation under the forms of trial for high treason was of course certain, should be barbarously dealt with. Her resolve can only be explained, though not excused, by the terror which these events had inspired in her. Her instructions on this point were conveyed from Burghley to Hatton to communicate to the judges:

> Besides this, she commanded me to write, that when the judge shall give the judgment for the manner of the death, which she saith must be done according to the usual form, yet in the end of the sentence he may say that such is the form usual, but yet considering this manner of horrible treason against her Majesty's own person hath not been heard of in this kingdom, it is reason that the manner of their death for more terror be referred to her Majesty and her Council.
>
> I told her Majesty that if the fashion of the execution shall be duly and orderly executed, by protracting of the same both to the extremity of the pains in the action, and to the sight of the people to behold it, the manner of the death would be as terrible as any other new device could be, but therewith her Majesty was not satisfied, but commanded me thus to write to you, to declare it to the judge and others of the counsel there.

The dreadful death that Burghley proposed was precisely what was dealt out to the first batch of seven of the condemned men. They were cut down after hanging only a short time, and disembowelled and mutilated while still alive. The second batch of seven, executed on the following day, were allowed to hang until they were quite dead before the revolting mutilations belonging to execution for high treason were performed. The volume of State Trials informs us that this was due to Elizabeth's intercession: 'the Queen, being informed of the severity used in the executions of the day before, and detesting such cruelty, gave express orders that these should be used more favourably'. That no doubt was policy, to give a terrible example to the multitude and then to make a parade of the Queen's merciful disposition. But the evidence above shows that it was Elizabeth herself who had clamoured for the most rigorous treatment possible for the con-

demned men, and that Burghley had seen to it that their punishment should be as brutal as the law would allow.

The trial, which lasted three days, began on September 13th,
1586, the commissioners including Hatton, Walsingham, the Lord
Chief Justice, the Lord Chief Justice of the Common Pleas and the
Lord Chief Baron of the Exchequer. Walsingham, however, took
no part in it and was possibly not present. The prisoners were
tried in two lots, and it appears that on the first day were taken
those of whom it was known, or thought likely from their confessions, that they would plead guilty.

The proceedings opened with Hatton asking the law officers
what order they would take in arraigning the prisoners. The
lawyers proposed to proceed with the trial of Savage, as 'he
meddled first in these matters'. Savage, being asked if he pleaded
guilty or no, replied that he was guilty of conspiracy with the
others, that he received letters from Morgan, William and Gilbert
Gifford provoking him to murder the Queen, but that he was not
guilty of consenting to it. The Lord Chief Justice pointed out that
he must plead guilty or not guilty to the whole indictment. Hatton
reinforced him:

> to say that thou art guilty to that and not to this is no plea; for thou
> must either confess it generally, or deny it generally. Wherefore,
> delay not the time, but say either guilty or not; and if thou say
> guilty, then shalt thou hear further; if not guilty, her Majesty's
> learned counsel is ready to give evidence against thee.

Savage then pleaded guilty. His confession, taken before Lord
Chancellor Bromley, Burghley, Hatton and Walsingham was then
read.

The most characteristic part of Savage's confession is the passage
about events after the arrest of Ballard. Babington came to him to
say that Ballard had been taken, and to urge him to go to Court
immediately and kill the Queen. 'Nay', said Savage, 'I cannot go
to-morrow, for my apparel is not ready, and in this apparel shall
I never come near the Queen', meaning that he would not be
admitted by the ushers. 'Go to', quoth Babington, 'here is my
ring and all the money I have, get the apparel and dispatch it.'
It is probably safe to say that no time or circumstance would have
suited Savage for the deed he had so recklessly undertaken. After
the reading of his confession, Hatton asked him if it had been

made without torture or threat of torture. Savage agreed, and Hatton then asked for the court to adjourn.

The next day Babington, Tichbourne, Salusbury, Barnewall, Dunne and Ballard were tried. As with Savage, Ballard endeavoured to plead guilty to part and not guilty to the rest, guilty of endeavouring to set Mary free and to alter the religion of the country, not guilty of the projected murder of Elizabeth. Whereupon Hatton said, 'Ballard, under thine own hand are all things confessed; therefore now it is much vanity to stand vaingloriously in denying it'. Ballard then confessed he was guilty. Babington followed with an eloquent account of the course of the plot.

Tichbourne refused to plead guilty to all counts. He knew of the treasons but was not guilty of anything else. He said, 'what I am guilty of, I plead guilty, and I will confess no more'. Hatton told him that he might plead not guilty. Tichbourne did so, and Hatton told him he should be tried after seeing what Salusbury and Dunne had to say. Henry Dunne, being asked if he were guilty or no, replied, 'when I was moved and made privy to these treasons, I always said that I prayed unto God that that might be done which was to His honour and glory'. Hatton quickly took him up: 'Then it was thus, that they said the Queen should be killed, and thou saidst "God's will be done".' Dunne: 'Yea, Sir.' Hatton: 'Oh wretch, wretch! Thy conscience and own confession show that thou art guilty.' Dunne then confessed his guilt. Salusbury also pleaded guilty, and Tichbourne's trial was resumed. He said, 'I beseech you, my Lords, give me leave to speak'. Hatton: 'Say what you will.' But Tichbourne, having said briefly that he had a lame leg which kept him in London, asked what probability was there that he had meant to kill the Queen, when if it had not been for his leg he would have been in Hampshire? After which feeble defence, he changed his mind and pleaded guilty.

Babington also said he was guilty, adding, 'by Ballard's persuasion'. Whereupon Hatton burst out, 'Oh Ballard, Ballard, what hast thou done? A sort of brave youths otherwise endued with good gifts, by thy inducement hast thou brought to their utter destruction and confusion'. Ballard, addressing Babington demurred, 'Yea, Mr. Babington, lay all the blame upon me, but I wish the shedding of my blood might be the saving of your life; howbeit, say what you will I will say no more'. And Hatton: 'Nay,

Ballard, you must say more and shall say more, for you must not commit High Treasons and then huddle them up. But is this thy *Religio Catholica*? Nay, rather, it is *Diabolica*.' Barnewall protested that what he had done was done for conscience' sake, and denied that he had ever intended any violence to the Queen's person. Whereupon, as Lord Campbell in his life of Hatton amusingly comments, Hatton volunteered some evidence himself:

O Barnewall, Barnewall, didst thou not come to Richmond, and when her Majesty walked abroad, didst not thou there view her and all her company, what weapons they had, how she walked alone? and didst traverse the ground, and thereupon coming back to London, didst make relation to Babington, how it was a most easy matter to kill her Majesty, and what thou hadst seen and done at the Court? Yea, I know thou didst so. How canst thou then say that thou never didst intend to lay violent hands on her Majesty?

This speech, shocking to a lawyer's ears, was not however so out of place in a sixteenth-century trial for high treason. Hatton may seem to be volunteering evidence; but it must be remembered that he had helped to examine Barnewall and was familiar with his confession.

The printed volume of State Trials preserves a summary of the speech made by Hatton at the conclusion of the day's proceedings; and it is of interest to observe that the Bardon Papers contain the heads of this speech, endorsed by a clerk, 'Your Honour's notes of the principal points of the conspiracy'. These points are drawn from various portions of the different confessions, and the mosaic, if not a good exposition of the main conception of the plot, serves, as it was intended, to give it a most lurid flavour. As summarized:

Then began Sir Christopher Hatton, and made an excellent good speech, in opening and setting forth their treasons, and how they all proceeded from the wicked priests, the ministers of the Pope. And first, he showed how these wicked and devilish youths had conspired to murder the Queen's most excellent Majesty; secondly, to bring in foreign invasion; thirdly, to deliver the Queen of Scots and make her queen; fourthly, to sack the city of London; fifthly, to rob and destroy all the wealthy subjects of this realm; sixthly, to kill divers of the Privy Council, as the Earl of Leicester, the Lord Treasurer, Mr. Secretary, Sir Ralph Sadler, Sir Amias Paulet; seventhly, to set fire on all the Queen's ships; eighthly, to cloy all the great ordnance; ninthly and lastly, to subvert religion and the whole state of government. The inventers and beginners whereof were these devilish priests and seminaries, against whom he doubted the Parliament had not yet sufficiently provided, who now-a-days do not go about to seduce the ancient and discreet men, for they (as the priests say) be too cold; but they assail with their persuasions the younger sort, and of those the most ripe wits, whose high hearts and ambitious minds do carry them headlong to all wickedness. In the end, he concluded with remorse for the youth of some of these unhappy men and with detestation of the facts [acts] of Ballard; and also showed forth a notable proof of the falsehood of these lying papists, which was a book printed at Rome and made by the papists, wherein they affirm that the English Catholics which suffer for religion be lapped in bear skins and bated to death with dogs; a most monstrous lie and manifest falsehood.

On the third day were taken those prisoners who had resolved to plead not guilty. They made a spirited defence. Edward Habington asked for a pair of writing tables to set down what was alleged against him, so that he might be able to answer properly. Sandys, the Clerk of the Crown, found no precedent for this: 'it was never the case here', he said, and Hatton pronounced, 'when you hear anything you are desirous to answer, you shall speak an answer at full, which is better than a pair of tables'. Hatton had, as already remarked, helped to examine the prisoners and take their confessions. The Attorney-General alluded to this. Addressing Hatton, he said, 'Mr. Vice-Chamberlain, you desired Abington to set down the truth of these things, whereupon he set down a great deal in writing, and yesterday he tore it in a hundred pieces; and here Mr. Lieutenant of the Tower hath given me the pieces and here they be'. Hatton: 'Abington, you be very obstinate, and seem indurate in these treasons.' Tilney and Habington both protested that Babington had accused them in the hope of benefiting himself. Hatton answered that Babington could have no such hope of his life, and that he had confessed 'for discharge of his conscience'. The Government, he argued, had to rely on such confessions, 'for had not Babington voluntarily named Abington, who could have named Abington? And had he not also willingly accused Tilney, who could have accused Tilney?' Habington immediately countered, quoting the Statute of Queen Elizabeth to the effect that those accused of high treason should be confronted with two lawful witnesses. The evidence of condemned men, Babington, Savage, Ballard, could not, he argued, count; and that Babington had appointed him as one of those chosen to kill the Queen did not prove that he knew of this, or had consented.

The Lord Chief Justice of the Common Pleas replied to this that he was not tried under the Statute of Elizabeth, but by the common law and the Statute of 25 Edward III, which required no such witnesses. By that Statute the Government could condemn anyone; and indeed the Solicitor-General practically admitted as much: 'If it should be as they would have it, then could never any treason be sufficiently proved . . . how then can that be proved by honest men, being a secret cognition which lieth in the minds of traitors? And such traitors will never reveal their cognitions unto honest men, but unto such as themselves, and they, I hope, be no honest men; so then they would have their treason never revealed.'

Tilney also made a spirited defence. He objected to his religion being dragged in. If he had been confessed, he said, so were all men in Henry VII's reign. But, the Solicitor-General replied, things were now quite different; the Pope was now the greatest enemy the Queen had, but it was not so then. Tilney asked, 'How know I the Pope is her greatest enemy?' And Hatton answered, 'Know not you how he invaded the realm of Ireland?' He was reminded of his oath as a Gentleman Pensioner, and replied that he was not then a Catholic.

Most of the prisoners made appeals that their wives and children should be provided for from their estates, or that their debts might be paid from money owing to them, knowing, of course, that their lands and goods were legally forfeit to the Crown. Charnock appealed to Hatton: 'I beseech your Honour, Mr. Vice-Chamberlain, to get her Majesty to pardon me.' Hatton: 'Charnock, thy offence is too high for me to be an obtainer of thy pardon, but I am sorry for thee. If thou hadst applied thyself the best way, thou mightest have done thy country good service.' Charnock: 'I beseech you then that six angels, which such a one hath of mine, may be delivered unto my brother to pay my debts.' Hatton: 'How much is thy debts?' Charnock: 'The same six angels would discharge it.' Hatton: 'Then I promise thee it shall be paid.' Something of Hatton's kindness of heart is allowed to peep out here among all the harsh cruelties of the trial.

Charles Tilney is one of the most interesting of the conspirators. He was the only son and heir of Philip Tilney of Shelley Hall,

Suffolk, who was Queen Elizabeth's fourth cousin, and had once entertained her during a progress. He was cousin of Edmund Tilney, the Master of the Revels, and of Sir George Buc who succeeded to that office. In the copy of *Locrine* in Dr. Rosenbach's collection there is an inscription, said to be in Buc's handwriting, to the effect that the play was written by his cousin Charles Tilney, so that Tilney, *antiqua generis claritate, unica spes familiae*, as Camden calls him, may have been a pioneer, with Marlowe, of the blank verse drama. His name is entered on the Roll of Gentlemen Pensioners of the year 1586, with the ominous note, 'removed the 21st of September'.

Chidiock Tichbourne, a man of ancient Catholic family, was one of Hatton's followers. This we know from his wife's statement, and from his own speech before his death. When his wife Jane (called wrongly in the printed version of the State Trials, Agnes) was examined on two occasions, once on Hatton's appointment by his dependant, Henry MacWilliam, she said that she took it that her husband belonged to Sir Christopher Hatton. And in the version of Tichbourne's confession made before his death, preserved among the Kenyon MSS., he is quoted as begging

> one Mr. Fulwell, one of Sir Christopher Hatton's gentlemen, that he would commend him to all his fellows, and ask them all forgiveness. And let not these my unnatural dealings be any way offensive unto them, and though it may be said that one of Mr. Vice-Chamberlain's men had attempted her Majesty's destruction, it can be no slander to them that be free of it. I desire his Honour to forgive me.

This part of his speech is omitted from the printed State Trials. Presumably it was not the sort of thing that Hatton wished to be circulated. But the following moving passage was allowed to stand. Recalling his friendship with Babington, he said:

> We lived together in most flourishing estate. Of whom went report in the Strand, Fleet Street and elsewhere about London but of Babington and Tichbourne? No threshold was of force to brave our entry . . . My dear countrymen, my sorrows may be your joy, yet mix your smiles with tears, and pity my case. I am descended from an house from two hundred years before the Conquest, never stained till this my misfortune.

He is remembered too for the pathetic letter he wrote to his wife on the eve of his execution, and for some moving verses which

he is said to have written in the Tower the night before he met
his end. They were printed by Thomas Kyd in 1586 in his *Verses
of Praise and Joy,* on the occasion of the disclosure of the plot; and
have found their way into the anthologies:

> My prime of youth is but a frost of cares,
>> My fest of joy is but a dish of pain:
> My crop of corn is but a field of tares,
>> And all my good is but vain hope of gain.
> The day is past, and yet I saw no sun;
> And now I live, and now my life is done.
>
> My tale was heard, and yet it was not told,
>> My fruit is fall'n and yet my leaves are green:
> My youth is spent, and yet I am not old,
>> I saw the world, and yet I was not seen.
> My thread is cut, and yet it is not spun;
> And now I live, and now my life is done.
>
> I sought my death, and found it in my womb,
>> I looked for life and saw it was a shade:
> I trod the earth, and knew it was my tomb,
>> And now I die, and now I was but made.
> My glass is full, and now my glass is run;
> And now I live, and now my life is done.

CHAPTER XXVIII

JEALOUSIES AT COURT

HATTON's relations with his Queen did not always run a smooth course. Elizabeth, though in general loyal and considerate to her ministers, was not an easy mistress. Those who served her groaned under the difficulties of keeping her to a consistent policy. No sooner had Burghley or Walsingham persuaded her, after days of argument, to some line of action, than she would change her mind, undo what had been done, cancel orders given, or send a fresh courier hotfoot on the heels of the first to delay or supersede some important dispatch. Then the heart-breaking task of making up the Queen's mind for her had to be begun all over again. In such long-drawn-out negotiations as those of the French marriage, or in a crisis like the decision to be taken on the fate of the Queen of Scots, the hesitations of the vacillating Queen drove her advisers almost frantic. Burghley would wring his hands, Walsingham utter gloomy prophecies, and Hatton on occasion burst into tears.

Hatton, unlike Burghley and Walsingham, had another relationship with Elizabeth, which led to situations of a more emotional kind than impersonal matters of State could do. He was a courtier as well as a statesman; he had to play the part of admirer as well as that of official. Such relations are not easy; and he was frequently out of favour at Court. Sir John Harington, the Queen's godson and, according to Bishop Aylmer, a friend of Hatton's, has preserved a tribute from Hatton to Elizabeth's disarming charm, and also one of his sayings, with Harington's comment which illustrates the rueful good-humour with which courtiers endured her tantrums. Speaking of Elizabeth's habit of weighing the advice of different councillors, and comparing each man's utterance with previously expressed opinions, 'Sir Christopher Hatton', Harington reports, 'was wont to say "the Queen did fish for men's souls, and had so sweet a bait, that no one could escape her network" . . . Hence she knew everyone's part, and by thus *fishing* as Hatton said, she caught many poor fish, who little knew what snare was laid for them'. The other story preserves one of Harington's puns. 'The Queen', he writes, 'seemed troubled to-day: Hatton came out of her presence with an ill countenance, and pulled me aside by the girdle, and said in secret way, "if you have any suit to-day, I pray you put it aside, the sun doth not shine".' Harington comments, "Tis this accursed Spanish business, so will I not adventure her Highness's *choler*, lest she should *collar* me also'. The passage has often been quoted — and misquoted. The pun was Harington's, not Hatton's. But even the precise Nicolas attributes it to the latter, while rebuking Lord Campbell for his carelessness in saying that the Queen once actually 'collared Hatton before the whole Court'.

However, few of Hatton's differences with the Queen seem to have been more serious than those that attend a flirtation, even one so elaborate as that of Hatton and Elizabeth. They were, in fact, lovers' quarrels. And they were occasioned, as such quarrels generally are, by the presence of a rival. Elizabeth's jealousy was aroused from time to time; as when, according to the Queen of Scots, Hatton played with the idea of courting Elizabeth Cavendish, Lady Shrewsbury's daughter, or when — Mary is again the witness — he was reported, during the French marriage crisis, to be a married man, discouraging in Elizabeth desire for the happiness he himself enjoyed. Hatton, for his part, displayed on occasion the established favourite's jealousy of a potential rival. As each new courtier attracted Elizabeth's eye, there was an envious stirring among the elder men. Leicester had seen Hatton rise suddenly to favour and challenge his position. And, if the stories of his sneers at Hatton's dancing are apocryphal, it seems to be the case that he tried to counter Hatton's influence by pushing the fortunes of Edward Dyer. But Dyer was never a great success at Court, and Hatton had not much to fear from him. Instead, he made of him a confidant, and sought his advice on how to act when a new star began to rise. Nor, after the first alarm, had Hatton any need to regard Oxford (if he were the subject of Dyer's letter) seriously as a possible rival. That erratic young man soon destroyed by his violence any chance he may have had of making a distinguished position for himself at Court.

Ten years passed, and a more serious rival blazed up suddenly in the person of an impecunious Devon squire, Walter Ralegh, a restless adventurer who for a time threatened to carry all before him. Ralegh is a much better known man than Hatton. He has had a score of biographers to Hatton's one, and has attracted the pen of a master of historical fiction. Scott in *Kenilworth* has drawn a picture, living though careless in detail, of Ralegh's rise to favour at the Elizabethan Court. Hatton has had to be content with an absurd role in *The Critic*, a verse from Gray, a tendentious sketch in one of the *Ingoldsby Legends*, a few words in one of Kipling's tales. But if literature and history have given their meed to the brilliant adventurer — soldier, sailor, Empire builder and writer — contemporary rewards were showered on his more sober rival.

Not as much information as we could wish is available of the course of Hatton's jealousy of Ralegh, but the little that we know or can surmise is both curious and amusing. It exhibits the quality of Hatton's flirtation with Elizabeth more vividly than any other incident in the history of the Queen and her courtier. It is a love passage, to our eyes almost incredible in its childishness, but to actors in a different age a delicate exchange of graceful compliments. Perhaps, however, only to the actors. Onlookers could be cruel enough in their laughter at the elderly Queen's coquetry. And her Scottish rival was one of the most merciless of her critics. Some account of Mary's celebrated letter to Elizabeth, written in the year 1584, has already been given. It may now be considered again as a preface to the story of Hatton and Ralegh.

In abusing Elizabeth, Mary gave more attention to Hatton as a target than to any other. She bracketed him with Leicester as one of the English Queen's lovers, and did not hesitate to include Alençon and Simier in the same list. She alluded to Hatton's courtship of Elizabeth Cavendish, which seems to have taken place about the year 1572 and perhaps in Mary's presence at Sheffield Castle; and recalled in a phrase that must have been particularly galling to Hatton, if he read it, that for fear of Elizabeth he had not dared to push his suit. Her letter then proceeded: 'as for Hatton, you forcibly pursue him, making the love you bear him appear so publicly that he is constrained to retire; and you boxed the ears of Killigrew, whom you sent after him, for not having brought him back when he departed in anger on account of some rude remarks of yours about the gold buttons on his coat'. Finally, Mary taxed Elizabeth with her lavishness to her favourites and to 'those who are mixed up with them, such as Gorge, one of your Chamber, to whom you gave a rent of £300 for bringing you the news of Hatton's return'.

Hatton as Elizabeth's supposed lover, and Hatton as prospective husband of Elizabeth Cavendish, later Countess of Lennox, have already been considered. Distorted as many of Mary's charges were, they contained a measure of truth — they would otherwise have been of no worth for purposes of vituperation. The two men she named, William Killigrew and Thomas Gorges, were Grooms of the Chamber, and Killigrew is mentioned below as the bearer of a message from Elizabeth to Hatton.

The mention by Mary, of all others, of Hatton wearing gold buttons and of Elizabeth making rude remarks about them inevitably recalls an episode in the life of Sir Henry Goodere, the father of Anne Goodere, Drayton's gracious lady. Goodere, who was friendly to the cause of the Queen of Scots, got into trouble with Elizabeth in consequence; and it appears that Mary had given him some gold buttons which he wore on his cap and doublet. This we learn from the confession of John Somerville, tried and executed in 1583 for his contemplated assassination of Elizabeth. Somerville, as was shown in a former chapter, was connected with the Ardens, who in turn were related to the Throckmortons and to Edmund Neville, involved in various conspiracies against Elizabeth's life. Hatton, it has been shown, had some contacts with these people, particularly with Hugh Hall, priest in the Arden household, while Arden Waferer, his friend and legal adviser, was a close relation of the Ardens, having an Arden for mother. It is not suggested, of course, that Elizabeth suspected Hatton of any concern in these plots. But, like others of his day, he was something of a trimmer, and Elizabeth must have known of or suspected his approaches to the Scots Queen. Remembering that it had just come out that Henry Goodere had received a present of gold buttons from Mary, we can well imagine Elizabeth's mockery when Hatton appeared in Court also wearing gold buttons.

It seems it was another set of buttons to which Hatton's old friend Sir Thomas Heneage, Treasurer of the Chamber, refers in a letter of July, 1581.

Heneage writes:

> For your buttons, which I bought for you and would have never worn if I had thought you would after have used them, I refer to your own best liking whether I shall return them, or pay for them; and how well soever they like me, I like better to please you than myself in a greater matter than this, as you shall ever find.

Trivial stuff, perhaps, but such trivialities illustrate the lighter side of Hatton's life, a life that had its share in the grim tragedies of the reign.

But, whatever the interpretation of the gold button episode, it appears that for some time Hatton had been irritated by Elizabeth's growing partiality for Ralegh and was jealous of his increasing influence. Hatton had left Court, ill or shamming illness. From his retreat he sent a letter to the Queen in October, 1582, through the medium of Heneage, who more than anyone was acquainted with the course of his relations with Elizabeth and had on other occasions carried letters between them. Hatton's message was accompanied by some 'tokens', symbolical of the actors in this sentimental comedy.

The tokens, which in their disparity suggest the contents of a modern Christmas cracker, were a diminutive bucket and a bodkin, the bucket signifying 'water', that is Walter Ralegh, whose Christian name was often so pronounced. The bodkin was a small dagger-shaped jewel to be worn in the hair. Its symbolism is doubtful, but it is likely that Mr. Edward Thompson in his life of Ralegh has correctly interpreted the episode as meaning that the Queen's 'bell-wether' would kill himself unless measures were taken to remove the water. Bucket and bodkin were accompanied by a book, the intention of which escapes us. Heneage brought these articles to the Queen who was about to ride forth into the Great Park (of Windsor?) to kill a doe. Expecting Ralegh's approach at any moment ('because I thought — as it happened — water should be so nigh her as soon as she came out of her drawing chamber') Heneage handed her the tokens with Hatton's letter. Elizabeth took them and said smiling, 'there was never such another'. She tried to put the bodkin in her hair but it would not stay, and she handed it back to Heneage with Hatton's letter. Presently she took the letter again and read it, 'and with blushing cheeks uttered many speeches, which I refer till I see you', half angry, half pleased, but finally deciding on Hatton's fidelity and determining never to give him cause to doubt her favour. She told Heneage to write to him, making elaborate play with the words 'water' or Ralegh, and *pecora campi*, an allusion to her pet-name for Hatton, her 'sheep':

> That she liked your preamble so ill, as she had little list to look on
> the bucket or the book; and that if Princes were like Gods (as they

should be) they would suffer no element so to abound as to breed confusion. And that *pecora campi* was so dear unto her that she had bounded her banks so sure as no water nor floods could be able ever to overthrow them. And, for better assurance unto you that. you should fear no drowning, she hath sent you a bird that (together with the rainbow) brought the good tidings and the covenant that there should be no more destruction by water. And further, she willed me to send you word, with her commendations, that you should remember she was a Shepherd, and then you might think how dear her Sheep was unto her.

The dove that Elizabeth sent was probably a jewel, and like Hatton's gifts is described as a 'token', for Heneage was ordered to give this reply together with the Queen's 'token' to Mr. Killigrew 'whom she meant to send to bring her word how you did'. This may therefore have been the occasion when William Killigrew, Groom of the Chamber, had his ears boxed by his irate mistress for coming back empty-handed.

In December Hatton was still playing at sulking, only half-heartedly out of temper and willing to be coaxed. He sent Elizabeth, again by Heneage, a present of a 'fish-prison', another symbol having reference to water, as Elizabeth immediately perceived, falling in with the game, and contrasting fish with flesh, that is Ralegh with Hatton in his role of sheep or bell-wether. Heneage writes:

> The fine fish-prison, together with your letter this bearer brought me, I presented immediately to the delightful hands of her sacred Majesty, who read it, well pleased to see you a little raised from your sour humour; and hath willed me to write unto you that the water and the creatures therein do content her nothing so well as you ween, her food having been ever more of flesh than of fish, and her opinion steadfast that flesh is more wholesome; and further that if you think not *pecora campi* be more cared for of her both abroad and at home, and more contenting to her than any waterish creatures, such a beast is well worthy of being put in the pound. Besides, but for stirring choler in you that for the most part carrieth men too far, her Highness told me she would have returned to you your token; but worn it is with best acceptance.

Concluding, Heneage is sure that Hatton retains the Queen's 'blessed favour', as always.

It was probably not long after this that Hatton again put in an appearance at Court, and his return at this point may have been the occasion when, to Elizabeth's delight, Thomas Gorges, Groom of the Chamber, brought him back, though we need not believe that the careful Queen made Gorges such a sum as £300 a year as a reward; Mary is perhaps thinking of Hatton's grant from Elizabeth of £400 a year, of which she may have heard a confused account. Still, Hatton's jealousy of Ralegh continued, and he was again out of humour in April, 1585, when once more he sought Heneage's offices as messenger to Elizabeth. He sent her some bracelets and a 'knot', which is explained by a note in the margin of the Letter Book as 'the true love knot'. The Queen, says Heneage in replying, expressed 'hearty and noble affection' for him and thought him 'the faithfullest and of most worth'. She complained of his long absence, and Heneage informed her that he heard from Varney (that is, Richard Verney, one of Hatton's men, grandson of Sir Richard Verney, the villain of Scott's *Kenilworth*) that Hatton had no place in the Court, then at Croydon, to rest himself, 'which, after standing and waiting, you much needed'. Elizabeth was very displeased and sent for an officer, who informed her that Sir Walter Ralegh had Hatton's lodging. She was furious with the Lord Chamberlain and spoke bitterly of Ralegh, saying she 'had rather see him hanged than equal him with you, or that the world should think she did so'. Hatton's true-love's knot was evidently a costly jewel, for Elizabeth declared 'you are a knave for sending her such a thing and of that price, which you know she will not send back again; that is the knot she most loves, and she thinks cannot be undone'.

Heneage concludes with some news that suggests that the Queen was contemplating some fresh preferment for Hatton: 'I keep the best to the last. This inclosed which it pleased her to read to me, and I must be a record of, which if I might surely see performed, I should have one of my greatest desires upon earth: I speak it faithfully.' Mendoza had reported two years before that Elizabeth had promised Hatton a reward for helping to save her from marriage with the Duke of Anjou. But what she may have designed at either time is unknown. The Lord Chancellorship, to which Hatton was appointed two years later, was not vacant, nor was he made a Knight of the Garter until three years after the date of this letter.

CHAPTER XXIX

THE TRIAL OF MARY STUART

IN 1586 Sir Christopher Hatton attended, as one of the commissioners, the trial of Mary Queen of Scots at Fotheringay. It was not his first meeting with Mary. Twenty years before, as a young man of six-and-twenty, he had been a member of the Earl of Bedford's mission which travelled to Stirling for the baptism of her infant son, the future James VI and I. He was now a very different man from the hot-headed youth who had been nearly tempted on that occasion to start a brawl that might have provoked a minor crisis between the nations. Twenty years' experience at Elizabeth's Court, that notable school of public affairs, and the moulding of a woman masterful and intelligent and a shrewd judge of men, had turned the handsome, impetuous youth, ready to fly out in a passion, into a diplomatist, suave and polished, dexterous and clear-headed. His contribution to the trial of the Queen of Scots was sufficiently important, for though the end was never in doubt and had indeed been predetermined, it was to Hatton's arguments that Mary bowed in consenting to acknowledge the competence of the Court and to plead before it.

There is some evidence that, loyal as he was in general to Queen Elizabeth, he had sought to reinsure himself with Mary, and had made some overtures to her. The masses of Mary's papers, seized by the Government, are said to have included communications from many an English knight and nobleman, paying court to her as the future sovereign. These papers Elizabeth wisely and generously burned, true to her maxim, *video sed taceo*. Hatton appears to have been one of the trimmers; but there is no need to condemn him more harshly than the other gamblers in reinsurance. The evidence, such as it is, is a memorandum among the papers of Nau, one of Mary's secretaries, dating from about the year 1582, and endorsed by Phelippes, Walsingham's spy, November, 1584. It contained 'notes of remembrance' of messages from the Queen of Scots for Nau to deliver in London to each councillor. It begins 'Hatton has done her several good offices; offering by the Countess of Shrewsbury that if the Queen of England should die, he would be ready to come and fetch the Queen of Scotland with the Guard'. But Lady Shrewsbury is not a very trustworthy witness, and Nau himself had some doubts of her: 'Tell him not to trust in her', he adds, 'and that she will do him wrong as she has done to all her friends, only keeping faith as long as it suits her.'

As in the hall of Fotheringay he faced the once beautiful Queen of Scots, now, though but 44, a woman prematurely aged, what thoughts may not have passed through Hatton's mind? Did he recall the gay pageantry of the Scotland of his youth, in which amid the solemn ceremonies of the cathedral service and the junketings that followed the baptism of the infant prince, heir to two kingdoms, could be discerned in the faces of the sullen Darnley and the grim Bothwell the shadows of the ghastly fates that were eventually to drag Mary to the scaffold? Did he bring to mind his visit six years later to the captive Queen at Sheffield Castle and his brief wooing of Elizabeth Cavendish, arrested before it could blossom by the imperious gesture of his possessive mistress? Did perhaps a glance from the Scots Queen, dignified in misfortune, fascinating yet in her ageing beauty, her charm still regal if tarnished by the ravages of guilty passions, recall to him that he too, among the throng of calculating statesmen who watched with absorbed interest the drama of the rival queens, had been prepared, if events had so fallen out, to throw cap in air and cry 'Long live Queen Mary'? But no flicker of recollection would appear in his level gaze, no reproach dwell in the eyes of a queen hardened by experience of the chancelleries of Europe to acquiesce in the cynicism of princes and courtiers. Again, one wonders, did Hatton recall that letter which Mary had written two years before to her rival, full of the coarsest abuse of the English queen, of unflattering references to the favourite who now confronted her? Had he indeed ever seen it? Perhaps not. The sagacious Burghley had filed it away within his capacious pigeon-holes. No need to trouble his royal mistress with such splenetic stuff. But Hatton? Could the veteran statesman, however cool-headed, have resisted the temptation to humiliate one who had once fancied himself as a rival? We can only guess.

Even before the trial of the Babington conspirators Burghley had been endeavouring to get Elizabeth to decide upon a place to which Mary might be removed and where she could be tried.

The Privy Council wanted to bring her to London, to the Tower, but Elizabeth would not listen to such a proposal. Finally, Fotheringay Castle in Northamptonshire was decided upon. About September 12th, 1586, Sir Amyas Paulet, Mary's gaoler, was ordered to remove her to the Castle where Sir Walter Mildmay, the Chancellor of the Exchequer, was directed to 'bestow' her. The commissioners were to meet at Westminster on the 27th for a preliminary sitting, and were then to leave for Fotheringay, stopping at Holdenby, Hatton's house, about October 3rd or 4th, and arriving at Fotheringay on the 5th.

The commission did not actually reach Fotheringay until October 11th. The castle was crowded with Paulet's soldiers and Mary's retinue, and the commissioners had to accommodate themselves as best they could. Hatton stopped at Apethorpe, the seat of Sir Walter Mildmay, about five miles away. There he received a letter from Elizabeth which 'a little daunted' him. As with the Babington trial, so with that of Mary, Elizabeth followed it closely and sought to control its details. She was, no doubt, a great nuisance to the commissioners. Hatton replied from Apethorpe on the 13th. It is the last letter we have from him to Elizabeth, and is not much more than an acknowledgment of her message, on the nature of which it throws but little light. Headed by his usual cipher when addressing her, four triangles, it begins:

> May it please your sacred Majesty, your princely goodness towards me is so infinite, as in my poor wit I am not able to comprehend the least part thereof. I must therefore fail in duty of thankfulness as your Mutton, and lay all upon God, with my humble prayers to requite you in Heaven and Earth in the most sincere and devout manner that, through God's grace, I may possibly devise. . . .

Hatton's main contribution to the trial of Mary, which began on the same day, was the argument by which he persuaded her to recognize the court that was to judge her. Mary had held that, as a sovereign queen of another country, the English commissioners had no competence to try her. Hatton addressed her:

> You are accused (but not condemned) to have conspired the destruction of our lady and queen anointed. You say you are a queen: be it so. But in such a crime the royal dignity is not exempted from answering, neither by the Civil nor Canon Law,

nor by the law of nations, nor of nature. For if such kind of offences might be committed without punishment, all justice would stagger, yea, fall to the ground. If you be innocent you wrong your reputation in avoiding a trial. You protest yourself to be innocent, but Queen Elizabeth thinketh otherwise, and that neither without grief and sorrow for the same. To examine therefore your innocency, she hath appointed for Commissioners most honourable, prudent and upright men, who are ready to hear you according to equity with favour, and will rejoice with all their hearts if you shall clear yourself of this crime. Believe me the Queen herself will be much affected with joy, who affirmed unto me at my coming from her, that never anything befell her more grievous than that you were charged with such a crime. Wherefore lay aside the bootless privilege of royal dignity, which now can be of no use unto you, appear in judgment and show your innocency, lest, by avoiding trial, you draw upon yourself suspicion, and lay upon your reputation an eternal blot and aspersion.

On the following day, after Mary had endeavoured to secure that her protestations of innocence might be admitted and allowed, and had been forced to be content with the ruling that it should be put on record but not allowed, she consented to the trial, as she was 'very desirous to purge herself of the crime objected against her, being persuaded by Hatton's reasons, which she had weighed with advisement'. He had but little further to do with her ordeal. Unlike previous trials for high treason, in which Hatton had represented Elizabeth, the conduct of Mary's trial was mainly in the hands of Burghley.

But if Hatton did not represent Elizabeth on this occasion, he did so in the House of Commons where, on November 3rd, he delivered a vehement attack on the Queen of Scots, whose trial, resulting in her condemnation, had just been concluded. We know a good deal of the circumstances in which he prepared this speech. As already pointed out, the collection of documents known as the Bardon Papers is a dossier concerning Mary, mainly, if not entirely, prepared for Hatton's use. Some of these documents are in his handwriting; others bear his endorsement. One of the longest and most lucid of them is a statement of the case against Mary, reviewing the whole series of plots in which she was directly or indirectly involved. It was prepared by Serjeant Puckering, Speaker of the House of Commons, who analysed briefly but without omitting any essentials, the evidence supplied by the Babington conspirators in their confessions, Mary's correspondence with Babington and other relevant documents. Hatton's shorter analysis in his own hand follows. It is Dr. Conyers Read's view, and it seems almost certainly correct, that this is Hatton's brief for his speech in the House of Commons. For the paper begins: 'First, her Majesty's instructions, uttered by the Chancellor', which accords with the order of proceedings of the House, as set forth in d'Ewes's *Journals*; while the second part, written across the back of the first, is a briefer summary of the case, headed: 'To acquaint the Parliament with the brief sum of the causes.'

We have here, therefore, what is probably, apart from similar notes for his Armada speech, a unique document, an important pronouncement in the making, by an Elizabethan statesman. First the full analysis of the documents which Serjeant Puckering follows closely and scrupulously; then Hatton's own précis of Puckering, which takes the form of an historical survey in short sentences, followed by the actual headings to be observed in his address. In these last brief notes, the orator is seen preparing to rise to the height of the occasion by underlining the importance of the events he is chronicling and by dwelling upon the miraculous preservation of Elizabeth's life and on her high courage:

> For a rarer cause than ever heretofore &c.
> God forbid that your ruin and change of King's life should have been before the chief argument of your assemblies.
> Her misfortune and undeserved calamity is such who never meant more harm to subject's life than to her own.
> Wonderful and miraculous stay of the [plot].
> That to her untolerable grief she hath seen stained the noble English nation with a foul plot of &c., which is stayed by God's providence.
> She chargeth you to acknowledge His admirable benefits, from whose goodness and no desert all this cometh.
> She voweth to God that the danger of her own breath never did equal that more.
> She hath thought meet to use you as a Council (for so you be) to be made acquainted with such things as may touch nearly both her and yourselves.

They are but disjointed sentences, and Hatton amends and polishes as he reads. In the fifth sentence he has written, above the line, for 'foul plot' the phrase 'so detestable crimes', and for 'God's providence' he has substituted 'Holy hand'. Then follow the heads of the arguments for Mary's guilt that he intends to present, sanctimoniously interlarded with Latin Scriptural tags.

When Parliament met on November 3rd, 1586, Hatton announced that it was summoned 'to consult for such matters as the like were never almost heard of, nor any Parliament called for, in former time, that can be found or read of'. Very excellently, plainly and effectually, as the record has it, he detailed 'the horrible and wicked practices and attempts caused and procured by the Queen of Scots, so called', to overthrow 'the true and sincere religion established in this realm' by promoting foreign invasion, rebellion and civil war; and, above all, to compass the English Queen's death — 'yea and withal (which his heart quaked and trembled to utter and think on) the death and destruction of the Queen's most sacred person, to the utter desolation and conquest of this most noble realm of England'. He asked that a speedy consultation concerning Mary might be taken by the House 'for the cutting of her off by course of justice', as otherwise Queen Elizabeth's life could not be preserved. He concluded with the ominous words, *Ne pereat Israel, pereat Absolon.*

As a result of this intimation of the Government's wishes, both Houses agreed to present a petition to Elizabeth, begging her to order Mary's execution. The petition was presented on the 12th; and on the 14th Hatton rose to communicate Elizabeth's wishes to Parliament. He said that 'moved with some commiserations for the Scottish Queen, in respect of her former dignity and great fortunes in her younger years, the nearness of her kindred to her Majesty, and also of her sex', Elizabeth would be well pleased 'to forbear taking of her blood', if Parliament could devise any other means of preserving Elizabeth's safety and the security of the realm. She left the House an unfettered judgment in the matter, collectively and individually, intimating that suggestions would be welcomed from any member by any of the Privy Council or by the Speaker, for submission to her. Hatton then moved the adjournment until the 18th, when the House again met and, after much discussion, came to the resolution 'that no other way, devise, or means whatsoever could or can possibly be found or imagined, that such safety can in any wise be had, so long as the said Queen of Scots doth or shall live'.

The precise degree of Elizabeth's responsibility for Mary's execution is difficult to determine. It is certain that she wished to escape the odium of ordering her rival to be judicially removed, and would have preferred if she could have been secretly put out of the way. Walsingham and Davison, the other Secretary of State, indeed wrote to Sir Amyas Paulet and Sir Drew Drury, Mary's gaolers, saying that Elizabeth noted in them a lack of that care and zeal for her service that she looked for, 'in that you have not in all this time (of yourselves without other provocation) found out some way to shorten the life of the Scots Queen', seeing the danger in which Elizabeth stood and her own reluctance to shed blood, especially that of a woman, a queen and a near relative; and reminding them of the Oath of Association that they, with others, had taken, to pursue to the death those who plotted against Elizabeth's life. Davison wrote the same day to Paulet, asking him to burn this letter, which however Paulet preserved with a copy of the reply. The two secretaries had mistaken their man. That stern Puritan was not at all likely to commit murder even on the Queen's instructions, a murder moreover that would certainly be disowned and the responsibility for which would be fastened upon him. Paulet wrote of his 'great grief and bitterness of mind, in that I am so unhappy in living to see this unhappy day, in which I am required by direction from my most gracious sovereign, to do an act which God and the law forbiddeth . . . God forbid I should make so foul a shipwreck of my conscience, or leave so great a blot on my poor posterity, and shed blood without law or warrant'. Elizabeth was disgusted at this reply. She complained of Paulet's and Drury's 'daintiness', and 'the niceness of those precise fellows'. But there was nothing for it but a legal process, and a warrant was accordingly prepared and given to Davison. Elizabeth afterwards repudiated her action, and Davison was made the scapegoat.

William Davison was an old friend of Hatton's. When he was the Queen's agent in Antwerp he had kept Hatton informed of events there, and had subsequently continued to correspond with him. So close was the friendship between the two men that Hatton had stood godfather to one of Davison's sons. This was Christopher Davison, born in December, 1581, who, like his brothers Francis and Walter, grew up a poet, though he did not contribute to *The Poetical Rhapsody*, edited by Francis, and is known only for his translations of some of the Psalms. Now, five years later, Hatton was to be intimately concerned in the events which led to poor Davison's disgrace.

It has been suggested that Davison was promoted to Secretary in order to make use of him for securing Mary's execution and then to repudiate him. A sentence from Davison's speech at his trial perhaps hints as much: 'The place I held, I protested I never sought for: it pleased her Majesty for some gracious opinion of me to prefer me thereunto.' However that may be, there seems little doubt that he was actually used as a cover, and it is certain that he was made the scapegoat. Elizabeth signed the warrant for Mary's execution, and handed it to him as Secretary to have it sealed under the Great Seal. He was to go to Walsingham who was lying sick in his house and tell him of it, because, as Elizabeth 'merrily said', 'the grief thereof would go near to kill him outright'. The explanation that Elizabeth afterwards gave for signing the warrant was that she wished to have it in readiness to be put into execution in the event of what she feared taking place, attempts at invasion in favour of the Scots Queen or conspiracies against her own life. If this was really her intention, it was not made sufficiently clear to Davison. She left herself a characteristic loophole for, after asking Davison to have the warrant sealed, she sent for her Groom of the Chamber, William Killigrew, to tell him not to seal it if that had not already been done. On Davison saying that it was already sealed, she exclaimed, 'What haste?' a phrase that, it was later argued, showed that she had not made up her mind. It was Davison's business, it was urged at his trial, to know the Queen's mind. Others wiser than he, Burghley and Walsingham, had spent a good part of their lives groaning under the difficulties of that very problem.

Davison was sufficiently alert to guess that his position was a difficult one, but not astute enough to avoid the snare set for his feet. He knew, of course, of the Queen's reluctance to proceed publicly against Mary. He knew also that Parliament and Government were determined on her execution. There could be no doubt that when the fatal act had been carried out, Elizabeth would be greatly perturbed and might well repudiate all responsibility. There would probably be a scapegoat, he reflected, as when Burghley had been blamed for Norfolk's death, and it looked uncommonly as if Mr. Secretary Davison were cast for that part. Revolving these things in his mind, he made a slip. Elizabeth had enjoined secrecy upon him. Did she intend him to act alone? The trap seemed to be closing on him. He felt he could not bear the sole responsibility, but must share it with others of the Privy Council. He could reasonably argue that the Queen's injunction of secrecy could not be intended to apply to her Council. But that is just what Elizabeth declared she had meant. The Lord Chancellor, to be sure, knew of the warrant, for he had sealed it, and Walsingham had been told of it by Elizabeth's own wish. It was argued that, as she had expressly excluded Walsingham from the condition of secrecy, she had meant that Davison was not to communicate her wishes to the other members of the Council. Nothing, probably, that the unfortunate Secretary could have done would have saved him. In taking the course he did, however, there seemed to be a reasonable chance of escape; at worst he would share responsibility with the others.

At any rate, Davison went to Hatton, told him all the circumstances and declared that he was determined not to proceed any further in the affair by himself, but would leave it to Hatton and the other members of the Council to decide what was to be done. Hatton reassured him, saying that 'as he was heartily glad the matter was brought thus far, so did he for his own part wish him hanged that would not join with Davison in the furtherance thereof, being a cause so much importing the common safety and tranquillity of her Majesty and the whole realm'. He and Davison sought conference with Burghley, and it was determined to assemble the Council the next day. Davison gave Burghley the warrant, Burghley undertook to draw up the letters which were necessary to accompany it, and the Privy Council was immediately assembled.

To the Council Burghley urged the need of executing the sentence, said that in signing the warrant the Queen had done as much as either reason or the law required of her, repeated what had taken place between her and Davison and that Davison had refused to act alone, and argued that, as they were all equally interested they ought to make common cause and dispatch the warrant without further reference to Elizabeth. They all agreed to share the responsibility, and the warrant was given to Beale, the Clerk of the Council, who was told to use the utmost haste in proceeding to Fotheringay. There Mary was executed on the morning of February 8th, 1587.

When Elizabeth heard the news of Mary's death, she sent for Hatton and protested that the execution was entirely contrary to her intentions. She was intensely indignant with all her ministers; but the blame fell, as Davison had feared, almost wholly on him. He was sent to the Tower and subjected to examination in which Hatton took part. But Hatton, with the other principal ministers, was absent from the Court of Star Chamber when Davison was tried for misprision and contempt, found guilty and sentenced to a heavy fine and imprisonment. The commissioners included a number of men who were certain to be unfriendly to the prisoner, Catholic conspirators like Lumley and Worcester, and Crofts, the notorious pensioner of the King of Spain.

Davison, ill and distraught, with his left arm in a sling from 'a late taken palsy', though speaking in an almost inaudible voice, made a dignified and sensible defence, maintaining his own interpretation of his orders and duties, but saying that it was not becoming for him to gainsay the Queen or contest her views, and praying for her mercy. The judges made long and learned speeches, with such pompous phrases as 'you did *justum*, but not *juste*' from the Chief Baron, capped by the Chief Justice, 'I think you meant well, and it was *bonum* but not *bene*'. Lumley impudently described the ministers who had signed the commission for Mary's execution as a nest of conspirators. He spoke of Mary as 'one of the greatest Princes in Europe, who had been unduly and presumptuously proceeded against'. Lord Grey, Hatton's cousin (was he perhaps prompted by his remorseful kinsman?) spoke up manfully for the prisoner. What would have been thought, he asked, if some attempt had been made on Elizabeth's life, and the warrant had been found in Davison's hands, signed but not executed?

Davison was eventually released; his fine was remitted, and he retained his fees as Secretary until his death. But his punishment had been heavy. Confined to the Tower, dismissed from the public service, ill and staggering under the threat of a huge fine, truly he had been ill served by his Queen and his friends. For the more one examines the case, the more certain it seems that Burghley and Hatton knew quite well what was happening, and how Davison was to be used. So far as anyone could know

Elizabeth's mind, never more irresolute than at this moment, they must have been aware of her secret wishes. The Council, at any rate, knew what they wanted; they were determined upon Mary's death. Elizabeth had got so far as to sign the warrant; if she changed her mind, or pretended to change it, they would bear the joint responsibility, and there was always Davison to sacrifice as a last resort. That may seem an unfair construction to place on their actions. But it is probably justified by the evidence. And there is this to be said. Burghley and Hatton were in a difficult position, and were fighting a hard fight. The irresolution of the Queen was intolerable. The country could not bear the strain of having Mary condemned worthy of death, and nothing done, while plots might brew and Elizabeth shirked a decision. They had the warrant, and that was enough. Each must trust to his own wits to fly the Queen's wrath should it explode in his direction. If Davison could not succeed in escaping from the danger zone, that was his look-out. So, consciously or unconsciously, argued the two elder statesmen, one of them Davison's friend and godfather to his son. It was not a very squeamish age.

CHAPTER XXX

HATTON AND IRELAND

IRISH history presents unusual difficulties for English readers. The strange names of people and places, often made more strange than they need be through the unstandardized efforts of English scribes to present their sounds, so different from what the Irish spelling conveys to English eyes, have tended to repel readers, even those who commonly find an interest in historical matters. And there is an even greater obstacle. For one who has read something of the history of England or of almost any European country, possessing some form of centralized administration and some connecting thread of internal and external policy, to turn to the story of Ireland with its multitude of warring native septs and rival Anglo-Irish houses, with their shifting allegiances and purely personal policies, is bewildering in the extreme. There seems to be no main clue to lay hold of and follow, no broad pathway that gives a view of the whole scene.

In Elizabeth's reign, however, some things begin to emerge more clearly in the Irish picture; and from the point of view of one who would follow Irish affairs only so far as they concern a statesman who had no special concern for Irish policy, a very slight acquaintance with the main trends will suffice. Hatton had only a limited interest in Irish matters. As a member of the Privy Council he was necessarily brought into contact with what his colleagues, the Irish Lord Deputy and the principal Secretary — Walsingham for the greater part of Hatton's official life — were doing. There were some attempts at foreign invasion of Ireland in Hatton's time, and references to these occur in the Hatton Letter Book. For four years Arthur Lord Grey of Wilton, was Irish Deputy. He was a distant kinsman of Hatton's, and some letters from him to Hatton have come down to us. Finally, Hatton, like many another Englishman, whether high official or adventurer, was interested in grants of Irish lands, and on the attainder of the Earl of Desmond, a large fief in Munster fell to his lot. Something must therefore be said of Irish affairs in Hatton's time and of his connection with them.

The most significant development in Ireland in Elizabeth's reign was the gradual growth of a national consciousness, a popular sentiment inevitably directed against the English people. The policy of expropriation, begun under Edward VI and under Mary who was the first to attempt English plantation on a large scale in Ireland, reinforced by the Catholic Counter-Reformation in Elizabeth's time, had tended to produce a weakening of tribal hostilities, a bringing together of the septs against the common political and religious enemy, and even to promote co-operation between such a national figure as the Irish Shane O'Neill and the Anglo-Irish Earl of Desmond. Such a growing consciousness of the need to combine against the oppressor looked to foreign support, and provided Elizabeth's continental enemies with abundance of troubled waters in which to fish.

Shane O'Neill had been killed in 1567. He was succeeded by his cousin, Turloch Luineach, who is mentioned in one of Grey's letters to Hatton, and in whose time Drake served in Ulster under Lord Essex. More important, as involving foreign interference, were the Anglo-Irish Desmonds. Gerald FitzGerald, fifteenth Earl of Desmond, descended from one of the most famous of the twelfth-century Anglo-Norman invaders, was at feud with Thomas Butler, Earl of Ormond, a connection through the Boleyns and a favourite of Queen Elizabeth. The English Government took Ormond's side, and arrested Desmond. His cousin, James FitzMaurice FitzGerald, raised the standard of revolt and appealed to Catholic and anti-English feelings. He was eventually forced to sue for pardon, only to proceed abroad to enlist foreign support against the English.

Meanwhile, an invasion of Ireland was attempted by Sir Thomas Stukeley, a soldier from Devon, a restless adventurer who had had some experience of Irish campaigning in Shane O'Neill's time. He had since seen continental warfare, notably at Lepanto, the most famous naval battle of the age, where he had commanded three galleys under Don John of Austria against the Turk. Stukeley planned an invasion of Ireland, with the aid of the Pope, who bestowed upon him the title of Marquis of Leinster, and of the Cardinal of Como, the Papal secretary; and set out on that mission in January, 1578, with a small fleet and six hundred men. The English Government were ready for him. They had ships lying in wait, and 2000 men at hand to throw into Ireland at short notice, while the Deputy, Sir Henry Sidney, was ordered to keep a strict look-out along the Irish coasts.

In June Walsingham wrote to Hatton about Stukeley. The Queen, he said, believed that the devotion to her of the nobility of Ireland was sufficient guarantee of Irish loyalty, holding it unlikely that 'so weak an instrument as Stukeley is shall be able to prevail against a Prince of her Majesty's power, armed with the goodwill of her subjects in that realm, as she doubted not but that she is'. At that time Stukeley had brought his small, unseaworthy fleet through the Mediterranean as far as Lisbon. Here Sebastian, King of Portugal, provided him with fresh ships, but induced him to join in his expedition against Abdulmelech, the Emperor of Morocco. As an enemy of Spain, the Emperor was in favour with Elizabeth. She had sent him an embassy bearing gifts, and had received a reassuring report from one of her agents that he was an earnest Protestant! At any rate, he proved useful in helping to fight Elizabeth's battles. For Stukeley fell at the Battle of Alcazar, both his legs being shot off by a cannon ball. With him fell also the Emperor of Morocco and the young King of Portugal. As Sebastian had no children, the heir to the throne of Portugal was his great-uncle, the Cardinal Henry, an old man, and next to him Philip of Spain. Hence Philip was presently able to add Portugal to his dominions, a good return from his point of view for the failure of Stukeley's expedition.

Meanwhile, Sir James FitzMaurice FitzGerald had been busy on the Continent, promoting an enterprise against the English in Ireland. The Pope blessed his plans, and appointed him Captain-General. King Philip unofficially approved them, and allowed him to recruit a force in Spain. The Jesuit, Nicholas Sanders, joined him with a consecrated banner presented by the Pope. In July, 1579, the joint expedition of Spanish and Papal filibusters landed at Dingle Bay in Kerry, and entrenched themselves at Smerwick. FitzMaurice was killed in August in a local fray; and the Munster rising was suppressed by Ormond and Sir William Pelham, with the assistance of Sir John Perrot, President of Munster, and Sir Peter Carew, an adventurer who was claiming vast tracts in Ireland on the strength of a mythical descent from one of the original grantees of the kingdom of Cork from Henry II. The little garrison at Smerwick clung on, awaiting reinforcements.

HATTON AND IRELAND

Hatton had no special concern in these Irish affairs. But, as a member of the Privy Council, he was naturally kept informed of developments by Walsingham, as the above letter shows. And he had some other contacts with Ireland. Before 1577 he had thought of that country as a field for one of those monopolies for which English courtiers possessed an insatiable appetite. He had been granted, as already narrated, a licence to export yarn from Ireland; but, when his licence expired, the Deputy, Sir Henry Sidney, refused to renew it, declaring that he would not be the first to break the Statute against such exports, which he had been instrumental in passing.

Some few years later, Hatton was in touch with affairs in Ireland through various agents and others passing backwards and forwards between the two countries. Barnabe Rich was one of these. He was related to an Irish gentleman, Robert Pyphoe, of Hollywood, co. Dublin, who was himself a cousin of Walsingham's; he thus possessed both English and Irish connections. He looked to some extent to Hatton as a patron, dedicated three of his books to him, and has left a description of Holdenby House in Hatton's time. He saw a good deal of service in Ireland; and in 1581, Sir Henry Wallop, Treasurer of the Wars in Ireland, sent him to Hatton to intercede for the Earl of Kildare who, though he had served against the rebels in the Nugent rebellion of that year, had promised aid to those who had planned with Rome the invasion of Ireland.

Another follower of Hatton's who turns up in Ireland in 1583, John Browne, 'servant to Mr. Vice-Chamberlain', executed a map of the town of Galway which still survives and another of co. Mayo. Describing himself as the first Englishman who has settled to dwell in Mayo, he petitioned for licence to inhabit and settle tenants in the 'decayed town of Athenry'. He was the ancestor of the Marquesses of Sligo, and is stated to have been a brother of Lord Montague. If so, he may be identified with 'young Brown, a base brother to the Lord Montacute' who was named in 1572 as a possible adherent of Stukeley in his designs on Ireland. Yet another of Hatton's men in Ireland was Jacomo di Francisci, the mysterious Captain Jaques of the Babington Plot. Of this sinister figure, Adam Loftus, Archbishop of Dublin, and later to be the first Provost of Trinity, Queen Elizabeth's Dublin foundation, wrote to Burghley commending 'Mr. Jacomo

319

di Francesqui, servant to Mr. Vice-Chamberlain, a forward and valiant gentleman'. Details of his relations with Hatton have already been given in the account of the Babington Plot.

In June, 1580, Arthur, Lord Grey of Wilton, was appointed Lord Deputy of Ireland. There are several letters from him in the Hatton Letter Book. In these he calls Hatton his cousin; and if the pedigrees can be trusted there was an extremely distant blood relationship between the two men. Hatton's great-grandmother, Elizabeth Holdenby, is said to have had for maternal grandfather Sir William Lucy; and the Holdenbys certainly impaled the arms of Lucy, the famous 'luces or pikes, haurient Argent' on which Shakespeare may have punned. Sir William Lucy's mother was a daughter of Richard Grey of Ruthin, a cadet of the house of Grey of Wilton; so that, according to this pedigree, Hatton's father and Arthur Grey of Wilton were no less than eighth cousins.

Hatton's interest in Ireland, strengthened no doubt by the appointment of his friend and kinsman to the responsible position of Lord Deputy, is shown in a remarkable letter that he wrote to Walsingham in September, 1580. There had been rumours of a great fleet being sent from Spain for the reinforcement of the garrison at Smerwick. Some agents forwarded to England accounts that eighteen ships and 12,000 men were assembled at Corunna and Santander; other estimates mentioned anything from forty to sixty ships. In the event, the force that landed in September and joined the Smerwick garrison consisted of but 600 men from two ships. But when Hatton wrote to Walsingham these rumours were taken seriously, and Elizabeth's admiral, Sir William Winter, had been sent with four ships of the Royal Navy to guard the Irish coasts. Believing that the insurrection had been crushed, he had sailed home without orders, as Hatton notes in his letter. He was immediately ordered to return to the coast of Kerry.

Hatton in this letter is all for vigorous action, emphasizing the importance of taking strong measures at the start, and not allowing things to drift; pointing to the strategical position of Ireland and Scotland as the postern gates of England, which a wise policy would bolt and bar; and laying the blame for the menacing developments of the time fairly and squarely on the shoulders of the Pope. There is no hedging here, no tenderness for Romish opinions. Whatever Hatton's religious views may have been ten years earlier, by 1580 he was apparently as uncompromising a Protestant as Walsingham himself. Something may be allowed for the fact that it is to Walsingham that he is writing; but he was now definitely of Walsingham's and Leicester's way of thinking, and had shaken off whatever allegiance he may once have held to Rome.

Scarcely more than a month later the little force of 600 men at Smerwick was attacked by Grey and, after three days' fighting, laid down its arms. Its members were almost to a man massacred in cold blood. This dreadful deed, the horror of which no less than Cromwell's slaughter at Drogheda has moved writers through the centuries to heated condemnation and equally vehement defence, has an added interest by reason of Grey's exculpation by one of the greatest of English writers. Edmund Spenser was his secretary, was present at Smerwick, and defended Grey in verse in Book V of the *Faerie Queene*, in prose in his *View of Ireland*. No one to-day can approve Grey's action, but by all the laws of war and all considerations of military security it is technically defensible. Such an episode, happening in our own times, when we imagine ourselves to possess a higher moral standard than the men of Elizabeth's day, would pass almost unnoticed.

Smerwick was the end of this attempt to invade Ireland, the last that concerns Hatton in any way. The leaders were killed or captured. Sanders the Jesuit died of starvation after wandering for months in the woods; the Earl of Desmond was eventually hanged, and to Hatton fell a share of his vast estates.

But, in spite of this exploit, Grey was not a success in Ireland. A strong Puritan, his remedy for Irish disaffection was the Mahommedan alternative of the true faith or the sword. The Queen, however, forbade him to interfere in matters of religion, and Grey felt in consequence that his efforts to pacify Ireland were futile. 'The wrong end is begun at', he reported gloomily. He had gone to Ireland much against his will; and, after numerous petitions to be relieved of his post, was recalled in 1584. His last letter to Hatton shows him on holiday at Northampton, enjoying the quiet of his 'poor lodge', and, thanks to Hatton, getting some hunting. Hatton, besides his estates in Northamptonshire, was Keeper of the Royal Forest of Rockingham; and so, when Grey writes, 'I have found by your officers and keepers hereabouts, your frank and friendly pleasure for my taking of sport in the games here under your commandment, of which offer as I have been bold to make trial, so have I found more than required therein afforded', he is probably referring to the Forest of Rockingham.

'The eagles . . . spread their wings for the Spanish Main; the vultures swooped upon Ireland.' A picturesque sentence that may hold for many of the adventurers who looked to grants from the estates of dispossessed Irish chieftains to redress the balance of unkind fortune in England. But, as Professor Pollard observes, the eagles were often the same men as the vultures. Ralegh, who had fought the Spaniard on the high seas as well as at Smerwick, was both. And, if Hatton was one of the vultures of that rhetorical phrase, so also was the poet Spenser who had a grant of Kilcolman, where he immortalized the scene in the *Faerie Queene* and in *Colin Clouts Come Home Againe*. Both Youghal, Ralegh's grant, and Kilcolman were parts of the immense estates of the Earl of Desmond, which fell to the Crown on his attainder in 1584, and of which Hatton got his share.

This was an area of some 10,000 acres in the Barony of Decies, co. Waterford, around Dungarvan and Cappoquin. Part of it, Cappoquin and neighbourhood, was escheated land of the Earl of Desmond; the Castle of Knockmoan (that is, Knockmaon, a townland in the parish of Whitechurch, adjoining Dungarvan) was escheated land of Richard FitzJohn FitzMaurice, a relative of Sir Gerald FitzJames FitzGerald of Dromana, lord of the Decies, a loyal subject who retained his estates; and other lands in the neighbourhood had been forfeited by various adherents of Desmond. Hatton's tenants numbered 53 Irishmen and 20 English, and his rent to the Crown was £60 7s. 6d. a year. His grant carried with it the post of Constable of the Royal Castle of Dungarvan. There is extant a muster roll of his, delivered by William Chapman (Deputy) Vice-Constable, the Vice-Constable John Tirrell being then absent in England. John Tirrell was the leader of Hatton's little force of twelve men that he sent to his nephew Sir William Hatton when he joined Anjou's expedition in the Netherlands in 1581. In that year also he was one of the defendants in a great tilting performance.

Hatton's title to some of his lands in Waterford was challenged by Gerald FitzJames FitzGerald of Dromana, lord of the Decies under the Earls of Desmond, whose great-great-grandfather, a younger son of James FitzGerald, seventh Earl of Desmond, had been granted the Decies by his father. Gerald FitzJames claimed as heir of his uncle, Maurice FitzGerald, created Viscount Decies in 1569. In 1590 the Queen issued a warrant to Sir William FitzWilliam, the Lord Deputy and to Adam Loftus, who with his Archbishopric of Dublin combined the office of Lord Chancellor of Ireland, concerning the grant to Sir Christopher Hatton, Lord Chancellor of England, of the Barony of Aughmean (?Knockmaon) and the lordship of Cappoquin, with other parts of the Decies in the county of Waterford, which were claimed by Garrett FitzJames FitzGarrett, heir male to the Viscount of Decies. They were directed to secure the surrender of these lands from FitzGerald, who was to be allowed to hold the Barony of Comragh.

In the same year Hatton wrote to Burghley, asking him to provide for the repair of the Castle of Dungarvan which, 'if it is to be preserved, must presently be looked to'. But he was apparently not very enthusiastic about his Irish grants, for he adds, 'otherwise as it shall please her Majesty, for he is not greedy of advancement in Irish honours'. At the same time he wrote to Sir Henry Wallop about the castle, which he described as the Queen's ruined castle of Dungarvan, and the cost of its repair, directing him to refund to Hatton or to John Tirrell, his Vice-Constable, the money expended on it, £259 3s. 4d. The Mayor of Bristol was to provide Tirrell with a barque for transporting to Ireland materials for the repair of the castle. Hatton thus undertook its restoration, his expenses being reimbursed by the Crown from the revenue of the Irish Establishment. After Hatton's death, it was certified by Sir Thomas Norris, the Vice-President of Munster, that his expenses for building had amounted to £690, presumably spent by him on behalf of the Crown.

Hatton's line, unlike that of Spenser, was not destined to continue in Ireland. His Irish estates passed, on his death in 1591, to his nephew, Sir William Hatton, who immediately sold them for £1600 to one Roger Dalton. Dalton's widow, Alison Dalton of Cappoquin, petitioned the Crown in 1597, complaining that Garrett FitzJames of Dromana, styling himself Lord of the Decies, and other Irish, had entered and occupied more than 6000 acres of her property. The FitzGeralds eventually got back a large part of these lands; and Gerald FitzJames's line is to-day represented by the family of Villiers-Stuart of Dromana.

CHAPTER XXXI

THE SPANISH ARMADA

IN 1587 the Spanish Armada was preparing for the invasion of England. The execution of Mary Stuart could not be ignored by the Pope and the Most Catholic King. Her death had cleared the way for a Spanish succession to the throne of England, claimed by virtue of descent from John of Gaunt, and of Mary's intended will (which, however, was never made) ceding her right to the English throne to Philip of Spain, in the event of her son not embracing the Catholic religion. So Philip prepared for war, and Sixtus V, who had the greatest admiration for Elizabeth, was reluctantly forced to back his schemes. 'What a valiant woman', the imperious Pope had exclaimed, 'she braves the two greatest kings by land and sea', and jesting at his own celibate state, he lamented the fact that he and Elizabeth could not marry to have children who would have 'mastered the whole world'. But Philip was pressing him to make common cause, and the Jesuits Allen and Parsons were urging him to help in the conquest of their native land. Allen, who had chosen himself as Archbishop of Canterbury and Lord Chancellor of conquered England, was made a cardinal in August, 1587; and in 1588 the Pope revoked the temporary licence for English Catholics to be loyal to Elizabeth, which Campion had managed to extract from Rome eight years before.

Parliament met on February 15th, 1587, a week after Mary's execution; and on the 22nd, by the Queen's command, Hatton made a long speech, in which he prepared the House for the coming of the Armada, declared that the dangers in which the nation stood arose from 'ancient malice against the Queen', and traced them to their origin in the agreement reached at the Council of Trent, by which the continental Princes had solemnly bound themselves 'to extirpate Christian religion which they termed heresy'. In the course of his speech Hatton gave a summary history of the plots against England and Elizabeth connected with the Queen of Scots; spoke of the danger to the Protestant religion both here and on the Continent from the

machinations of the Pope and the members of the League; out-
lined the course of relations between England and Spain, dwelling
on Spanish provocations of England and glossing over English
assaults on Spain; and warned the House of the danger of a
Spanish invasion, giving an estimate of the dimensions of the
coming Armada.

Drake's raid on Cadiz in April, in which he sunk or burned
two of the largest Spanish vessels and thirty-one smaller ones, and
carried off four laden with prisoners, prevented the Armada from
sailing in 1587. His action was an illustration of the new naval
strategy of attacking the enemy at his base instead of waiting for
him to come to the shores of England. But Drake was a century
or two ahead of his time, and was not in command of a sufficiently
organized fleet to follow up his success. The danger had but been
postponed. In August Leicester, who had gone to the Netherlands when Elizabeth reluctantly decided to take them under
her protection, came home. He had accomplished nothing except
to widen the breach between the two countries by an act of war
against the King of Spain. Hatton, as Lord Lieutenant of
Northamptonshire, had been responsible for levying 200 men
within the county to be sent to Leicester; and with Leicester, as
a volunteer, had gone Hatton's nephew and heir, William
Newport or Hatton, as well as Hatton's dependant Churchyard,
the poet. Philip Sidney too, the flower of his age, had taken part
in the campaign, only to lose his life at Zutphen.

On October 28th, Hatton, now Lord Chancellor, made a
speech in the Star Chamber on the subject of the coming invasion. Of this speech a report, communicated to the King of
Spain, is among the Spanish archives. Hatton said that Philip
and the Pope had resolved to invade England, and for that
purpose had a most potent Armada at sea. He therefore admonished everybody to be on the alert, inferring that the sons of
David were with the English, and the Holy Scriptures on their
side, 'with other persuasions and remonstrances of the same sort,
all pronounced with much severity'. The report of Hatton's
speech goes on to say that he enjoined the noblemen and
others then in London on business at the law courts to return
home, and defend their wives, children and fatherland, for the
Queen, he said, was now certain that the Pope and the Kings
of Spain and France were in league to ruin her, because of her

religion. She therefore ordered those who had official positions in the counties to go there, and muster foot and horse, the lists of which should be sent to her within a month.

The Armada had long been expected, and the Government had been energetically putting the country into a state of defence. Besides his general activities as a member of the Privy Council, as the spokesman of the Queen in the House of Commons and, since 1587, as Lord Chancellor, Hatton had a special responsibility as Lord Lieutenant of Northamptonshire and as Admiral of the Isle of Purbeck, for the districts under his charge. By Letters Patent in September, 1586, he had been constituted Lord Lieutenant of his native county. It was Burghley's county too where he had made his home and where he was 'no new planted or new feathered gentleman', and he was sore at being passed over. Hatton was given authority to levy all subjects first for military service, to train and array them, and put them in readiness with necessary arms, and to muster from time to time men of arms, horsemen, archers and footmen; to declare martial law and to put down any rising within the county, with powers of life and death at his discretion. He was assigned as deputy lieutenants, Sir John Spencer (who shortly afterwards died, and was succeeded by Sir Thomas Cecil, Burghley's eldest son), Sir Richard Knightley and Sir Edward Montague.

In October, 1586, the Privy Council instructed Hatton to enrol 1000 foot of the most substantial householders in the county, under captains, 'the fittest gentlemen, best affectionated in religion', every band of 100 men to consist of 40 shot, 20 armed pikes and 40 bows and bills. General instructions were issued to Lieutenants of counties, Hatton among them, on choosing and training men. They were told to administer an oath to all soldiers and captains; to disarm all papists and other suspected persons; to see that the privileged towns (eight in number in Northamptonshire) had a supply of powder in store; and last — the detail best remembered to-day — to see that the beacons (five for Hatton's county) were built and well kept. In December Knightley writes to Montague asking for a certificate of the number of trees needed for a beacon to be sent to him, directed to Mr. Vice-Chamberlain Hatton. He thought that Montague would have to reckon more than three trees to a beacon, unless those in Montague's part of the county were larger than his.

The church towers, built of Northamptonshire ironstone, were selected as sites; and so all was in readiness against the day of ordeal, when beacon would answer to beacon against the summer sky.

When Sheridan in *The Critic* laughed at amateur playwrights he chose Tilbury Fort at the time of the Armada for the scene of Mr. Puff's ridiculous effort. Hatton and Ralegh, of course, figure in it. Puff explains, 'You'll know Sir Christopher by his turning out his toes — famous, you know for his dancing. I like to preserve all the little traits of character'. Hatton opens with

> True, gallant Ralegh!
> But oh, thou champion of thy country's fame,
> There is a question which I yet must ask:
> A question which I never asked before —
> What mean these mighty armaments?
> This general muster? and this throng of chiefs?

Without waiting for an answer, he proceeds to a description of the warlike scene before him, ending:

> I cannot but surmise — forgive, my friend,
> If the conjecture's rash — I cannot but
> Surmise the State some danger apprehends!

And so on; the ludicrous dialogue explaining for the benefit of the audience matters of which the speakers are, of course, well aware.

The papers which tell the story of the levying by Hatton of the Northamptonshire contingent have been printed by the Northamptonshire Record Society. Similar instructions were issued throughout the length and breadth of the country. And so England prepared for the coming of the Armada. It had been again delayed by the death in January, 1588, of its appointed commander, Santa Cruz. As his successor was chosen the Duke of Medina Sidonia, a soldier ignorant of the sea, under whom the Armada was to go down in defeat. There faced him on the English side Lord Howard of Effingham, a competent sailor who, as Charles Howard, had jousted with Hatton in the tilt-yard in earlier days; and to Effingham's competence was added the genius of Drake, Hatton's one-time protégé. This is not the place to describe the nine days' fight, from July 19th to 27th, the first great naval battle under sail. That wonderful story has been told a thousand times. The victory was won by superior seamanship and gunnery, and completed by the wreck of the Great Armada, badly handled on a stormy coast as it sought flight around the northern margins of Scotland and Ireland. *Flavit Deus et dissipati sunt.*

On August 25th, when the danger was over and the county contingents were returning home, the Privy Council wrote to Hatton to express the Queen's 'princely thanks' for what he and his deputy lieutenants had done in choosing and equipping their men. Elizabeth had visited Hunsdon's camp at Islington and seen the Northamptonshire forces with the others. Earlier in the month, as the Spanish records tell us, reviews were held of the forces which had been raised by private persons for the national service, forces which the defeat of the Armada had now rendered unnecessary. The first to be reviewed was Hatton's contingent, which was mustered on August 9th in the Queen's presence. Hatton entertained Elizabeth to dinner at his house in Ely Place, and there presented to her his company of a hundred men-at-arms, well accoutred, in uniforms of red and yellow. Burghley, Leicester and the other great men of the kingdom followed suit, including Elizabeth's young favourite, Essex, whose company, according to the Spanish King's informant, was the best of them all: sixty musketeers, sixty harquebusiers on horseback, and 200 light horse, in uniforms of orange-coloured cloth, with facings of white silk, several of the light horsemen having surcoats of velvet of the same colour, trimmed with silver. These reviews were appropriately followed by a joust.

Parliament met on November 12th, and was prorogued till February 4th, 1589. On that day the Queen attended in person, accompanied by Lord Chancellor Hatton, who explained the reason for its being summoned. He made a fine speech, the main object of which was to warn the country that the danger was by no means past. In it he included an impressive statement of the importance of sea-power to England. The early part of this speech, a full-blooded attack, in keeping with the sentiments of the times, on the Pope, Cardinal Allen and the Catholic clergy, is not printed in the Parliamentary Journals. The following account of it has been found by Professor J. E. Neale, and is quoted from his *Queen Elizabeth*:

He struck the note of the time, a fierce vituperative hatred of the Pope and all his works. He inveighed against the raging Bull and slanderous calumniations of that monster Pius V; against the tag and rag of seminary priests sent hither pell-mell, thick and three-fold, to increase the number of potential rebels under pretence of planting popery; against the unchristian fury of the Pope — 'that wolfish bloodsucker' — and of the Spaniard — 'that insatiable tyrant' — turned against a Virgin Queen, a famous lady, and a country which embraced without corruption in doctrine the true and sincere religion of Christ; and against the machinations and writings of that shameless atheist and bloody Cardinal Allen, a savage and barbarous priest. He was shocked that Englishmen — 'those bloody priests and false traitors' — should turn against their native country: 'I think it was never heard of amongst the very Scythians. It is said that the snakes in Syria will not bite nor sting the people that are born there; but these most venomous snakes you see do not only labour to bite and sting us, but, as a generation of cruel vipers, to tear us in pieces and to feed themselves with our blood.' He went on to praise the Queen's government and review her life-story as the object of Catholic hatred. God had blessed where papists had cursed, and multiplied His innumerable benefits upon England. He had defended Elizabeth and her realm, 'making the very birds of the air' — a felicitious description of Walsingham! — as it were to reveal the conspiracies of her enemies.

The speech is of interest on another account. As the notes for Hatton's statement in Parliament against the Queen of Scots have come down to us, so, it would appear, have those for the conclusion of this 'Armada Speech'. At any rate, there is among the Bardon Papers a document in Hatton's hand, evidently the abstract of a statement to be delivered in Parliament, urging the taking of measures of defence. Dr. Conyers Read considers that this paper is probably a collection of notes for part of that speech, for portions of it, as reported in the Lords' Journals, correspond roughly with these notes. Hatton said that peace had ever been the object nearest the Queen's heart, and that neither the infant state of Scotland, the treachery of France, the divisions of her enemies, nor the frequent solicitations of the Dutch, had provoked her to make war; and that, while she was endeavouring to keep the peace with Spain, the Armada had prepared to invade the country. He gave a graphic description of its great size, and of its defeat and final dispersion:

Behold a vast navy of Spanish ships was seen on our English coasts. Such a navy that for numbers and greatness of the ships, for quantity of arms and military forces, and for all kinds of necessary stores, was never seen to float on the ocean before. But God Almighty, her Majesty's hope, defender and preserver rendered this vast Armado of her enemies vain and useless. For the British navy, by far inferior in number and strength, happily attacked, once and again, those huge raised-up rocks and mountains of ships; and, at the third conflict, so dispersed, shattered and disabled them that, never thinking to renew the fight, they fled for it and took a long course hitherto unheard of; for they steered round Scotland, Ireland and the most northern regions, and by those means hoped to regain the Spanish coasts. But what shipwrecks they suffered, what hardships they bore, how many ships, soldiers and seamen they lost, neither can they yet know, nor we for certain learn. Some few ships escaped to Spain; but so shaken, shattered and forlorn, as they can never be of use to them again. The soldiers and sailors who have survived were so miserably harassed by hunger, thirst and other hardships, that they cannot of a long time recover former health.

The danger, however, he insisted, was not over. To quote again from Professor Neale's narrative:

The King of Spain, to the wonder of all Europe, had suffered great loss and dishonour. He was unlikely to make himself a by-word to posterity by acquiescence. Consequently they must prepare their defence. Their noble predecessors, though lacking their means, had been able to defend England, and in their day had been most worthy conquerors. 'Shall we', he asked, 'now suffer ourselves with all dishonour to be conquered? England hath been accounted hitherto the most renowned kingdom of valour and manhood in all Christendom, and shall we now lose our old reputation? If we should, it had been better for England we had never been born.'

Of the answer, Professor Neale resumes there was not a doubt. Among thousands of the poorer sort who, willy-nilly, had gone to the wars by sea and land, there were hundreds who had gladly ventured and were yet to venture, and die. 'In troth, they were young gentlemen, yeomen and yeomen's sons and artificers of the most brave sort, such as did disdain to pilfer and steal, but went as voluntary to serve of a gaiety and joyalty of mind, all which kind of people are the force and flower of a kingdom.'

In his peroration Hatton again urged the importance of taking steps so as to be prepared for the renewed assault by the armed forces of Spain, which was thought to be certain:

> But to what end do I by this recital endeavour to make you secure and void of fear? Do not you imagine, I say, that they are ardently studious of revenge, and that they will not employ the power, the strength, the riches of Spain, and the forces of both Kingdoms, to accomplish it? Know you not the pride, fury and bitterness of the Spaniard against you? Yes, this is the great cause of summoning this Parliament; that in this most full assembly of the wisest and most prudent persons, called together from all parts of this Kingdom, so far as human counsel can advise, a diligent preparation may be made, that arms and forces and money may be in readiness; and that our Navy, which is the greatest bulwark of this Kingdom, may be repaired, manned and fitted out for all events, with the utmost expedition.

English statesmen taught by the exertions of Drake and his fellows, had at last grasped the importance of sea-power, and were beginning to think and say with Shakespeare,

> Let us be backed with God and with the seas
> Which He hath given for fence impregnable.

CHAPTER XXXII

LORD CHANCELLOR

ALL Hatton's biographers have agreed that the last and crowning honour of his life, his appointment as Lord Chancellor, is the most astonishing event of his career. Astonishing, certainly; that the son of an obscure country squire, having no eminence in the law and indeed but little knowledge of it, should be selected for the leadership of the legal profession is remarkable enough. But the ground of his biographers' bewilderment is not well taken. They think it necessary to explain why Elizabeth should appoint a man, whom they regard as an incompetent, to a great legal position. They must also find a reason for Hatton's acceptance of a post which, whatever its eminence, removed him from that personal contact with the Queen in which so much of his influence lay. They have to represent Bench and Bar as being scandalized at his elevation to the Woolsack, and to draw pictures of sullen Serjeants refusing to plead before him.

The truth of the matter is that in choosing Hatton Elizabeth was making not a legal but a political appointment, and that she presumably thought him the man best fitted for the post in the circumstances of the moment. Lord Chancellor Bromley died on April 12th, 1587. The Queen's first choice of a successor lit, according to Camden, upon Edward Manners, Earl of Rutland, who was a learned man and a profound lawyer, but he died six days later. The one man being dead, who combined to statecraft a knowledge of the law, Elizabeth turned to consider the claims of those who were not professional lawyers.

It was a critical time. The Armada was expected that year or the next, and the foreign situation was, in consequence, more troubled than ever. But the matter which loomed largest in the Queen's mind in guiding her choice of a Chancellor was not foreign but domestic. It was the religious question at home. With the execution of Mary Stuart, the English Catholic problem had indeed become less urgent, though a foreign invasion of England would, of course, bring the Catholic question to the fore again. But apart from such a calamity, the principal ecclesiastical problem, as Elizabeth saw it, was the attitude of the Puritan party.

She had always disliked them. Indifferent to matters of dogma, more Catholic at heart than anything else, she had been driven by the logic of events to a Protestant position, to fill, much as it might irk her, the role of Protestant champion of Europe. But the Puritan claim to self-government in the Church ran counter to all her prejudices. It challenged the royal authority in the most important sphere and, if successful, would in her view strike the shrewdest of blows at the divine right of princes.

John Whitgift, who had become Archbishop of Canterbury in 1583, and had in 1586, perhaps partly through Hatton's influence, been sworn of the Privy Council, was specially chosen by Elizabeth to restore discipline in the Church of England, and to secure uniformity in worship. He was, in Professor Pollard's estimation, one of the ablest statesmen who ever sat in the chair of St. Augustine; and to her 'little black husband', as Elizabeth called him (he had once been her 'White gift', in her favourite game of nicknaming her courtiers) she turned over the business of dealing with the Puritan pretensions that threatened her authority. Whitgift, on Rutland's death, is said to have been Elizabeth's second choice for Lord Chancellor. He refused the post, and, according to Sir George Paule, recommended Hatton to the Queen. Paule, who was comptroller of Whitgift's household and wrote his life, is probably a good authority here, and it is likely that it was to Whitgift's recommendation as much as to Elizabeth's own confidence and partiality that Hatton owed his elevation to the Woolsack.

Though Puritan doctrine was not uncongenial to Whitgift, he had no sympathy with the Puritans' claims when they conflicted with the Book of Common Prayer or the Act of Uniformity. He became their intolerant persecutor; and in 1583, when he succeeded the weak Grindal, who professed a sympathy with them that enraged the Queen, she had to her hand the instrument that she required for bringing them to their senses. A stout ally of the formidable Archbishop was Richard Bancroft, who was to succeed Whitgift at Canterbury a generation later. He was Whitgift's chaplain, according to Paule, but in 1584 we find him occupying the same position in Hatton's household, with a chamber in Ely House. His relations with Hatton were close. In 1584 he was acting on behalf of Adam Loftus, Archbishop of Dublin, in supporting his remonstrances to Burghley against the proposal of Sir John Perrot, the Irish Deputy, to appropriate the site and

333

endowments of St. Patrick's Cathedral, Dublin, for the purpose of founding a University. Bancroft, among his other emoluments, held a prebendal stall in St. Patrick's. He, therefore, as well as Loftus, stood to suffer financial loss if Perrot's proposal were adopted; and Loftus showed his usual astuteness in choosing Bancroft, a man with influence at Court, to bear his letter to Burghley and explain his point of view. But, though in this letter Loftus professes the highest regard for Perrot and his motives, he was in reality his bitter opponent. And one cannot help wondering whether Loftus's choice of Bancroft as his emissary was not to some extent due to the calculation that Hatton's influence would be likely to be cast against any schemes of his enemy Perrot. If this be so, Hatton may have to bear some of the blame for postponing the foundation of Trinity College for eight years, a critical period in Irish history when the Catholic Counter-Reformation was reaping its fruits, and an Irish university to train men for the Protestant ministry was sadly needed. Trinity was eventually founded in 1592, without involving the sacrifice of St. Patrick's; it is perhaps only a coincidence that the great Irish university had to wait for Hatton's death before it could come into being.

Strype, the ecclesiastical historian, following Paule, tells us that Whitgift 'in his weighty business had the encouragement and cordial friendship of Sir Christopher Hatton', and that Hatton sent him a collection of notes on the petitions for reform that were to be brought before Parliament, so that the Archbishop could study them and prepare replies, if needed.

On April 29th, 1587, the Queen delivered the Great Seal to Sir Christopher Hatton, and appointed him Lord Chancellor of England. The Court was then at the Archbishop of Canterbury's house at Croydon; and about four o'clock in the afternoon, in a private ambulatory or gallery near her private chamber, and in the presence of the Archbishop and of some other persons of high rank, her Majesty took the Seal, which was lying in a red velvet bag in a window, into her own hands and carried it to the centre of the gallery. She then delivered it to Hatton, but immediately received it back again, and commanded it to be taken out of the bag. The Seal was then affixed to an instrument and replaced in the bag, when the Queen re-delivered it to Hatton; and she 'then and there made and constituted the said Sir Christopher Hatton, Lord Chancellor of England'.

The following day, Burghley's son Robert Cecil brought a message of congratulation to Hatton from 'my lady', presumably Lady Burghley. Pleasant passages passed on this occasion between him and Hatton, who acknowledged his friendship for and indebtedness to Lord Burghley. 'He hath left his hat and feather', Cecil reports to his father, 'and now wears a flat velvet cap, not different from your Lordship's.'

Sir George Paule seems to be the only authority for the statement that Hatton was Whitgift's choice for the Lord Chancellorship. But from the facts given above the conclusion seems inescapable that Hatton's appointment had Whitgift's approval, if it were not actually his suggestion. There is no need therefore to credit this appointment to the machinations of enemies who wished to get Hatton out of the way, to kick him upstairs. Camden is the author of this extraordinary explanation of the Queen's choice, an explanation which Sir Harris Nicolas has accepted. Camden's words are: 'Hatton was advanced thereunto through the cunning Court practices of some, that by his absence from Court and troublesome office of so great a magistracy, for which they knew him to be insufficient, his favour with the Queen might be abated.'

The story that Hatton's appointment caused a flutter of the legal dovecotes is probably more substantial, but is almost certainly exaggerated. No doubt there were jealousies and searchings of heart among the men of the Bar. But the later developments of the legend, that some of the lawyers carried their hostility so far as to refuse to plead before him take no account of human nature, legal as well as lay, which has an inveterate dislike of quarrelling with its bread and butter. Camden's is the soberest version: 'The great lawyers of England took it very offensively, for they, ever after the ecclesiastical men were put from this degree, had with singular commendations for equity and wisdom, borne this highest place of gowned dignity, bestowed in old time for the most part upon churchmen and noblemen.' Fuller embroiders the tale:

> The gownsmen, grudging hereat, conceived his advancement their injury, that one not thoroughly bred to the laws, should be preferred to the place. How could he cure diseases, unacquainted with their causes, who might easily mistake the justice of the Common Law for rigour, not knowing the true reason thereof? Here-

upon it was that some sullen Serjeants at the first refused to plead before him, until partly by his power, but more by his prudence, he had convinced them of their errors and his abilities.

It is, however, certain that Hatton himself had some doubts, engendered by rumours of the Queen's misgivings. The day after Lady Burghley's message of congratulation, one of Burghley's suit waited on Hatton to present Burghley's own felicitations, and reported Hatton's mood:

> His lordship willed me to let your lordship understand that he findeth himself much troubled and grieved with a message his servant Mr. Varneie brought to him yesterday from the Court, from divers of his good friends there; which was that her Majesty should [i.e. did] much repent of her committing of the Great Seal unto him, as that an occasion was thereby given to the world to talk diversely thereof; which should be [i.e. was] often and publically spoken by her Majesty; and therefore he is this afternoon gone to the Court (as he willed me also to let your lordship know) with a resolution that if he found her Majesty to continue that conceit, to deliver up the Seal again, rather than to keep it with her discountenance to his disgrace. . . .

On May 3rd, the first day of Trinity Term, Hatton rode in great state to Westminster from his house in Ely Place to take the oath as Chancellor. He was preceded by about forty of his gentlemen dressed in blue liveries, wearing gold chains, and with them were several of his corps of Gentlemen Pensioners and, on foot, gentlemen of the Court. He was attended by the officers and clerks of the Chancery. On his right hand rode Lord Burghley and on his left the Earl of Leicester; and he was followed by nobles and knights, the Judges and a great retinue of others.

Hatton, though he had spent a few years at the Inns of Court, was not a trained lawyer. But he was a man of affairs, and had the good sense to secure expert assistance. Fuller tells us that he was guided by the advice of Richard Swale, whom he describes as his 'servant friend'. Swale, a Fellow of Caius College, Cambridge, was a man of Catholic sympathies, so that his views were presumably more or less in harmony with what we know of Hatton's private feelings, though at this time Hatton was very far from being a practising Catholic. Swale's leanings are sufficiently indicated by the fact that he and Thomas Legge, the President of

Caius, were charged with perverting the youth of Cambridge to popery. So strong was the feeling against these two men that in 1581 the Fellows asked for a Visitation. Hatton interfered on Swale's behalf, supported his candidature for Proctor, and asked the Visitors to see that his election was not upset. Swale, however, offered some rudeness to the Visitors, and Burghley, the Chancellor of the University, cancelled his appointment and compelled him to apologize. Burghley writes vigorously to Hatton about Legge and Swale who, he says, have abused him in many ways and are corrupting the youth of Cambridge. Swale, he adds, 'is, as I perceive, now your man'. Here again we are conscious of that undercurrent of irritation between the two men, that came occasionally to the surface. It must have been intolerable to Burghley that Hatton, who had no particular status in Cambridge at that time, should be laying down the law in this way, and ignoring the Chancellor. But, if he did not get his way in this matter, Hatton had the satisfaction of seeing Swale elected instead President of Caius in the same year. That was five years before Hatton became Lord Chancellor.

Fuller's statement, that Hatton as Lord Chancellor was indebted for help to Swale, is supported by the facts of Swale's subsequent career. Immediately on Hatton's appointment he left Cambridge, and came to London, to the law. Through Hatton's influence he was appointed a Master in Chancery in May, 1587, and in July was made LL.D. by his University. The following year he became Member of Parliament for Higham Ferrers, Hatton's old seat. His further career as lawyer and Government envoy abroad was distinguished; he was knighted by James I.

With Swale at his elbow, Hatton got on well enough. He was used to the procedure of the Star Chamber, where he had been accustomed to sit as a Privy Councillor. To this Court, according to usage, he devoted Wednesdays and Fridays. On other days he sat for Equity in the Court of Chancery; in Westminster Hall in the mornings and in his own house in the afternoons. He made an order that Masters in Chancery, who had been negligent in their attendance, should always be present and sit on the Bench with him, four in Court daily, and two in the afternoons, three days a week at his own house, to assist him in the cases heard before him. He thus had plenty of help, and was cautious in other ways, 'not venturing to wade beyond the shallow margin of Equity, where he could distinctly see the bottom'.

Hatton indeed displayed a businesslike attitude towards his new duties. There is some evidence that he concerned himself with the reform of procedure in the Courts in the direction of expedition and the accessibility of justice to the poor. The eulogistic verses of Robert Greene, written on Hatton's death, cannot perhaps be cited as a good witness. After speaking of his incorruptibility as a judge, Greene goes on to refer to his speeding up of business in the Courts and his zeal for the cause of the poor suitor:

> The poor man's cry he thought a holy knell.

But this testimony is not unsupported, for David Lloyd, writing it is true eighty years after Hatton's death, says 'he reduced the Chancery and all other Courts to rules'. Such evidence is not, of course, conclusive, but it is fair to observe that reforms of this kind had been advocated by Hatton, speaking under the Queen's direction, from his seat in Parliament. Moving the adjournment of the House in December, 1584, he urged those members who were engaged in the Law to consult together and use their best endeavours 'to devise some good laws to abridge and cut off the long and tedious courses, and extreme chargeable circuits, and superfluous delays of suits of law'.

Lord Campbell has found an order of Hatton's as Lord Chancellor which shows his concern for the business of his Court:

> For the avoiding of such great numbers of suitors and others as do daily pester the Court in the time of sitting, by reason whereof heretofore it hath many times happened that the due reverence and silence which ought to be kept and observed in that honourable Court hath been undutifully neglected, and contrariwise much unmannerly and unseemly behaviour and noise hath been there used, to the hindrance of the due hearing of such matters and causes as were there to be handled, and to the great derogation of the honour of this Court and due reverence belonging to the same,

he made a number of regulations, by which none was to come into Court but counsel, attorneys, officers and their clerks and parties, who were 'to continue so long as the cause shall be in hearing, and no longer; and all other suitors whatsoever (except noblemen and such as be of her Majesty's Privy Council) were to stand without the Court, and not suffered to come in without special licence'.

Only one case in which Hatton presided as Lord Chancellor has been reported to us, the trial of his old friend Sir Richard Knightley, who got into trouble over the publication of the Martin Marprelate Tracts. As this case closely concerned both Whitgift and Hatton, and as it was to deal with matters of Puritan intransigeance that the Queen had appointed them to their respective posts, it will not be amiss to say something about it here. Sir Richard Knightley of Fawsley, in Northamptonshire, we have already met as one of Hatton's deputy lieutenants; it was he who led the Northamptonshire contingent to London at the time of the Armada. The two men were neighbours and friends, and Hatton stood godfather to one of Knightley's sons by his second wife, Elizabeth, daughter of Protector Somerset. He was not able to attend at the baptism in person, so in a charming letter he asked Lady Knightley's brother to act for him.

The Martin Marprelate Tracts bring together for a moment on the crowded Elizabethan stage four of the figures of our story: Whitgift, the stern Archbishop who had waived the offer of the Chancellorship in Hatton's favour; Bancroft, his right-hand man, connecting link between him and Hatton, all three bent on restoring Church discipline and discomforting the Puritans; and Knightley, Hatton's friend and neighbour, a man of strong Puritan sympathies who had helped the cause by allowing some of the Tracts to be printed on presses concealed in his house at Fawsley. The Tracts attacked in coarse but vigorous English the Church policy of the Bishops. Whitgift was the principal target; Bancroft was the busiest of those who hunted down the authors; Knightley for his Puritanical zeal found himself landed in the Star Chamber; and Hatton tried him.

The first of the Tracts was issued from Robert Waldegrave's press at Kingston-on-Thames in October, 1588. In November the press was removed to Fawsley, Knightley's house, where a second Tract was printed. Thence it was again removed to John Hales's house at Coventry, whence in February, 1589, a third Tract was issued, and in March a fourth, *Hay any Worke for Cooper?*, an answer to Bishop Cooper's official reply to the first two Tracts. The press was then transferred to Roger Wigston's house at Wolston in Warwickshire, where the fifth and sixth Tracts were printed in July. The press was seized at Warrington in August while *More Worke for the Cooper* was being printed, and the seventh and last Tract was published in September, having apparently been printed at Wolston in July. The identity of the authors was never fully established. John Penry, a clever young Welsh minister, and Job Throckmorton, a cousin of the Catholic conspirator, Francis Throckmorton, had certainly a share in the preparation of the Tracts if they were not, indeed, the authors of some of them. John Udall, a Puritan divine, was also suspected of complicity. But the trial in February, 1590, of Knightley, Hales and Wigston, did not throw any real light on the problem of the authorship, though it sufficiently established the responsibility for harbouring the printing presses. It was due to Bancroft that the presses were dragged into the light; and he also, it is said, was the author of the idea of replying to the Tracts in like satirical vein, commissioning Thomas Nash, Gabriel Harvey, Robert Greene and their fellows to write *Pappe with a Hatchet*, *An Almond for a Parrot* and other papers directed against them.

The trial of Knightley, Hales, Wigston and his wife took place before Hatton in the Court of Star Chamber. Knightley was fined £2000, Hales 1000 marks, Wigston, who was ruled by his wife, 'for obeying his wife and not discovering it', 500 marks, and Mrs. Wigston £1000, while all were imprisoned during the Queen's pleasure. At the close of the trial Hatton made a speech:

> The Lord Chancellor gave the assembly that stood by to note that these prisoners were not the devisers and makers of these books, for if they had, another place had been fit for them, and not this; but the county of Northampton did swarm with these sectaries . . . whereby he concluded it was necessary to prevent such mischief and to make example of it; and desired the judges to notify his action herein in their circuits abroad, to the end the whole realm might have knowledge of it, and the people no more seduced with these lewd libellers.

Penry died on the scaffold. Thomas Cartwright, the celebrated Puritan, brother-in-law of John Stubbs who had lost his hand for writing a tract against the French marriage, was committed to prison in 1590, in spite of his repudiation of the Martinists. Udall was condemned to death for a libel on the Bishops and other ecclesiastics. A letter from Cartwright to Hatton occurs in the Hatton Letter Book. It is undated, and apparently belongs to an earlier period than this. He writes to Hatton as a lover of the Gospel and a hater of foreign power and papacy. He complains that his liberty has been restrained for six years on suspicion of disloyalty and subversive writings against Church government; and refers to his writings as testimony that these charges were misconceived.

Hatton appears in a rather favourable light in these affairs. At any rate, while doing his duty, he found opportunity to show his kindly and merciful nature. After the first disclosures involving Knightley he made occasion to warn his friend of the peril in which he stood; and when Job Throckmorton, one of the suspected authors of the Tracts, petitioned Hatton he wrote that he is 'encouraged by hearing of divers that in the like distress have found favour' at Hatton's hands. Hatton too took a prominent part, according to Strype, in saving Udall from the gallows. Udall and some others had been tried and condemned to death in March, 1591. Hatton, pitying them, as Strype tells us, was instrumental in moving the Privy Council to decide that if Udall and his associates would confess their errors, they would recommend mercy to the Queen. But Udall has himself left a long account of interrogations put to him, which leaves little doubt that he was not the man to change his opinions for fear or favour. Sir George Paule tells a different story from Strype's. Whitgift, he says, 'drew upon him the dislike of his dear and honourable friend, Sir Christopher Hatton', in urging Udall's pardon on the Queen. He was, in fact, pardoned, but it was too late; he died in prison a few days afterwards.

One last glimpse of a Puritan being examined by Burghley, Hatton, Whitgift and Aylmer, the Bishop of London, may be given here, as it shows Hatton in an amusing light, impatient at Burghley's adroit cross-examination which demanded scriptural proof for all the prisoner's statements; and, not too well-informed, venturing to dispute the derivation of a Greek word. The Puritan in question was Henry Barrowe, who at Whitgift's instance had been arrested with John Greenwood and John Penry. Barrowe, who had been influenced by the Brownist movement, has been claimed on rather slender evidence as the author of some of the Martinist Tracts and as the founder of Congregationalism. With Penry and Greenwood he was hanged in 1593. He has left us an account of his examination when, being a close prisoner in the

Fleet, he was brought in haste by a Mr. Raglande, a gentleman of the Lord Chancellor's, to Hatton's chamber in the Court at Whitehall. There he was confronted by Burghley, Hatton, Whitgift and Aylmer. To Barrowe's statement that 'your Church is not governed by the word of God but by the Romish courts', Hatton irritably remarked that 'he never heard such stuff in all his life'. Later, he burst forth, 'there must be straiter laws made for such fellows'. Aylmer in his cross-examination asked, 'Why? What is the word, presbyter, I pray you?' Barrowe: 'An elder.' Aylmer: 'What, in age only?' Hatton: 'Presbyter is the Latin for a priest.' Barrowe: 'It is no Latin word, but derived, and signifieth the same as the Greek word doth, which is an elder.'

There is but little more to relate of Hatton's conduct of the office of Lord Chancellor. Lord Campbell has discovered a speech made by him on the elevation of a Mr. Robert Clarke to the dignity of Serjeant-at-Law. It is an excellent discourse for a formal yet friendly occasion, both dignified and kindly:

No man can live without Law, therefore I do exhort you that you have good care of your duty in the calling, and that you be a father to the poor; that you be careful to relieve all men afflicted. You ought to be an arm to help them; a hand to succour them. Use uprightness and follow truth. Be free from cautel [i.e. quibble]. Mix with the exercise of the law no manner of deceit. Let these things be far from your heart. Be of an undaunted resolution. Be of good courage, and fear not to be carried away with the authority, power or threatenings of any other. Maintain your clients' cause in all right. Be not put to silence. As it is alleged out of the Book of Wisdom, *Noli quaerere fieri Judex, ne forte extimescas faciem potentis, et ponas scandalum in agilitate tua.* Know no man's face. Go on with fortitude. Do it in uprightness. *Redde cuique quod suum.* Be not partial to yourself. Abuse not the highest gifts of God, which no doubt is great in equity. These things be the actions of nobility. He that doth these things duly deserves high honour, and is worthy in the world to rule. Let truth be familiar with you. Regard neither friend nor enemy. Proceed in the good work laid upon you. And the last point that I am to say to you, use diligence and carefulness. And although I have not been acquainted with the course of the Law, albeit in my youth I spent some time in the study thereof; yet I find by daily experience that diligence brings to pass great things in the course and proceeding of the Law; and contrarily, negligence overthrows many good causes. Let not the dignity of the Law be given to men unmeet. And I do exhort you all that are here present not to call men to the Bar, or the Bench, that are so unmeet. I find that there are now more at the Bar in one House than there were in all the Inns of Court when I was a young man.

He concluded with an exhortation to avoid Chancery, and to settle disputes in the Common Law Courts:

> We sit here to help the rigour and extremities of the Law. The holy conscience of the Queen for matters of Equity in some sort is by her Majesty's goodness committed to me, when *summum jus* doth minister *summam injuriam*. But the Law is the inheritance of all men. And I pray God bless you, and send you as much worship as ever had any in your calling.

As illustrating an even lighter side of Hatton's life as Chancellor is one of his witticisms, which Bacon has preserved in his *Apothegms*. Though not specially amusing, it must have caught the public ear, and so has chanced to be remembered:

> In Chancery, one time when the counsel of the parties set forth the boundaries of the land in question, by the plot; and the counsel of one part said, 'We lie on this side, my Lord'; and the counsel of the other part said, 'And we lie on this side': the Lord Chancellor Hatton stood up and said, 'If you lie on both sides, whom will you have me to believe?'

Nearly a hundred years after Hatton's death there was published in 1677, *A Treatise concerning Statutes, or Acts of Parliament, and the exposition thereof; written by Sir Christopher Hatton, late Lord Chancellor of England*. It was printed for Richard Tonson at his shop under Grey's Inn Gate. It has been doubted if this book was really Hatton's work. But, on the face of it, it would seem likely enough that he was the author. There could be but little reason for ascribing it to him unless it were his, for it was presumably intended chiefly to appeal to lawyers, to whom Hatton's name would be but little recommendation. Lord Campbell, who has missed the point that it was by nearly a century a posthumous work, says 'to give the public a notion that he had attended to the study of the law, he actually published' this book; 'but it was well known to be written by another, and was withal a very poor production'. But Daines Barrington, the correspondent of Gilbert White, in his

Observations on the More Ancient Statutes, says 'it must be allowed to be not entirely destitute of merit'. That sounds more like a description of Hatton's work than that of a professional lawyer. Some slight additional evidence that the book may indeed have been Hatton's is the reference in it to 'Sir Edward Saunders, late Chief Baron, of worthy memory'. Saunders, who died in 1576, was first cousin of Hatton's mother.

CHAPTER XXXIII

THE GARTER; CHANCELLOR OF OXFORD

THE last honour Hatton received from Queen Elizabeth was the Order of the Garter. On St. George's Day, April 23rd, 1587, in a Chapter of the Order he had been chosen by the Companions, receiving eight, the greatest number of votes. But, as the Queen refused to attend when the scrutiny was taken on the excuse that she was not attired in the mantle of the Order, no election took place. It was obvious that Hatton would be elected on the next occasion, and when the Earl of Leicester, who had still a year to live, added a codicil to his will, dated September 30th, 1587, appointing Sir Christopher Hatton, his brother, the Earl of Warwick, and Lord Howard of Effingham the overseers of his will, he left Hatton his Garter in anticipation of his election. He speaks of him most affectionately: 'To my Lord Chancellor, mine old dear friend, I do give one of my greatest basins and ewers gilt, with my best George and Garter, not doubting but he shall shortly enjoy the wearing of it, and one of his armours which he gave me.'

The following April, 1588, Hatton's election was secured. On St. George's Day in a Chapter held at Greenwich, four knights were elected by the Companions, and on the following day, April 24th, the Queen chose Robert Devereux, Earl of Essex, Thomas Butler, Earl of Ormond, President of Munster, and Sir Christopher Hatton, Lord Chancellor, as Knights of the Garter. Being introduced into the Chapter, the kneeling knights elect were invested by the Queen with the insignia of the Order, and were installed on May 23rd. There is a reference to this election among the manuscripts of the Duke of Rutland, a letter from one Robert Berton in London to Elizabeth, Countess of Rutland, which says, 'I looked for the jewels which, if they had been sent up, might have saved £40. For at this St. George's Feast, three knights were elected of the Order, namely Lord Essex, Lord Ormond and the Lord Chancellor, who would willingly have bought them or most of them'.

In June, 1589, Sir Christopher Hatton's nephew, Sir William
Hatton, son of his sister Dorothy by her husband John Newport
of Hunningham in Warwickshire, was married. His wife was
Elizabeth, daughter and heiress of Sir Francis Gawdy, Justice of
the King's Bench, and the marriage took place at Holdenby. The
Lord Chancellor attended the ceremony; and two or three contemporary letters mention the marriage and Hatton's presence at
it. One of these, that of Francis Allen, written to Anthony Bacon,
contains an interesting personal detail, which is probably the
inspiration of Gray's well-known lines in his *Long Story*. Allen
says: 'My Lord Chancellor's heir, Sir William Hatton, hath
married Judge Gawdy's daughter and heir; and my Lord Chancellor danced the measures at the solemnity. He left the gown in
the chair, saying "Lie thou there, Chancellor".' Gray's lines are:

> Full oft within the spacious walls,
> When he had fifty winters o'er him,
> My grave Lord Keeper led the brawls,
> The Seals and maces danced before him.
>
> His bushy beard, and shoe-strings green,
> His high-crown'd hat and satin-doublet,
> Mov'd the stout heart of England's Queen,
> Tho' Pope and Spaniard could not trouble it.

But the scene of the revelry Gray places at Stoke Poges in Bucking-
hamshire, which was never Hatton's, but was leased by Sir
Edward Coke who married the second wife and widow of Sir
William Hatton, Sir Christopher's nephew.

On Leicester's death, September 4th, 1588, the Chancellorship
of the University of Oxford fell vacant. According to Sir George
Paule the heads of the University first made choice of Archbishop
Whitgift for their new Chancellor, but Whitgift (as in the case of
the Lord Chancellorship) declined, and recommended Hatton to
them. Be that as it may, on September 20th Hatton was chosen
by Convocation as Leicester's successor. A deputation from the
University waited on him at Ely Place. Richard Bancroft,
Hatton's chaplain, afterwards Archbishop of Canterbury, has left
us a most interesting account of the proceedings. Bancroft had a
chamber in Hatton's house in Ely Place, and writes as an eye-
witness of the ceremony he describes. His account was copied by

Matthew Stokes, Esquire Bedell of Cambridge, an antiquary who made some academical collections. This was in turn copied in 1771 by the Rev. William Cole, whose manuscripts are in the British Museum.

On Thursday, October 3rd, 1588, about 2 o'clock in the afternoon, Bancroft tells us, the Vice-Chancellor, accompanied by the Heads of Colleges, the Proctors and the other Regents to the number of twenty-four, came to Mr. Flower's lodgings in Ely Place in Holborn, where Hatton, my Lord, as he is called throughout Bancroft's manuscript, was walking in his gallery with John Wolley, the Latin Secretary to Elizabeth. The Vice-Chancellor was attired in his scarlet gown; three Bedels walked before him, and he was accompanied by eight Doctors also in scarlet gowns, the two Proctors in their Regents' hoods, Mr. Case also in his Regent's hood, and other graduates, Bachelors of Divinity with hoods 'cast over them as in time of disputation', and Masters of Arts with hoods worn in the usual manner. They passed through both the courts to the Bishop's Hall, the ancient Hall of the palace of the Bishops of Ely, all bare-headed, Hatton watching them from the window of his gallery. When they came into the gallery, they stood still about twenty feet away, and Hatton then came forward to meet them, taking off his hat and, shaking hands with the Vice-Chancellor, Doctors, Proctors and Mr. Case, bade them welcome 'in very kind sort'. Hatton then turned and sat down in his chair, where he usually sat at the side of the gallery about the middle of its length. This was the Great Gallery, a characteristic room in the larger Elizabethan houses; and it appears from this account that Hatton at Ely Place was accustomed to walk in it, talking to friends and visitors, and that he had a favourite chair there where he sat to receive guests.

All now approaching, Case made a Latin oration, saying that the University had conferred upon Hatton the degree of Master of Arts, and presented him to the Vice-Chancellor and the others. The two Proctors, speaking together, then said, *Dabis fidem te observaturum Privilegia et Consuetudines Academiae Oxoniensis*. Hatton, who was still seated, made no answer. Was his Latin, perhaps, a little rusty? But silence being taken to signify consent, the Vice-Chancellor began his oration, and admitted him Master of Arts. He then declared that the University had chosen Hatton as their Chancellor, and produced a public instrument which he gave to the Orator to read. The Orator read the grant, written on parchment and sealed with the University seal, and after kissing it, handed it to Hatton. The Vice-Chancellor continued, saying that the University most humbly besought Hatton to accept the position of Chancellor, and, also kissing it, handed him a letter to that effect. Hatton took the letter, and read it to himself. The Vice-Chancellor then went on to say that the University's choice involved four especial points, Faithfulness, Justice, Wisdom and Authority. These were symbolized by four objects lying on a stool covered with damask: a bunch of keys, a book, two seals and one of the Bedels' staves. The first three, being principal virtues, they were assured, he said, that they would find in Hatton, handing to him first the keys of all the treasure and evidences of the University; second the Statute Book, in assurance of his justice; third, the seals, one for passing leases, the other used for matters of learning, in assurance of his wisdom, quoting the Epistle, *Ad quintum fratrem, sit annulus tuus non minister alienae voluntatis, sed testis tuae.*

Then, turning to the company, the Vice-Chancellor said that it was fitting that they should give Hatton authority also and, taking up one of the Bedels' staves, handed it to him as *virgam* or *symbolum authoritatis*. On it, he said, were written two words which comprehended his Lordship's charge: *scientia, mores*, and, handing him the staff, pronounced that he was to maintain learning and punish disorders. He then concluded, thanking Hatton for accepting the degree and office, and proclaimed him High Chancellor of the University of Oxford.

Hatton who, Bancroft tells us, looked not for such solemnity, replied at first modestly, speaking in English. He belittled himself, saying he was unlearned and not worthy of so great an honour. He thanked the University and the present company, promising that what he lacked in ability he would supply by goodwill. And then, perhaps rather tactlessly, considering the occasion, he began, in Bancroft's words, 'to take already like a Chancellor upon him'. He said that, according to reports, 'their University was fallen very greatly through many abuses from the old and honourable reputation which heretofore it hath had'. He spoke of Colleges making havoc, and decaying their ancient revenues. He complained also, that there was great contempt among them: in the Bachelors of Divinity of the Doctors, Masters of Arts of the

Bachelors, Bachelors of Masters, Scholars of Bachelors; 'how in his time there was no such abuse; how every man was known by his Habit approximated unto his Degree &c.' The reference is to the notorious laxity — due to Puritan influence — that prevailed at Oxford in the wearing of the appropriate gowns. There were other disorders also, he said, which he would not go into at the moment. He was bound to redress such 'enormities'. He asked them to let him know of any abuses springing up, and said he would take care to encourage good and diligent students and to be severe towards the others. He argued that the quiet estate of the whole realm greatly depended upon the good government of the Universities, and as the Queen had made him 'a man of state', he as Chancellor of the University would take care to suppress factions there. He returned the keys, the book, the seals and the staff to the Vice-Chancellor, keeping the letters patent of his office. He asked for a copy of the Statutes, and concluded by again thanking them and bidding them all 'very lovingly farewell'.

Mr. Case in the above account is presumably John Case, Fellow of St. John's and a well-known figure in the Oxford of his day. He was one of those who contributed to an Oxford anthology of poems on Hatton's death in 1591. Francis Flower, to whose rooms in Hatton's house in Ely Place the deputation from Oxford came on its way to make him Chancellor, has occurred several times in these pages.

Laurence Humfrey, President of Magdalen, who corresponded with Hatton from time to time, in particular about the studies of Hatton's nephew, William Newport when an undergraduate at Magdalen, had been Vice-Chancellor. In 1587 he became Dean of Winchester, and was succeeded as Vice-Chancellor by Dr. William James, Dean of Christ Church. James is the Vice-Chancellor in the proceedings recorded above. He was also Rector of Kingham, the parish adjoining Churchill, Hatton's Oxford-shire manor; and a letter from him written from that place to Samuel Cox, Hatton's secretary, occurs in the Hatton Letter Book. Humphrey was of the Calvinist party, who were engaged in purging Oxford of Catholicism. Anthony Wood says that he stocked his College 'with such a generation of Nonconformists as could not be rooted out in many years after his decease'. Hatton, once a Catholic, was at this time mainly interested in helping Whitgift to suppress the Puritans; and, on succeeding to the Chancellorship of Oxford, he emphasized the need of conformity in religion. Sir George Paule records that Whitgift ever found him 'a great assistant in bridling and reforming these novelists [Puritans]', who, by the countenance of Leicester, etc., 'were now grown to a strong head'. William James, Hatton's Vice-Chancellor, was of a similar way of thinking, being 'a bitter enemy of those called Calvinists'. He and Hatton presumably got on well together, but not much is recorded of Hatton's relations with his University.

Hatton also succeeded Leicester in 1588 as High Steward of Cambridge University. But long before that he had busied himself with Cambridge affairs. His interference on behalf of Dr. Swale, his legal assistant, has already been chronicled; and on other occasions he used his influence to promote the fortunes of those in whom he was interested. And, though he sent his nephew to Oxford, he placed his kinsman Thomas Saunders of Sibbertoft, Northamptonshire, at Cambridge. In 1589 this man was specially admitted to the Inner Temple on the recommendation of Lord Chancellor Hatton. A letter from Hatton addressed to the Treasurer and other members of that society, says that he had had the care of his kinsman's education, and had sent him to Cambridge 'where (as some tell me) he hath not spent his time altogether unprofitably; and therefore he being now both for age and understanding (as I hope) fit enough for the study of the law, I am desirous to have him follow the same rather in that House, whereof myself was and am, than in any other'.

CHAPTER XXXIV

HATTON'S DEATH

HATTON's health, never very robust, began to decline towards the latter half of the year 1591. Some mention of his illness is made in a letter he wrote from London on September 5th of that year to Sir Henry Unton, the English Ambassador in Paris. Unton is said to have been employed by Hatton, who recommended him to the Queen. He was an intimate friend of Hatton's nephew, Sir William Hatton, and both were with Leicester in the Netherlands and were present at the affair at Zutphen, where Sir Philip Sidney lost his life. It appears from Hatton's letter to him that Unton also was ill at this time with jaundice; and Hatton writes anxiously to inquire how his friend is, and to convey the Queen's sympathy. He then intimates that he himself is in bad health: 'I have been visited myself of late with some distemperature of body.'

Hatton's death has been ascribed by romantic biographers to the Queen's insistence on his paying the debts he owed her. He was indebted to the Crown in an immense sum due on his accounts as Receiver of Tenths and First Fruits. Camden says he had hopes that Elizabeth would forgive him this debt, and that her refusal to do so was a contributory cause of his death. 'It brake his heart', says Fuller, 'that the Queen (which seldom gave boons and never forgave due debts) rigorously demanded the payment of some arrears, which Sir Christopher did not hope to have remitted, but did only desire to be forborne. Failing herein in his expectation, it went to his heart and cast him into a mortal disease.' But men who live so chronically in debt as Hatton had always done are not so easily depressed by their financial obligations. Another report was that of the Jesuit Parsons, who hinted that his death was due to poison, administered apparently by the Puritans who disliked his Catholic sympathies. But Parsons and his friends, authors of such propagandist works as *Leycester's Commonwealth*, saw poison everywhere. There can be no doubt that Hatton died of disease, and there is sufficient evidence to say that the disease was cystitis.

He seems to have had a long-standing weakness of this kind,

351

for it was presumably a similar trouble in 1573 of which Gilbert Talbot reported vaguely, 'it is doubted [i.e. thought] it is in his kidneys'. He was so ill then that he had to go to Spa for a cure. There are incidental references to ill-health from time to time in the intervening years, but no details. David Lloyd, not a contemporary witness, reports that he was a corpulent man. Camden is the authority for the statement that he died of diabetes. But this is not the diabetes of to-day's usage; and the term in Camden's Latin is precisely rendered in the English version of his work as 'a flux of his urine'. This complaint is what the other evidence indicates. There is one other possible indication of a symptom, but it is not easy to interpret and is probably irrelevant. He once reported to the Queen, perhaps in 1573 when he was at Spa, 'Your Mutton is black; scarcely will you know your own, so much hath this disease dashed me'.

Hatton had a premonition that his end was near. Burghley, two years before his own death, quotes a saying of his on the point. The Queen's devoted old servant, writing 'with a weary head', to his son Sir Robert Cecil, says that if necessary he will venture his life to go to the Queen, who had summoned him; 'though at my return from that house, I may follow my Lord Chancellor Hatton in saying and proving that I shall never see Richmond again'.

Hatton was well enough to attend to affairs on October 5th when he wrote to Robert Earl of Essex, then Lord General of the English army in Normandy, reiterating the Queen's insistence that Essex should return home.

The first mention of his fatal illness is on October 31st, when Thomas Phelippes, one of Walsingham's agents whom we have met with in the Babington Plot, wrote to Thomas Barnes who was busy in the Government interest hoodwinking Charles Paget, once Mary Stuart's ardent supporter in France. Phelippes suggests a letter for Barnes to write to Paget. Such letters contained various items of news to make them seem more natural, and this one says, 'The Chancellor is very sick with a strangury, and not likely to recover'. Sixteen years after Hatton's death there is another reference to his illness in a letter from Lord Northampton to the Earl of Mar. Henry Howard, Earl of Northampton, brother of the ill-fated Duke of Norfolk, had known Hatton well, and his letters to Hatton when he was in prison in 1584 for supposed complicity in Catholic plots have been quoted in a previous chapter. He is writing now about the Earl of Shrewsbury, son of Mary Stuart's gaoler. He says:

> My Lord of Shrewsbury . . . hath been desperately sick, not of the strangury, but withal of such frurres symptomatical out of such smart and agony, insomuch as it is not possible that he should live long in this torment, if it continue, for the neck of the bladder is so raw as it should appear by excoriation (which is the disease whereof Hatton, the Chancellor, deceased) as unless they can by lenitives diminish some part of that acrimony which brings on those frurres and enforceth him to roar at every avoidance, which is every hour, *violentia* cannot be *perpetua*.

These gruesome details leave little doubt of the nature of Hatton's disease.

When the Queen heard of Hatton's serious condition, she showed all her old affection and that real tenderness of heart which was apt to discover itself unexpectedly in one apparently so unsympathetic. Camden says she visited and comforted him; according to John Phillips's poem she stayed with him five days, and she was certainly at his house in Ely Place on November 11th. A week from the anniversary of her accession, usually the gladdest day of the year for Elizabeth and her friends, found queen and dying courtier together for the last time. All tender-hearted woman at the last, she who had so often dealt roughly with her wayward favourite, only to forgive again, read a foolish letter from him, lay in her bosom some trinket warm from his hand, and then forget jealousies and vexations in the dance they loved when they were young together. She brought to the dying man's bedside, 'as some say' (so Fuller reports) 'cordial broths unto him with her own hands, but all would not do. Thus no pulleys can draw up a heart once cast down, though a Queen herself set her hand thereunto', paraphrasing Camden's 'having once cast him down with a harsh word, she could not raise him up again'.

Hatton died on November 20th, and was buried with great pomp in St. Paul's Cathedral, between the Lady Chapel and the south side. His body was preceded to the grave by a hundred poor people, on whom were bestowed gowns and caps provided for the occasion; and more than three hundred gentlemen and yeomen in gowns, cloaks and coats, the Lords of the Council, and

z

eighty of the Queen's Guard, Hatton's old corps, attended the funeral. Sir William Hatton, his nephew and heir, erected an elaborate monument in his memory. This was lost in the fire that destroyed Old St. Paul's, but its appearance and the inscription on it have been preserved by Dugdale in his history of the cathedral. Dugdale's illustration of this imposing tomb shows Hatton lying on a pedestal, a bearded figure in armour. Above is a long Latin inscription, flanked by various shields of arms; and above this is a small rectangular tablet with the coat of Sir Christopher Hatton, quarterly of twelve, in a shield surrounded by the motto of the Garter, and supported by two horses. Over the shield is a helm and the Hatton cognizance, a hind. Above this again, on each side of the monument stands a horse supporting a small shield, bearing the garbs of Hatton. Above all is the hind, standing at the top of the monument. Beside the tomb is a column with a tablet affixed with a eulogistic poem in English, the work of Hatton's follower Francis Flower.

The grandeur of Hatton's tomb called forth some contemporary comment. The contrast with the neighbouring monuments to Sir Francis Walsingham and to his son-in-law Sir Philip Sidney, whom posterity at any rate has judged the greater men, made even the groundlings feel dimly that things were out of scale.

> Sir Philip, Sir Francis, have no tomb,
> For great Christopher takes all the room,

ran a doggerel ballad which has come down to us in more than one version. It first appears in the *Survey of London* (1598) by John Stow, who says, 'some merry poet wrote thus'; and Holland, in his *Monumenta Sepulchraria Sancti Pauli* (1614), conjectured that the 'merry poet' was 'the merry old man Stow himself'. A further note of criticism is sounded by Bishop Corbet, poet and wit, who thus addressed the shade of a brother prelate, Ravis Bishop of London, who has some small fame for undertaking part of the translation of the New Testament:

> Nor needs the Chancellor boast whose pyramis
> Above the host and altar rearèd is;
> For, though thy body fill a viler room,
> Thou shalt not change *deeds* with him for his *tomb*.

Hatton's death was the occasion for a remarkable series of eulogies, which were printed in 1591 and the following years. The

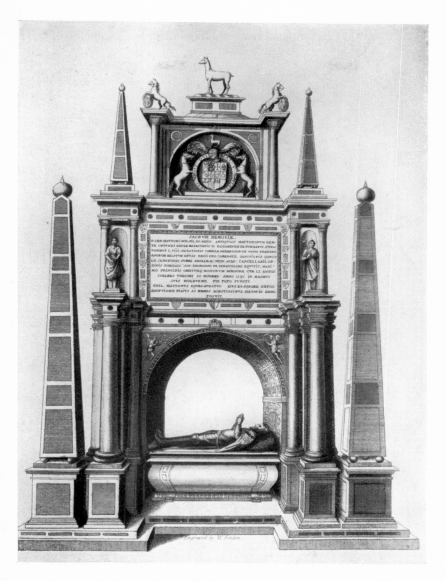

SIR CHRISTOPHER HATTON'S TOMB IN OLD ST. PAUL'S

From Dugdale's *History of St. Paul's Cathedral*

earliest is *A Lamentable Discourse of the Death of the Right Honourable Sir Christopher Hatton, Knight, late Lord Chancellor of England*. The entry in the Stationers' Register is 'November 24th, 1591, Richard Jones, entered for his copy under the hands of Thomas Crowe and Richard Watkins'. Richard Jones was the well-known printer who had published *The Book of Honour and Arms*, dedicated to Hatton. Nothing seems to be known of this 'Lamentable Discourse'. It was apparently rushed through the press a few days after Hatton's death to supply an expected demand; and it is probably to it and others like it, pamphlets and manuscripts, that Robert Greene refers in the dedication of his *Maiden's Dream*, the next eulogy of Hatton in point of date. Greene says, 'while I thus debated with myself, I might see (to the great disgrace of the poets of our time) some mechanical wits blow up mountains and bring forth mice, who with their follies did rather disparage his honour than decipher his virtues'.

Robert Greene's *A Maiden's Dream upon the Death of my late Lord Chancellor* is entered in the Stationers' Register under date December 6th, 1591, 'Thomas Nelson, entered for his copy under the hands of Mr. Francis Flower and Mr. Walkins', which shows that Hatton's follower Francis Flower had a share in sponsoring the work.[1] The book has an added interest from its authorship. It was one of Greene's last compositions, for he died less than a year after Hatton, in great poverty and misery. Greene had been one of the literary men commissioned to answer the Martin Marprelate Tracts, and it is possible that he may have been moved to write this elegy from the consciousness of having done some work for Hatton, Whitgift and Bancroft, the men most concerned in prosecuting the authors and publishers of the Tracts. Greene did not dedicate any of his works to Hatton, and in his dedicatory epistle to this elegy, addressed to Lady Hatton, wife of Sir William, he says he had received no private benefit from him. Nevertheless, he was known to Hatton, the patron of literary men, as we can gather from the passages in the poem, in which he calls Hatton his friend and claims that Hatton had honoured him. And, even discounting the compliments which needy authors must pay to the great ones of the earth, there is a note of sincerity in Greene's

---

[1] It is of interest to note that in the same year (1591) another publisher, Thomas Newman, who had acquired a manuscript version of Sidney's sonnets issued them with a dedication to Francis Flower.

tribute, which makes it difficult to dismiss it as merely formal. Greene's testimony to Hatton's amiability, fairness, integrity and compassion reinforces that of such different witnesses as the sober Camden and the sprightly Harington. That Hatton had his traducers may be gathered from Greene's dedication, in which he speaks of 'base report who hath her tongue blistered by slanderous envy begun as far as she durst, now after his death, to murmur, who in his life time durst not once mutter'.

Another eulogy of Hatton was *A Commemoration on the Life and Death of the Right Honourable Sir Christopher Hatton*, by John Phillips, 1591. The author was a Cambridge man, a student of classics and divinity, the composer of some epitaphs and poems in the *Mirror for Magistrates*. His epitaph on Hatton exists in a unique copy, formerly in the possession of Sir Charles Isham of Lamport Hall, Northamptonshire. It was reprinted with some other pieces, as *A Lamport Garland*, for the Roxburghe Club in 1881. The Ishams were neighbours of the Hattons, and it was natural that a copy should find its way to them, and be preserved at Lamport with other rare books and the precious collection of Elizabethan and Jacobean costume, now in the Victoria and Albert Museum. Phillips's poem is dedicated to Sir William Hatton, 'son adopted and heir' to Sir Christopher. No connection between Hatton and Phillips has been traced, but the piece, though dull, contains some interesting particulars not elsewhere on record, which there is no reason to question. Besides testimonies to Hatton's virtues, his sense of duty, justice, loyalty, kindliness and helpfulness to the poor, particularly in his solicitude for the rights of poor legal suitors, his early performances in the tilt-yard are noticed. In an interesting passage Phillips comments on the care Hatton took of his men of the Queen's Guard, and states that he induced Elizabeth to raise their pay from 1s. 4d. to 1s. 8d. a day, and for three months in the year to 2s. There is a reference also to the Babington Conspiracy, the credit for the unravelling of which popular opinion seemed inclined to bestow on Hatton rather than Walsingham, on account of the prominence of the former at the Trial. Hatton's part in these events is celebrated in the quaint lines:

> Those wily wolves untrusty to the Crown
> By justice he threw topsy turvy down.

There follows an account of Hatton's pious death. The Queen,

the poet says, came from Richmond to visit him and remained
with him for five days, leaving him before the end to the physicians
and great divines:

> He took his leave of his most gracious Queen,
> And praisèd God she had his comfort been.

Anthony Wood in his account of Hatton in his *Athenae* states that
soon after his death appeared a little book of verses by several
hands, entitled *Musarum Plangores*. Nothing is known of this work,
unless possibly it is the same as *Oxoniensium Στεναγμός, sive Carmina
ab Oxoniensibus conscripta, in obitum illustrissimi Herois D. Christophori
Hattoni Militis, summi totius Angliae nec non Academiae Oxoniensis Can-
cellarii*. This work, which is described by Falconer Madan in his
Oxford Books from a unique copy in the Lambeth Library, was
printed by Barnes, the Oxford printer, in 1592. It was dedicated
by the editor, John Dove, to Lord Buckhurst, who had succeeded
Hatton as Chancellor of Oxford. It consists of Oxford poems on
Hatton's death, and it is possible, Falconer Madan surmises, that
it was never publicly issued, being perhaps regarded as too small
a collection to be an adequate memorial of the Chancellor. Fifty-
six persons contributed poems to it, among them the heads of
Balliol, Magdalen and St. John's, and John Hoskins the poet.

The last of the testimonies to Hatton was issued four years after
his death, in a curious and interesting work: *Polimanteia, or the
Means lawful and unlawful to judge the Fall of a Commonwealth
against the frivolous and foolish conjectures of the Age. Whereunto is added a Letter from England to her three daughters, Cambridge, Oxford and the Inns of Court etc.*, 1595. It bears the
initials W.C., and the author has been identified as William
Clarke, a Cambridge man and miscellaneous writer. It is dedicated to Robert Devereux, Earl of Essex, the favourite of Elizabeth's old age. This rare work was reprinted by Grosart in his
Select Ancient English Poems. It contains a eulogy of the Universities
and of the Inns of Court, the third University of England as
Elizabethan writers, William Harrison and others, regarded them.
Its main interest in literary history is its early mention of Shake-
speare: 'sweet Shakespeare', Harvey, Nash and 'divine Spenser'.
It is pleasant to find Hatton in such company:

> Then name but Hatton, the Muse's favourite, the Church's music,
> learning's patron, my once poor Island's ornament, the courtier's

grace, the scholar's countenance, the Guard's Captain. Thames, I dare avouch, will become tears: the sweetest perfumes of the Court will be sad signs: every action shall accent grief; honour and eternity shall strive to make his tomb, and after curious skill and infinite cost, engrave this with golden letters, *Minus merito*; the fainting Hind untimely chased, shall trip towards Heaven, and *tandem si* shall be virtue's mot.

Here Hatton's love of letters, music and learning is again emphasized. His cognizance, the hind, again makes its appearance with his motto, *Tandem Si*.

Hatton was never married. A letter from Dr. Thomas Wilson, who was joint Secretary of State with Walsingham, written in 1581, refers to him as a bachelor. Wilson had intended at this time to visit Hatton at Court, but being too ill himself he sent his two daughters to him instead. It looks as if he had matrimonial designs in mind: ' . . . In the meanwhile I have sent thither my two daughters, my only treasure; which I write unto you as a bachelor, to whom maidens cannot be unwelcome. . . .'

Hatton's brief wooing of Elizabeth Cavendish, as reported by Mary Queen of Scots in her famous letter to Queen Elizabeth, has already been mentioned. That courtship, if it ever took place, was probably in the year 1572. But Mary is not a very trustworthy witness. In 1579 she wrote to the Archbishop of Glasgow about Elizabeth's proposed marriage to the Duke of Alençon, adding, 'Leicester and Hatton are married secretly, which hath so offended this Queen it is thought she hath been led upon such miscontentment to agree to the sight of the Duke of Alençon'. But there seems to be no truth in this statement. On his tomb, and the wording is his nephew's, he is described as *coelebs*. But though David Lloyd says that his life was chaste, it may be that he had an irregular connection, and that it was this that had come to Elizabeth's ears, and had been inaccurately reported to the Queen of Scots.

There is in fact some evidence that Hatton had an illegitimate daughter. In the heraldic visitation of Wales written by Lewys Dwnn, it is said that Sir John Perrot, the Deputy of Ireland, had a daughter (illegitimate), Elizabeth the wife of Hugh Butler of Johnstown, by Elizabeth daughter of Sir Christopher Hatton. Though Dwnn was a contemporary, writing of Welsh family history with which he was familiar, his evidence, if it stood alone, would scarcely be final. But it is clear from the testimony of Naunton, who married Perrot's granddaughter, that Hatton and Perrot were enemies. At any rate Robert Dunlop, the Irish historian, accepted the story of the seduction by Perrot of Hatton's daughter, and found in it an explanation of Hatton's hostility to him; and Professor Polland has accepted it also. But there is apparently no authority save Dwnn's statement for it. There seems, however, to be a small scrap of evidence bearing on this matter, which may be significant. The will of Perrot's son, Sir Thomas Perrot, speaks of an agreement dated in May, 1583, between Sir John Perrot knight, of the one part, Sir Thomas Bromley the Lord Chancellor and others, of the second part, and Arden Waferer, Esq., of the third part. The nature of the agreement is not disclosed. But Arden Waferer, the legal adviser of Lodowick Bryskett (the friend of Spenser and Sidney), was also Hatton's lawyer and a member of his circle. He was a witness in 1579 to one of the settlements of Hatton's estates, and was busy with Hatton's affairs in 1577. This we know from a letter from Burghley to Hatton, who says he has known Waferer since he was first at the Inner Temple fourteen or fifteen (in reality seventeen) years before. It may be added that Arden Waferer, like so many of Hatton's friends, belonged to an intensely Catholic circle. His mother was an Arden, aunt of Edward Arden, the uncle of Edmund Neville, the conspirator and the father-in-law of John Somerville who had aspired to assassinate Queen Elizabeth. A Francis Waferer, no doubt of this family, was at Rheims, 1584, priest 1585. May not Sir John Perrot's agreement of 1583 have been some sort of a settlement in connection with Hatton's daughter?

Apart from this presumed daughter, there is no evidence of Hatton having had any children. The Oxford University Register shows a William Hatton, son of a knight, from Northamptonshire, matriculating in 1577 or 1578; and as Sir Christopher was the only knight of the name of Hatton living at the time, and the county is Northamptonshire, Foster in his *Alumni Oxonienses* surmised that this William might be a son of Sir Christopher; but it is certain that he was his adopted son William Newport alias Hatton who was, we know, at Magdalen at this time.

The inquisition taken on the death of this Sir William Hatton, the Chancellor's heir, states that Hatton's estates were 'extended', or valued in connection with the debt he owed the Queen from his office of Receiver of Tenths and First Fruits, which he had held from the year 1578. The amount of this debt is variously stated in different documents. It is given in one place as £42,139 5s.; in another record the 'great debt' is thus divided:

		£	s.	d.
To the Queen	..	18,071	12	2
To the subject	..	23,647	8	5½
	Total	41,719	0	7½

These two totals agree closely enough, and we may therefore put the debt at about £42,000. This too is the amount indicated by the figures given concerning the position of the estate in the time of the eventual heir, Sir Christopher Hatton. In this statement it is said that the Queen is to receive a yearly rent of £1500 until £40,000 is paid. Elsewhere, however, the great debt is put at £48,037, 'which debt to the Queen before his death grew to £4000 more'. Only one reference to the Chancellor's personal effects has been discovered. Sir William Hatton is said to have sold to Lady Shrewsbury and others all Hatton's jewels, 'saving one blue sapphire which he used to wear at his shirt string, which only came to my Lady Hatton's hands'.

As Sir William Hatton left no son, the Hatton estates passed on his death in virtue of the settlement to Christopher Hatton, son of the Chancellor's first cousin John Hatton of Stanton, Cambridgeshire, by his wife Jane, daughter of Robert Shute, Baron of the Exchequer and Justice of the Common Pleas. This young man was an undergraduate at Cambridge when Sir William died. He became the Queen's ward, and the Government kept him very short of money. So we learn from several documents, including a letter of the year 1599 to Sir Robert Cecil, Burghley's son, then Principal Secretary, from Hatton's old associate Richard Bancroft, then Bishop of London. Bancroft entreats Cecil 'to favour the heir of mine old good friend and master, the late Lord Chancellor'. Young Christopher is, he says, at Cambridge by Burghley's direction, but though he is the Queen's ward, he has not received anything for his maintenance. Hatton has been in London in connection with his affairs, but has had nothing but fair words. 'Who would have thought', Bancroft concludes, 'that within seven years the Lord Chancellor's heir should have been brought to such an exigent?'

However, he obtained an Act of Parliament in 1605 to enable him to sell part of his inherited lands. In 1608 accordingly he conveyed Holdenby to trustees for the use of the King for life, remainder to Charles Duke of York, the future Charles I, in tail male. It was in virtue of this conveyance that Holdenby passed to the Crown. Another condition of the sale was that the King should grant to Christopher Hatton all his Majesty's interest and reversion in any of the Lord Chancellor's lands, which the King held on account of his debts to Queen Elizabeth, provided the residue of the debt should be paid off at the rate of £1500 a year.

Christopher Hatton was created by Charles I Baron Hatton of Kirby. His son, another Christopher, was created Viscount Hatton of Gretton. The latter left no male issue and his titles became extinct. His only daughter Anne married Daniel Finch, Earl of Nottingham and Winchilsea; and their younger son, the Hon. Edward Hatton, assumed the name of Hatton and succeeded to Kirby. From him descends the present Earl of Winchilsea and Nottingham. The Hatton muniments which went with the property were briefly calendared by the Historical Manuscripts Commission. The older deeds and charters are now in the British Museum, and the late Lord Winchilsea deposited many of the more recent documents with the Northamptonshire Record Society. Both divisions of these records have been consulted in writing the foregoing pages.

CHAPTER XXXV

SAMUEL COX

As a footnote to the life of Sir Christopher Hatton, it seems a pious duty to say something of his secretary, Samuel Cox. For it is due to Cox that we have so many letters, written by Hatton or to him over a period of years from March, 1578, to 1587 when Hatton became Lord Chancellor. And Cox's life is of interest in itself.

Hatton's Letter Book, which Cox kept, is entitled 'Book of Letters received by Sir Christopher Hatton, Vice-Chamberlain to the Queen's Majesty, from sundry persons, and procured by him to be written in this book'. It was purchased by the British Museum at Upcott's sale in 1846, and now forms Addl. MS. 15,891. It was printed with other letters, drawn from various sources, and notes by Sir Harris Nicolas in 1847. Its previous history is unknown. Upcott was a great collector, who acquired manuscripts from many quarters, and there is no indication of the origin of many of the documents in his collection. It may be that the Letter Book passed to one of Cox's heirs, perhaps Samuel Warcopp of English and Nuffield, Oxfordshire, and was purchased by Upcott from a descendant of that family.

As the Letter Book begins in March, 1578, it may be supposed that Cox became Hatton's secretary not long before that date. And this supposition is borne out by other evidence. Writing to Hatton in October, 1584, when he was in temporary disgrace with his master, Cox says that he has spent seven summers and as many winters in Hatton's service. That would date the beginning of his employment with Hatton from the winter of 1577. It will be remembered that Thomas Doughty, who sailed with Drake in November, 1577, claimed that he had been Hatton's secretary. Whether or not his statement was true, it agrees with the deduction that Cox did not enter Hatton's service until the end of 1577 or beginning of 1578. Hatton was made Vice-Chamberlain in November, 1577, and knighted on December 1st. This was probably the occasion for taking a secretary into his employment. In any case, the title of the Letter Book shows that it must have been begun after December 1st, 1577, when Hatton was Vice-Chamberlain and a knight.

Samuel Cox, or Cocks, was the eldest son of William Cocks, citizen and haberdasher of London, whose will was made and proved in the year 1569. In it he names his sons, Samuel, to whom he left his dwelling-house, and John Cox, and his seven daughters. His children were then all under age. The will is of interest because, besides leaving money to the London hospitals of Christ's, St. Bartholomew's and St. Thomas's, Southwark, and for poor strangers of the French and Dutch churches in London, he gave £30 to support two poor scholars studying divinity in Oxford and Cambridge.

But little is known of the younger son, John Cox. In 1578 Walsingham writes to William Davison, Hatton's friend, the English Agent at Antwerp, recommending a suit of his connected apparently with the Netherlands; presumably he had some business interest there. Walsingham concludes, 'The Marquis [i.e. Charles Philippe de Croy, Netherlands envoy to England] promised me that some order should be taken for the contentment of Cox. I wish the more care taken therein, as Mr. Vice-Chamberlain is very earnest in the matter; for Cox's brother serves him in place of secretary'. There is also a reference to John Cox in the Hatton Letter Book. In 1582 a correspondent, whose name is not given, writes to Samuel Cox from the Court at Windsor, scolding him for not having made a promised visit and begging him to come and bring his brother with him. John Cox must have died before Samuel, and without surviving issue, for on the latter's death in 1612 his heirs were found to be the various descendants of his numerous sisters. It is possible that John Cox is the Mr. Cox, a citizen of London, lately dead in October, 1583, leaving a daughter in great poverty, on whose behalf Hatton then wrote to the Lord Mayor.

Samuel Cox, who shows himself in his voluminous letters to be a well-informed man with a good knowledge of Latin, classical and English history, diplomatic practice and law, was almost certainly educated at one of the universities. A man of this name matriculated in 1565 at Pembroke College, Cambridge, and it is likely that this is he. If he were fifteen or sixteen at matriculation, he would be a minor in 1569, as his father's will requires. If this is a correct identification, we may take it that he was born about the year 1550; and this corresponds with his intimation in a love-letter to one Mistress E., quoted below, that he was about forty in 1590. In 1578, when he became Hatton's secretary, he would have been about twenty-eight. He had already served under the English Ambassador in France. This we learn from a letter written by him in 1599, long after Hatton's death, addressed to a Mr. T., who is identified below. Cox says that he has 'served her Majesty first under her Ambassador Mr. Dale in France, and then under her Vice-Chamberlain, Sir Christopher Hatton, as a poor scribe in Court, twenty years together, without any manner of recompense'. Valentine Dale, an eminent lawyer and civilian, was Ambassador from 1573 to 1576. Cox's service with him would have fallen between these dates. He may possibly have become acquainted with Hatton when the latter was on his way to Spa in 1573. At any rate, on Dale's return to England, Cox transferred himself to Hatton's service; and at the beginning of this employment we find him in 1578 asking in Hatton's interest the advice of Dale and of Dr. William Aubrey on a legal point. In his later career Dale sat on several commissions in cases of high treason, with Hatton as a colleague. He was present at the trials of William Parry, 1585, and of the Babington conspirators and of Mary Stuart, 1586.

Cox's diplomatic connections are further illustrated by the fact that he had a cousin and namesake, Samuel Cox the younger, who in 1588 was an Ambassador elect. Cox writes to him on that occasion, exhibiting in his letter all that sententiousness and display of learning which make his correspondence, taken in small doses, entertaining reading. After a homily on the honours and dangers of the employment to which his young relative is called, he reviews the office of Ambassador from the classical era, which however 'is not to be stained with the comparison of this ignorant, barren age of ours'. Our Ambassadors 'are little better than grammarians and sophisters *qui verborum flosculis nulla rerum scientia pollent*'. He goes on to speak of his kinsman's delicate health, his poverty and his youth as impediments, reminding him that he is not yet twenty-five, but concluding by wishing him luck. The younger man is not to be overawed by this heavy artillery, but solemnly caps his cousin's classical examples and allusions, dwelling complacently on the importance and privileges of an Ambassador's position. Samuel Cox the younger does not appear in any lists of ambassadors, and it seems probable that the disabilities that his older relative mentions prevented him from taking up the post. Perhaps this good young man died early, as no further mention of him has been found.

Another relative of Cox's who seems to have been in the diplomatic service was one Robin Calveley, who got into trouble with Hatton for his rough treatment of the deputies of the Low Countries in 1584. Cox defends his kinsman in a long, wordy letter to Hatton. He admits that Calveley should not have used 'violence or any such rigorous course' against the Deputies, but he launches out at interminable length to correct Hatton for calling the Deputies ambassadors. With a wealth of classical and historical example he puts his master right, a course scarcely tactful in a dependant. Nothing else about Calveley's conduct in this affair has been found, nor any particulars of his diplomatic service. He is possibly the Calveley of whom Lord Hunsdon writes to Burghley in 1570 saying that Burford and Calveley, who are with him at Berwick, have used him ill and will not serve in one place, and have been discharged. Hunsdon, who was Warden of the East Marches with headquarters at Berwick, had just defeated Leonard Dacre, one of the leaders of the Northern Rebellion, and was engaged in the campaign on the Scottish Border that followed Dacre's flight across it.

About the year 1581 Cox procured through Hatton's influence a preferment of some kind in the gift of Magdalen College, Oxford. The President of Magdalen, Dr. Laurence Humfrey, in writing to Cox, says it had formerly been held by his predecessor, and intimated that it was very unwillingly conferred upon Cox. Humfrey had succeeded Coveney at Magdalen in 1561. His life touched Hatton's at several points. In October, 1580, he was made Dean of Winchester; and an undated letter from him to Hatton seems to refer to a promise of this appointment, and suggests that his coming preferment was through Hatton's influence. This letter is probably to be dated about 1579, as Humfrey reports to Hatton on the progress of his nephew William Newport or Hatton, who was at that time at Magdalen, having matriculated in 1577 or 1578. Hatton was therefore, to some extent, Humfrey's patron, and in a position to ask for a favour for Cox or for his friend, Edward Dyer. About Dyer, Humfrey writes to Hatton to say that he has busied himself in Dyer's favour with Winchester College; he has delayed writing, he says, as he has been busy

composing a reply to Campion and his accomplices. This reply
was Humfrey's *Jesuitismi Pars Prima*, which appeared in 1582. In
March of that year Cox was sent by Hatton to visit Sir Thomas
Tresham, a Catholic recusant then in the Fleet, and to remonstrate with him on the conduct of his brother who had shown
great ingratitude and insolence to Hatton, and had annoyed the
Queen by leaving the realm without permission. This amusing
interview has been described in a previous chapter.

Cox, as Hatton's secretary, was naturally often approached by
suitors of various sorts as a way to the ear of the great man. One
of his most persistent correspondents of this kind was Toby
Mathew, who on the death in 1581 of Dr. Thomas Wilson, the
Secretary of State, who also held the Deanery of Durham, kept
up a constant bombardment of Hatton *via* Cox for the latter post,
which he eventually obtained in 1583. The following year he was
concerned in procuring a lease for Cox, no doubt in return for
Cox's assistance.

Towards the end of the year 1584 Cox got into serious trouble
with Hatton. It was charged against him that he had taken fees
from suitors seeking Hatton's influence. Perhaps Toby Mathew's
lease was the occasion. Cox's accusers were some of his fellow
servants on Hatton's staff; he calls them his enemies, and the
whole course of the correspondence shows that he was a troublesome fellow to live with. As a punishment, Hatton dismissed or
suspended him. In writing to his master Cox says that he under-
stands that he is charged with selling 'such justice and favour as
your Honour was wont to afford to your friends and poor suitors'.
He denies that he has offended in this way, and claims that he has
done no more than take an occasional small fee for expediting the
business of a client. It is the custom of the age:

> There liveth not so grave nor so severe a Judge in England, but he
> alloweth his poor clerk under him, even in the expedition of
> matters of greatest justice, to take any reasonable consideration
> that should be offered him by any man for his pains and travail.
> It is the poor man's whole maintenance, and without it he could
> not live. I know your Honour will think it reason he should have
> it. If this be to sell justice and favour, sometimes to take a gratuity
> of ten shillings for one letter among one hundred, sometimes more,
> sometimes less, according as the party was benefited, or as myself
> had deserved, I then confess with all humbleness, that as a poor

scribe under your Honour (though unworthy), not knowing how else to live, I ignorantly erred (as all the rest of your servants have done).

He continues, 'I never charged you with any kind of wages, nor other gift or bounty of your own whatsoever; I was never worthy to be any of those whom you have advanced to reputation and wealth by your service'. In seven years he has had nothing from the Queen through Hatton's influence, except a lease in reversion which had yielded him some £200.

From all this it appears that Cox got no salary from Hatton for his services, and Hatton must have known that he had to make what he could. It may be surmised that it was something more than this customary system of taking fees which had got Cox into trouble. His real offence was his quarrelsome nature, which had helped to foster jealousy and turmoil among Hatton's staff.

To this and other communications Hatton makes a dignified and forceful reply. Though in Cox's letters he finds 'some show of your love towards me', he discovers in his actions no proof of a real disposition towards a reconciliation. His main complaint relates to Cox's quarrels with his fellow servants, regardless of his master's comfort: 'It seems you be not only reckless, little weighing me, whom the quiet of this concord might most comfort . . . But for conclusion I say, alter the course or you may not be mine. That you have been hardly handled I will not deny; and that you have deserved it, I must likewise needs confess.' As for the charges of corruption, Hatton admits that he does not take them too seriously: 'For causes touching myself I will first tell you, I find them not so forcibly proved as they were plainly informed; neither am I of so light belief that thereby I will be carried to leave the men I have loved for such reports as have been uttered. I will not touch your fame without the warrant of justice, nor be your enemy before I feel your injury.' He concludes by telling Cox to report his compliance with Hatton's requirements to Mr. Bruskett, when he will hear further from him. 'Bruskett' is Sebastian Bryskett, one of Hatton's followers, brother of Lodowick Bryskett, the writer, friend of Spenser and Sidney.

Hatton, persisting in his refusal to employ Cox again, unless he should make his peace with the men with whom he had quarrelled, Cox at length consented to a reconciliation, and wrote a long letter in November to one of Hatton's staff, whose name is not given, showing himself prepared to forgive and forget. He says he had written to this man who had told him that after his return from Northampton (perhaps he was going to Holdenby on Hatton's business) he would meet him and discuss matters. This man was Francis Flower, for in the letter which Cox writes to Hatton later in the month and which concludes the affair, he says that the day before he and Mr. Flower (through whose name, however, in the copy in the Letter Book he has run his pen) met together in Hatton's house in Holborn and were reconciled; and that Flower had then written to Mr. Marv—— and John, two other men with whom Cox had fallen out, to effect a similar reconciliation and to meet together with Mr. Bancroft, Hatton's chaplain, later Bishop of London and Archbishop of Canterbury, in Hatton's house. But these two men had pleaded that they were too busy to come, and Cox fears they will not bury the hatchet unless Hatton orders them to do so. Something about Francis Flower, Gentleman Pensioner and follower of Hatton's, has been said in a previous chapter.

When Leicester went to the Netherlands in 1586, Hatton's nephew William Hatton accompanied him. He and his friend Henry Unton behaved with great gallantry, and were both knighted by Leicester. It was probably because his nephew was with this expedition that Hatton sent Cox to the Netherlands. At any rate there is evidence that he was for a time with Leicester and brought home some of his dispatches to Hatton, Walsingham and Burghley. Thus Leicester writes to Walsingham, 'I pray you let me hear from you by Coks'. Three days later he writes again, urging the recall of Sir John Norris with whom he had quarrelled, and suggesting that he should be sent to Ireland, adding, 'I have imparted to Coxe, Mr. Vice-Chamberlain's secretary, some matter concerning this, both to tell his master and you'. A month after this Burghley writes to Leicester, who had been asking for instructions from the Queen, 'By some late letters written from your Lordship to her Majesty and by some conference had with Coxe, who brought the same letters, her Majesty hath had sundry earnest consultations with Mr. Vice-Chamberlain, Mr. Secretary [Walsingham] and me, upon divers things contained in your Lordship's letters'.

To the Parliament of 1586 Cox, like his rival Flower, was returned through Hatton's influence. His seat was Richmond in

Yorkshire. But when Hatton became Lord Chancellor in the following year, Cox left his employment. He left Parliament also, and settled down as a country gentleman. The estate he retired to was in Oxfordshire. In 1586 he had bought a hundred acres of pasture and a hundred of woodland in Charlbury, at the same time acquiring from Sir Henry Unton, Hatton's follower and Sir William Hatton's friend, and from Unton's elder brother Edward, forty acres of pasture and 120 of woodland in the same place and in Chadlington, as well as a much more extensive estate. This latter, also bought from Sir Henry Unton and Dorothy his wife, and from Edward Unton and Catherine his wife, consisted of the manors of Fulbrook and Westhalhill, not far from Burford, with fifty messuages and gardens, forty tofts, a mill, four dovecotes, 2000 acres of land, 600 of meadow, 3000 of pasture, 200 of woodland and 2000 of heath, all lying in Fulbrook, Swinbrook, Westhall and Westhalhill, Taynton, Upton, Leafield and Asterlee. The price is given as £160, £160 and £680 for the three properties, or £1000 in all. The figures recorded in such transactions, fines as they are technically called, are not always to be taken at their face value; they are often conventional. But the amount, at least £5000 of our money, indicates that, for all his protests, Cox had not done too badly for himself in Hatton's service.

Richard Beckingham had bought the manor of Pudlicote in the parish of Charlbury from his cousin William Beckingham, a descendant of an ancient family which had owned Pudlicote from the middle ages. Towards the close of Elizabeth's reign it was sought to upset this purchase by alleging that it had involved a fraud on William Beckingham, who was a man of weak mind. The proceedings, carried on at great length in the Courts of Chancery and Star Chamber, are of some interest, but we are not concerned with them here, save to notice that one of the charges made was that William Tipper had bought the pretended title of William Beckingham to the lands he had sold. Tipper was Hatton's associate in the matter of the grant for the hosting of merchant strangers, and had later received a patent in association with Edward Dyer for 'discovering concealed lands', that is, endeavouring to upset in the interest of the Crown titles to estates. It may be that Cox had heard of the Charlbury property through Tipper, for, as is shown below, Tipper was subsequently to harass Cox about his Fulbrook estate. Hatton had already secured a

stake in Oxfordshire by his purchase of the manor of Churchill in
the north of the county four years before, at the same time as his
friend Sir Henry Lee bought Ditchley. But he does not seem to
have ever lived at Churchill, and so Hatton's example could have
been no reason for Cox's purchase of Fulbrook and Westhalhill.
Cox himself says in a letter to Sir Henry Lee, 'I have made choice
to live near you for the special regard which I bear to your virtue,
and (though I speak it of yourself) I have not been a little proud
of the comfort of so singular a friend and so good a neighbour'.
But this may be dismissed as rhetorical, for it occurs in a letter
admitting a quarrel and seeking a reconciliation.

Sir Harris Nicolas has relegated to an appendix a number of
private letters of Cox's which occur in the Letter Book. To anyone
who has acquired a taste for Elizabethan letter-writers they are
most entertaining reading; but it would be out of place to enlarge
on them here, and for those interested they are available in
Nicolas's book. They are of all sorts: appreciations of foreign
politics and home affairs, with long and learned historical dis-
quisitions; on religion — Cox was like his master at this time, a
supporter of the Elizabethan settlement, but disliking both
Catholics and Puritans; homilies to friends and acquaintances on
their manners; letters of commiseration in bereavement; advice
on medical matters; and, since he has become a country gentleman, on agriculture; and all written in the sensible though
pompous manner which we have come to expect of Samuel Cox.
As his quarrel with his fellow servants shows, he was a prickly
fellow, and many of his letters chronicle disputes and skirmishes.

Others are a humane intervention on behalf of an old soldier
pressed to go to the wars — this was in 1589, the year of Essex's
expedition to Corunna; and a letter fulminating against plays and
players. 'I must confess unto you', he writes, 'I am somewhat
scrupulous for the tolerating of these stage plays, which are nowadays without respect of person, time or place, so much used and
allowed among us.' After a characteristic diatribe, he goes on:
'I could wish that players would use themselves nowadays as in
ancient, former times they have done, which was only to exercise
their interludes in the time of Christmas, beginning to play in
the holidays and continuing until Twelfthtide or at the furthest
until Ash Wednesday.' He then proceeds to an historical excursus
on the development of the drama in England. Though in his

strictures he thus makes exceptions which would excuse Hatton's acting in his student days during the Christmas Revels at the Inner Temple, Cox's attitude is very unfavourable to the drama, unlike Hatton's ten years before, when he tried to befriend the players whom the authorities had decided to suppress.

Cox's first letter from Fulbrook and Westhalhill is dated November 2nd, 1587, and this confirms the other evidence from the Letter Book that he ceased to be Hatton's secretary on his patron's elevation to the Woolsack in April. He was succeeded by George Carew, a Gentleman Pensioner, of the house of Carew of Antony in Cornwall. Carew was called to the Bar and later knighted. Besides Lord Chancellor Hatton he served his successors, Sir John Puckering and Sir Thomas Egerton as secretary. But though Cox had left Hatton's employment, he still went up to London, where he had lodgings in Cornhill, and was occasionally at Court.

In the year 1590 Cox fell in love with a certain Mistress E. He writes from Westhalhill, and it seems that she was a neighbour, for he speaks of forbearing to visit her. She was unmarried. 'How dearly I love you,' he says; and, in his emotion he lays aside for once some of his pomposity, though he cannot refrain from a classical allusion here and there. 'You may see it is not my profession to make love, and my years (as you know) require other cares . . . There was a law among the Lacedaemonians that he which loved youthfully at forty should lose the liberty as a citizen till fifty'; and he has incurred the perils of that law. Forty in 1590 would make him born about 1550, and that is what we have already deduced. There are three more letters to Mistress E. Cox is an unfortunate suitor, and he complains that when he calls she is not at home. In one letter he seems to refer to having received a valentine from her, and makes a playfully ponderous reply. Then the correspondence comes to an end. Mr. Cox was fated to die a bachelor.

Another letter is from Dr. William James, Rector of Kingham, a parish adjoining Churchill, Hatton's manor. James was Dean of Christ Church and Vice-Chancellor under Hatton of Oxford University. Sir Harris Nicolas disguises the writer by reading his name as Seames. The matter of his letter is unimportant, except perhaps for a phrase, 'I will either be glad to see you here at a Scholars' Commons, or meet you where you shall appoint'. The words 'Scholars' Commons' must be taken figuratively and as a compliment to Cox's learning, for the letter is written from Kingham and not from Oxford; and Cox, as we have seen, was probably from Cambridge.

The examples given above show that the names of a number of Cox's correspondents are omitted, and without a detailed knowledge of some of the minor figures and incidents of the time, it would be impossible to name them. But there can be no doubt of the identity of 'Mr. T.' to whom Cox addresses the last of his letters from Fulbrook, April 29th, 1599.

'Mr. T.', he says, 'I have received your letter, and though I have no cause to thank you for your news (as you say yourself), yet the remembrance of old friendship, that hath been of long time between us, makes me take anything kindly that comes from one who I think meaneth honestly.' T's letter evidently called in question Cox's title to the manors of Fulbrook and Westhalhill. Cox says he has 'but one poor thing to live on, which I have bought and overbought once or twice already, even to my utter ruin and undoing, and yet cannot enjoy it quietly for statute and other encumbrances'. He then comes to the threat to his title and speaks of

> this untimely tossing and tumbling up of men's estates; this ransacking of old titles, and raking up, as it were, dead men's bones out of their graves ... If her Majesty knew how many poor men are like to be hurt and utterly ruined in this case, some by ancient warranties which have been made in the sale of these lands to others; some by statute, some by recognizances, and some by infinite suits of law

he is persuaded that she would rather lose than pursue such claims.

> To make an end, I have but a piece of a poor manor to live upon, and God knows indeed but a very small portion. I have sold a great part of it to supply my wants, the rest hath been extended for debt ever since I bought it, till within this year or two, and I owe yet, I protest unto you, above a thousand pounds upon interest, which the rent of Fulbrook will not discharge.

Then comes the passage, already quoted, about his service with Dale and Hatton. He signs himself 'your old fellow and friend most assuredly'. There can be no doubt that 'Mr. T.' is William Tipper, Hatton's servant and the patentee for 'the discovery of concealed lands'. He was no doubt blackmailing the unfortunate Cox, on account of some supposed flaw in his title.

Samuel Cox lived well on into James I's reign. He made his will in 1611, describing himself as Samuel Cox of Fulbrook, Esquire. As he was unmarried he left his lands according to a settlement made between him and George Gascoigne of the Middle Temple, London. He names some of his relatives and leaves the residue of his property to his nephews and executors, Nicholas Wheeler and Samuel Warcopp, who proved the will the following year. George Gascoigne, who here acts as Cox's trustee, was a witness to some of Hatton's deeds of settlement and other legal instruments. He was the father of Richard Gascoigne, the antiquary, and came of the same family as George Gascoigne, the poet, of whom he was a distant kinsman.

After Cox's death the usual inquisition on the decease of a tenant in chief was taken. It was found that he possessed the manors of Fulbrook and Westhalhill and lands adjoining, which he had purchased from Sir Henry Unton. The settlement on his nephews was quoted, and it was stated that he died on April 1st, 1612, in the parish of St. Giles in the Fields, London. Although he had settled his estates, the inquisition, as was usual, named his heirs in blood. These were his sister Avis Hales, widow, who by her first husband, John Wheeler of Burford, Oxfordshire, and formerly a merchant and citizen of London, was mother of Nicholas Wheeler; Rodolph Warcopp, the elder brother of Samuel Warcopp, sons of Rebecca Warcopp deceased, another of Cox's sisters; and various descendants of another sister, Sarah Wootton.

A few days after the taking of this inquisition, Nicholas Wheeler and Samuel Warcopp petitioned the King in the Court of Star Chamber, and unfolded a lurid tale of Cox's last hours. They said that he had for many years been familiarly acquainted with one Hugh Ithell, now of the parish of St. Giles in the Fields, gentleman, the two men having been fellow servants attending upon the Rt. Hon. Sir Christopher Hatton, knight, late Lord Chancellor of England. Having to go to London to attend to legal affairs, Cox had in October last gone to lodge with Ithell in High Holborn. He brought with him 'divers chests, trunks, books, plate, apparel, ready money and other necessaries fit for a man of his degree and calling'. They go on to say that Ithell was a needy man who, seeing that Cox was ill, determined to get some of his property into his hands. On the day before Cox died, about eleven or twelve at night, when he 'lay most extremely languishing' and past all hope of recovery, Ithell sent all his servants to bed and said that he would watch the night by the dying man. Cox had a servant, James Fludd, who was drowsy with overmuch watching by his master's bedside, so that Ithell was able 'in very secret manner' to abstract from the pocket of Cox's gown, hose or doublet, or from some other place near his bed the keys of his trunk containing his will, the inventory of his goods, as well as 'great store of jewels, plate, ready money, apparel and other things of good and great value' worth a thousand pounds at least, including a bag with fifty pounds or so in cash. Ithell then locked the trunk again and restored the key to Cox's pocket. Ithell, according to this story, had also attempted to enter into a plot with Cox's heirs in blood, the same as those named in the inquisition, including Nicholas Wheeler's mother, Avis Hales, and Samuel Warcopp's brother Rodolph, suggesting that if they would pay him six hundred pounds, he would suppress the will and inventory. We are not told the upshot of this case, but Cox's lands, at any rate, descended to Wheeler and Warcopp by virtue of the settlement. Wheeler died a year later, leaving his half share to his wife.

Leonard Warcopp, the father of Rodolph and Samuel Warcopp, was of an ancient family from Yorkshire, which had acquired the manor of English in Oxfordshire by marriage with the heiress of English of English. He was heir to his brother Rodolph Warcopp of English which is in the parish of Nuffield, whence the present Lord Nuffield takes his title. Leonard's eldest son, Rodolph, inherited English. The half of Fulbrook and Westhalhill went to the younger son, Samuel, under Cox's settlement. The pedigree of Warcopp of English is entered in the *Heralds' Visitation of Oxfordshire*. It shows Leonard Warcopp as married to a daughter of one Cocks of London, merchant. Samuel Warcopp, Cox's heir, is given as marrying Anne, daughter of William Lenthall of Creslow, Oxfordshire, sister of the well-known Speaker of the Long Parliament. By her he had twenty-one children. He succeeded eventually to the estate of English also, died in 1662 aged eighty, and was buried in Nuffield Church. It is possible that the Hatton Letter Book was purchased by Upcott from one of his descendants.

SOURCES

CHAPTER I. The earliest biographical references to Hatton are contained in William Camden's *Annales* in Latin, with English translation, *Annales: or the History of Elizabeth*. The first biography is the sketch included in Sir Robert Naunton's *Fragmenta Regalia*. Camden and Naunton are contemporary writers. So in a sense is Thomas Fuller who, in his *Worthies of England*, has preserved contemporary impressions of Hatton's life. Of later writers, David Lloyd wrote seventy years after Hatton's death. His sketch in *State Worthies* is not of much value, but makes a few points, such as Hatton's corpulence and chaste life, that may be based on evidence not now extant. The first full-length biography is that of Lord Campbell, who included an account of Hatton in his *Lives of the Lord Chancellors* (1845), a lively performance but unsatisfactory from the point of view of accuracy. Sir Harris Nicolas's *Memoirs of the Life and Times of Sir Christopher Hatton* (1847) is not strictly speaking a life, but a running biographical commentary introducing the various letters in Hatton's Letter Book, of which Nicolas's work is in the main a transcript. The most accurate and up-to-date account of Hatton's life is J. M. Rigg's in the *Dictionary of National Biography* (1908).

CHAPTER II. For the two places named Hatton in Cheshire, see Ormerod's *Cheshire*. For the family see the *Heralds' Visitation of Cheshire* (1580) published by the Harleian Society. The Hatton-Holdenby connection is proved by the inquisitions taken after the deaths of William, Joyce and John Holdenby and of William Hatton, which are in the Public Record Office. The first has been abstracted in the printed Calendar, the others are unprinted. The agreement of 1514 between John Holdenby and John Hatton is referred to in that of 1516 which, with that of 1518, is in the British Museum (Addl. Charters 21,975, 21,977). The Subsidy Roll of 1522-4 is in the Public Record Office. The wills of John and William Hatton are among the Northamptonshire wills in the Probate Office at Birmingham (Books C. f. 124 and M. f. 13). For the tombs and inscriptions in Holdenby church see Bridges, *Northamptonshire*, i. 529. Lease of Harrington by William Saunders: Brit. Mus., Addl. Charter 21,994. Marriage settlement on Thomas and Ursula Hatton: Finch-Hatton MSS. no. 2,586, on deposit with Northamptonshire Record Society.

APPENDICES

CHAPTER III. Hatton's matriculation: Wood's *Athenae Oxon.* edn. Bliss i. 582. Admission to the Inner Temple: W. H. Cooke, *Students admitted to the Inner Temple.* For Sir Edward Saunders, see Foss, *Lives of the Judges* and *D.N.B.* The quotation from Lytton Strachey is from his *Elizabeth and Essex*, p. 23. For Naunton and Perrot, see *D.N.B.* For life in the Inns of Court see J. Bruce Williamson, *The History of the Temple*, and authorities cited. Sir Edmund Chambers's remarks on the mask of 1562 from his *Elizabethan Stage*, iii. 457.

CHAPTER IV. For Sackville and Norton see *D.N.B.* The 'recent writer' quoted on *Gorboduc* is the author of the article on Sackville in *The Times Literary Supplement* of January 25th, 1936. Order for Hatton's armour: State Pap. Dom., Eliz. vol. 34. Rolls of Gentlemen Pensioners in Public Record Office. Pedigrees of Parr and Lane: *Visitation of Northamptonshire*, edn. Metcalfe. Catherine Parr's letter: Salisbury MSS. vol. 1 (Hist. MSS. Commn.). For a history of the Gentlemen Pensioners see Sir Henry Brackenbury, *The Nearest Guard*.

CHAPTER V. Tilts in which Hatton took part: Nichols, *Progresses of Queen Elizabeth*; Chambers, *Elizabethan Stage*. George Delves's account of the tilt of 1571: Rutland MSS. (Hist. MSS. Commn.), i. 92. Hatton's armour: Dillon, *An Almain Armourer's Album*; Cripps-Day, *Fragmenta Armamentaria*, i. part ii. Hatton's costume as a Gentleman of the Privy Chamber: Ashburnham MSS. (Hist. MSS. Commn.). Hatton's New Year's gifts: Nichols, *Progresses*.

CHAPTER VI. Father Crichton's memoir: J. H. Pollen, *Mary Queen of Scots and the Babington Plot*. Norfolk on Hatton's kindness: Nicolas, *Memoirs of Sir Christopher Hatton*, p. 9. Henry Bradley on rustic pronunciation at Court: *Shakespeare's England*, ii. 541; George Gordon on Shakespeare's English in *Shakespearean Comedy*. Gossip about Hatton by his Northamptonshire neighbours: Salisbury MSS. (Hist. MSS. Commn.), vol. ii. Ralph Lane calls Hatton his cousin: *ibid.* Tate pedigree: *Visitation of Northamptonshire*, edn. Metcalfe. For Henry MacWilliam see Strype, *Life of Cheke*, p. 133. Francis Flower's printing licence: *Stationers' Register*, edn. Arber, i. 111. Wentworth's speeches: D'Ewes, *Journals*, *passim*. *A Book of the Heir Apparent*: State Pap. Dom., Eliz., vol. 240.

CHAPTER VII. *Visitation of Northamptonshire*, 1564, edn. Metcalfe. Scoring sheet of the tilt of 1571: Bodleian Library, Ashm. MSS. 845. The quotation about J. H. Round and his parchments is from Lytton Strachey's study of Froude in his *Six English Historians*. Bostock's Cheshire collections: Brit. Mus., Harl. MS. 139; from it the correspondence between Hatton and Dutton has been printed, with some errors in transcription, in *Memorials of the Duttons*. Hatton's proposal to search the muniments of Christ Church: Nicolas, p. 76. Search in London muniments: *Remembrancia Rolls*, p. 425.

CHAPTER VIII. Scandal about Leicester in 1570: Lodge, *Illustrations*, i. 514. Mather and Berney: Salisbury MSS. (Hist. MSS. Commn.), vol. ii. Archbishop Parker's report: Brit. Mus., Lansd. MSS. 15, art. 43. Mary Stuart's letter: Labanoff, *Letters of Mary Stuart*, vi. 50. Gilbert Talbot's letter: Lodge, *Illustrations*, ii. 17. Edward Dyer's letter in Nicolas from Harl. MS. 787, f. 88. For Oxford's life generally see *D.N.B.* and B. M. Ward, *The Seventeenth Earl of Oxford*; and for the Knyvet affair see Sir Edmund Chambers's life of Sir Henry Lee.

CHAPTER IX. Gilbert Talbot's letter: Lodge, *Illustrations*, ii. 17. Characters in Dyer's poem 'Amarillis' see Kenneth Thorpe Ross in a contribution to *Papers of the Michigan Academy of Science, Arts and Letters* (1939); *cf.* Ralph M. Sargent, *At the Court of Queen Elizabeth*. Privy Council order: Acts of the Privy Council, 1571-5, p. 108. Hatton's letters to Elizabeth are printed in Nicolas. Hatton's cipher: Martin Hume, *Courtships of Queen Elizabeth*, p. 354, and Professor Neale's *Queen Elizabeth*, p. 214. The Northall Mimms affair: Nicolas, p. 113. The supposed letters from Elizabeth to Hatton: Nicolas, p. 30; Harington, *Nugae Antiquae*, p. 115. T.G.'s letter: Salisbury MSS. (Hist. MSS. Commn.), ii. 54; *cf.* also B. M. Ward in *Review of English Studies*, 1928. Bertrand de la Tour: Strype, *Annals*, vol. ii, part i. p. 376.

CHAPTER X. Burchet's confession: Brit. Mus., Lansd. MSS. 17, no. 88. Bacon on Burchet: Spedding, *Letters of Bacon*, i. 203. Sir Thomas Smith on attempts on Hatton's life: Wright, *Queen Elizabeth and her Times*, i. 492. For a criticism of Mr. Ward's conclusions regarding the authorship of *A Hundreth Sundrie Flowres*, see C. T. Prouty, *George Gascoigne* and Dr. Prouty's edition of his *Flowres*.

CHAPTER XI. Hatton's Star Chamber case: Public Record Office, Star Ch. H. 53/24, 49/38 (1583). Walsingham's letter: State Pap. Dom., Eliz., vol. 45. Grant of Brancksea: Acts of Privy Council, 1575-7, p. 192. Privy Council to Poole: *ibid.* Callis the pirate: State Pap. Dom., Eliz., vol. 112; C. L'Estrange Ewen, *The Golden Chalice*. Burghley on Callis: Salisbury MSS. (Hist. MSS. Commn.), ii. 156. Lord Thomas Howard to William Pitt: Corpn. of Weymouth MSS. (Hist. MSS. Commn.). Hawley a commissioner in Ralegh's case: Brit. Mus., Harl. MS. 6,849, f. 183. Hatton Hawley's verses on death of Queen Elizabeth: Falconer Madan, *Oxford Books*, *sub anno* 1603.

APPENDICES

CHAPTER XII. The Queen's progresses are collected in Nichols, *Progresses of Queen Elizabeth*; *cf.* Sir Edmund Chambers, *Elizabethan Stage*; *Letters of Philip Gawdy* (Roxburgh Club, 1906). For Burghley's expenses at a progress, see Peck, *Desiderata Curiosa*, p. 25. For Hatton's bearward see William Kelly, *Notices illustrative of the Drama . . . at Leicester.*

CHAPTER XIII. Burghley on Hatton, 'a lover of learned men': Nichols, *Progresses*, ii. 110. Father Crichton: 'a learned man'; J. H. Pollen, *Mary Queen of Scots and the Babington Plot.* For the Elizabethan literary patron see *Shakespeare's England*, ii. ch. xxii. For Churchyard's life G. Chalmers's life in his edition of the *Chipps*, and *D.N.B.* Sources for Barnabe Rich: *D.N.B.* For Dr. Dee, see Charlotte Fell Smith, *Life of John Dee* and *D.N.B.*

CHAPTER XIV. For the authors and works mentioned see in general *D.N.B.* George Whetstone's *Heptameron*: *Collectanea Anglo-Poetica*, v. 387 (Chetham Society). Lupton's *Siuqila*: Grosart, *Select Ancient English Poems*, vol. ii. For George Saunder's murder see my article in *Notes and Queries*, clxxiv. 182. Flower's patent: *Stationers' Register*, edn. Arber, i. 111. Harington's anecdote of Hatton: *Nugae Antiquae*, p. 210.

CHAPTER XV. For Hatton House see E. Williams, *Early Holborn.* Bishop Cox's letters: Strype, *Annals*, vol. ii, part i. 533; part ii. 564. North's letter to Cox: Salisbury MSS. (Hist. MSS. Commn.), ii. 120. Hatton to the Master of Requests: in Cal. State Pap. Dom., Eliz. Addenda, vol. 29. Hatton's leases at Peterborough: Acts of the Privy Council, 1571-5, p. 341.

CHAPTER XVI. For Holdenby House see J. Alfred Gotch, *Old English Houses* and *Early Renaissance Architecture in England*, and Emily S. Hartshorne, *Memorials of Holdenby.* Charter of 1576: Brit. Mus., Addl. Charter 21,996. Hatton's letter to Burghley, Dec., 1578: Nicolas from Murdin's State Papers, p. 318; Cal. Salisbury MSS. (Hist. MSS. Commn.), vol. ii gives date as 1579. Burghley's reply: State Pap. Dom., Eliz., Addenda, vol. 25. Privy Council on Puritans in Northampton: Acts of Privy Council, 1578-80, p. 218. Survey of 1587: Finch-Hatton MSS., quoted in Baker's *Northamptonshire*. Sale to James I in Baker. Norden's account: *Delineation of Northamptonshire.* Parliamentary Survey: Public Record Office, E. 317, no. 55 and in Hartshorne, *Memorials of Holdenby.* Tombs in Holdenby church: Bridges' *Northamptonshire*, i. 529.

CHAPTER XVII. Hatton to be a Privy Councillor: State Pap. Dom., Eliz., Addenda, vol. 25. Sworn and appointed Vice-Chamberlain: Acts of the Privy Council, 1577-8, p. 85. De Champagny in England: Cal. Spanish Pap., 1568-79, p. 529. Mary Stuart on Hatton's supposed marriage: Labanoff, *Letters of Mary Stuart*, v. 94. Mendoza on Simier's arrival: Cal. Spanish Pap., 1568-79, p. 655; on Bromley's appointment: *ibid.*, 659; suggests presents to Privy Council: *ibid.*, 668-9. Appletree fires at the Queen's barge: Nichols, *Progresses*, ii. 110 from Stow. Mendoza on Hatton's speech to the Queen: Cal. Spanish Pap., 1580-6; on Elizabeth's gratitude: *ibid.*

CHAPTER XVIII. For Drake's voyage see Julian Corbett, *Drake* and sources cited, and James A. Williamson, *The Age of Drake*; the latter book incorporates the discoveries of E. G. R. Taylor from *The Missing Draft Project of Drake's Voyage* (Geographical Journal, Jan., 1930), *Master John Dee, Drake and the Straits of Anian* (*Mariners' Mirror*, 1929) and *More Light on Drake* (*ibid.*, 1930). Doughty's will: P.C.C. 40 Bakon. Hatton's share in Drake's booty in Murdin, p. 539. Hatton's share in Fenton's and later expeditions: Cal. Colonial Papers.

CHAPTER XIX. Deposition of Zachary Jones: State Pap. Dom., Eliz., vol. 123. For Campion see life by Richard Simpson. Pound's letter to Hatton is printed (with some mistakes in transcription) with other documents in Foley, *Records of the English Province of the Society of Jesuits*, iii. 565; the original is in State Pap. Dom., Eliz., vol. 142.

CHAPTER XX. Tresham Papers: Hist. MSS. Commn. For George Gilbert see Foley, *Records of the English Province of the Society of Jesuits*, vol. iii and *D.N.B.* Grafton Estate Book, by John Humphreys (Birmingham Arch. Society, vol. 44, 1918). Ralph Dutton and Gilbert: State Pap. Dom., Eliz., vol. 148. Cases of Lady Egerton and Margaret Countess of Derby in Nicolas; the letter to John Dutton and those about Dutton and his wife and about Lady Egerton are also in Peck, *Desiderata Curiosa*, pp. 130, 142, 158, presumably from the originals.

CHAPTER XXI. Dr. Dale on his salary as Ambassador: Duke of Manchester, *Court and Society*, i. 251. Hatton's grant to import yarn from Ireland: Sidney Papers, i. 159. Grant of import duty on wine: State Pap. Dom., Eliz., vol. 140. Tipper's services with Lady Laxton: Charles J. Sisson, *Thomas Lodge*. Documents about his hosting patent: State Pap. Dom., Eliz., vol. 130 and Acts of Privy Council, *passim*. Tipper and Munslowe: State Pap. Dom., Eliz., vol. 157. Memorandum by Robert Ardern: *ibid.*, vol. 181. Application for Samuel Cox as Packer: *Remembrancia Rolls*. Sir James Mervyn's case, *ibid.* Tipper's patent for concealed lands: State Pap. Dom., Eliz., vol. 241.

CHAPTER XXII. For Parry see J. H. Pollen in *The Month*, July, 1902, Conyers Read, *Walsingham*, and *D.N.B.* His trial in *State Trials*. Fleetwood on Hatton's speech: Wright, *Queen Elizabeth*, ii. 244. Hatton's speeches in Parliament: D'Ewes, *Journals*. For Edmund Neville see *D.N.B.* Lupold von Wedel on Parry: Trans. R. Hist. Society (New Series), ix. pp. 255 fol. For Parry's use of the word 'settled' see my letter on *Leycester's Commonwealth* in *Times Literary Supplement*, December 26th, 1942.

CHAPTER XXIII. Ralegh's letter to Cecil about Essex: Nicolas, p. 438 from Murdin's State Papers, p. 811. For Henry Percy see *D.N.B.* Inquiry on his death: *State Trials*.

CHAPTER XXIV. For Henry Howard, Charles Arundel and Lord Arundel see *D.N.B.* For the relations between the Howards and Charles Arundel and Lord Oxford see B. M. Ward, *The Seventeenth Earl of Oxford*. For Solomon Aldred see Father Parsons's memoirs, Edn. J. H. Pollen (Cath. Rec. Socy. Miscellanea II, pp. 33, 34), Charles J. Sisson, *Thomas Lodge*.

CHAPTER XXV. Maude as de Monte Alto: J. H. Pollen, *Mary Queen of Scots and the Babington Plot*. Sandys case: State Pap. Dom., Eliz., vol. 158, Nicolas and Froude. Captain Jaques: Pollen, *op. cit.*; Sadler Papers, ii. 478; *Journal* R. Soc. Antiquaries Ireland (1858-60, 1860-1). Leicester in the Netherlands: Leicester Correspondence (Camden Society, 27). Bacon's letter to Essex: Spedding, *Life and Letters of Bacon*, ii. 42. Sir William Stanley's letter to Jaques: *Cardinal Allen's Defence of Sir William Stanley* (Chetham Society, vol. 25). Anthony Copley on Jaques: Strype, *Annals*, iv. 279. Jaques in Antwerp, 1592: Salisbury MSS. (Hist. MSS. Commn.), vol. 5.

CHAPTER XXVI. George Gifford and Nix: State Pap. Dom., Eliz., vol. 160. Poley's relationship to Christopher Blount in Trans. Worcestershire Arch. Socy., 1943. Edward Windsor's letter to Hatton: State Pap. Dom., Eliz., vol. 201

CHAPTER XXVII. *The Bardon Papers*, edited by Conyers Read for the Royal Historical Soc., 1909. Babington trial: *State Trials*. For Tilney see 'George Buc' by Mark Eccles in *Thomas Lodge*, ed. Charles J. Sisson. Gentlemen Pensioners' Roll of 1586 in Public Record Office. Examination of Jane Tichbourne: Cal. Scottish and Mary Queen of Scots, vol. 8. Tichbourne's speech: Kenyon MSS. (Hist. MSS. Commn.).

CHAPTER XXVIII. Harington's anecdotes in *Nugae Antiquae*. Heneage's letters in Nicolas.

CHAPTER XXIX. Nau's memorandum about Hatton: Cal. Scottish and Mary Queen of Scots, vol. 7. Mary's trial: *State Trials*. Hatton's speeches in Parliament: D'Ewes, *Journals*. Hatton, godfather to Davison's son: State Pap. Dom., Eliz., vol. 150. Davison's trial: *State Trials*.

CHAPTER XXX. For Irish history at this period see A. F. Pollard in *Political History of England*, vol. 6, ch. 22. For Stukeley see Froude and *D.N.B.* Barnabe Rich and Jacomo di Francisci in Ireland: Cal. Pap. Ireland, *passim*; for Rich's relationships see W. H. Welply in *Notes and Queries*, August 26th, 1944. For John Browne, see Cal. State Papers, Ireland, Wright's *Queen Elizabeth and her Times*, i. 472 and Mrs. O'Sullivan's *Old Galway*. Pedigree showing Hatton's descent from the Greys: Brit. Mus., Harl. MS. 890, f. 36. Hatton's letter to Walsingham in Nicolas, p. 158. Hatton's grants in Co. Waterford: Cal. Pap. Ireland, *passim*; Salisbury MSS. (Hist. MSS. Commn.), vol. 4; State Pap. Dom., Eliz., Addenda, 1597; Acts of Privy Council, 1586-7, p. 364, 1589-90, pp. 41, 43; *cf.* W. H. Gratton-Flood in *Journal Waterford, etc. Arch. Socy.*, ix. 56.

CHAPTER XXXI. Hatton's speech in Parliament, Feb. 15th, 1587: D'Ewes *Journals*. In Star Chamber, Oct. 28th, 1587: Cal. Spanish Pap., 1587-1603. Musters in Northamptonshire printed by Northamptonshire Record Society. Hatton's entertainment of Elizabeth after the Armada: Cal. Spanish Pap., 1587-1603. Hatton's speech in Parliament: part in Neale's *Queen Elizabeth*, part in D'Ewes, *Journals*.

CHAPTER XXXII. For Whitgift see *D.N.B.* and Paule's and Strype's biographies. Hatton's misgivings about the Lord Chancellorship in Murdin, p. 589. For Martin Marprelate Tracts see Arber, *The Martin Marprelate Controversy*; Pierce, *Historical Introduction to the Marprelate Tracts*; and Pollard in *Political History of England*, vol. 6. Knightley's trial: *State Trials*. For Hatton and Udall see Strype, *Whitgift*, ii. 97. Udall's examination: *State Trials*. Barrowe's examination: Arber, *Martin Marprelate Controversy*.

CHAPTER XXXIII. Hatton's election to the Garter: Nicolas, p. 476; Rutland MSS. (Hist. MSS. Commn.), i. 248. Allen to Bacon on William Hatton's marriage: Birch, *Memoirs of Queen Elizabeth*, i. 56. Hatton's installation as Chancellor of Oxford: Brit. Mus., Addl. MS. 5,845, p. 455; *cf.* Falconer Madan, *Oxford Books*, vol. ii, *sub anno.* 1588. Hatton's letter to Inner Temple about Thomas Saunders: W. H. Cooke, *Students admitted to the Inner Temple*.

CHAPTER XXXIV. Hatton's letter to Unton: Nicolas, p. 491. Parsons's report: in his work *Andreas Philopater*. Hatton's foreboding of death: State Pap. Dom., Eliz., vol. 186. Phelippes on his illness: *ibid.*, vol. 240. Northampton on Hatton's disease: Mar and Kellie MSS. (Hist. MSS.

Commn.), p. 53. Bishop Corbet on Hatton's tomb in his *Iter Boreale*. 'A Lamentable Discourse': *Notes and Queries*, 3, series 1, 142. Mary Stuart on Hatton's alleged marriage: Labanoff, *Letters of Mary Stuart*, v. 94. For Perrot and Hatton see article on Perrot in *D.N.B.* and Pollard, *Political History of England*, vol. 6, p. 434, Sir Thomas Perrot's will: P.C.C., 14 Dixy. For Arden Waferer and Lodowick Bryskett, see Deborah Jones in *Thomas Lodge*, ed. Charles J. Sisson. Hatton's debts: i.p.m. on Sir William Hatton in Public Record Office; *cf.* Alice Dryden, 'Sir Christopher Hatton and his Homes', in *Memorials of Old Northamptonshire*; Salisbury MSS. (Hist. MSS. Commn.), vol. 10; Neale: *Queen Elizabeth*. Hatton's jewels: Alice Dryden, *op. cit.*: she gives no reference. Letter from Bancroft on Christopher Hatton, the Chancellor's cousin: Salisbury MSS. (Hist. MSS. Commn.), vol. 9.

CHAPTER XXXV. Will of William Cox, 1569: P.C.C., 20 Sheffield. Walsingham to Davison on John Cox: Cal. State Pap. Foreign. Hatton to Lord Mayor of London on death of one Cox: Remembrancia of the City of London, p. 60. Matriculation of Samuel Cox at Pembroke, 1565: Venn, *Alumni Cantabrigienses*. Hunsdon to Burghley on Calveley: Cal. State Pap. Foreign. Bryskett: Sebastian Bryskett witnesses one of the Hatton documents among the Finch-Hatton MSS.; *cf.* Deborah Jones in *Thomas Lodge*, edited by Charles J. Sisson. Cox with Leicester in the Netherlands: Leicester Correspondence (Camden Society). Cox's estates in Oxfordshire: Feet of Fines, Oxon., Easter 29 Eliz. in Public Record Office. Beckingham Law Suits: St. Ch. Jas. I, 6/5 in P.R.O. For George Carew see *D.N.B.* Cox's will: P.C.C. 28 Fenner. His *inquisitio post mortem*: 10 Jas. I in P.R.O. Star Chamber case about his estate: St. Ch. Jas. I, 8, 305/15.

THE HATTON PEDIGREE

THE following notices of Hattons of Hatton near Daresbury in Cheshire may be collected here. In 1440-1 Peter de Hatton, yeoman, of Hatton near Daresbury, received pardon of outlawry (Cheshire Recognizance Roll, Vol. II). In 1487 John Hatton and others granted to Peter Hatton of Hatton their capital messuage in Hatton near Daresbury for life, remainder to his sons; Thomas Hatton of Crooton to give seisin (Turner and Coxe: Charters in the Bodleian Library). In 1501-2 Richard de Hatton granted to Richard Aston of Aston a messuage in Hatton near Daresbury. In 1524 John Danyell of Daresbury, Esq., granted to Rondolph Hatton and another, churchwardens and reeves of Daresbury Church, arrears of rent for certain church-lands (P.R.O., Ancient Deeds, A.5616). Thereafter there are numerous records of Hattons of Hatton and Quisty Birches in Daresbury.

John Danyell of Daresbury was the owner of the principal estate in Daresbury. When Christopher Hatton entered his pedigree in 1564 he gave the name of his great-great-grandfather as Laurence Hatton of Duddon, and said that his wife was a daughter of John Danyell of Daresbury (an earlier John Danyell, of course, than the one mentioned above). Laurence was a family name among the Hattons of Quisty Birches. Laurence Hatton of that place, whom Bostock interviewed in 1573, left a will which was proved in 1574.

The above-mentioned records disclose a family of Hatton, yeoman, living at Hatton and Quisty Birches from the fifteenth century at any rate. It may be presumed that they were descended from the ancient lords of Hatton. And on the whole it seems likely that the Hattons of Holdenby were in fact descended from the Quisty Birches line.

To the records of the first Hattons of Holdenby may be added the following: In 1511 Richard Hatton, gentleman, quitted claim to any rights he might have in the manors of Holdenby and Old and all other premises of William Holdenby, as in the agreement concluded between John Holdenby and Elizabeth Gyles and George Hatton (Brit. Mus., Addl. Charter 21,971). As any claim of Richard Hatton could only have come through Elizabeth Gyles, it is obvious that he must have been her son (Gyles being her second husband), a younger brother of George and John Hatton. He is the ancestor of Christopher Hatton's second cousins, the Hattons of Northampton mentioned in the settlement of Christopher Hatton's estates.

According to the pedigrees, Joan the wife of John Hatton of Blechingley, Christopher Hatton's grandmother, was a daughter of John
Westby of Kent. But it is doubtful if the heralds had any evidence for
this. When Christopher Hatton entered his pedigree in 1564 he gave
her name, but said she was of Surrey. There is an agreement, or as it
is technically called a fine, of the year 1507 regarding some land in
Nutfield, Surrey, in which the vendors are John Hatton and Joan his
wife, Richard Wenright and Clemence his wife, John Vese and Margaret his wife, and Anne Merssher, who dispose of a house, garden and
land there. As Nutfield adjoins Blechingley it seems fairly certain that
this is our John Hatton and his wife. The wording of the fine indicates
that the four women were the joint heiresses of this small estate, the
last of them being presumably unmarried. It is likely therefore that
Merssher was Joan Hatton's maiden name.

According to the agreements providing for a future marriage and the
statements in the heralds' pedigrees, William, Christopher Hatton's
father, first married Mary daughter of John Holdenby of Ravensthorpe.
It is certain however that Christopher Hatton's mother was Alice
Saunders of Harrington. And there is some evidence that before he
married Alice Saunders William was married secondly to Elizabeth,
daughter of one John Coke. This appears from a fine of the year 1530,
in which William Hatton and Elizabeth his wife, one of the daughters
and heirs of John Coke, sell some lands in Nortoft and East Haddon,
adjoining Holdenby.

The Hattons parted in 1532 with the manor of Old, which had come
to the Holdenbys from their de la Carvaile ancestors. William Hatton
and William Haynes and Alice his wife, selling the manor to Edward
Montague. Alice Haynes was the widow of George Hatton, William
Hatton's uncle; in the sale of the manor her rights of dower had to be
considered.

THE HOLDENBYS

A MAGNIFICENT series of charters and deeds concerning Hatton's ancestral estate of Holdenby descended to the Earls of Winchilsea and Nottingham, the representatives of Christopher, second Baron and first Viscount Hatton. These deeds are mentioned, though not calendared, in the first Report of the Historical Manuscripts Commission, issued in 1870. The earlier deeds were subsequently purchased by the British Museum, and are now among the Additional Charters. With their aid it would be possible to form a connected pedigree of the family of Holdenby of Holdenby, or de Haldenby as they are generally styled in the medieval documents, from Robert de Holdenby who flourished in the reign of Henry III, to the time when the Hattons inherited the manor.

Many of the seals of the lords of Holdenby are preserved on these deeds. They bear a coat of arms, showing five cinquefoils arranged in the form of a cross. These are the arms of Holdenby which Laurence Bostock, when he visited the place in 1573, found on their tombs in Holdenby Church, in stained glass in the church windows and in Hatton's house at Holdenby, that is the old Holdenby manor house beside the church, which Hatton superseded by Holdenby House. Bostock tricked them as: Azure, a cross of five cinquefoils Argent. They are among the arms quartered by Hatton on his seal and on the heraldic achievement on the gateways of Holdenby House. Sometimes the Holdenbys used a seal with a single cinquefoil and the motto, *un pour toutes*, the one cinquefoil doing duty for the five.

Passing over the intermediate generations, which the pedigrees show marrying into the families of Zouch and Verdon, thus accounting for the impaling of their arms by the Holdenbys, we come to Robert de Holdenby who flourished at the end of the fourteenth and beginning of the fifteenth century. He married Maud, the daughter and heiress of William de la Carvaile, who brought into the family the manor of Old (written Wolde in medieval days) not far from Holdenby. The seal of Maud's guardian during her minority, John de la Carvaile, the King's escheator in Northamptonshire, is preserved in the British Museum. It shows three bends, with a triple-towered castle on a canton. In Holdenby Church Bostock found the tomb of Robert de Holdenby, a marble gravestone and the inscription: *Hic jacet Robertus de Holdynby qui obiit die Jovis, quarto die Junii, anno domini* 1411, *cujus anima propicietur Deus.* It bore the arms of Holdenby impaling 'bendwise of eight pieces Argent and Sable, a canton in chief Sable, a castle Argent'. Elsewhere, more accurately he reads the arms as bendy of six pieces, that is the three bends shown on the shield, and correctly interprets them as those of de la Carvaile, or de la Carnell as the name was sometimes improperly rendered. A man impales his wife's arms, and so Robert de Holdenby is portrayed on his tombs as impaling the arms of his wife, Maud de la Carvaile. These arms were also seen by Bostock in Hatton's manor house at Holdenby, and they are on his achievement on the gateway of Holdenby House.

This Robert's son William is shown in the pedigree as having married into the family of Raven of Whipsnade, Bedfordshire, whose arms are impaled by Holdenby on the font in Holdenby Church. William's son John de Holdenby married Joan, daughter of John Mortimer the elder of Grendon, Northamptonshire, and of Eakley manor in Stoke Goldington, Buckinghamshire. Hence the arms of Mortimer of Grendon: Ermine, on a fess Azure three cross crosslets Or, on the gateway of Holdenby House and on the font.

William, the son of this John de Holdenby, is shown in the pedigrees as marrying Agnes daughter of Sir William Lucy, thus accounting for the impaling of the Lucy arms. In the same pedigrees (Brit. Museum, Harl. MS. 890, f. 36) Sir William Lucy's mother is given as Katharine daughter of Richard Grey of Ruthin, thus explaining Hatton's relationship with Arthur, Lord Grey of Wilton.

William's son, another William de Holdenby, died in 1498. Bostock found his tomb in Holdenby Church, an alabaster gravestone with the representation of a man in armour, and a woman by him, with the following inscription: *Hic jacet Willelmus de Holdynby et Margareta uxor ejus, que quidam Margareta obiit . . . die mensis . . . anno domini mcccclxxx, et Willelmus obiit . . . die mensis . . . anno domini mcccclxxxx, quorum animabus propicietur Deus* (the date of William's death is incorrectly given) and the arms of Holdenby impaling: Azure on a fess Gules three escallops Azure. These are the arms of Margaret, William's wife. In the pedigree she is said to have been a daughter of Robert Jakes of co. Leicester, and these are the arms of Jakes of Wellesborough in that county.

This William was the brother of Elizabeth, who by her marriage with a Hatton brought Holdenby to that family. The details of his will are known from a copy printed in Miss Hartshorne's *Memorials of Holdenby* (1868), the original being apparently now lost. It names his son John (who died young), his daughter Joyce (who succeeded her father and married her kinsman, John Holdenby of Ravensthorpe), and his sister Elizabeth, the Hatton ancestress. We read in it also that the testator left to Richard Hutton £5, with £4 yearly for three years for his schooling and to bind him apprentice to a suitable craft. It is likely that the name was misread by the copyist, and should be Richard Hatton, the youngest of Elizabeth's three sons.

In Baker's *Northamptonshire* is a description of the font in Holdenby Church, which showed the following coats of arms:

1. Holdenby, impaling Gules, a chevron Or between ten bezants (Zouch).
2. Holdenby, impaling Sable, a lion rampant Argent (Verdon).
3. Holdenby, impaling de la Carvaile.
4. Holdenby, impaling Sable, a raven within a border Argent (Raven).
5. Holdenby, impaling Mortimer of Grendon.
6. Holdenby, impaling Gules, semée of cross crosslets Or, three lucies or pikes haurient Argent (Lucy).
7. Hatton, impaling Holdenby.

THE SETTLEMENT OF HATTON'S
ESTATES

BESIDES his hereditary manor of Holdenby, Hatton possessed large properties in Northamptonshire granted by Queen Elizabeth (Nicolas, from Patent Rolls). They included the manors of Church and Chapel Brampton and of Little Weldon, the demesne of Naseby, the site of the Abbey of Sulby and the Keepership of the Forest of Rockingham. In Dorset he was given the castle of Corfe; in Oxfordshire the site of the Abbey of Bruern; in Middlesex the manor of Drayton; Ely House in Holborn; and a large fief about Dungarvan in Ireland. He added to these estates by purchase. About the year 1575 he bought the manor of Kirby from the Staffords, and in 1581 that of Gretton from Sir William Catesby (P.R.O., Anc. Deeds, A. 4779, 4780). In 1588 he added to his Northamptonshire estates the manor of Great Weldon. In Oxfordshire he bought in 1583 from the Barentines the manors of Churchill and Little Haseley and other lands, eventually retaining only Churchill (Feet of Fines, Oxon., Trim. 25 Eliz.). He also purchased some manors in Cheshire, no doubt to emphasize his connection with that country, among them Warmingham, bought from Edward de Vere, Earl of Oxford, and Bartomley. Both were sold by his heirs to Sir Randle Crew.

As he was unmarried, Hatton settled in his lifetime (by deeds of date, 1573 and 1584) the way in which his estates were to descend (i.p.m. Sir William Hatton and John Hatton, 1597, P.R.O.; Finch-Hatton deeds 2029, 3075). Failing any sons and daughters which he himself might have, he chose as his heir his nephew William Newport, son of his sister Dorothy by John Newport of Hunningham, Warwickshire. This nephew he adopted and had him change his name to Hatton. Failing heirs male of the nephew, Hatton then looked to the descendants of his father's brother, his uncle John Hatton of Gravesend. This man had had two sons, William Hatton of Gravesend and John Hatton of London, later of Stanton, Cambridgeshire. William Hatton was dead, leaving an only son Edward, and Edward Hatton was accordingly named as next heir in Hatton's settlement. But Edward died in Hatton's lifetime without issue, and so the next heir was Christopher Hatton, son of John Hatton of Stanton. He and his descendants eventually succeeded to Hatton's estates.

But he made a further provision, in case these lines should fail. He named in remainder his second cousins, three brothers, John of Northampton, William and Richard, grandsons of Richard Hatton, his grandfather's younger brother. And failing these, he named as heir Thomas Hatton of Monkton Foregate near Shrewsbury. This man was son of Richard Hatton of the same place, whose father, another Richard, was son of Peter Hatton of Quisty Birches. According to the pedigree which deduces the Hattons of Holdenby from those of Quisty Birches, Thomas of Monkton Foregate was Hatton's third cousin.

In 1579 John Hatton of Stanton made a settlement of his contingent interest in accordance with Hatton's wishes. The trustees were Sir Walter Mildmay, Francis Saunders, Esq., and William Doddington. They were the same trustees as those of Hatton's final settlement of 1584. Mildmay was Chancellor of the Exchequer, Saunders was a kinsman, probably Francis Saunders of Welford, Northamptonshire. William Doddington is presumably the man of that name who married Walsingham's sister. A letter from him occurs in the Letter Book, and a marginal note says that he committed suicide by throwing himself from St. Sepulchre's steeple in Holborn. Hatton had sold him the manor of Breamore in Hampshire, and Sir John Oglander in his Note Books tells us that his grandson Henry Doddington was also mad and killed his own mother.

These deeds of settlement are witnessed by a number of Hatton's men. That of 1579, for instance, includes many of those who occur in the foregoing pages: Henry MacWilliam, the Gentleman Pensioner; Robert Colshill mentioned in Burghley's letter to Hatton about his entertainment at Holdenby; Samuel Cox, Hatton's secretary; Anthony Ashley, later Clerk of the Council, who dedicated his *Mariner's Mirror* to Hatton; Arden Waferer, a legal friend who looked after some of his affairs; and Francis Flower, also a Gentleman Pensioner, who wrote an epitaph for Hatton in St. Paul's. An interesting witness is Sebastian Bryskett. He was the elder brother of Lodowick Bryskett, the friend of Spenser and Sidney (Deborah Jones in *Thomas Lodge*, ed. Charles J. Sisson). He was evidently a member of Hatton's retinue, and is so referred to as 'Mr. Bruskett' in a passage in the Letter Book.

The estate in Churchill formed the subject of two inquisitions taken in 1597 (P.R.O.; Cal. i.p.m.). They state that Sir Christopher Hatton died without lawful issue on November 20th, 1591, that the premises in Churchill descended in virtue of the settlement to his nephew Sir William Hatton, and that they were extended, that is valued, and seized into the Queen's hand for debts owed to her by Sir Christopher, contracted in connection with his office of Receiver and Remembrancer of First Fruits, which he had held from the year 1578. Under the terms of the settlement Hatton's heir was found to be Christopher Hatton, son of John Hatton of London, aged 16.

The grandfather of this young man was John Hatton, younger brother of Sir Christopher's father. His will was proved at Rochester in Kent in March, 1557 (Rochester wills in Somerset House). By this it appears that he was of Milton next Gravesend in that county. He had three daughters and two sons, William to whom he left half the goods in his shop, and John, then a minor, to whom he gave five quarters of barley. The shop and the meagre legacies sufficiently indicate the humble position of this scion of an alleged courtly house.

The elder son William, of Gravesend, yeoman, made his will in 1570 (P.C.C., 12 Lyon). He left a son Edward and two daughters. He seems to have been a fisherman, for he left as legacies 'the profit of his tide', and a half boat called a tilt boat. The title deeds of his lands in Essex and Kent he left to his brother John until his son Edward should come of age. This Edward died young.

The heir under the settlement was now the above William Hatton's younger brother John, whose marriage Sir Christopher promoted in the year 1581 to Jane, daughter of Robert Shute, Esq., second Baron of the Exchequer, settling an annuity on them from the manor of Kirby in Northamptonshire (Brit. Mus., Addl. Charter 19,885). John and Jane Hatton were the parents of Christopher, the Chancellor's eventual heir.

Of the other people mentioned in Hatton's settlement but little is known. Of the three brothers, his second cousins, John Hatton was of the parish of All Hallows, Northampton, draper, whose will was proved in 1589, when he died, leaving issue. A William Hatton of Earl's Barton, Northamptonshire, whose will was made in 1617, was probably a son of William Hatton, the second brother. The third brother is probably Richard Hatton of Kingsthorpe, Northamptonshire, whose will, proved in 1640, mentions a son Christopher. Thomas Hatton of Abbey Foregate near Shrewsbury, Hatton's third cousin according to the pedigrees, died in 1601, leaving a will (P.C.C. 76 Woodhill) which, however, throws no light on the family history.

HATTON'S ARMS

THERE seems to be little doubt that the arms: Azure, a chevron Or between three garbs Or, were those of Hatton of Hatton. There is in the British Museum a loose seal, *temp.* Ed. III, of Hatton, showing a chevron between three garbs. In Hatton Hall, Waverton, Cheshire, which was rebuilt by Sir Piers Dutton, 1539-42, there were carved shields on the entrance porch showing the arms of Dutton impaling a chevron between three garbs, the arms of Hatton, from whom the Duttons inherited the manor. In Harl. MS. 2151 are a number of tricks of arms which were in Hatton Hall in 1572. They include this coat.

It is of interest to note that Christopher Hatton had a coat of arms for Hatton in the old Holdenby manor house, quite different from the coat he adopted after Bostock had compiled a pedigree for him. This coat: Sable, a cross engrailed Ermine, which Bostock saw in February, 1573 is in fact the same as that which the heralds tricked against Hatton's name on the scoring sheet for the tilt of May, 1571. Hence it appears that, as the circumstances of the compilation of the pedigree suggest, the adoption of the ancient coat of Hatton of Hatton was an afterthought.

The Hatton coat that Bostock found in Hatton's manor house he included among Hatton's quarterings, and ascribed it to Hallum, one of his supposed Cheshire ancestors. There is some evidence that the coat of the Cheshire Hallums was in fact the same as that assigned in 1571 to Hatton of Holdenby. It occurs in 1572 in Minshull church, Cheshire, and was then attributed (by Erdwicke?) to Hallum. When Bostock visited Daresbury church in 1574 he saw this coat in a window, and underneath it written 'Ranulph Plumley, John Hallum'. It is possible that when the heralds first assigned a coat to Christopher Hatton they took this from Daresbury church, on Hatton's statement that he was descended from the Danyells of Daresbury.

Bostock in his memorandum of May, 1574, setting forth the arms of Christopher Hatton 'as justly descended unto him and marshalled in his shield as he may rightly bear them', assigned to him a shield quarterly of ten: Hatton of Hatton, Golburne, Brune, Rixton, Hallum of Hallum, Hellesby of Hellesby, Bostock of Moberley, Holdenby, de la Carvaile, and Washingley. Of these, the first seven are Cheshire families who appear in the pedigree of Hatton of Hatton. Holdenby's arms were Hatton's to quarter by right of his descent from the heiress of Holdenby. Those of de la Carvaile came in from a Holdenby ancestress, and those of Washingley from a de la Carvaile ancestress (Harl. MS. 890, f. 36).

The six quarterings on Hatton's seal are Hatton, Hallum, Hellesby, Holdenby, de la Carvaile and Washingley. The shields of fourteen quarterings on the gateways at Holdenby and those on his portraits, on his monument in St. Paul's and on plates in books dedicated to him, differ by the addition or subtraction of certain coats. The most elaborate achievement is that marshalled by Segar, Garter King of Arms, which gives a few more quarterings, and assigns Hatton the motto, *Virtus tutissima cassis*. On the plate in the book that John Dee dedicated to him is the variant, *Cassis tutissima virtus*. What seems to be a later motto is *Tandem Si*. It is on the coat of arms of Hatton as Lord Chancellor in Dugdale's *Origines Juridicales*, and also above his arms in *The Book of Honour and Arms*, 1590. It is found too on the curious portrait of Hatton, now in Northampton, and in one of the preliminary pages of *Oxoniensium Στεναγμός*, verses published in his honour after his death. It is referred to also in the passage on Hatton in *Polimanteia*, 1595.

HATTON'S PORTRAITS

A NUMBER of portraits of Sir Christopher Hatton are known. They may be classified in four groups: (*a*) Hatless, with piked ruff; (*b*) Hatted, with high-standing embroidered collar; (*c*) A miscellaneous group; and (*d*) a curious allegorical picture, with the head different from the others.

To the first group belongs the beautiful family portrait, in the possession of the Earl of Winchilsea and Nottingham, presumably the earliest in date. It is said to be by Cornelius Ketel, and shows Hatton full length, life size, apparently in the dress of a Gentleman Pensioner: white doublet with gold stripes, black coat and trunks embroidered with pearls, gold embroidered hose, pinked nether stocks drawn over knee, black pantoffles, white ruff and cuffs. Round his neck is a long gold chain, of which he holds in his right hand the lowest link, which is replaced by a medallion containing a head of Queen Elizabeth. His left hand rests on his sword hilt and holds a black cap with jewelled rim, white feather and jewelled brooch. A small dog lies at his feet.

Lord Winchilsea's portrait was exhibited at the Tudor Exhibition, 1890, the description above being largely taken from Mr. H. A. Grueber's account in the catalogue. It is reproduced in Fletcher and Walker's *Historical Portraits* and in E. M. Tenison's *Elizabethan England*. From it was engraved the half-length portrait in Nicolas's *Memorials of Sir Christopher Hatton*. If this portrait is Ketel's, it must have been painted during his stay in England, 1573-81; the title on it, 'Christ[r] Lord Chanc[l] Hatton' is in any case a later addition, for immediately on becoming Chancellor, Hatton, Robert Cecil reports, abandoned his hat and feather, and wore a flat velvet cap (but see below for a portrait of Hatton as Chancellor, 1589 where he wears a cap and feather).

This portrait is presumably that which was the subject of a letter from John Dugdale in 1666 (Addl. MS. 29,551, f. 171). Dugdale's father, the famous antiquary Sir William Dugdale, was closely associated with Christopher Hatton, first Lord Hatton of Kirby, who was also a keen antiquary. Lord Hatton did not die till 1670, but his son Christopher, later Viscount Hatton of Gretton, must have been looking after the family affairs in 1666, for he had agreed to lend the then Lord Chancellor, that is Edward Hyde, Lord Clarendon, the historian, the portrait of Lord Chancellor Hatton. Dugdale's letter is as follows:

2, June, 1666. Sir, My father having told me that you were pleased to lend my Lord Chancellor the picture of my Lord Chancellor Hatton, I presume to send this bearer for it, my Lord being very impatient for it. You shall have it safe returned as soon as a copy can be taken from it. . . .

For the Rt. Hon. Christopher Hatton, Esq., at Hatton House in Holborne.

Nothing is known of Clarendon's copy, if it were ever made.

Almost identical with Lord Winchilsea's portrait is that formerly in the possession of Lord Dillon at Ditchley Park, Oxfordshire. It seems in fact to be a copy. It came to Lord Dillon from his ancestors the Lees of Ditchley. It is reasonable to suggest that Hatton made a present of a copy of Ketel's portrait to his friend Sir Henry Lee. Lord Dillon's portrait was sold in 1933 after his death. It has now fittingly found a home in the Inner Temple, where Hatton studied law as a young man. A third portrait belonging to this group is that reproduced in the Catalogue of Portraits of Lord Liverpool at Kirkham Abbey, 1905. Another comes from the Brudenell collection at Deene Park, Peterborough.

To the second group belongs a portrait in the National Portrait Gallery (no. 2,162). Hatton, as in his Gentleman Pensioner days, has a long chain round his neck, having in it a portrait of the Queen, and wears a similar cap with jewels round the rim and a brooch and feather in it. He holds in his hand the George of his Knighthood of the Garter, which would date the portrait as after May, 1588. This agrees with the inscription, 'Lord Chancellor Hatton, 1589'. In the right-hand corner is Hatton's coat of arms of eleven quarterings. The portrait, which was acquired in 1927, came from the collection of Brigadier-General E. H. Finch-Hatton.

A second portrait belonging to this group is that reproduced in John Thane's *British Autography* (1788-93), which shows the same head as the last, only reversed (perhaps the same portrait). It is from an original at that time in the possession of Sir Thomas Hatton of Long Stanton, Cambridgeshire, a descendant of a younger brother of Christopher Hatton, the father of the first Lord Hatton of Kirby. A third portrait of this type, from the collection of Miss Essex Finch-Hatton and Mrs. A. Z. Newenham, was sold at Christies in 1945. Another was exhibited by Mrs. Henrietta Coffin in 1866 at the South Kensington National Portrait Exhibition.

The third group is one of miscellaneous portraits. It includes a second portrait in the National Portrait Gallery (no. 1,518). This is a very interesting picture. It shows Hatton as Chancellor of Oxford University, and is therefore to be dated 1588-91. Hatton, dressed in black with a gown, presumably his M.A. gown, stands at a sort of parapet or coping. Just in front of him the parapet is lowered to make a recess in which stands the hind, his cognizance. On either side of this recess his hands rest on the parapet, the right hand holding the George of the Garter suspended from a cord round his neck, and the left a shield of arms of Oxford University. Above to his right are the Hatton arms with the motto of the Garter round them, and to his left the arms of the city of Oxford. But the most remarkable feature of the portrait is the series of verses inscribed on it. Under Hatton's coat of arms, for instance, are verses which conclude:

> The oxe, the toyle, the shefe, the fruite,
> His threefold virtues showes,
> Whose nature, art and industrie,
> With treble graces flowes.

The allusion is to the three corn-sheafs of Hatton's arms, and to the ox which is apostrophized in verse below the arms of Oxford. Beneath the George are verses about the slaying of the dragon, and proceeding:

> Sir Christopher, who Hatton hight,
> Saint George's worthy knight,

to whom falls the task of subduing the dragons that stand in the way of justice. Under the hind are verses to 'this noble beast' and to the 'worthy wight' who has taken it for his badge. Finally, the famous seat of learning has its tribute in lines beneath the arms of Oxford University. This portrait, which is labelled on the back as coming from Corfe Castle, is reproduced in Mr. B. M. Ward's edition of *A Hundreth Sundrie Flowres*.

Another portrait is in a panel at Knole, apparently similar to the Clamp engraving in *Harding's Biographical Mirror*, 1795, from a picture in the collection of the Rev. R. Masters of Land Beach, Cambridgeshire. Yet another shows Hatton standing to the right, in Garter robes. This in 1822 was in the possession of G. Finch-Hatton, Esq. (? the 10th Earl of Winchilsea). It is apparently the portrait now in the possession of Major J. C. Wynne-Finch, having been purchased in 1825 by the Rev. Daniel Heneage Finch-Hatton, who bequeathed it to Charles Wynne-Finch, father of the present owner. It is a full-length figure, rather more sombre than the others, wearing dark cloak and breeches, dark cap with brooch, a flowered ruff, and the usual chain and medallion round the neck. Hatton wears the Garter, and so the portrait can be dated after May, 1588. It has been attributed to Zucchero, but as Zucchero left England in 1578 the attribution is incorrect. The portrait is reproduced in the Northamptonshire Record Society's volume of Musters, Beacons and Subsidies in that county during Hatton's time.

Of Miniatures there is one in the Duke of Rutland's collection at Belvoir Castle. Hatton is shown wearing the Garter, thus again dating the portrait as after 1588. This miniature was described and reproduced by Lady Victoria Manners in the first volume of the *Ancestor*: 'Sir Christopher Hatton is a most curious full-length picture; the Great Seal is lying on a table near him, and a small dog is at his side. It is not signed, but is most probably by Nicholas Hilliard (an almost exact replica of this portrait is now in Mr. Salting's fine collection).' The Salting miniature, to which Lady Victoria refers, is now in the Salting Collection in the Victoria and Albert Museum. Is it the same as the miniature lent by Mr. J. Lumsden Propert to the Tudor Exhibition, 1890, when it was described as being by Hilliard?

Perhaps the most interesting of all the portraits of Hatton is a curious allegorical picture, which was exhibited at Christie's in 1929 when it was bought by Sir Algernon Tudor-Craig, from whom it was acquired in the same year by the Northampton Art Gallery. It is a head and shoulders in a circle, showing Hatton wearing a long black cap and white ruff. Around the circumference are the signs of the zodiac; above, the motto *Tandem Si*. In the left-hand corner are the words *Natus, Exoratus, Inhumatus*, under each other, but no dates are filled in. On the right is Hatton's heraldic achievement, quarterly of eleven, surmounted by his cognizance, the hind. In the bottom left-hand corner is seen the artist at an easel painting the portrait, and in the right-hand is a gowned figure, presumably an astrologer, contemplating an astrolabe. The obverse shows some curious imagery. In the top panel a winged male figure, with wings also on his feet, stands on a cloud. He represents Time, and above him is the word *Tempus*. The middle panel shows, on the left, a man and woman joining hands and about to dance, with a minstrel standing by, holding a lute. In the middle, one of the Fates is seen spinning, with a distaff, and beside her are the words *Lachesis trahit*. To the right is a glass or metal lamp with a round flame. In the bottom is a disquisition in Latin on Time, headed *Tractatus de Tempore*. This has been identified as a loose translation of an epigram given in the Greek Anthology (see *Notes and Queries*, cxc. 40).

Besides the portraits enumerated above, a miniature is recorded at the Earl of Carlisle's at Naworth, and a portrait at Shardeloes, the Buckinghamshire seat of the Tyrwhitt-Drakes. This is of interest, for the ancestor of that family is Richard Drake, to whose son Sir Christopher Hatton stood godfather, as we learn from the Hatton Letter Book. A portrait of Hatton in the possession of the Drakes is thus naturally accounted for. This portrait was recorded as being at Shardeloes in 1703 in an inventory made after the death of Montague

Drake (information from Mr. G. Eland of the Buckinghamshire Archaeological Society). An article on Shardeloes in *Country Life* (July 5th, 1913), has a photograph of the drawing-room showing the Hatton portrait hanging over the door leading to the library. In this portrait Hatton is seated; he wears a large ruff, has a white beard, and looks rather old.

Finally, Lyson's *Environs of London*, 1795, has a reference to a portrait of Hatton at Ken Wood, then Lord Mansfield's house; and, according to the *Topographer* (ii. 148) there was in 1790 a portrait of Hatton at Ashridge Abbey, Bucks, the seat of Lord Chancellor Ellesmere.

INDEX

ABINGTON. (*See* Habington)

Agas, Ralph, 145

Alasco, Albertus, Free Baron of Lasco, 132-3

Aldred, Solomon, 258-9

Alençon, Duke of. (*See* Anjou, Duke of)

Allen, Francis, 346
—— William, Cardinal, 61-2, 82, 84, 234, 236, 238, 246, 256, 268, 273, 324, 328

Alva, Duke of, 269

Anjou, Duke of (Alençon), 85, 95, 168 fol., 300, 304, 322, 358

Appletree, ——, 173

Arden, Edward, 236, 257-8, 301, 359

Ardern, Robert, 227

Armada, The, 17, 134, 136, 182, 324 fol., 339

Arundel, Charles, 89-90, 217, 251-3, 255
—— Earl of. (*See* Henry FitzAlan; Philip Howard)
—— Sir Matthew, 251

Ashley, Sir Anthony, 138, 389

Association, Bond of, 234, 270, 311

Aubrey, John, 90, 225
—— William, 225, 364

Audley End, Royal Progress to, 18, 107, 121-2, 135

Aylmer, John, Bishop of London, 17, 132, 174, 197-201, 204-6, 298, 341-2

BABINGTON, ANTHONY, 217, 231, 246, 264-5, 267, 270-1, 274, 276-7, 280-8, 291-2, 294-6, 309
—— Plot, 17, 21, 137, 217, 231-2, 251, 256, 260 fol., 270 fol., 309, 319-20, 352, 356
—— Trial, 288 fol., 364

Bacon, Anthony, 346
—— Sir Francis, 104, 136, 163, 267, 343
—— Sir Nicholas, 101-2, 226

Bailiff, Thomas, 194, 244, 247-9

Baker, George, 160-2, 165

Ballard, John, 265, 270, 275-85, 288, 291-5

Bancroft, Richard, Hatton's chaplain, afterwards Archbishop of Canterbury, 18, 264, 333-4, 339-40, 346-8, 355, 360-1, 368

Bardon Papers, 20, 65, 231, 234, 271, 293, 308, 329

Barker, Christopher, 142

Barnes, Thomas, 279, 352

Barnewall, Robert, 281, 283, 286, 292-3

Barrowe, Henry, 341-2

Bath, Marquess of, MSS., 170

Bayly, Dr., 131

Baylye, Thomas, 194

Beale, Robert, 313

Bear-baiting, 121, 138

Bedford. (*See* Francis Russell)

Belgrave, Dorothy, 165
—— George, 165

Bendlowes, Serjeant, 119

Berney, ——, 83

Bertie, Peregrine, 109

Berton, Robert, 345

Best, George, 135-6, 193, 284

Blount, Sir Christopher, 273, 282

Bond, Thomas, 111

Bostock, Laurence, 26, 75, 77-81, 165, 216

Bothwell, Earl of, 56, 306

Bradley, Henry, 66

Brewer, John, 188-9, 191-2

Briant, Alexander, 206

Bromley, Sir Thomas, Lord Chancellor, 65, 91, 128, 171, 173, 229, 247, 288, 291, 332, 359

Browne, Anthony, Lord Montague, 203, 319
—— John, 319
—— Mary, 203

Brownsea (Brancksea) Island, 113

Brudenell, Sir Edmund, 159

Bryskett, Lodowick, 359, 367, 389
—— Sebastian, 367, 389

Buc, Sir George, 296

Buchanan, George, 56

Burbage, James, 143

Burchet, Peter, 61, 104

Burghley, Lady, 86, 91, 335-6
—— Lord. (*See* Cecil, William)

Butler, Elizabeth, 358
—— Hugh, 358
—— Thomas, Earl of Ormond, 86, 88, 317-8, 345

Bynneman, Henry, 18, 135-7, 140-2, 193

Byrd, William, 18, 142

CALLIS, JOHN, 114-5, 194

Calveley, Robin, 365

Camden, William, 16, 18-19, 62, 104, 124, 161, 171, 173, 175, 208, 235, 244, 247, 249, 257, 277, 296, 335, 351-3, 356, 375

Campbell, Lord, 13, 15, 28, 30, 33, 104, 293, 299, 338, 342-3, 375

399

INDEX

INDEX

INDEX